영어와 한글로 읽는
교양 세계사
BILINGUAL KOREAN-ENGLISH
HISTORY OF THE WORLD

영어와 한글로 읽는

교양 세계사

1판 1쇄 발행 2022.1.3

지은이 박찬영, 나일수, 차주호, 송영심, 이화영, 정대연, 최서연
옮긴이 Robert Young
펴낸이 박찬영
편집 이다정, 최나래, 김지은, 조태강, 정예림
디자인 박민정
마케팅 조병훈, 최진주, 박민규
발행처 (주)리베르스쿨
주소 서울시 성동구 왕십리로 58 서울숲포휴 11층

BILINGUAL KOREAN-ENGLISH

HISTORY OF THE WORLD

Author Park Chan-young, Na Il-soo, Cha Ju-ho, Song Young-shim, Lee Wha-young, Jung Dae-yeon, Choi Seo-youn
Translator Robert Young
Publisher Park Chan-young
Editor Lee Da-jeong, Choi Na-rae, Kim Ji-eun, Jo Tae-gang, Jeong Ye-rim
Designer Park Min-jung
Marketer Jo Byoung-hoon, Choi Jin-joo, Park Min-kyu
Issued by Liberschool
Address 11th floor, 58, Wangsimni-ro, Seongdong-gu, Seoul, Republic of Korea

등록번호 Registration Number   2013-000016호
전화 Phone   02-790-0587, 0588
팩스 Fax   02-790-0589
홈페이지 Website   www.liber.site
커뮤니티 Community   blog.naver.com/liber_book(블로그)
이메일 E-mail   skyblue7410@hanmail.net
ISBN   978-89-6582-334-6(04900), 978-89-6582-333-9(SET)

Youtube   https://www.youtube.com/channel/UCnCu_Vdwopl1y1rwPJsPnHQ

Youtube Link

영어와 한글로 읽는

교양 세계사

BILINGUAL KOREAN-ENGLISH
HISTORY OF THE WORLD

박찬영 나일수 차주호 송영심 이화영 정대연 최서연

새로운 세계사적 관점이 당신의 생각을 바꾼다!
A New World View on History Will Change Your Thoughts!

㈜리베르
Liberschool

세계사는 모든 독서의 기초입니다

이 책은 우리가 태어나기 훨씬 전에 이 세상에 어떤 일이 일어났는지 궁금증을 풀어 주는 세계사 이야기입니다. 눈앞의 작은 세계만 보고 큰 세계를 자신의 시각으로 확대 해석할 경우 우물 안 개구리처럼 자기중심적인 세계관을 가질 수도 있습니다. 따라서 세상을 바라보는 눈을 넓히고 사고에 깊이를 더하여 지나간 시대를 전체적으로 조망할 수 있는 능력을 길러야 합니다.

역사는 세상에서 가장 재미있는 이야기이며 세상에서 가장 중요한 뉴스거리를 모아 놓은 것이기도 합니다. 정치, 경제는 물론 일반인들의 생활과 관련이 있는 문화도 역사 가 될 수 있습니다. 이 모든 것들이 오늘의 우리를 있게 한 토대이기 때문입니다. 세계사 는 세상사의 중요한 사건들을 모아 놓았으므로 모든 독서의 기초가 됩니다. 그렇다면 세계사는 어떻게 읽어야 할까요?

역사적인 이야기의 맥락과 행간을 살필 수 있도록 그림, 사진, 지도, 일화 등을 다양하 게 활용해야 합니다. 역사적인 지식의 틀이 제공된다 하더라도 수많은 이야기들이 시 간이나 공간 차원에서 연결되지 않는다면 물 위에 뜬 기름처럼 머릿속에 제각각 떠다 니게 될 뿐입니다.

이 책에는 정치, 경제, 문화 등 다양한 주제의 지도를 제시하였습니다. 지도를 보며 사 건이 일어난 장소를 확인하고 역사적 사건을 시간과 공간 속에서 이해하며, 역사에 관 하여 폭넓게 생각할 수 있도록 하였습니다. 또한 세계사의 주요 사건을 생생하게 전달 할 수 있도록 이야기 자료를 풍부하게 실었습니다.

World History Is the Basis of All Reading

This book is a world history that will satisfy your curiosity about what had happened in the world long before you were born. If you see only the small world in front of your eyes and stretch the meaning of the big world based on your narrow viewpoint, you are likely to build a self-centered worldview like a frog in a well. Therefore, it is important to broaden your worldview and add depth to your thoughts so that you can see past eras as a whole.

History is the most captivating story of all in the world, and it is also a collection of the world's most important news. Politics, economy, as well as culture that is associated with the livelihood of ordinary people can all be part of history, because they are the foundation that made what we are today. World history is the basis of all reading, because it is a collection of important events that happened in the world. So, the question is, what is the right approach to reading world history?

You must use pictures, photos, maps, anecdotes, and other materials in a wide variety of ways so that you can read between the lines and context of historical events. Even if the frame of historical knowledge is set in place, many other stories will randomly float around in your head like oil on water if you cannot connect them in terms of time and space.

This book includes maps of diverse topics such as politics, economy, and culture. Maps are there to help you think about history in broader terms while confirming the locations of historic events on the maps and understanding them within the context of time and space. The book contains many story materials so that major events in world history can come home to you more realistically.

세계사는 영어로 읽어야 합니다

　현대인들은 세계를 여행하며 견문을 넓힐 일이 많아졌습니다. 이제는 다른 문화를 접하는 데서 한걸음 더 나아가 세계 각국의 역사를 서로 연결 지을 수 있는 안목이 필요합니다. 또한 세계와 소통하는 글로벌 리더가 되기 위해서는 세계사적인 시각을 갖출 필요가 있습니다.

　『영어와 한글로 읽는 교양 세계사』는 세계사를 한국어와 영어로 읽을 수 있도록 구성하였습니다. 역사는 가장 효율적인 언어 학습 텍스트이기 때문입니다. 역사는 인문학은 물론 예술, 과학, 생활까지 모두 아우르는 학문입니다. 세상의 사건, 문화유산, 지식 가운데 인류에게 가장 크게 영향을 끼친 것들만 선별되어 역사로 기록됩니다. 역사에는 세상에서 중요한 모든 것이 포함되어 있는 셈입니다. 따라서 세계사 책에서는 각 분야에서 가장 중요한 어휘와 용어가 다루어질 수밖에 없습니다. 역사의 맥락 속에서 어휘와 용어를 익히면 영어도 더 효율적으로 학습할 수 있습니다.

　『영어와 한글로 읽는 교양 세계사』는 ㈜리베르스쿨의 역사 교과서를 주요 내용으로 삼아 구성하였습니다. 또한 역사적 논쟁거리도 의미 있게 다루었습니다. 전문가들에게 검증을 받은 내용이므로 이야기 세계사이면서도 내용의 신뢰도가 높습니다.

　이 책으로 역사를 여행하면서 온 세상이 공부의 마당이라는 깨달음을 얻게 된다면 더이상의 기쁨이 없겠습니다.

지은이 드림

World History Should Be Read in English

People in today's society have more opportunity to travel the world and broaden their horizons. Modern society requires us to take a step further from experiencing other cultures and develop an insight to connect histories of countries around the world. In addition, now is a time when everybody needs to build a global history perspective to become a global leader who can communicate with the world.

"Bilingual Korean–English History of the World" tells world history both in Korean and English. It is because history can offer the most efficient language-learning texts. History is a subject that covers all humanities subjects as well as art, science, and living. Among the events of the world, cultural heritages, and knowledge, those that left the most important influence on mankind are selected and recorded in history. That means history is a compilation of all the important things of the world. As a result, the world history book is bound to include the most important terms and vocabulary in various academic disciplines. When you learn those terms and vocabulary within the context of history, you can learn English more efficiently as well.

"Bilingual Korean–English History of the World" is written based on the history textbooks published by Liberschool. It also contains meaningful historical controversies. Therefore, the contents were all verified by experts and are as reliable as history textbooks.

We couldn't be happier if you traveled through history with this book and realize that the whole world is a classroom where you can learn.

By the authors

차례

머리말   **4**

CONTENTS

IV. Imperialist Invasions and Nation-state Building Movements

V. World War and Social Changes

VI. Progress and Tasks of the Modern World

Ⅰ

문명의 발생과 고대 세계의 형성

역사란 과거와 현재의 끊임없는 대화이다.

과거에 일어난 사실과 현재에 살고 있는 역사가의 상호 작용이 중요하다.

– 에드워드 헬릿 카(1892~1982)

↓ **포로 로마노** | 로마의 공회장(Foro)은 신전, 바실리카(공회당), 기념비 등으로 구성된 공공 생활의 중심지였다.
Foro Romano | Foro Romano was the center of communal life for Roman citizens, surrounded by the ruins of temples, basilica, and monuments.

↓ 사투르누스 신전
Temple of Saturn

↓ 원로원 Senate

I

The Birth of Civilization
and the Development of the Ancient World

History is a constant conversation between the past and the present.
The interaction between what happened in the past
and the historian living in the present is important.

– Edward Hallett Carr(1892–1982)

↓ 팔라티노 언덕 Palatine Hill

↓ 콜로세움 Colosseum

역사의 의미

01 역사의 의미

역사에는 사실의 역사, 기록의 역사가 있다

역사는 과거에 일어난 수많은 사건들로 이루어져 있다. 현재의 우리는 과거의 모든 사건을 직접 경험할 수 없다. 대신 과거의 사람이 남긴 기록이나 유물·유적 등을 통해 과거에 어떤 사건이 일어났는지 알 수 있다. 이처럼 역사에는 '사실의 역사'와 '기록의 역사'라는 두 가지 의미가 있다.

사실의 역사는 실제로 과거에 일어난 사실을 뜻하고, 기록의 역사는 과거에 일어난 사실에 대한 기록을 뜻한다. 사실의 역사가 변하지 않는 사실인 반면, 기록의 역사는 바라보는 사람의 관점에 따라 조금씩 다를 수 있다.

역사가들은 역사를 어떤 입장에서 바라봤나요?

레오폴트 폰 랑케
역사가는 오직 역사적 사실만을 찾아내고 말해야 해요. 그러려면 자신의 생각을 죽이고 과거가 본래 어떠한 상태에 있었는지 객관적으로 밝히는 것이 중요하지요. 오직 역사적 사실이 스스로 이야기하도록 해야 합니다.

베네데토 크로체
역사에서 인간의 인식은 중요한 부분입니다. 실제로 일어난 일들은 인간의 사유를 거쳐야 비로소 역사로 남을 수 있어요. 즉 인간이 정신적 욕구에 따라 사유하고 반성하고 탐구한 것만이 참된 역사가 되지요.

에드워드 헬릿 카
역사란 과거와 현재의 끊임없는 대화입니다. 역사적 사실과 역사가의 관점 중 어느 한 쪽이 일방적으로 중요한 것이 아닙니다. 과거에 일어난 사실과 현재에 살고 있는 역사가는 상호 작용을 해야 합니다.

1

The Significance of History

01 The Significance of History

History as a Truth vs. History as Documentation

History is a compilation of events that occurred in the past. Living in the present time, we cannot personally experience any event that has already happened. However, we can glean a good idea about what happened in the past by studying history books, relics, and historic sites. There are two types of history: history as a truth and history as documentation.

History as a truth is all about facts that forever remain unchanged, while history as documentation can be different depending on the viewpoint of the person who wrote it.

◉ **How Did Historians View History?**

Leopold von Ranke
The historian has to determine and state only historical facts. To do that, it's important to exclude their own thoughts and objectively reveal what the past was like. Let historical facts speak only for themselves.

Benedetto Croce
Human perception is an important part of history. What actually happened only remains in history through human thought. In other words, only what humans think, reflect, and explore according to their mental needs becomes true history.

Edward Hallett Carr
History is a constant conversation between the past and the present. Neither the historical facts nor the historian's point of view are unilaterally important. What happened in the past and the historian living in the present must interact.

02 역사의 연구 방법
역사 연구 방법은 사료의 형태에 따라 다르다

문자 기록이 없는 선사 시대를 연구할 때는 주로 유물이나 유적을 과학적으로 분석하는 고고학이나 인류학의 연구 방법을 이용한다. 문자를 사용한 역사 시대를 연구할 때는 유물·유적을 발굴하여 연구하는 방법뿐만 아니라 문자로 남겨진 기록을 읽고 그 의미를 해석하는 방법도 이용한다. 기록에는 기록한 사람의 견해와 관점이 반영되어 있기 때문에 기록을 검토할 때에는 비판적이어야 한다.

역사를 탐구할 때에는 사료를 바탕으로 역사적 사실을 철저하게 조사하고 비판적으로 분석해야 한다. 또한 자기 주도적인 자세로 탐구에 임하여 역사를 바라보는 자신의 관점을 확립해 나가야 한다.

⊘ **문자가 발명되기 전 인류의 흔적은 어디에서 찾을 수 있나요?**

눈 덮인 운동장에 찍혀 있는 발자국을 보고 누군가 먼저 학교에 왔다는 사실을 추측할 수 있는 것처럼 오래전 일이라도 근거만 뚜렷하면 어떤 일이 일어났는지 추측해 볼 수 있다. 문자가 발명되기 이전에 살았던 사람들에 관해서는 유물과 유적을 보고 짐작할 수 있다. 유물은 과거의 인류가 남기고 간 물건인데 대체로 형태가 작아 운반이 가능한 토기, 석기, 금속기를 뜻한다. 유적은 과거의 인류가 생활하던 장소인데 형태가 크고 위치를 변경할 수 없는 주거지, 무덤 등을 뜻한다.

크로마뇽인 두개골   주먹도끼(국립중앙박물관)   빌렌도르프의 비너스(오스트리아)
A Skull of Cro-Magnon   Hand Axe(National Museum of Korea)   Venus of Willendorf(Austria)

02 Research Methods of History

History Research Methods Differ Depending on the Historical Materials

When studying prehistoric times that have no written records available, archeological and anthropological research methods are utilized to scientifically analyze relics and historic sites from those periods. When studying the history of times when written records were available, the method of reading and deciphering these written records in addition to various methods of excavating and researching relics and historic sites are used. When researching records, one has to make sure to examine them with a critical eye because the records are filtered through the viewpoints and opinions of those who recorded them.

When exploring history, one must meticulously research and critically analyze historic facts based on historic resources. In addition, one must assume a self-directed learning attitude so that one can establish one's own viewpoints regarding history.

⚜ **Where Can Traces of Humanity Be Found before the Invention of the Letters?**

Just as we can guess that someone came to school before us by looking at the footprints on the snow-covered playground, we can guess what happened long ago if the evidence is clear. We can infer things about the people who lived before the invention of writing by looking at artifacts and ruins. Relics are objects left behind by humans in the past, and generally refer to earthenware, stoneware, and metalwork that can be transported due to their small shape. Ruins are places where humans lived in the past, and refer to dwellings and tombs that are large in shape and cannot be relocated.

세계의 선사 문화와 고대 문명

01 세계의 선사 문화

인류가 세계 각지로 이동하다

인류가 지구상에 출현한 시기는 약 400만 년 전으로 추정된다. 아프리카 동남부 지역에 등장한 오스트랄로피테쿠스 아파렌시스가 최초의 인류로 여겨지고 있다. 유인원과 달리 두 발로 서서 걷고 손으로 간단한 도구를 만들었기 때문이다.

약 180만 년 전 아프리카, 유럽, 아시아의 여러 지역에 흩어져 살았던 호모 에렉투스는 불을 이용하여 음식을 익혀 먹고 언어도 사용하였다. 약 20만 년 전에는 현생 인류의 조상인 호모 사피엔스가 아프리카 지역에 처음 등장하여 세계 각지로 흩어졌다. 이들은 각 지역의 자연환경에 따라 서로 다른 신체적 특징을 지니게 되었고, 이후 다양한 인종으로 진화하였다.

✿ 최초의 인류는 누구일까요?

최초의 인류는 1974년 에티오피아 아파르 지구에서 발굴되었다. 당시 발굴대가 즐겨 듣던 노래 가사를 따 '루시'라고 이름 지었다. 루시는 키 107cm, 몸무게 28kg인 성인 여성으로 밝혀졌다. 근처에서 더 큰 두개골이 발견되었는데, 남성으로 추정되어 루시앙으로 불린다.

루시는 약 318만 년 전에 살았고 직립 보행을 하였다. 외양과 두뇌가 침팬지에 가깝고, 수습된 뼈가 인간 골격의 28%에 지나지 않는다는 점 등 논란 속에서도 '최초의 인간'이라 불렸다.

그러다 1992년, 루시가 발견된 지역 인근에서 '아르디'가 발굴되었고, 루시는 아르디에게 최초의 인류 자리를 내주었다. 아르디는 약 440만 년 전에 살았고, 직립 보행을 하였으며, 물건을 세게 쥘 수 있었던 것으로 추측된다.

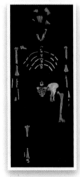 

'루시'의 유골
Lucy's Remains

'아르디'의 유골
Ardi's Remains

Prehistoric Cultures of the World and Ancient Civilizations

01 Prehistoric Cultures of the World

Humanity Moves Throughout the World

It is estimated that the first human ancestors appeared on Earth about 4 million years ago. Australopithecus afarensis, who lived in Southeastern Africa, is believed to be the first human species, because unlike apes, Australopithecus afarensis could walk, stand on two legs, and used their hands to make tools.

Homo erectus, who lived about 1.8 million years ago in various parts of Africa, Europe, and Asia, used fire to cook food, and also used language. About 200,000 years ago, Homo sapiens, which are considered the ancestor of modern human beings, made their first appearance in Africa and spread all over the world. They developed different physical characteristics according to the natural environment of each region, and eventually evolved into various races.

◉ Who Were the First Humans?

The first human was excavated in the Afar district of Ethiopia in 1974. It was named 'Lucy' after the lyrics of a song that the excavation team enjoyed listening to. Lucy was found to be an adult woman, 107cm tall and weighing 28kg. A larger skull was found nearby, presumed to be male and called Lucien.

Lucy lived about 3.18 million years ago and walked upright. Despite the controversy surrounding the appearance and brain are close to chimpanzees, and that only 28% of the human skeleton was located, it has been called the 'first human'.

Later, in 1992, 'Ardi' was discovered near the area where Lucy was found, and Lucy made way for Ardi as the first human specimen. Ardi lived about 4.4 million years ago, walked upright, and is believed to have been able to grasp things.

구석기 시대, 사냥과 채집을 하다

구석기 시대에는 몸돌에서 돌조각을 떼어 만든 뗀석기를 사용하였다. 처음에는 하나의 뗀석기를 여러 용도로 사용하다가 점차 쓰임새에 맞는 도구를 제작하였다. 사냥할 때는 찍개, 주먹도끼 등을, 음식을 다듬거나 조리할 때는 긁개, 밀개 등을 사용하였다.

이들은 사냥, 채집, 고기잡이로 식량을 구하였기 때문에 이동 생활을 하였다. 주로 막집 임시로 간단하게 막처럼 꾸민 집, 동굴, 바위 그늘 등에서 살았는데 사냥의 성공, 풍요, 다산 등을 기원하며 동굴 벽화를 남기기도 하였다. 대표적으로 프랑스의 라스코 동굴 벽화와 에스파냐의 알타미라 동굴 벽화가 유명하다.

⚜ **구석기 시대 사람들이 그린 그림은 무엇을 의미할까요?**

구석기 시대의 벽화가 그려진 동굴은 유럽에 200여 곳 이상 있는데, 대부분이 프랑스와 에스파냐에 분포한다. 그중 라스코 동굴 벽화와 알타미라 동굴 벽화는 크로마뇽인이 남긴 예술 작품이다.

라스코 동굴 벽화에서는 약 800점의 그림이 발견되었는데, 1~5m까지 크기가 다양하다. 주술사, 들소, 말, 사슴, 염소 등이 표현되어 있는데, 동물을 화살, 덫과 함께 표현한 것을 보면 그림에 사냥이 잘 되기를 바라는 주술적인 의미를 담은 것으로 보인다.

알타미라 동굴 벽화에도 매머드, 들소, 사슴 등 동물이 표현되어 있다. 묘사가 생생하고 입체적이며 색채가 아름답다.

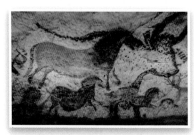

라스코 동굴 벽화(프랑스)
A Mural in Lascaux Cave(France)

알타미라 동굴 벽화(에스파냐)
A Mural in Altamira Cave(Spain)

The Paleolithic Age of Hunting and Food Gathering

During the Old Stone Age, which is also known as the Paleolithic Age, humans created stone tools made by breaking stones. At first, they used simple multi-functional pebble choppers, but later, they created more diverse stone tools for various purposes. For example, they used pebble chopper and hand axe when hunting larger games, and scraper and end-scraper when chopping and cooking food.

They were nomadic because they had to travel to hunt, gather food, and fish. Mostly they lived in huts, caves, and rock overhangs, and left paintings of animals on the cave walls wishing for successful hunting, abundance, and fertility. Some of the most famous Paleolithic cave paintings can be found in Lascaux Cave in France and the Cave of Altamira, Spain.

◎ What Did the Paleolithic People's Paintings Mean?

There are more than 200 caves with murals from the Paleolithic Age in Europe, and most of them are distributed in France and Spain. Among them, the murals in Lascaux Cave and Altamira Cave are works of art left by the Cro-Magnons.

About 800 paintings were found in Lascaux Cave, varying in size from 1 to 5m. Shaman, bison, horse, deer, and goats are represented. Seeing that animals are represented in conjunction with arrows and traps, it seems that the pictures contain the magical meaning of hoping for a successful hunt.

Animals such as mammoths, bison, and deer are also represented on the murals in the Cave of Altamira. The description is vivid and three-dimensional, and the colors are beautiful.

신석기 시대, 농경과 목축을 시작하다

아프리카에서 유라시아로 이주한 호모 사피엔스는 매머드를 비롯한 큰 동물들을 사냥해서 먹고 살았다. 약 1만 년 전 빙하기가 끝나고 기후가 점차 따뜻해지면서 해수면이 높아졌다. 큰 동물이 줄어들고 빙하가 녹아 강물이 들판을 뒤덮기 시작하였다. 이러한 자연환경의 변화에 따라 인류는 순록같은 동물을 사냥하거나 바닷가에서 물고기나 조개를 잡으며 생활하였다. 간석기^{날 부분이나 표면 전체를 갈아서 만든 석기}와 토기 등의 도구를 사용하였고 사냥과 채집 이외에도 농경과 목축을 통해 식량을 얻었다. 이 시기를 신석기 시대라고 한다.

농경은 서남아시아에서 처음 시작된 이래 전 세계로 확대되었다. 신석기인들은 돌괭이로 밭을 갈아 밀, 보리, 조, 수수, 콩 등의 잡곡을 재배하였고, 돌낫, 뼈 낫 등을 이용하여 수확하였다. 수확한 곡식은 돌 갈판과 같은 간석기를 사용하여 가공하였다. 또한 곡식의 보관과 음식 조리를 위해 토기를 만들었다.

이처럼 농경과 목축을 통해 먹을거리를 생산함으로써 나타난 인류 생활의 큰 변화를 신석기 혁명이라 한다.

◎ 스톤 헨지는 누가 세웠을까요?

스톤헨지는 높이 2~7m, 무게 50t에 달하는 거대한 석상 80여 개로 이루어져 있다. 거대한 규모 때문에 외계인이 만들었다는 설까지 나왔다. 스톤헨지 주변 무덤에 묻힌 유골의 주인공들이 아시아 계열이라는 연구 결과가 있어 만주와 한반도의 고인돌 문화와 관련이 있다는 주장도 제기되었다. 영국 곳곳에서 한반도 고인돌과 비슷한 형태의 고인돌들이 발견되기도 했다.

한반도의 북방식 고인돌과 유사한 풀나브론 고인돌(영국 아일랜드)
Poulnabrone Dolmen Similar to the Northern Style
Dolmens of the Korean Peninsula(Ireland, UK)

스톤헨지(영국 윌트셔) Stonehenge(Wiltshire, England)

The Neolithic Period of Farming and Livestock

Homo sapiens migrated out of Africa to Eurasia, where they hunted large animals including mammoth. The last Ice Age came to an end roughly 10,000 years ago, and the temperature and sea levels began to rise. The population of large animals declined rapidly, and the melting glaciers allowed rivers to flow over the fields. Humans adapted to these changing natural environments by hunting animals such as reindeer or living near the sea catching fish and shellfish for food. They also started creating and using polished tools and pottery, and their food sources began to include farming and livestock in addition to hunting and fishing. This period is called the Neolithic period, or the New Stone Age.

Agriculture started in Southeast Asia and spread throughout the world. During this period, humans cultivated land with stone picks, grew crops such as wheat, barley, millet, sorghum, soybeans and others, and harvested them using sickles made of stones or bones. The harvested crops were processed with polished stone implements such as stone mills. The humans of this age also made pottery to cook food and store crops.

The great changes that happened in people's lifestyles as the result of producing food through farming and livestock are collectively referred to as the Neolithic Revolution.

◎ Who Built Stonehenge?

Stonehenge is made up of about 80 massive standing stones that are 2-7 meters tall and 50 tons each. The massive weight and nature of the arrangement made some theorists believe that it must have been built by aliens. Some people suggest that it is related to the dolmen culture of Manchuria and the Korean Peninsula, because studies have shown that the remains buried in graves around Stonehenge are of Asian origin. Meanwhile, dolmens similar to those found in the Korean Peninsula have also been found in various parts of England as well.

02 도시 국가의 등장

청동기를 사용하고 도시 국가가 등장하다

기원전 3500년경 메소포타미아에서 청동기를 사용하기 시작하였다. 부족들은 청동 무기를 사용하여 활발한 정복 전쟁을 벌이고 세력을 확장하였다. 그 과정에서 도시 국가가 출현하였다. 도시를 중심으로 왕, 제사장, 전사, 농민, 노예 등의 계급이 생겨났고, 도시 국가 간에는 교역이 활발하게 이루어졌다.

한편 중요한 일을 기록하기 위해 문자가 만들어졌는데, 이로 인해 인류 문명은 급속하게 발전하기 시작하였다. 고대 문명은 메소포타미아 지역, 나일강 유역, 인더스강 유역, 황허강 유역 등에 있었다. 이들 지역은 모두 기후가 따뜻하고 큰 강을 끼고 있어 농사짓기에 알맞은 곳이었다.

🧭 **세계 4대 문명 가운데 중국 문명만 지속된 이유는 무엇일까요?**

인류의 고대 문명은 티그리스 · 유프라테스강, 나일강, 인더스강, 황허강 등 큰 강의 유역에서 시작되었다. 이들 강 주변의 비옥한 토지로 인구가 유입되면서 고대 문명은 비약적으로 발전했다. 하지만 기원전 2000년부터 기온이 급격히 상승하면서 티그리스 · 유프라테스강, 나일강, 인더스강 유역에서는 사막화가 진행되었고 사람들은 흩어지기 시작했다. 황허강 유역의 북쪽도 사막화가 진행되었다. 하지만 황허강의 서쪽은 고원과 산맥이고 남쪽은 아열대 우림지역이며 동쪽은 바다이다. 이에 중국은 기후변화의 영향을 덜 받고, 외부의 침입도 적게 받았다. 지리적 환경 덕분에 중국은 문명을 이어갈 수 있었다.

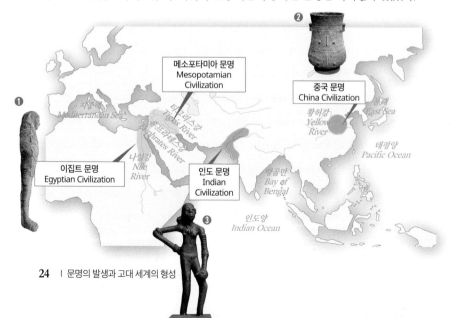

02 Emergence of City States

The Use of Bronze and the Emergence of the City State

People started using bronze in Mesopotamia around 3500 BC. Tribes used bronze weapons during war to aggressively occupy land and expand territory. During this process, the city state emerged. In cities, people belonged to different classes such as nobility, priests, warriors, farmers, and slaves. These City states were also dynamically involved in trading.

In the meantime, several alphabets were invented to record important events and contributed to the rapid development of human civilizations. Ancient civilizations were born near rivers in Mesopotamia, in regions by the Nile River, the Indus River, the Yellow River, and so on. All of these regions had perfect conditions for farming because they were characterized by warm climates and ample water supply.

....

 Why did only the Chinese civilization last among the world's four major civilizations?

The ancient civilizations of mankind began in the basins of large rivers such as the Tigris and Euphrates rivers, the Nile River, the Indus River, and the Hwanghe River. As the population flowed into fertile land around these rivers, ancient civilizations developed rapidly. However, as temperatures rose sharply from 2000 BC, desertification progressed in the Tigris, Euphrates, Nile, and Indus basins, and people began to disperse. Desertification also progressed in the north of the Hwanghe River basin. However, the west side of the Hwanghe River is a plateau and mountain range, the south side is a subtropical rainforest, and the east side is the sea. As a result, China was less affected by climate change and less invaded from outside. Thanks to the geographical environment, China was able to continue its civilization.

❶ 이집트의 미라 Egyptian Mummy ❷ 상의 청동 제기 Utensils Used in Ancestral Rites of the Sang Dynasty ❸ 모헨조다로 유적의 춤추는 여인상(뉴델리 국립박물관) Dancing Woman Statue of Mohenjodaro Ruins(National Museum of New Delhi) ©Joe Ravi

03 문명의 발생과 국가 형성

티그리스강과 유프라테스강 유역에 메소포타미아 문명이 형성되다

티그리스강과 유프라테스강 사이의 땅을 뜻하는 메소포타미아 지역은 토지가 비옥하여 일찍이 농경이 발달하였다. 기원전 3500년경 이 지역에서 수메르인이 인류 최초의 도시 국가를 세웠다. 이들은 천체의 움직임을 연구하여 **점성술과 태음력** 달이 지구를 한 바퀴 도는 시간을 기준으로 만든 역법을 발전시키고, 60진법을 사용하였으며, 점토판에 **쐐기 문자**로 기록을 남겼다. 또한 지구라트라는 신전을 세워 각 도시의 수호신을 섬겼다. 신의 대리인인 왕은 강력한 **신권 정치**를 펼쳤다. 메소포타미아 지방은 사방이 트여 있어 교역이 활발하였지만 이민족이 자주 침입하였다. 그래서 죽은 이후의 세상보다는 살아 있을 때의 안정적인 삶을 더 중요하게 여겼다.

아무르인이 세운 **바빌로니아 왕국의 함무라비왕**은 기원전 18세기에 메소포타미아 전역을 통일하고 법전을 편찬하는 등 왕국을 크게 발전시켰다. 함무라비왕이 죽은 후 바빌로니아 왕국은 급속히 쇠퇴하였고 철제 무기로 무장한 히타이트인에게 멸망하였다.

🏵 함무라비 법전비에는 어떤 이야기가 담겨 있을까요?

함무라비 법전에는 태양신으로부터 법전을 건네받는 함무라비왕의 모습이 조각되어 있다. 함무라비 법전의 조항은 매우 엄격한 편인데, 기본적으로 보복의 원칙을 따르며 신분에 따라 처벌이 달랐다.

195. 아들이 아버지를 때렸을 때에는 그 손을 자른다.
196. 평민이 귀족의 눈을 빼면 그의 눈을 뺀다.
198. 귀족이 평민의 눈을 빼면 은화 1미나를 지불한다.

195. If a son should strike his father, his hands shall be hewn off.
196. If a man put out the eye of a nobleman, his eye shall be put out.
198. If a nobleman put out the eye of a freed man, he shall pay one mina of silver.

함무라비 법전비(루브르 박물관) Code of Hammurabi(Louvre)

03 Birth of Civilizations and Establishment of States

Mesopotamian Civilization Blooms by the Rivers of Tigris and Euphrates

Agriculture started and developed early on in the Mesopotamia region because, situated within the Tigris–Euphrates river system, the area had fertile soil. Around 3500 BC, the Sumerians established the first city state in the history of mankind. They studied the movement of the celestial bodies to develop astrology and a lunar calendar, used the sexagesimal system, and left written records by carving wedge-shaped marks called cuneiform onto clay tablets. They built huge temple towers called ziggurats in their city states as well. The Sumerian kings established powerful theocracy because they were considered agents of their gods. The Mesopotamia area had dynamic trading activities because it was open in all four directions, but this also made it subject to constant invasions by other ethnic groups. Therefore, a secure life mattered more than the world after death to the Mesopotamians.

The Babylonian Empire founded by the Amur began its rise to power after King Hammurabi, whose feats included the unification of the entire Mesopotamian region and the enactment of a set of laws among many others during his reign in the 18th century BC. The Babylonian Empire quickly declined after the death of King Hammurabi, until it fell into the hands of the Hittites who were armed with iron weapons.

⊚ **What Is the Story Behind the Code of Hammurabi?**

In the Hammurabi's Code, there is a sculpture of King Hammurabi who was handed a code from the deity of the sun. As the provisions of the Hammurabi Code are very strict, they basically follow the principle of retaliation with the punishment differing according to status.

나일강이 이집트 문명을 선물하다

주기적인 범람으로 비옥해진 나일강 유역에는 일찍부터 여러 도시 국가가 형성되었다. 기원전 3000년경에는 통일 왕국이 성립되었고, 고왕국, 중왕국, 신왕국을 거치며 기원전 7세기까지 통일 국가를 유지하였다. 이 지역은 사막과 바다로 둘러싸인 폐쇄적인 지형이었기 때문에 이민족의 침입을 거의 받지 않았다.

이집트에서는 왕을 태양신 '라'의 아들로 여기고 파라오라고 불렀다. 파라오는 살아 있는 신으로 군림하면서 절대적인 권력을 행사하였다. 이집트인은 태양신을 비롯하여 여러 신을 섬겼다. 또한 사후 세계를 믿어 미라를 만들고 죽은 사람을 위한 안내서인 「사자의 서」를 남겼다. 이들은 파피루스에 상형 문자 사물의 형상을 본떠 만든 문자를 기록하였다.

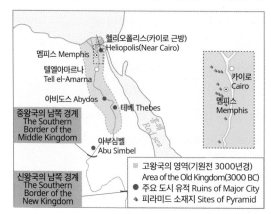

이집트 문명의 범위 Scope of Egyptian Civilization

나일강의 범람 시기를 예측하고 농경지를 정비하는 과정에서 천문학, 측량술, 기하학 등이 발달하였으며 10진법과 태양력을 사용하였다. 미라를 제작하는 과정에서 의술도 발달하였다.

💮 투탕카멘이 자신의 무덤을 발굴한 사람에게 저주를 내린 것일까요?

파라오의 관에는 보통 '사자(死者)의 안녕을 방해하는 자에게 저주가 있으라!'라는 문구가 쓰여 있지만, 이집트 제18왕조 12대 왕이었던 투탕카멘의 관에는 '왕의 이름을 알리는 자에게 복이 있으라!'라는 말이 쓰여 있었다. 그러나 투탕카멘의 무덤 발굴과 관련된 사람들이 잇달아 의문의 죽음을 당하였고 사람들은 이를 '투탕카멘의 저주'라고 불렀다. '저주'에 대해 고대 바이러스설, 미발견 질병설, 미지의 독극물설 등이 제기되었지만 지금까지 결론은 나지 않았다.

투탕카멘의 황금 마스크(이집트 박물관) Golden Mask of Tutankhamun

Egyptian Civilization, a Gift from the Nile River

Many city states were established along the Nile River in Egypt because the river's annual flooding ensured fertile soil for growing crops. The first Pharaoh of Egypt solidified Egypt into a single kingdom about 3000 BC, and the kingdom remained unified as it wound its way through the periods of the Old, Middle, and New Kingdoms. Surrounded mostly by deserts and oceans, this closed area was rarely invaded by other ethnic groups.

Egyptians called their kings Pharaoh, because they believed that their kings were the sons of 'Ra', the ancient Egyptian deity of the sun. In life, the Egyptian Pharaohs had absolute authority while being treated like gods. The ancient Egyptians served many gods including the deity of the sun. They also made mummies of dead bodies and kept a book called 'Book of the Dead' because they believed in the afterlife. They created records in hieroglyphic writing on papyrus as well.

They used a decimal numerical system and solar calendar, and were able to develop and advance astronomy, surveying techniques, and geometry while trying to predict when the Nile was going to flood and manage agricultural land. They also advanced medical science through the mummification process.

....

◉ Was Tutankhamen Cursing the Man who Excavated His Grave?

A Pharaoh's coffin usually reads, 'Curse those who interfere with the well-being of the dead!', but the coffin of Tutankhamuns', 12th king of the 18th dynasty of Egypt, said 'Blessed are those who make known the king's name!' However, people involved in the excavation of his tomb suffered mysterious deaths one after another, and people began to call it 'the curse of Tutankhamun'. Ancient virus rumors, undiscovered disease rumors, and unknown poison rumors have been raised about the 'curse', but no conclusions have been made so far.

∞ 메소포타미아인과 이집트인은 왜 다른 세계관을 가졌나요?

메소포타미아 지역은 개방적인 지형이었기 때문에 이민족의 침입을 많이 받았다. 메소포타미아인은 현재의 삶이 언제 끝날지 모른다고 생각하였기 때문에 현세를 중시하였다. 반면 이집트 지역은 사막과 바다로 둘러싸인 폐쇄적인 지형이어서 이민족의 침입을 거의 받지 않았다. 오랫동안 통일 국가를 안정적으로 유지하면서 이집트인은 죽음 이후의 세계에 관심을 가졌다.

길가메시 부조(루브르 박물관)
Gilgamesh Relief(Louvre)

메소포타미아의 「길가메시」 서사시

반신반인의 영웅 길가메시는 영원한 생명을 찾기 위해 광야를 떠돌았다. 지쳐 있던 길가메시를 본 한 여인은 그에게 말하였다.

"…… 길가메시여, 당신은 영원한 생명을 찾을 수 없을 것입니다. 신들이 인간을 만들 때 인간에게 죽음도 함께 붙여 주었습니다. 하지만 생명만은 그들이 보살피도록 남겨 두었지요. 좋은 음식으로 배를 채우십시오. 밤낮으로 춤추며 즐기십시오. 잔치를 벌이고 기뻐하십시오. …… 당신의 손을 잡아 줄 자식을 낳고, 아내를 당신 품 안에 꼭 품어 주십시오. 왜냐하면 이 또한 인간의 운명이니까요."

이집트의 「사자의 서」와 스카라베

고대 이집트인들은 사람이 죽으면 저승의 신인 오시리스 앞에서 심판을 받는다고 믿었다. 심장을 진실의 깃털과 함께 저울에 달았을 때 깃털이 더 무거우면 죄가 없는 것으로 보아 오시리스의 왕국에 들어갈 수 있다. 반면 심장이 더 무거우면 죄가 많은 것으로 여겨 암무트라는 괴물에게 심장을 먹히고 만다. 이때 죽은 사람의 심장이 스스로 입을 열고 신에게 죄를 고백할 수도 있기 때문에 이집트인들은 스카라베라는 부적을 만들어 죽은 사람의 심장 위에 올려 두었다.

「사자의 서」 'Book of the Dead'

스카라베의 앞면과 뒷면(이집트 박물관)
Front and Back of Scarab
(Egyptian Museum)

👀 Why Did the Mesopotamians and Egyptians Have Different Worldviews?

The Mesopotamian region was highly open to immigrants because of its open terrain. The Mesopotamians valued their present life because they thought that their present life would end. On the other hand, the region of Egypt is a closed terrain surrounded by desert and sea, so it was hardly ever invaded by immigrants. Due to maintaining a stable state for extented periods, Egyptians became interested in the afterlife.

Epic of '*Gilgamesh*' from Mesopotamia

Gilgamesh, the hero of the demigods, wandered the wilderness in search of eternal life. A woman, seeing the weary Gilgamesh, told him.

"⋯⋯ Gilgamesh, you will never find eternal life. When the gods made humans, they also attached death to humans. But only life was left for them to take care of. Satisfy your hunger with good food. Enjoy dancing day and night. Feast and rejoice. ⋯⋯ Give birth to a child who will hold your hand, and hold your wife in your arms. Because this is also human destiny."

Egyptian '*Book of the Dead*' and Scarabs

The ancient Egyptians believed that when a person died, he was judged before Osiris, the god of the underworld. When the heart is placed on a scale with the feather of truth, if the feather is heavier, it is considered innocent and enters the kingdom of Osiris. On the other hand, if the heart is heavier, it is considered sinful, and the heart is eaten by a monster named Ammut. At this time, the heart of the dead could open its mouth and confess sins to the gods, so the Egyptians made an amulet called a Scarab and placed it on the heart of the dead.

인더스강 유역에 인도 문명이 형성되다

기원전 2500년경 인더스강 유역에서는 드라비다인이 건설한 것으로 추정되는 도시 문명이 발달하였다. 이곳에서 발굴된 하라파 유적과 모헨조다로 유적은 성벽, 포장도로, 배수 시설 등을 갖춘 계획도시였다. 당시 사람들은 다양한 청동기와 채색 토기, 문자를 사용하였고, 메소포타미아 지역과 교류하였다.

기원전 1500년경 중앙아시아의 아리아인이 인도 북부로 이동하여 인더스강 상류 지방에 정착하였다. 이들은 기원전 1000년경 동쪽으로 이동하여 갠지스강 유역까지 진출하였다.

브라만 Brahman
(사제 Priest)

크샤트리아 Kshatriya
(왕족, 무사 Royalty, Warrior)

바이샤 Vaishya
(평민 Common)

수드라 Sudra
(하층민 People of the Lower Classes)

카스트 제도의 계급 피라미드 Caste System

아리아인은 철제 농기구를 이용하고 관개 사업을 실시하여 농업 생산력을 크게 향상하였다. 아리아인은 태양, 물, 불 등의 자연 현상을 섬겼는데, 이를 바탕으로 『베다』를 경전으로 하는 브라만교가 만들어졌다. 한편 아리아인은 피정복민을 지배하기 위해 신분 제도인 카스트 제도를 만들었다.

◉ 고대 계획 도시 모헨조다로가 사라진 이유는 무엇일까요?

4만여 명의 사람들이 모여 살던 모헨조다로에 이상한 일이 벌어졌다. 집과 도시를 버려둔 채 모두 어딘가로 사라져 버린 것이다. 그렇게 수백 년이 흘러 거대한 성채 도시마저 모래와 먼지에 뒤덮여 흔적도 없이 사라졌다. 후대의 고고학자들이 인더스 강 유역에서 이 도시를 찾아냈지만 그곳에 살던 사람들이 왜 사라졌는지는 정확히 알아내지 못하였다. 인구 급증과 무분별한 산림 파괴로 인해 연이은 홍수에 시달리다가 사람들이 도시를 버린 것으로 추측할 뿐이다.

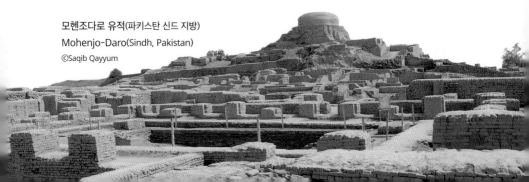

모헨조다로 유적(파키스탄 신드 지방)
Mohenjo-Daro(Sindh, Pakistan)
ⓒSaqib Qayyum

Indian Civilization Is Formed on the Banks of the Indus River

Around 2500 BC, an urban civilization was developed in the area of the Indus River, supposedly by the Dravidians. Archeological sites excavated in the area, such as Harappa and Mohenjo-Daro, showed they were planned cities with ramparts, streets, and drainage facilities. People at the time used various brass tools, painted pottery, and a writing system, and traded with the Mesopotamian region.

By 1500 BC, the Aryans migrated from central Asia to the north of India and settled in the upper region of the Indus River. By 1000 BC, they advanced as far as the eastern Ganges River.

The Aryans had greatly improved their agricultural productivity through the use of iron farming tools and irrigation facilities. The Aryans worshiped natural phenomena that involved the sun, water, and fire, and from their faith in those elements came Brahmanism, whose hymns and religious texts are known as "*Vedas*". Aryans also concurrently created a caste system to rule the people that they'd conquered.

....

⊚ Why Did the Ancient Planned City of Mohenjodaro Disappear?

A strange thing happened in Mohenjodaro, a city of 40,000 people. They all disappeared leaving their houses and the entire city behind. Hundreds of years later, even the massive fortress city disappeared without a trace, covered in sand and dust. Later archaeologists found the city along the Indus River, but they couldn't figure out exactly why the people who lived there had disappeared. It is only speculation that people abandoned the city after suffering a series of floods due to a surge in population and reckless deforestation.

황허강 유역에 중국 문명이 형성되다

기원전 2500년경 중국에서도 청동기를 사용하고 성을 쌓는 등 초기 국가의 모습이 나타났다. 황허강 유역에서는 최초의 왕조인 하가 나타났다고 전해진다.

기원전 1600년경에는 황허강 중·하류 지역에서 상이 출현하였다. 상은 청동으로 무기와 제기 ^{제사에 쓰는 그릇}를 만들었고, 달력을 제작하여 제사를 지내고 농사를 짓는 데 활용하였다. 상은 나라에 중요한 일이 있을 때 하늘의 뜻을 묻기 위해 점을 쳐서 결정하는 신권 정치를 행하였다. 이때 점을 친 내용과 결과를 동물의 뼈와 거북딱지에 새겼는데, 이것이 한자의 기원이 된 갑골문이다.

기원전 11세기경 상을 멸망시킨 주가 호경 ^{현재의 시안}을 중심으로 황허강 유역을 지배하였다. 주는 넓은 영토를 효율적으로 다스리기 위해 봉건제를 시행하였다. 한편 주는 천명사상 ^{하늘이 덕 있는 사람을 선택하여 권력을 맡겼다는 사상}과 덕치주의 ^{덕으로 백성을 감화하여 다스림}를 내세워 왕권을 정당화하였는데, 이는 이후 중국 역대 왕조의 기본적인 통치 이념이 되었다.

⚙️ 주의 봉건제는 어떤 제도였나요?

봉건제란 도읍 일대는 왕이 직접 통치하고, 지방의 땅(봉토)은 왕의 혈연인 왕족이나 공신을 제후로 삼아 맡기는 통치 제도를 말한다. 제후는 왕을 천자로 받들며 세금을 내고 군사적 충성의 의무를 다하였지만 자신이 다스리는 지역에서는 왕과 같은 권력을 누렸다. 제후 아래에는 경, 대부, 사가 있었는데 이들 사이에서도 같은 관계가 맺어졌다.

-- 상의 세력 범위 Sphere of Shang Kingdom
— 주의 세력 범위 Sphere of Zhou Kingdom

상과 주의 세력 범위 Sphere of Shang Kingdom and Zhou Kingdom

주는 봉건제를 이용해 넓은 영토를 다스렸어요. 봉건제는 종법제에 바탕을 두고 운영되었지요. 종법제란 집안을 계승하는 적장자가 아버지의 지위를 이어받아 대종이 되고 적장자 이외의 자식은 소종이 되어 한 등급 낮은 작위를 받는 것을 말해요.
The Zhou Kingdom ruled a large territory using feudal system. The feudal system was operated based on clan rules. The clan rules refer to the eldest son inheriting the father's position to become the Daizong, and all children other than the eldest son become the Xiaozong and receive a title one rank lower.

Chinese Civilization Is Formed by the Yellow River

Around 2500 BC, an early form of a state emerged in China, established by people who used bronze tools and built castles. The records also show that the first kingdom, Xia, emerged on the banks of the Yellow River.

Around 1600 BC, the Shang Kingdom was established in the middle and lower regions of the Yellow River. People of the Shang Dynasty used weapons and utensils made of bronze and a calendar to keep track of the timing for religious rites and farming. The Shang Dynasty is characterized by a shamanistic theocracy, wherein the king made important decisions based on divination from the Oracle. The results of these divinations were carved onto animal bones or turtle shells, which came to be known as the 'Shell-and-bone characters' which eventually evolved into the current Chinese characters.

Around the 11th century BC, the Zhou Kingdom brought down the Shang Kingdom and ruled the regions around the Yellow River with Haojing(today's Xian) as its capital. A feudal system was developed during the Zhou for better management of the vast amounts of land. In the meantime, the Zhou kings justified their legitimacy by advocating the Mandate of Heaven and the principle of benevolent government. These two principles became the fundamental ruling principles for all of the kingdoms that followed in China.

⊚ What Was the Feudal System of the Zhou Kingdom?

The feudal system refers to a system of governance in which the king directly governs the area of the capital and entrusts the royal family or officials who are the king's blood ties to the local land. The feudal lords paid taxes and fulfilled their military allegiance duties by treating the king as a celestial deity, but they enjoyed the same power as the king in the area they ruled. Under the monarch, there were Ministers, Grand Masters, and Servicemen, and this same relationship was established between them.

๑๑ 인류 4대 문명보다 앞선 랴오허 문명은 어느 나라가 형성하였나요?

중국은 1980년대 랴오허 강(요하) 부근에서 대규모 유적지들을 발견하였다. 이것이 인류 4대 문명보다 1,000년이나 앞서는 랴오허 문명이다. 중국에서는 동북공정의 일환으로 '중국 문명은 랴오허 문명과 황허 문명 등이 융합하여 형성되었다.'라고 주장하고 있다. 이는 랴오허 지역 사람들이 남하하여 황허 문명을 만들었다는 것을 의미한다.

랴오허 지역은 한국 최초의 국가인 고조선, 강성한 고대 제국 고구려, 고구려를 계승한 발해의 강역이었다. 이곳에서 발견된 빗살무늬 토기, 계단식 돌무지무덤, 치(雉)가 있는 석성, 비파형 동검, 옥결(옥고리) 등은 중국 중원에서는 발견된 적이 없고 만주와 한반도에서만 발견되었다.

싱룽와 · 차하이 유적(기원전 6200~기원전 5200년경)에서 발견된 빗살무늬 토기와 옥결은 한반도에서 발견된 것들과 동일한 형태를 지니고 있다. 이로써 랴오허 문명의 근원이 중국 중원에 있다는 주장은 설득력을 잃게 되었다.

홍산 문화(기원전 4700~기원전 3000년경)를 대표하는 뉴허량 유적에서 발견된 피라미드식 돌무지무덤은 고구려와 백제의 돌무지무덤과 유사하다. 뉴허량 유적의 여신상 옆에서는 곰 형상들이 발견되었는데, 이는 고조선 단군 신화의 웅녀족과 관련이 있는 것으로 추정한다.

샤자뎬(하가점) 하층 문화(기원전 2000~기원전 1500년경)에 속하는 싼쭤뎬과 청쯔산에는 치가 있는 석성 수천 개가 널려 있다. 이 석성은 고구려와 백제에 영향을 주었고, 조선 시대에 쌓은 공심돈에서도 그 흔적을 찾을 수 있다.

싱룽와 유적에서 발견된 빗살무늬 토기(왼쪽)
Comb-patterned Earthenware from Xinglongwa Historic Sites(Left).
함경북도 서포항에서 발견된 빗살무늬 토기
Comb-patterned Earthenware from Seopo Port, North Hamgyeong Province, Korea.

차하이 유적의 옥결(왼쪽)과 강원도 고성 문암리의 옥결
Jade Disc from the Chahai Historic Sites(Left) and Jade Disc from Munam-ri, Goseong, Gangwon Province

👓 **Which country formed the Liaohe civilization ahead of the four major human civilizations?**

China discovered massive historic sites near the Liaohe River in the 1980s. This is the Liaohe civilization that predates four other human civilizations by 1,000 years. China claims that Chinese civilization was formed by the fusion of the Liaohe civilization and the Yellow River civilization. This means that the people of Liaohe region moved south to create the Yellow River civilization.

The Liaohe region was a stronghold of Old Joseon(Korea's first state), Goguryeo, and Balhae. Comb‑patterned earthenware, stone mound tombs, stone fortifications with rectangular bastions, lute‑shaped bronze daggers, and jade discs were found only in Manchuria and the Korean Peninsula, but never in China.

Comb‑patterned earthenware and jade discs discovered at Xinglongwa and Chahai historic sites(6200‑5200 B.C.) have the same shape as those found on the Korean Peninsula. This broke the belief that the source of Liaohe civilization lies in the Chinese midfield.

The pyramid‑style stone‑set burial chamber discovered in Niuheliang, which is an important site of the Hongshan culture(4700‑3000 B.C), is similar to the burial chambers from Goguryeo and Baekje. Bear figurines were discovered next to the statue of a goddess in the Niuheliang site, and it is presumed to have connection to the bear‑totem group from Dangun mythology of Old Joseon.

Thousands of stone fortifications with rectangular bastions are scattered throughout the Sanzuodian and Chengzi mountain that belonged to the lower Xiajiadian culture(2000‑1500 B.C.). These stone fortifications influenced Goguryeo and Baekje. The evidence can be found at the fortress Gongsimdon built during the Joseon period.

뉴허량 유적에서 출토된 여신상(왼쪽) Clay Statue of a Goddess from Niuheliang Historic Sites(Left).
뉴허량 유적에서 출토된 곰 발 소조상 Clay Statue of a Bear's Foot from Niuheliang Historic Sites

3

고대 제국들의 특성과 주변 세계의 성장

01 페르시아 제국의 발전

페르시아가 서아시아를 지배하다

티그리스강 상류 지역에서 성장한 **아시리아**는 기원전 7세기에 메소포타미아와 이집트를 정복하여 서아시아 지역의 대부분을 통일하였다. 아시리아는 피정복민에게 무거운 세금을 매기고 가혹한 형벌을 내렸다. 이에 각지에서 반발하였고 결국 아시리아는 신바빌로니아에 의해 멸망하였다.

신바빌로니아는 기원전 18세기에 함무라비왕이 세운 바빌로니아의 문화를 받아들였다. 네부카드네자르 2세는 수도 바빌론에 이슈타르의 문과 왕비를 위한 공중 정원을 만들었고 유대와 예루살렘을 정복하였다. 유대인은 두 차례에 걸쳐 바빌론으로 끌려갔다(바빌론 유수).

기원전 6세기에 **키루스 2세**가 메디아를 정복하고 **아케메네스 왕조 페르시아**를 세웠다. 이어 바빌로니아를 정복하고 서아시아를 다시 통일하였으며 유대인을 예루살렘으로 돌려보냈다. 기원전 5세기에 **다리우스 1세**는 이집트, 인도의 인더스강에 이르는 대제국을 이루었다. 페르시아는 중앙 집권 체제를 확립하고 이민족에 대한 포용 정책을 펼쳐 번영을 누렸다.

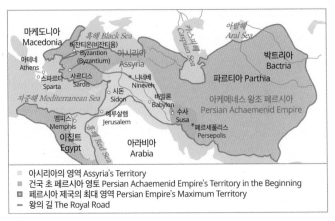

- ■ 아시리아의 영역 Assyria's Territory
- ■ 건국 초 페르시아 영토 Persian Achaemenid Empire's Territory in the Beginning
- ▣ 페르시아 제국의 최대 영역 Persian Empire's Maximum Territory
- ― 왕의 길 The Royal Road

페르시아 제국의 최대 영역 Persian Empire's Maximum Territory

Characteristics of Ancient Empires and the Growth of Surrounding Civilizations

01 Development of the Persian Empire

Persia Rules West Asia

Assyria is an empire that grew in the upper region of the Tigris River and unified most of West Asia by conquering Mesopotamia and Egypt in the 7th century BC. The Assyrians imposed heavy taxes on the people they conquered and subjected them to severe punishments. Consequently, people from all over the conquered lands rebelled against the Assyrians until the empire was itself conquered by the Babylonians.

Neo-Baylonian Empire accepted Babylonian culture founded by King Hammurabi in the 18th century B.C. Nebuchadnezzar II built a hanging garden for the queen and Ishtar gate in Babylon, the capital, and conquered Judea and Jerusalem. The Jews were taken to Babylon twice.

In the 6th century BC, the Persian Achaemenid Empire was established by Cyrus II of Persia with the conquest of Median. Cyrus II conquered Babylonia and reunified West Asia and sent Jews back to Jerusalem. The Persian Empire reached its peak during the reign of Darius I when it included much of Greece, Egypt, and the banks of the Indus River. The Persian Empire thrived with a centralized government system and a policy of embracing other ethnic groups.

공중 정원 Hanging Gardens of Babylon

이슈타르 문 Ishtar gate

아케메네스 왕조 페르시아가 그리스 원정 실패로 쇠퇴하다

페르시아 제국은 서쪽으로 세력을 확장하기 위해 그리스 원정에 나섰다. 하지만 그리스 연합군의 저항으로 세 차례에 걸친 원정은 실패하였다. 이후 페르시아는 점차 쇠약해지다가 기원전 4세기 말 알렉산드로스의 침입으로 멸망하였다.

기원전 3세기 중엽에 메소포타미아 동부에서 이란계 유목민이 **파르티아**를 세웠다. 파르티아는 비단길을 이용한 한과 로마 사이의 중계 무역으로 번영을 누렸다. 하지만 페르시아 제국의 부흥을 꾀한 **사산 왕조 페르시아**에 의해 멸망하였다. 사산 왕조 페르시아도 중계 무역으로 번영을 누리며 비잔티움 제국과 경쟁하였다.

> 파르티아는 앞면에 왕의 초상을 새긴 금속 주화를 사용하였어요.
> Parthia used gold coins with the King's portrait on the front.

파르티아의 금화
A Gold Coin of the Parthia ©PHGCOM

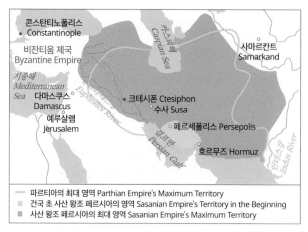

----- 파르티아의 최대 영역 Parthian Empire's Maximum Territory
■ 건국 초 사산 왕조 페르시아의 영역 Sasanian Empire's Territory in the Beginning
■ 사산 왕조 페르시아의 최대 영역 Sasanian Empire's Maximum Territory

사산 왕조 페르시아 제국의 최대 영역 Sasanian Empire's Maximum Territory

◉ 페르시아 제국이 200여 년이나 유지된 이유는 무엇일까요?

페르시아 제국은 강력한 중앙 집권 제도를 실시하였다. 전국을 20개의 주로 나누어 총독을 보내고 감찰관을 파견하여 감시하였다. 또한 화폐와 도량형을 통일하여 지역 간의 교류가 원활하도록 하였다. 도로를 건설하여 전국의 주요 지역을 연결하였고, 지방에 명령을 신속하게 전달하기 위한 교통 · 통신 기관인 역참을 정비하였다. 피정복민에게는 정해진 세금을 내면 고유한 종교, 풍습, 언어 등을 존중하는 관용 정책을 실시하였다.

Achaemenid Empire Declines in the Aftermath of a Failed Expedition to Greece

The Persian Achaemenid Empire launched expeditions against Greece to expand its territory to the west. But all three of their expeditions ended in failure due to the strong resistance of the allied Greeks. In

살라미스 전투 Battle of Salamis

the aftermath of the failed expeditions, Persia slowly began to decline until it was invaded and conquered by Alexander the Great in the late 4th century.

In the mid–3rd century BC, Iranians established the Parthian Empire in the east of Mesopotamia. Positioned between the Chinese Han Empire and the Roman Empire, the Parthians enjoyed prosperity through intermediate trade between east and west. However, the empire was overthrown by the Sasanian Empire who dreamt of reestablishing the Persian Empire. The Sasanian Empire also enjoyed prosperity through intermediate trade and even competed with the Roman Empire.

Why Did the Persian Empire Last for Over 200 Years?

The Persian Empire implemented a strong centralized government system. The entire country was divided into 20 provinces, and governors and inspectors were sent to monitor each one. In addition, currency and weights and measures were standardized to facilitate exchanges between regions. Roads were constructed to connect major regions across the countries and postal stations, which served as transportation and communication institutions, were reorganized to deliver orders quickly to local areas. When the conquered people paid a fixed tax, their religion, customs, and language were respected.

페르시아에서 국제적인 문화가 발전하다

페르시아는 바빌로니아·아시리아·이집트 문화뿐만 아니라 그리스 문화까지 받아들여 국제적 성격의 문화를 발전시켰다. 아케메네스 왕조 페르시아의 수도인 **페르세폴리스** 그리스어로 '페르시아의 도시'라는 뜻의 왕궁 유적에서 이를 확인할 수 있다.

페르시아에서는 금·은 가공 기술이 발달하였는데, 사자나 새와 같은 동물 모양을 새긴 정교한 공예품을 많이 만들었다. 사산 왕조 페르시아에서는 은과 유리로 그릇을 만들었고, 이는 비잔티움 제국은 물론 중국, 우리나라, 일본에도 전해졌다.

● 페르시아 문화는 어떤 특징을 지니고 있나요?

페르시아 문화는 다른 나라의 풍습과 문물을 적극적으로 수용하여 국제적인 성격을 지녔다. 페르세폴리스 궁전의 입구에서는 아시리아 양식의 황소 몸 조각상, 이집트의 영향을 받은 연꽃 무늬, 그리스 건축의 영향을 받은 기둥의 세로선을 볼 수 있다. 궁전의 부조에는 각 나라 사절단이 조각되어 있다. 또한 페르시아에서는 사자를 비롯한 동물 모양이 장식된 황금 공예품을 많이 만들었다. 이는 주변 지역의 문화를 두루 흡수한 보편적인 페르시아 미술 양식을 보여 준다.

페르세폴리스 궁전의 부조
Relief of Persepolis Palace

연꽃무늬 Lotus Pattern

기둥의 세로선
Vertical Lines of Column

페르세폴리스의 '만국의 문'과 돌기둥
Persepolis' 'Gate of All Nations' and Stone Pillars ©Alborzagros

페르세폴리스 유적 전경 (이란) Panoramic View in Persepolis(Iran)

Persia Develops Internationalized Culture

Persia was able to develop an internationalized culture because it accepted the diverse cultures of Babylonia, Assyria, and Egypt, as well as Greece, as testified to by the remains of its royal palace discovered in Persepolis, the capital of Persia during the Achaemenid Empire.

Persians also left a great deal of elaborate artwork of animals such as lions and birds because they utilized advanced gold and silver crafting techniques. During the Sasanian Empire, they made a large number of silver and glass bowls, which were introduced to the Byzantine Empire as well as China, Korea, and Japan.

What Are the Characteristics of Persian Culture?

Persian culture has an international character by actively accepting the customs and cultures of other countries. At the entrance to Persepolis Palace, you can see the bull-body statues of Assyrian-style, the lotus patterns of Egyptian-style, and the vertical lines of columns influenced by Greek architecture. Foreign envoys are carved in the reliefs of the Palace. Also, in Persia, many golden crafts decorated with lions and other animals were created. These show the universal Persian art style that absorbed the culture of the surrounding area.

❶ 날개 달린 사자 장식 뿔잔(이란 국립박물관) A Rhyton Decorated with Winged Lion(National Museum of Iran) ❷ 사사 장식 금잔(이란 국립박물관) A Golden Vessel Decorated with Lion(National Museum of Iran) ❸ 사자 머리 장식 단검(이란 국립박물관) Dagger Decorated with Lion's Head(National Museum of Iran)

조로아스터교가 여러 종교에 영향을 주다

페르시아인들은 기원전 6세기경 예언자 조로아스터(자라투스트라)가 창시한 조로아스터교를 널리 믿었다. 페르시아의 왕들은 자신이 선한 신 아후라 마즈다로부터 권력을 부여받았다고 주장하였다. 그래서 선한 신의 상징인 불을 소중하게 다루었다. 사산 왕조 페르시아는 조로아스터교를 국교로 삼아 체계적인 종교로 발전시켰다.

조로아스터교의 교리 가운데 선과 악의 대결, 구세주의 출현, 천국과 지옥, 최후의 심판 등은 유대교, 크리스트교, 이슬람교에 영향을 주었다.

◎ '매직(Magic, 마법)'이 조로아스터교에서 유래된 이유는 무엇인가요?

조로아스터교는 세상을 선의 신 아후라 마즈다와 악의 신 아리만이 대결을 벌이는 곳으로 보았다. 페르시아인은 최후의 심판이 다가오면 이 대결에서 아후라 마즈다가 승리할 것이고, 아후라 마즈다를 믿고 따르면 천국으로 갈 수 있다고 믿었다.

조로아스터교인들은 아후라 마즈다가 불 속에서 산다고 생각하여 제단의 불이 늘 꺼지지 않도록 하였는데, 이 불을 지키는 사제들을 'Magi(마기)'라고 불렀다. 마기들은 종교 의례를 담당하고 징조나 꿈을 해석하는 역할도 하여 불가사의한 일을 해결할 수 있다고 여겨졌다. 바로 이 Magi(마기)에서 Magic(매직, 마법)이라는 단어가 유래하였다.

> 페르세폴리스 유적에 조로아스터교의 신 아후라 마즈다가 새겨져 있어요.

> 아후라 마즈다가 사산 왕조 페르시아 왕에게 왕권의 상징인 링을 건네고 있어요.

아후라 마즈다 부조
Relief of Ahura Mazda ©Radiokafka

페르시아 왕권을 묘사한 부조
Relief Depicting the Persian Kingship

Zoroastrianism Influences Various Religions

Beginning in the 6th century BC, the Persians believed in the Zoroastrianism founded by the Prophet Zoroaster(Zarathustra). The kings of Persia claimed their power was bestowed upon them by the supreme god Ahura Mazda. For that reason, because fire was the supreme symbol of their god, sacred fires were maintained in their temples. The Sasanian Empire made Zoroastrianism the state religion and developed it systematically.

Major creeds of Zoroastrianism, such good and evil, messianism, heaven and hell, and the final judgment, influenced other religions such as Judaism, Christianity, and Islam.

⊚ Why Did 'Magic' Come from Zoroastrianism?

The Zoroastrianism regarded the world as a place where only the god of good, Ahura Mazda, and the god of evil, Ahriman, confront each other. The Persians believed that Ahura Mazda would win this confrontation when the last judgment came, and that if they believed in Ahura Mazda, they could go to heaven.

The Zoroastrians thought that Ahura Mazda lived in fire, so the fire on the altar was kept alight in perpetuity and the priests who kept this fire were called 'Magi'. They were considered to be able to solve mysteries by taking charge of religious rites and interpreting signs and dreams. The word 'Magic' stems from these Magi.

The Zoroastrian god Ahura Mazda is engraved on the ruins of Persepolis.

Ahura Mazda is handing a ring, a symbol of royal authority, to the Sasanian Persian king.

02 춘추·전국 시대의 사회 변화

춘추·전국 시대가 시작되고 사회가 변화하다

혈연관계를 중심으로 운영되던 주의 봉건제는 시간이 지나 주 왕실과 제후 간의 혈연관계가 멀어지면서 점차 붕괴되었다. 기원전 8세기 초 견융족의 침입을 받은 주가 수도를 동쪽의 낙읍(뤄양)으로 옮기면서 주 왕실의 권위가 크게 약해졌다. 그러자 중국 각지의 제후들이 제각기 독립하여 서로 경쟁하였는데, 이 시기를 춘추·전국 시대라고 한다.

춘추 시대에는 주 왕실의 권위가 어느 정도 인정되었으나, 전국 시대에 이르면서 각 제후들은 주 왕실을 무시하고 치열하게 세력 다툼을 벌였다.

춘추·전국 시대의 영역
Territory of the 'Spring and Autumn Period' and the 'Warring States Period'

■ 춘추 시대의 영역 Territory During the Spring and Autumn Period
■ 전국 시대의 영역 Territory During the Warring States Period
● 춘추 5패 Five Hegemons
■ 전국 7웅 Seven Warring States

◉ 춘추·전국 시대의 특징은 무엇인가요?

춘추 시대에는 많은 제후국이 있었다. 그중 주 왕실에 충성하여 오랑캐를 물리친다는 명분을 내세운 춘추 5패가 패권을 차지하였다. 전국 시대에는 전국 7웅이 주변 제후국을 통합하였다. 춘추·전국 시대에는 무기가 발달하여 경쟁적으로 영토를 넓혔다. 철제 농기구와 소를 이용하여 농업 생산량도 늘었다.

춘추·전국 시대에 사용된 화폐로 농기구의 모습을 본떠 만들었어요.
Spade Coins are currency used in the Spring and Autumn Period and the Warring States Period, and they were made after the appearance of agricultural implements.

포전 Spade Coins

02 Social Changes During the 'Spring and Autumn Period' and the 'Warring States Period' of China

The 'Spring and Autumn Period' and the 'Warring States Period' Begins and Brings Changes to Society

The Zhou Dynasty had a kinship–based feudal system, but the system gradually declined as the familial ties between the Zhou kings and feudal lords grew thinner over the generations. Then, in the early 8th century BC, the Zhou Dynasty moved its capital east to Luoyi(modern day Luoyang) after it was invaded by the Quanrong tribe, which resulted in weakening the power of the dynasty. Feudal lords took advantage of this to become independent from the central government and began warring with each other during the periods that came to be known as the 'Spring and Autumn Period' and the 'Warring States Period'.

During the Spring and Autumn Period, the Chinese monarchy maintained a certain degree of authority, but during the Warring States Period that followed, regional rulers ignored the Zhou kings and engaged in fierce wars with each other over power.

....

◉ What Are the Characteristics of the 'Spring and Autumn Period' and the 'Warring States Period'?

There were many kingdoms governed by feudal lords in the Spring and Autumn Period. Among them, the Five Hegemons were loyal to the main royal family and took supremacy through the cause of defeating the barbarians. During the Warring States Period, the Seven Warring States united the surrounding kingdoms. During the 'Spring and Autumn Period' and the 'Warring States Period', the kingdoms developed weapons and expanded their territory competitively. The use of iron farming tools and cattle increased agricultural production as well.

치열한 경쟁 속에서 다양한 사상가들이 등장하다

춘추·전국 시대의 제후국들은 치열한 경쟁에서 살아남고 부국강병을 이루기 위해 국적과 신분에 관계없이 뛰어난 인재를 모았다. 그 결과 다양한 사상가와 학파가 등장하였는데, 이를 제자백가라고 한다. 제자백가는 이후의 중국 사상과 학문뿐만 아니라 정치와 문화에도 많은 영향을 끼쳤다. 제자백가 중에서도 특히 유가, 도가, 법가, 묵가가 대표적이다.

공자와 맹자가 발전시킨 유가는 '인', '예', '충'을 중시하며 도덕 정치를 추구하는 사상이었다. 유가는 중국, 한국, 일본 등 동아시아 여러 나라의 통치 이념이 되었다. 노자와 장자의 사상인 도가는 자연에 순응하는 삶을 추구하였고, 중국의 종교와 예술에 큰 영향을 미쳤다. 법가는 엄격한 법률과 형벌로 사회 질서를 유지해야 한다고 주장하였다. 한비자가 발전시킨 법가는 강력한 군주권을 확립하고자 하는 제후국들에 환영 받았다. 특히 진은 법가를 통치 이념으로 정하기도 하였다. 묵자를 대표로 하는 묵가는 차별 없는 사랑과 평화를 추구하고 전쟁을 반대하였다.

◎ 춘추·전국 시대 사상가들은 무엇을 주장하였나요?

What Were the Beliefs of the Thinkers During the 'Spring and Autumn Period' and the 'Warring States Period'?

공자 군주가 백성에게 인과 예를 가르치고 덕을 베풀면 세상이 평화로워질 것입니다.
Confucius The world will be at peace if the monarch teaches people 'advocated kindheartedness' and 'appropriate behavior' and imbues 'virtues'.

노자 도덕이나 법 등 인위적인 것은 오히려 세상을 혼란스럽게 합니다. 자연스럽게 살아가면 혼란이 해결될 수 있습니다.
Laozi Artificial things such as morality or law confuse the world. Confusion can be resolved by living naturally.

한비자 세상이 어지러운 것은 인간의 본성이 악하기 때문입니다. 법을 어기면 엄격히 처벌해야 좋은 세상이 됩니다.
Han Feizi The world is confusing because human nature is evil. Those who violate the law must be punished strictly for a good world.

묵자 전쟁을 멈추고 모든 사람이 서로 차별 없이 사랑한다면 평화가 찾아올 것입니다.
Mozi If we stop war and everyone loves each other without discrimination, it will bring peace.

Emergence of Numerous Thinkers Amidst Fierce Competition

During the Spring and Autumn Period and the Warring States Period, regional rulers recruited talented people regardless of their nationality and social class so that they could ensure their survival, as well as their prosperity and strong military power, in the climate of fierce competition. As a result, the periods witnessed the emergence of 'a Hundred Schools of Thought'. They had great influence on Chinese philosophy and academics as well as politics and culture. Some of the major schools of thought born during these periods include Confucianism, Legalism, Taoism, and Mohism.

Confucianism, which is the body of thoughts formulated by Confucius and Mencius, 'advocated kindheartedness', 'appropriate behavior', and 'loyalty', as the most important guidelines for moral politics. It became the ruling principle in countries around East Asia including Korea, Japan, and China. Taoism, which was formulated by Laozi and Zhuangzi, was about living in harmony with the natural world and greatly influenced the Chinese religion and arts. Legalism was about preserving the social order by imposing discipline and strict enforcement of laws. Formulated by Han Feizi, it was widely accepted by regional rulers who were trying to establish a powerful monarchy. In particular, the Qin Dynasty adopted legalism as its official governing philosophy. Mohism, which was represented by Mozi, advocated engagement in impartial care, the practice of collective love and peace, and stood against war.

공자를 모신 중국의 대표적인 사당이에요. The Temple of Confucius in Qufu is the largest and most renowned temple of Confucius.

공묘 대성전(중국 산둥성 취푸) Temple of Confucius(Qufu, Shandong Province, China)

03 진의 통치 체제 마련

진, 최초로 중국을 통일하고 군현제를 실시하다

중국 서북쪽의 약소국이었던 진(秦)은 법가 사상으로 통치 체제를 정비하고 국력을 키워 전국 7웅 중 하나가 되었다. 진은 500여 년 동안 분열되어 있던 중국을 통일하였다(기원전 221). 통일을 달성한 진왕은 자신의 업적을 널리 알리고 왕권을 강화하기 위해 왕이라는 칭호를 황제로 바꾸었다. 또한 스스로를 최초의 황제, 즉 **시황제**^{첫 황제}라 칭하였다.

시황제는 광대한 영토의 중국을 효율적으로 통치하고, 강력한 중앙 집권 국가로 만들기 위하여 여러 정책을 시행하였다. 전국을 36개의 군으로 나누고 그 아래에 현을 설치한 뒤 중앙에서 관리를 파견하는 군현제를 실시하였고, 전국의 문자를 통일하였다. 당시에는 여러 번 수레가 지나가면서 생긴 바퀴자국을 따라 수레를 몰아야 하였는데, 국가마다 수레바퀴의 폭이 달라 통행이 어려웠다. 이에 시황제는 **수레바퀴의 폭**을 통일하고 전국에 도로를 건설하였다. 또한 지역마다 달랐던 **도량형**과 화폐를 통일하여 지역 간 교역을 원활하게 하였다.

◎ 시황제는 왜 수천 명의 병사와 함께 땅에 묻혔을까요?

시황제의 무덤 속에는 실물 크기의 기마상, 수천 명의 병사상 등 당시 시황제의 군사 규모가 거의 그대로 재현되어 있어요. 병사는 각자의 복장, 머리 모양 등이 다른데, 진의 군대가 다양한 민족으로 구성되었음을 알 수 있지요. 병마용은 최대 72만 명의 인부가 약 39년 동안 만들었는데, 이는 시황제의 권력을 보여줍니다.

시황제의 병마용갱과 병마용(중국 산시성 시안)
Mausoleum of the Qin Shi Huang and the Terracotta Army(Xian, Shaanxi Province, China)

03 Qin Establishes Governing Systems

Qin Unifies China for the First Time and Adopts a Commandery-county System

Qin was a small state situated in the northwestern part of China but became one of the Seven Warring States by building structured political power and a large military supported by the ruling principle of legalism. Around 221 BC, Qin unified a divided China. Once it had united China, the king of Qin called himself an emperor to promulgate his accomplishment and strengthen his royal authority. He also called himself Qin Shi Huang, whose meaning is 'The First Emperor' in Chinese.

Qin Shi Huang implemented various policies in order to effectively govern China over vast territories and transform itself into a powerful centralized government. After dividing the country into 36 counties, prefectures were installed under each the Commandery-county system, in which officials were dispatched from a centralized authority, was instituted, and the language across the country was unified. At that time, carts had to be driven along the wheel ruts worn into the roads, but the width of the cart was different in each country, making it difficult to pass. Accordingly, Qin Shi Huang unified the axle length of carts and constructed roads across the country. In addition, by unifying weights and measures and currency that differed from region to region, trade between regions was facilitated.

....

⚉ Why Was Qin Shi Huang Buried in a Grave with Thousands of Soldiers?

Inside the Qin Shi Huang's tomb, there are life-size statues of horses and soldiers, all of which are recreated almost as they were. Each soldier has a different outfit and hairstyle, which shows that Qin's army was made up of various ethnic groups. The Terracotta Army was created by up to 720,000 workers over a period of about 39 years, demonstrating the power of the Qin Shi Huang at the time.

가혹한 통치를 시행하다

시황제는 흉노족진(秦)·한(漢)대에 몽골고원에서 활동하던 기마 민족의 침입을 막기 위해 **만리장성**을 쌓고 거대한 무덤을 만드는 등 대규모 토목 공사를 실시하였다. 시황제가 **법가 사상**을 내세워 가혹한 통치를 계속하고 불로장수를 위한 도술에 빠지자 유학자들은 이를 비판하였다. 그러자 시황제는 법가 사상 관련 도서와 실용서를 제외한 모든 책을 태우고 유학자들을 산 채로 묻는 **분서갱유**를 단행하였다.

지방을 순시하던 시황제가 갑자기 죽으면서 진은 혼란에 빠졌다. 시황제의 아들이 제위에 올랐으나, **진승·오광의 난**중국 역사상 최초의 농민 반란을 비롯한 백성들의 항거가 계속 이어졌다. 결국 진은 중국을 통일한 지 15년 만에 멸망하였다(기원전 206).

....

✏ 분서갱유가 무엇인가요?

시황제는 많은 책을 금지하고 불 태웠으며 학자들을 처형하였다. 일반 백성들이 가지고 있는 서적 가운데 의학, 점복, 농업, 임업과 관련 있는 것을 제외하고 모두 불태워 버렸다(분서). 또한 국가의 명령을 거역하고 황제의 통일 정책을 비판하거나 국법을 어긴 460명을 수도 선양에 묻어 죽이고(갱유), 이를 온 천하에 알려 후세까지 경계하도록 하였다. 이러한 분서갱유는 엄청난 문화적 손실이었다.

시황제는 시서와 백가의 저서를 몰수하여 불태우고 우민 정책을 추진하였다. 이를 비판하는 자들은 구덩이를 파고 묻어 버렸다.
- 『사기』 「이사·왕전 열전」
Qin Shi Huang confiscated the collections of poetry, calligraphy, and books of many schools and burned them. He dug a pit and buried those who criticized him.
- "The Records of the Grand Historian", 'A Series of the Grand Historian: Li Si and Wang Jian'

분서갱유 Burning Books and Burying of Scholars

Execution of a Cruel Reign

Qin Shi Huang also launched large-scale construction projects including massive tombs and the Great Wall to defend his dynasty against the Xiongnu barbarians. However, Qin Shi Huang was criticized by many Confucian scholars because he enforced a cruel reign in accordance with Legalism and became obsessed with magic and alchemy in his search for the elixir of immortality. In response, Qin Shi Huang had all books, except for those dealing with legalism and practical references, burned and had Confucian scholars buried alive in what came to be known as the 'Burning of Books and Burying of Scholars' incident. He also had Confucian scholars buried alive.

Qin Shi Huang's sudden death during an inspection tour led to great chaos in the Qin Dynasty. Even though Qin Shi Huang's son took the throne, the dynasty was constantly under attack by rebellions, including the Uprising of Chen Sheng and Wu Guang, until the Qin Dynasty collapsed 15 years after unifying China(206 BC).

◉ What Is Burning of Books and Burying of Scholars?

Qin Shi Huang banned and burned many books and executed numerous scholars. He burned all of the books held by the general people except those related to medicine, occupation, agriculture, and forestry. In addition, over 460 people who disobeyed the state's order, criticized the emperor's unification policy, or violated the national law were buried in Shenyang, the capital. This was announced to the entire country so that future generations would be wary. The burning of books and burying of scholars was a massive cultural loss.

04 한의 통치 체제 마련

한, 통치 체제를 정비하다

진 말기의 혼란으로 분열된 중국을 한이 다시 통일하였다(기원전 202). 초의 항우를 누르고 중국을 다시 통일한 한 고조(유방)는 **군국제**를 실시하였다. 군국제는 군현제와 봉건제를 절충한 제도였다. 수도 부근과 군사적 요충지는 황제가 직접 관할하고, 나머지 지방은 제후가 대신 다스렸다.

한은 무제 때 국력이 크게 성장하여 전성기를 맞았다. 무제는 모든 지역에서 군현제를 실시하여 강력한 중앙 집권 체제를 확립하였다. 또한 정복 전쟁에 나서 남월국을 정복하고 고조선을 멸망시켰으며 북방의 흉노를 공격하여 중앙아시아까지 세력을 떨쳤다.

거듭된 전쟁에 막대한 비용이 사용되면서 국가의 재정이 부족해지자 무제는 군수법과 평준법을 도입하여 경제를 통제하였다. 또한 소금과 철을 국가가 전매_{국고 수입을 위하여 국가가 어떤 재화의 생산과 판매를 독점하는 일}하는 제도를 시행하였다.

한의 오수전
Five-zhu Coin of Han

한 무제 때 만들어진 오수전은 당 초기인 621년까지 사용되었어요. 중국 역사상 가장 오랜 기간에 걸쳐 유통된 화폐였지요.
Five-zhu coin, which was created during the period of the Emperor Wu, was used until 621, in the early days of Tang. It was the currency that has been in circulation over the longest period in Chinese history.

❂ 한 무제는 재정 확충을 위해 어떤 제도를 도입하였나요?

한 무제
흉노족을 비롯한 오랑캐와의 전쟁이 끊이질 않으니 국가의 재정 확충을 위해 다음과 같은 정책을 시행하고자 합니다.
국가가 지방의 특산물을 조세로 거둔 후 다른 지방에 판매하여 유통을 돕고 이익을 거두겠습니다(균수법).
또한 물가가 쌀 때 국가에서 물건을 사두었다가 오르면 판매하는 방법으로 물가를 조절하겠습니다(평준법).
앞으로 이익이 많이 남는 소금과 철의 판매는 정부가 독점하겠습니다(전매제).

04 Han Establishes Government Systems

Han Organizes a Government System

China was a divided country at the end of the Qin Dynasty, but it was reunited again by the Han Dynasty(202 BC). Emperor Gaozu(Liu Bang) united China after defeating the last rebellion led by Xiang Yu of the insurgent Chu State, and adopted a system of commandery and princedom, which was a mix of commandery and feudal systems. Under this system, strategic military posts and capital areas were under the direct command of the emperor while the rest were under regional rulers.

The Han Dynasty became a great power and reached its peak during the reign of the Emperor Wu of Han. He was able to build a strong and centralized state thanks to the Commandary-county system that covered the entire territory. He also launched conquest campaigns and defeated Nanyue and Old Joseon, and went on to invade Central Asia as well as the northern Xiongnu barbarians.

When the significant cost of repeated wars drained the national revenue, Emperor Wu controlled the economy through the standardization of the transport system and the price of goods via special regulations. He also had the state monopolize the production, transport, and sale of salt and iron.

◈ What Kind of System Did Emperor Wu Introduce to Expand Finances?

Emperor Wu of the Han Dynasty
Since the war with the Xiongnu and other barbarians is constant, the following policies will be implemented to expand the national finances.
After the state collects local specialties as tax, the state will sell them to other regions to help with distribution and make profits. In addition, when prices are low, the state will adjust prices by buying goods in the country and selling them when they are higher. In addition, the state will monopolize the sale of salt and iron to generate profit.

한이 흉노와 대립하면서 다양한 종족과 문화를 통일하다

한대에는 북쪽의 유목 국가인 **흉노**가 자주 쳐들어왔다. 어느 정도 흉노에 대하여 군사적 우위에 서게 된 한 무제는 흉노와 전쟁을 벌여 일시적으로 흉노를 고비 사막 너머로 쫓아냈다.

무제는 흉노와의 전쟁에 앞서 대월지와 손을 잡기 위해 **장건**을 서역으로 보냈는데 이 과정에서 한에서 서역으로 연결되는 길이 개척되었다. 이후 이 길을 통해 동서 문화의 교류가 시작되었고, 한의 비단이 로마까지 전해져 **비단길**로 불렸다.

한은 주변의 종족과 문화를 통일하는 과정에서 유교적 통치 이념과 **화이관** _{중국의 중화주의적 세계관}을 바탕으로 한 책봉과 조공 관계를 적용하였다. 책봉과 조공은 다분히 형식적이어서 주변 나라들은 별다른 거부감 없이 이를 수용하였다. 한은 이러한 외교 의례를 거부할 때는 무력을 행사하여 직접 지배를 도모하기도 하였다.

한의 영역과 장건이 다녀온 길 Territory of Han Dynasty and Zhang Qian's Path

----

🌐 비단길은 어떻게 개척되었나요?

장건은 대월지와 동맹을 맺기 위해 서역으로 갔다. 그러나 평화를 누리고 있던 대월지는 흉노 공격을 위한 동맹을 원하지 않았다. 동맹을 맺는 데 실패한 대신 장건은 서역의 물품과 정보를 가지고 귀국하였다. 이를 본 무제는 서역에 흥미를 느끼고 서역과 교류하기 위해 노력하였다. 그 결과 새로운 교역로인 비단길이 열렸다.

장건(좌)과 한 무제(중국 둔황 석굴 벽화의 일부, 우)
Zhang Qian(Left) and Emperor Wu of Han(Part of Mural Painting at the Mogao Caves in China, Right)

Han Unifies Diverse Ethnic Groups and Cultures While Fighting Against the Xiongnu Tribe

The Han Dynasty was constantly raided by northern nomadic people called the Xiongnu tribe. After building a military force that surpassed the Xiongnu tribe, Emperor Wu waged war with them and drove them beyond the Gobi Desert, if only temporarily.

Before the war with the Xiongnu, Emperor Wu dispatched Zhang Qian to the Western Regions to build an alliance with the Yuezhi against the Xiongnu. During this journey, a road that connected Han and the Western Regions was established. Later on, the cultures of the East and the West were exchanged through this road and the silk made in Han was introduced to Rome, thereby giving it the name the Silk Road.

Founded upon the Confucian governing principles and a value system called Huayiguan (lit. Chinese superior, others inferior), Han applied the tributary system and title conference system on its quest to unify surrounding tribes and their cultures. Being rather a matter of formality only, the surrounding tributary states accepted them without much resistance. However, Han turned to force to deal directly with the tributary states that refused to follow these diplomatic formalities.

How Was the Silk Road Established?

Zhang Qian went to the Western regions to form an alliance with Yuezhi. But Yuezhi did not wish an alliance to attack Xiongnu. Instead, Zhang Qian returned to the Han Dynasty with supplies and information from the Western regions. Seeing this, Emperor Wu became interested in the Western regions and tried to exchange with them. As a result, a new trade route, the Silk Road, was opened.

| Now I'm leaving for the Western regions. | Go and make an alliance with Yuezhi. |

황건적의 난을 계기로 한이 멸망하다

무제 이후 외척 어머니 쪽의 친척과 환관 궁정에서 일하는 내관이 정치에 개입하면서 정치가 혼란해지고 황제권이 약화되었다. 결국 외척 왕망이 황위를 빼앗고 신을 세웠다(8). 그러나 신은 얼마 못 가 멸망하였고 이후 광무제가 다시 한을 세웠는데 이를 후한이라 부른다.

후한 말에 이르러 어린 황제들이 계속해서 즉위하자 외척과 환관의 권력 다툼이 심해졌다. 정치의 혼란으로 중앙의 통제력이 약해지자 지방에서는 호족 지방에서 대토지를 소유하고 권력을 누리던 사람들 세력이 성장하였다. 호족이 더 많은 토지를 소유하고 서로 다투기 시작하며 농민의 생활은 어려워졌다. 결국 황건적의 난(184)을 비롯한 농민 봉기가 일어났고 호족들의 다툼이 지속되어 후한이 멸망하였다(220).

◉ 황건적의 난이 삼국(위·촉·오) 탄생의 배경이 되었나요?

후한은 호족 연합 정권이어서 황제는 허수아비에 불과했고 농민은 호족의 착취 대상이 되었다. 이때 나타난 태평도의 교주 장각은 신도와 농민을 규합하여 황건적(노란 수건을 두른 도적)의 난을 일으켰다. 중앙 정부는 지방 호족들에게 난의 진압을 명령했고 이때 조조, 유비, 손견 등이 두각을 드러냈다. 십상시(10명의 환관)의 난까지 일어나 한은 이미 기울었고 중원을 차지하기 위한 싸움이 벌어졌다. 그 이야기가 바로 나관중의 『삼국지』이다.

유비, 관우, 장비 세 사람은 복숭아밭에서 의형제를 맺고 황건적 토벌에 나섰어요. 이후 유비는 제갈량을 영입하여 촉(蜀)을 세우고, 위(魏)의 조조, 오(吳)의 손권 등과 함께 패권을 다투었지요.
Liu Bei, Guan Yu, and Zhang Jiang took an oath of fraternity in a peach orchard and together set out to crack down on the Yellow Turban rebels. Later on, Liu Bei recruited Zhuge Liang to found Shu(蜀) and competed for supremacy with Cao Cao of Wei(魏) and Sun Quan of Wu(吳).

『삼국지』의 '도원결의(桃園結義)' 장면
Scene of the 'Oath of Fraternity in the Peach Garden' as Described in the "Romance of the Three Kingdoms"

The Yellow Turban Rebellion Brings Down the Han Dynasty

The royal authority of the kings that succeeded Emperor Wu grew weak because consort kin and eunuchs started getting their hands into politics. Eventually, a consort kin named Wang Mang seized the throne and founded the Xin Dynasty(8). However, the Xin Dynasty soon perished, and after that, Gwangwu revived Han to become what is called the Later Han Dynasty.

Towards the end of the Later Han Dynasty, the power struggle among the consort kin and eunuchs intensified because the succeeding kings took the throne at very young ages. While the central government's power grew weak as a result of deepening political chaos, powerful local landowners started growing their influence. Life became harder for peasants because of the tyranny and exploitation of the powerful landowners. Eventually, the situation led to numerous revolts by peasants, including the Yellow Turban Rebellion(184), while the power struggle among local landowners continued until the Later Han Dynasty was overthrown(220).

⊚ Did the Yellow Turban Rebellion Contribute to the Founding of the Three Kingdoms(Wei, Shu, Wu)?

The Later Han was a state run by a coalition of wealthy landowners, where the emperor was just a figurehead, and the farmers were exploited by the landowners. At the time, the founding leader of the Way of the Great Peace Zhang Jue united his followers and peasants to incite the Yellow Turban Rebellion. The central government ordered local landowners to crack down on the rebels, and it was during this time that Cao Cao, Liu Bei, and Sun Jian emerged as warlords. Then came the rebellion by the Ten Attendants(the Ten Eunuchs). By then, the power of the Han Dynasty was already declining, and wars broke out to occupy the land. Their stories are written in the Chinese classic "*Romance of the Three Kingdoms*" by Luo Guanzhong.

유학이 통치 이념으로 자리 잡고 중국 문화의 기틀이 마련되다

진의 시황제에게 탄압받았던 유학은 한대에 크게 발전하여 통치 이념으로 자리 잡았다. 무제는 유학자 동중서의 건의를 받아들여 유학을 국가의 통치 이념으로 삼았다. 또한 수도 장안에 유학 교육 기관인 태학을 설립하고 오경박사 제도를 운영하였다. 한대에는 진대에 있었던 분서갱유의 영향으로 유학의 경전을 해석하고 주석을 달아 정리하는 훈고학 고서의 문자나 어구를 해석하여 본래의 사상을 이해하는 학문이 발달하였다.

한대에는 학문과 과학 기술이 발전하여 중국 전통문화의 기틀이 마련되기도 하였다. 사마천은 『사기』를 편찬하였는데, 『사기』의 서술 방식인 기전체는 이후 역사서 집필의 표준이 되었다. 또한 채륜이 종이 만드는 방법을 개량하여 종이의 생산이 쉬워졌다. 한 이전에는 주로 죽간, 목간, 비단 등에 문자를 기록하였는데, 이 재료들은 비싸거나 구하기 어려웠다.

과학 기술이 발전하여 해시계와 지진계도 발명되었다. 장형은 세계 최초의 지진계인 지동의를 발명하여 지진의 발생 방향을 측정하였다.

🌀 사마천의 『사기』는 어떤 책인가요?
What Kind of Book Is Sima Qian's *"The Records of the Grand Historian"*?

『사기』는 신화 시대부터 한 무제 시대에 이르기까지 중국 역대 왕조의 역사와 주변 국가의 역사를 기록한 책입니다. 황제의 업적을 다룬 '본기', 제후들의 전기를 다룬 '세가', 제도와 문물을 다룬 '서', 각 분야의 유명 인물들을 다룬 '열전' 등으로 구성되어 있는데, 이러한 구성 방식을 '기전체'라고 해요.

"The Records of the Grand Historian" is a book written about the history of the successive dynasties of China and surrounding countries on everything from the myths to the Emperor Wu of the Han Dynasty. It consists of the 'Basic Annals', which deals with the emperor's achievements, the 'Hereditary Houses', which deals with the biography of feudal lords, the 'Monographs' which deals with institutions and cultures, and the 'Biographs' which deals with famous people in each field. This configuration method is called 'Jizhuanti style'.

『사기』 *"The Records of the Grand Historian"*

Confucianism Becomes the Main Political Ideology and Foundation of Chinese Culture

Confucianism was suppressed by the first Emperor of the Qin Dynasty, Qin Shi Huang, but it advanced greatly during the Han Dynasty. At the proposal of a Confucian scholar named Dong Zhongshu, Emperor Wu acknowledged Confucianism as the dominant political ideology of the Han Dynasty. In addition, an imperial academy dedicated to Confucian learning called the Taixue was established in the capital city of Changan, where a program called 'Erudite of the Five Classics' was introduced. After having experienced the 'Burning of books and burying of scholars' incident during the Qin Dynasty, a textual exegesis(currently called philology) was developed during the Han Dynasty to decipher the meaning of Confucian texts and analyze them.

The advancement in academic studies and scientific technology during the Han Dynsaty laid the groundwork for traditional Chinese culture to flourish. A Chinese historian of the early Han Dynasty named Sima Qian penned "*The Records of the Grand Historian*". He wrote this book in the Jizhuanti style, which was about presenting history in a series of biographies. This style became the standard for writing history books later on. Production of paper was made easy during this period after Cai Lun invented modern paper and advanced the papermaking process. In the past, they left written records on bamboo poles, wooden tablets, or silk, but these were expensive and not widely available.

Development in science and technology also resulted in the invention of the sundial and the world's first seismograph. Invented by Zhang Heng, the seismograph, named the Didongyi, made it possible to measure the movements of the Earth.

05 고대 그리스의 민주주의 체제와 문화

그리스에서 에게 문명이 발달하다

에게해의 크레타섬과 그리스 본토의 미케네에서 오리엔트 '해가 뜨는 곳'이라는 뜻 문명의 영향을 받아 청동기 문명이 일어났다. 기원전 2000년경 크레타인들은 여러 지역과 교류하며 자유롭고 생동감 넘치는 문명을 꽃피웠다. 크레타 문명은 그리스 본토 주민의 침입과 자연재해로 멸망하였다. 미케네인들은 크레타섬을 점령하고 트로이 전쟁에서 승리하였다.

미케네 문명은 기원전 1200년경 철기로 무장한 도리스인의 공격을 받아 파괴되었다. 에게 문명이 몰락한 이후 그리스 지역은 수 세기 동안 암흑기를 거쳤다.

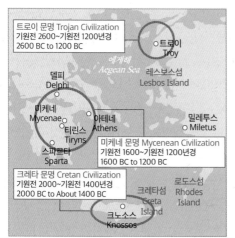

에게 문명 Aegean Civilization

· ·

🌀 **트로이 전쟁은 정말 황금 사과 때문에 벌어진 전쟁이었나요?**

트로이 전쟁을 기록한 호메로스의 「일리아드」에 따르면 전쟁의 발단은 아름다움에 대한 여신들의 경쟁 때문이었다. 불화의 여신이 놓고 간 '가장 아름다운 여신에게'라고 적힌 황금 사과를 두고 헤라, 아프로디테, 아테나가 다투었다. 트로이의 왕자 파리스가 아프로디테를 사과의 주인으로 택하였고, 그 대가로 가장 아름다운 여인을 아내로 맞이하였다. 그러나 그 여인은 스파르타의 왕 메넬라오스의 부인 헬레네였다. 아내를 빼앗긴 메넬라오스는 미케네의 왕이자 자신의 형 아가멤논에게 트로이를 공격하라고 호소하였다. 이에 그리스 연합군과 트로이 간에 전쟁이 발생하였다고 한다.

그러나 트로이 전쟁은 바다의 패권을 차지하려는 해상 국가의 욕심 때문에 벌어진 전쟁이었다. 당시 에게해를 지나 흑해로 가고 싶어 했던 미케네 왕국은 흑해의 길목에 있는 트로이가 걸림돌이 되자 헬레네 납치 사건을 빌미로 전쟁을 일으킨 것이다.

05 Democratic System and Culture of Ancient Greece

The Advancement of the Aegean Culture in Greece

Influenced by the Eastern civilizations, the Bronze Age civilization developed around the island of Crete in the Aegean Sea and Mycenae on the mainland of Greece. Around 2000 BC, the Cretans nourished a liberal and dynamic civilization while interacting with people from various regions. The Cretan civilization was destroyed after numerous invasions by the mainland Greeks and several natural disasters. The Myceneans occupied the island of Crete and claimed victory in the Trojan War.

The Mycenean civilization was subsequently destroyed by the Dorians, who were equipped with iron weapons. Greece went into a Dark Age that lasted several centuries after the fall of all of the Aegean civilizations.

....

🏺 Was the Trojan War Really a War for a Golden Apple?

According to Homer's the '*Iliad*', a record of the Trojan War, the start of the war was due to the goddess' competition for beauty. Hera, Aphrodite, and Athena quarreled over a golden apple that said 'To the most beautiful goddess' left by the goddess of discordia, and Paris, the prince of Troy, chose Aphrodite as the owner of the apple. In return, he would have the most beautiful woman as his wife. But the beautiful woman was Helene, wife of Menelaus, king of Sparta. Having lost his wife, Menelaus appealed to his brother Agamemnon, king of Mycenae, to attack Troy. This led to war between Greece and Troy.

However, the Trojan War was waged because of the greed of the maritime states to seize the hegemony of the sea. At that time, the kingdom of Mycenae, which wanted to go to the Black Sea through the Aegean Sea, started a war with the abduction of Helen when the path of the Black Sea became an obstacle.

파리스의 심판 Judgement of Paris

그리스에 도시 국가들이 나타나다

그리스에는 산지와 섬이 많아 통일된 국가가 세워지기 어려웠기 때문에 폴리스 그리스어로 '성채'를 뜻함라는 크고 작은 도시 국가들이 생겨났다. 그리스인은 기원전 8세기 중엽부터 해안에 가까운 평야 지대에 자리 잡고 언덕에 성이나 요새를 쌓았다.

이렇게 형성된 폴리스의 중심부에는 신전이 조성된 **아크로폴리스**가 있었고, 그 아래에 시민이 회의를 열거나 상거래를 하는 **아고라**가 있었다.

그리스는 수많은 폴리스로 이루어져 있었지만 그리스인은 같은 언어를 사용하고 동족 의식도 강하여 스스로를 **헬레네스** 헬렌(그리스 신화에 나오는 그리스인의 시조)의 후손이라는 뜻라고 불렀다. 이들은 4년마다 **올림피아 제전**을 열어 유대감을 다졌다.

◉ 올림피아 제전에서는 어떤 경기가 열렸나요?

올림피아 제전은 펠로폰네소스반도 서쪽에 자리 잡은 올림피아에서 처음 시작되었다. 기원전 776년에 시작된 이래 기원후 393년까지 1,100여 년 동안 한 번도 거르지 않고 열렸다. 아킬레우스가 친구의 죽음을 애도하기 위해 경기를 시작한 이후 스파르타, 아테네 등의 도시들과 식민지들도 참가하였고, 기원전 6세기에 이르러서는 그리스 전체의 민족 제전이 되었다. 이는 단순한 운동 경기가 아니라 자신의 몸을 단련하여 신에게 바치는 종교적 의미가 강하였기 때문에 '올림피아 제전'이라고 하였다.

올림피아 제전은 그리스인들의 민족적 자부심을 고취하고, 그리스인을 결속하는 데 큰 역할을 하였다. 당시의 경기 종목인 경주, 투창, 원반던지기, 도약, 레슬링 등은 지금의 올림픽 경기에까지 계승되고 있다.

아크로폴리스는 성벽으로 둘러싸여 있어 유사시 시민들의 피난처로 이용되기도 하였어요.
The Acropolis was surrounded by walls and was used as a refuge for citizens in case of emergency.

원반 던지는 사람(영국 박물관, 복제)
Discobolus(British Museum, Replica)
ⓒLivioandronico2013

그리스 아테네의 아크로폴리스
Acropolis of Athens, Greece

City States Emerge in Greece

Greece had numerous small and large city states called Polis because, with its territory consisting mostly of islands and mountains, it was difficult to establish a unified nation. Beginning in the mid-8th century BC, the Greeks settled in flatlands near the oceans and built castles and fortresses on hills.

Within a polis built this way, there was an urban center called the Acropolis built upon an area of elevated ground with temples, and below the acropolis, there was an Agora where citizens gathered for meetings or commercial trade.

The Greeks called themselves Hellenes, because, even though Greece consisted of a number of poleis, they spoke the same language and shared a strong sense of identity. They built their solidarity by getting together for the Olympic Games that happened once every four years in the city of Olympia.

What Kind of Games Were Held at the Olympia Games?

The Olympic Games began in Olympia, located west of the Peloponnesos. From its beginning in 776 BC to 393 AD, it has been opened for over 1,100 years. After Achilleus started the games to mourn his friend's death, cities and colonies such as Sparta and Athens began to participate. By the 6th century BC, it had become a national festival for the whole of Greece. This is not a simple sporting event, but because it has a strong religious meaning to train one's body and dedicate it to the gods, it was called the 'Olympic Games'.

The Olympic Games inspired the national pride of the Greeks and played a major role in uniting them. Races, javelin, discus throwing, a long jump, and wrestling, which were the events of the time, have been handed down to the current Olympic Games.

아테네에서 민주 정치가 발전하다

기원전 6세기 무렵 그리스의 대표적인 폴리스인 아테네는 활발한 해상 활동을 벌였다. 이 과정에서 재산을 모은 평민들은 스스로 무장을 하여 귀족들과 함께 전쟁에 참여하였고 그로 인해 평민의 영향력은 확대되었다. 이 무렵 **솔론** 계층 간의 갈등을 조절하려 한 조정자로 평가받음 은 재산 소유의 정도에 따라 일부 평민도 정치에 참여할 수 있게 하였다. 기원전 6세기 말에는 **클레이스테네스**가 **참주** 비합법적인 방법으로 독재권을 장악한 지배자를 말함의 출현을 막기 위하여 **도편 추방제**를 도입하였다.

아테네 민주 정치는 **페리클레스** 때 전성기를 맞이하였다. 페리클레스는 정치 참여 자격에서 재산 기준을 없애고 시민이 참여하는 민회 중심의 직접 민주주의를 정착시켰다. 하지만 아테네에서 여성, 노예, 외국인은 정치에 참여할 수 없었다.

⟡ **페리클레스의 민주 정치에는 어떤 한계가 있나요?**

페리클레스는 아테네의 황금시대를 연 인물이다. 그는 시민이 참여하는 직접 민주주의를 정착시켰지만 페리클레스의 민주 정치에는 한계가 있었다.

우선 아테네에서는 시민권을 가진 남성에게만 참정권이 주어졌고, 여성과 아이는 정치 참여가 불가능하였다. 외국인도 납세의 의무는 있었으나 정치에는 참여할 수 없었다. 노예는 정치 참여가 불가능하였고, 거주 이전의 자유도 없었다. 또한 다수결의 원칙이었기 때문에 다수의 의견이 잘못될 경우 이를 바로잡을 기회가 없다는 한계가 있었다. 대표적으로 중우 정치에 희생된 소크라테스가 있다.

소크라테스는 국가에서 인정하는 신을 믿지 않고 청년들에게 나쁜 영향을 미친다는 죄목으로 고소되었어요. 배심원들의 투표로 사형을 구형받았지요. 그는 도주할 수도 있었지만 독배를 마시고 생을 마쳤어요.

소크라테스의 죽음(메트로폴리탄 미술관) The Death of Socrates(Metropolitan Museum of Art)

Development of Democratic Politics in Athens

Around the 6th century BC, there was a boom of maritime trade in the leading polis named Athens. Some of the common people who were able to build wealth during the boom raised their own armies and participated in wars along with members of the aristocracy, consequently increasing the clout of the common people greatly. It was around this time that an Athenian statesman named Solon allowed some of the wealthy commoners to participate in politics. Then towards the end of the 6th century BC, Cleisthenes introduced ostracism to forestall the recurrence of tyranny.

Athenian democratic politics were at their peak during the reign of Pericles. Pericles eliminated wealth as a requirement to participate in politics and laid the groundwork for a direct democracy centering on an assembly in which citizens could participate. In Athens, however, women, slaves, and foreigners were not allowed to participate in politics.

◉ What Were the Limits to Pericles' Democracy?

Pericles is the person who opened the golden age of Athens. He established a direct democracy involving citizens, but Pericles' democratic politics had limitations.

First of all, in Athens, suffrage was given only to men with citizenship. Women and children were unable to participate in politics, and while foreigners were also obligated to pay taxes, they were unable to participate in politics. Slaves were unable to participate in politics and had no freedom of residential mobility. In addition, since it was a principle of majority vote, there was no opportunity to correct the opinions of majority if they were wrong. A representative example is Socrates, who was killed by the ochlocracy.

> Socrates was accused of not believing in the gods recognized by the state and for adversely affecting young people. He was sentenced to death by a jury vote. He could have escaped, but he ended his life by drinking poison.

스파르타가 군사 국가로 성장하다

도리스인이 세운 스파르타는 강력한 군사 제도를 바탕으로 소수의 시민이 많은 원주민을 다스렸다. 스파르타 시민은 원주민의 반란에 대비해 엄격한 군사 훈련을 받았다. 남성은 어릴 때부터 집을 떠나 아고게라는 학교에서 단체 생활을 하면서 군사 훈련을 받았다. 여성도 건강한 아이를 출산하기 위하여 체력 훈련을 받았다.

스파르타는 왕과 소수의 귀족이 정치를 맡았지만 국가의 주요 정책은 민회에서 결정하였다.

● '스파르타식 교육'이라는 말은 무슨 의미인가요?

기원전 약 900년경 스파르타에 리쿠르고스라는 사람이 있었다. 그는 스파르타를 위대한 도시 국가로 만들기 위해 여러 나라를 돌아다니며 강한 나라를 만드는 비결을 배웠다. 리쿠르고스가 내린 결론은 먹이를 풍족하게 주고 키운 개보다 먹이를 스스로 찾아 먹도록 만든 개가 더욱 강하다는 것이었다.

스파르타로 돌아온 리쿠르고스는 여러 가지 개혁을 실시하였다. 그중 스파르타식 교육법이 있었다. 이는 사자가 새끼를 언덕 위에서 떨어뜨려 살아남는 새끼만 키우는 것과 비슷하였다.

리쿠르고스가 정한 법률에 따라 스파르타에서는 아기가 태어나면 먼저 건강 상태를 검사하였다. 허약한 아기들은 타이게토스산에 버리고 강한 아기들만 길렀다. 그렇게 자란 아기가 일곱 살이 되면 국가에서 운영하는 군대식 교육 기관에 들어가 예순 살이 될 때까지 공동생활을 해야 하였다. 교육 기관에서는 고통을 참는 법을 가르치기 위해 심한 매질을 하였고 아무리 배가 고파도 배불리 먹지 못하도록 하였으며, 추운 날씨에도 옷을 따뜻하게 입지 못하도록 하였다. 감정을 쉽게 드러내는 것도 금기였고 대답은 짧고 간결하게 해야 하였다.

운동하는 스파르타 젊은이들(런던 내셔널 갤러리)
Young Spartans Exercising(The National Gallery, London)

Sparta Grows into a Military State

Sparta, the capital of a polis created by the Dorians, ruled a great number of occupied dwellers with a small number of its citizens supported by its powerful military forces. Spartan citizens were subject to strict military training in preparation for the revolts by native dwellers. Spartan children were removed from their parents and placed in a rigorous military-style educational system called 'Agoge'. Spartan women were also required to maintain athleticism so that they could give birth to healthy babies.

Sparta's king and aristocrats were in charge of politics, but important government decisions were made in their assembly.

◉ What Does 'Spartan Education' Mean?

About 900 BC, there was a man named Lycurgus in Sparta. He traveled around many countries in order to make Sparta a great city-state, learning the secrets of building a strong country. He came to think that dogs that were made to find and eat food on their own were stronger than dogs that were given food.

Returning to Sparta, Lycurgus made several reforms. Among them was the Spartan teaching method. It was similar to a lion dropping its cubs on a hill and raising only the survivors.

In accordance with the law set by Lycurgus, in Sparta, a baby was first tested for health. Weak babies were thrown off of Mount Taygetus, and only strong babies were raised. At the age of seven, a baby raised in this way had to enter a military-style educational institution operated by the state and live in a communal style until the age of sixty. In order to teach them how to endure pain, educational institutions used severe beatings, prevented them from eating even when they were hungry, and prevented them from wearing warm clothes even in cold weather. It was also taboo to show emotions easily and answers were to be short and concise.

그리스 - 페르시아 전쟁과 펠로폰네소스 전쟁이 일어나다

페르시아가 지중해 동부로 진출하자 아테네는 이오니아가 페르시아에 맞서 일으킨 반란을 지원하였다. 페르시아는 반란을 진압하고 그리스를 공격하였다(그리스-페르시아 전쟁).

그리스의 폴리스들은 힘을 모아 3차에 걸친 페르시아의 침략을 막아 냈고 페르시아의 침략에 대비하기 위해 델로스 동맹을 맺었다. 델로스 동맹을 주도한 아테네는 지중해 무역을 독점하며 세력을 확장하였다. 이에 불만을 품은 일부 폴리스들이 스파르타를 중심으로 펠로폰네소스 동맹을 강화하였다.

두 세력의 대립은 결국 펠로폰네소스 전쟁으로 이어졌다. 오랜 전쟁 끝에 스파르타가 승리하였지만 폴리스 간의 싸움은 계속되었다. 이후 그리스는 쇠퇴의 길로 접어들었고 기원전 4세기 중엽 마케도니아에 의해 정복되었다.

- ■ 페르시아 제국 Persian Empire
- ■ 그리스 동맹 지역 Greek Alliance Area
- ■ 이오니아 반란 지역 Ionian Revolt Area
- ✳ 주요 격전지 Main Battlefield
- → 페르시아군의 2차 침입 Second Persian Invasion
- → 페르시아군의 3차 침입 Third Persian Invasion

그리스-페르시아 전쟁 Greco-Persian Wars

🌐 마라톤 전투의 승전보를 전하고 죽은 병사 이야기는 사실인가요?

기원전 490년, 페르시아군은 아테네를 공격하기 위해 아테네 동북부에 있는 마라톤 해안에 상륙하였다. 아테네 시민들은 소수였지만 페르시아군과 격전을 벌여 대승을 거두었다. 아테네의 병사 페이디피데스는 승전보를 알리기 위해 전속력으로 아테네를 향해 달렸고, 시민들에게 승리의 소식을 전한 뒤 곧바로 숨을 거두었다. 이를 기념하기 위해 마라톤 경기가 시작되었다고 한다. 하지만 헤로도토스의 『역사』에는 페이디피데스가 200km를 이틀 동안 달려 스파르타에 도움을 요청하였다는 사실만 기록되어 있다.

한편 마라톤 전투에서 패한 페르시아의 후예 이란은 마라톤 경기에 참여하지 않고 있다.

스파르타에 도움을 요청하러 간 페이디피데스(루브르 박물관)
Pheidippides Went to Sparta for Help(Louvre)

The Outbreak of the Greco-Persian Wars and Peloponnesian Wars

When Persia advanced to the eastern Mediterranean, Athens helped Ionia to revolt against Persia. Persia suppressed their revolts and attacked Greece(the Greco-Persian Wars).

The poleis in Greece united and stopped the Persians, who invaded them three times, and formed the Delian League in preparation for further invasions. Athens, the leadership polis of the Delian League, monopolized the Mediterranean trade and expanded its influence. Some of the poleis that were not happy about this development joined the Peloponnesian League under the leadership of Sparta.

The two forces eventually collided in the Peloponnesian War. Sparta claimed victory in the long war, but the battle between the poleis continued. Before long, Greece began to decline until it was occupied by Macedonia in the mid-4th century BC.

....

◉ Is the Story of the Soldier who Died after Delivering the News of the Marathon Victory True?

In 490 BC, Persian forces landed on the coast of Marathon in northeast Athens to attack it. Although there were few citizens in Athens, they fought a fierce battle with the Persian army and won a great victory. The Athenian soldier Phedippides ran at full speed from the site of the battle to Athens to announce the victory and died immediately after delivering the news of the victory to the citizens. It is said that the marathon race was begun to commemorate this. However, in Herodotus' *"Histories"*, it's simply said that he ran 200km over two days and asked Sparta for help.

Meanwhile, Iran, a descendant of Persia, who lost the marathon battle, does not participate in the marathon.

인간 중심적인 그리스 문화가 발달하다

그리스인들은 신도 인간의 모습과 감정을 지닌 존재로 생각하였다. 호메로스는 「일리아드」와 「오디세이아」에서 신의 인간적인 모습과 영웅들의 활약상을 소개하였다. 건축과 조각에서는 조화와 균형을 중시하여 파르테논 신전과 같은 건축물을 만들었다.

자연과 인간에 대해 토론하는 과정에서 철학이 발전하였다. 진리가 상대적인 것이라고 주장하는 소피스트 '지혜로운 자라는 뜻'들에게 맞서, 소크라테스는 절대적이고 객관적인 진리가 존재한다고 주장하였다. 그의 철학은 플라톤과 아리스토텔레스로 이어졌다.

🧭 라파엘로의 그림 '아테네 학당'에는 어떤 사람들이 있나요?
What Kind of People Are in Raffaello's Painting 'The School of Athens'?

플라톤 Plato
철학자가 다스리는 국가가 이상적인 국가다.
A utopian city-state is ruled by a philosopher-king.

소크라테스 Socrates
너 자신을 알라.
Know yourself.

아리스토텔레스 Aristotle
인간은 사회적 동물이다.
Human beings are social animals.

아테네 학당(바티칸 미술관)
The School of Athens(Vatican Museum)

Development of the Human-centric Greek Culture

The ancient Greeks believed that gods were just as emotional as humans and also looked like humans. The author Homer introduced the human-like gods and feats of ancient heroes in his books, the '*Iliad*' and the '*Odyssey*'. To the Greeks, proportion and symmetry were some of the most important principles behind their architecture and sculpture, and Parthenon is considered the embodiment of these principles.

During the course of discussing nature and man, the Greeks were able to develop and advance philosophy. While a group of teachers called Sophists developed a view of truth as relative, Socrates searched for objective and absolute truths. His philosophy was carried on by his pupils, who included Plato and Aristotle.

◉ 파르테논 신전의 기둥은 왜 곡선으로 만들어졌나요?
　Why Were the Pillars of the Parthenon Made Curved?

> 파르테논 신전은 아테네의 수호신인 아테나를 모시는 신전으로 비례와 균형이 잘 잡혀 있어요. 신전의 기둥들은 가운데 부분이 볼록하게 제작되어 멀리서 보면 직선으로 보이도록 하였지요.
> The Parthenon is a temple dedicated to Athena, the guardian deity of Athens, and is well balanced and proportional. The pillars of the temple were made to be convex in the middle so that they looked straight when viewed from a distance.

파르테논 신전(그리스 아테네)
The Parthenon(Athens, Greece) ©Steve Swayne

06 헬레니즘 시대

알렉산드로스, 대제국을 건설하다

마케도니아의 **알렉산드로스**는 그리스 전역을 통일한 후 동방 원정에 나섰다. 그는 이집트와 아케메네스 왕조 페르시아를 무너뜨리고 인더스강 유역까지 진출하여 불과 10년 만에 유럽, 아시아, 아프리카에 이르는 대제국을 세웠다.

하지만 알렉산드로스가 죽은 후 제국은 후계자들에 의해 마케도니아, 시리아, 이집트로 나뉘었다. 알렉산드로스가 원정을 시작한 때부터 이집트가 로마 제국에게 정복 당할 때까지의 약 300년 동안을 **헬레니즘 시대**라고 부른다.

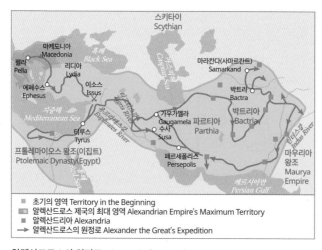

- ■ 초기의 영역 Territory in the Beginning
- ■ 알렉산드로스 제국의 최대 영역 Alexandrian Empire's Maximum Territory
- ■ 알렉산드리아 Alexandria
- → 알렉산드로스의 원정로 Alexander the Great's Expedition

알렉산드로스의 원정로 Alexander's Expedition

🌐 알렉산드로스는 어떤 정책을 펼쳤나요?

알렉산드로스는 정복지 주민을 포용하는 정책을 폈다. 페르시아에서는 페르시아식 왕관과 옷을 입었고, 페르시아 왕의 딸과 결혼도 하였다. 이집트에서는 스스로를 파라오라 칭하며 동방의 전제 군주제를 수용하기도 하였다.

알렉산드로스 동상(이스탄불 고고학박물관)
Statue of Alexander the Great(Archaeological Museum, Istanbul)

06 The Hellenistic Period

Alexander the Great Builds a Great Empire

After conquering Greece, Alexander the Great of Macedonia set out on an eastern expedition. He brought down Egypt and Persia and advanced to the banks of the Indus River until he was able to establish a great empire that extended to Europe, Asia, and Africa in just ten years.

However, after he died, the empire was split into Macedonia, Syria and Egypt by his successors. The period that spans about 300 years beginning with the expedition of Alexander the Great to the occupation of Egypt by the Roman Empire is called the Hellenistic period.

◎ What Policy Did Alexander the Great Carry Out?

Alexander the Great had a policy of embracing the conquered people. In Persia, he wore a Persian crown and robe, and he married the daughter of a Persian king. In Egypt, he called himself pharaoh and embraced the Eastern monarchy.

> 페르시아의 다리우스 3세와 싸우는 모습을 그린 모자이크 벽화입니다. 알렉산드로스는 뛰어난 전술가이자 영웅이라는 평가를 받기도 하지만, 한편으로는 정복지 주민을 학살하고 페르세폴리스를 파괴하여 '잔인한 정복자'라는 평가를 받기도 합니다.
> This is a mosaic mural depicting Alexander the Great fighting Darius III of Persia. Although Alexander the Great is considered a great tactician and hero, he was evaluated as a 'cruel conqueror' because he slaughtered residents of the conquered area and destroyed Persepolis.

이소스 전투의 알렉산드로스
Alexander in the Battle of Issus

동서 문화가 융합된 헬레니즘 문화가 나타나다

대제국을 건설한 알렉산드로스는 정복한 지역에 그리스인들을 이주시키고, 그리스의 문화를 전파하였다. 그 과정에서 그리스 문화와 동방 문화가 결합된 헬레니즘 문화가 나타났다.

공동체 의식이 약해지면서 개인주의적인 경향도 나타났다. 개인주의는 철학에도 영향을 주었다. 진정한 행복을 위해 이성에 따른 금욕을 내세우는 스토아학파와 정신적 쾌락을 강조하는 에피쿠로스학파가 등장하였다.

헬레니즘 시대의 미술은 그리스 예술을 바탕으로 하면서도 사실적이고 생동감 넘치는 것이 특징이다. 밀로의 비너스, 사모트라케의 니케, 라오콘 군상 등이 대표적이다. 헬레니즘 미술은 인도의 간다라 미술, 중국과 우리나라의 미술에도 영향을 주었다.

밀로의 비너스(루브르 박물관) Venus de Milo(Louvre)

🔎 헬레니즘 문화의 특징은 무엇인가요?

사랑의 여신인 비너스 조각상이에요. 에게해의 밀로섬에 묻혀 있었기 때문에 '밀로의 비너스'라는 이름이 붙었어요. 이 조각상은 얼굴과 신체가 실제 사람과 매우 비슷하고, 상체와 하체가 1:1.618의 황금 비율로 표현되었답니다. This is a statue of Venus, the goddess of love. It was named 'Venus de Milo' because it was buried on Millo island in the Aegean Sea. This statue has a face and body very similar to a human, and the upper and lower bodies are expressed in the golden ratio of 1:1.618.

니케 조각상은 그리스 사모트라케섬에서 발견되었어요. 신체와 옷주름이 매우 사실적으로 표현되었지요. 사모트라케의 니케는 영화 「타이타닉」의 여주인공이 취한 포즈의 모티브가 되었고 나이키 브랜드의 로고는 이 조각상 날개의 모습에서 고안하였다고 해요. The statue of Nike was found on the island of Samothrace, Greece. The body and the folds of drapery were very realistic. Nike of Samothrace was the motif used for the pose taken by the heroine in the movie *Titanic*, and it is said that the Nike brand logo was also devised from the shape of this statue's wings.

사모트라케의 니케(루브르 박물관) Nike of Samothrace(Louvre)

Hellenistic Culture Brings the East and the West Together

After establishing a vast empire, Alexander the Great moved the Greeks to occupied territories and spread the Greek culture. During this process, the Hellenistic culture that represented a fusion of the Ancient Greek world with that of East Asia was born.

As the sense of community weakened, an individualistic tendency also appeared. Individualism also influenced philosophy. For the sake of true happiness, the Stoic school, which emphasized abstinence according to reason, and the Epicurean school, which emphasized mental pleasure, appeared.

Founded upon the Greek arts, the Hellenistic culture was characterized by realistic and lively representation. Some of its well-known artworks include the Venus de Milo, the Nike of Samothrace, and Laocoon and His Sons. Hellenistic art also influenced the Gandharan arts of India, as well as the arts of China and Korea.

....

🌀 What Are the Characteristics of the Hellenistic Culture?

라오콘은 트로이 아폴론 신전의 사제였어요. 트로이 전쟁 때 그리스군의 목마를 성안으로 들이는 것을 반대하였다가 신의 노여움을 사 두 아들과 함께 큰 뱀에게 물려 죽었지요. 이 조각에는 고통받고 있는 인간의 표정이 생생하게 표현되어 있어요.
Laocoon was a priest at the temple of Apollo. During the Trojan War, he opposed bringing the trojan horse into the city and he, along with his two sons, was bitten by a large snake due to God's anger. This sculpture vividly depicts the human face in pain.

라오콘 군상(바티칸 미술관) Laocoon and His Sons(Vatican Museum)

👀 더 알아보기

👀 불상의 모습은 서양인일까요, 동양인일까요?

간다라 지방은 오늘날 파키스탄 북부와 아프가니스탄 남부 일대를 말한다. 초기 불교 도들은 부처님을 발바닥, 연꽃 등의 모습으로 표현하였다. 불교 예술은 발달하였지만 부처의 모습을 조각상으로 만드는 것은 불경스럽다고 여겼기 때문이었다. 그래서 부처에 대한 인물상이 구체적으로 드러나지 않는 대신 깨달음 혹은 신성함을 상징하는 나무, 발바닥 등을 조각하였다.

그런데 알렉산드로스가 간다라를 침략한 이후 부처의 모습이 바뀌었다. 헬레니즘 문화의 영향을 받아 부처를 인간의 모습으로 표현하기 시작한 것이다. 이때 만들어진 불상은 몸이 날씬하고 머리가 곱슬곱슬하며 코가 오똑하다는 특징이 있다. 서양인의 외모로 표현되었고, 옷도 그리스식의 옷을 입고 있다. 그러다 점차 몸이 크고 둥근 모습으로 변화하였다. 이러한 모습은 중국을 거쳐 우리나라의 삼국에 영향을 주었고, 이는 통일 신라까지 이어졌다.

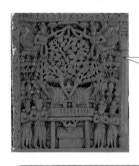

부처님은 6년간 고행한 후 보리수나무 밑에서 명상을 하다 7주일 만에 깨달음을 얻었다고 해요.
The Buddha is said to have gained enlightenment after seven weeks of meditating under a bodhi tree after practicing asceticism for six years.

산치 대탑의 보리수 조각 Bodhi Tree Sculpture of the Buddhist Monuments at Sanchi ⓒBiswarup

불교 초기에는 부처님의 모습을 발바닥이나 연꽃으로 표현하였어요. 발바닥에 표현된 수레바퀴는 '법륜'을 뜻해요.
In the early days of Buddhism, the image of Buddha was expressed as a sole or lotus flower. The wagon wheel expressed on the sole of the foot stands for 'Dharma cakra'.

부처님 발바닥과 연꽃무늬(인도) Buddha's Sole and Lotus Pattern(India)

산치 대탑(인도) Buddhist Monuments at Sanchi(India)

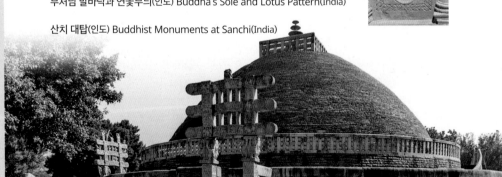

∞ Is the Image of the Buddha Western or Asian?

The Gandhara region today refers to northern Pakistan and southern Afghanistan. Early Buddhists expressed the Buddha in the form of feet, lotuses, etc. Although Buddhist art was developed, it was considered irreverent to make the image of a Buddha into a statue. So, instead of revealing the figures of Buddha in detail, trees and the soles of feet were carved to symbolize enlightenment or sacredness.

However, after Alexander the Great's invasion of Gandara, it was influenced by the Hellenistic culture and expressed the Buddha in human form. The Buddha statues created at this time are characterized by a slim body, curly hair, and a straight nose. They are expressed through the appearance of Westerners, and the clothes are also in the Greek style. Then, the body gradually changed into the large and round shape we know today. This appearance had an influence on Three Kingdoms in Korea through China, and the influence continued through to Unified Silla.

물결형의 곱슬머리, 한쪽 어깨에 걸친 형태의 옷, 옷 아래로 드러난 신체의 곡선 등에서 그리스 조각의 영향을 받았음을 알 수 있어요.
Bodhisattva Maitreya was influenced by the Greek sculpture in the wavy curls, the shape of the clothes over one shoulder, and the curves of the body under the clothes.

신체가 크고 사실적이며 얼굴의 이목구비가 또렷한 모습이에요.
The body is large and realistic, and the features on the face are clear.

간다라 보살상(국립중앙박물관) Bodhisattva Maitreya (National Museum of Korea)

석굴암 본존상(한국) Principal Statue of Sakyamuni in Seokguram Grotto(Korea)

07 로마의 정치적 변화

로마에 공화정이 수립되다

로마는 기원전 8세기 무렵 이탈리아 중부 테베레강 강가의 작은 도시 국가에서 출발하였다. 로마는 왕정을 거쳐 기원전 6세기 말에 공화정을 수립하였다. 공화정 초기에는 귀족이 **콘술**(집정관)행정과 군사를 맡아보던 장관과 **원로원**실질적인 지배 기관으로 내정과 외교를 지도함을 독점하였다. 이후 전쟁을 통해 평민의 영향력이 확대되면서 평민의 정치 기관인 **평민회**가 구성되고 **호민관** 평민회의 투표로 뽑았으며, 원로원이나 집정관의 결정에 대하여 거부권을 가짐이 선출되었다.

기원전 3세기에 이탈리아반도를 통일한 로마는 카르타고와 벌인 세 차례의 포에니 전쟁에서 승리한 이후 지중해 일대를 장악하였다. 점령지로부터 값싼 곡물이 들어오고 귀족들이 노예를 이용하여 대농장인 **라티푼디움**을 경영하면서 자영농은 토지를 잃고 빈민이 되었다. 자영농의 몰락으로 귀족과 평민의 갈등이 깊어졌다.

호민관으로 선출된 **그라쿠스 형제**는 대토지 소유를 제한하고 농민에게 토지를 재분배하여 자영농을 육성하려 하였으나 대토지 소유자의 반대로 실패하였다. 개혁이 실패한 후 로마는 군인 정치가들이 권력 다툼을 벌이면서 혼란에 빠졌다.

⚜ 그라쿠스 형제는 왜 개혁에 나섰을까요?

호민관이 된 티베리우스 그라쿠스는 자영농을 위한 정책을 펴다가 귀족들에게 살해되었다. 형의 뒤를 이어 호민관이 된 가이우스 그라쿠스는 가난한 시민들에게 싼값에 곡물을 공급하는 정책을 펴다가 귀족들의 위협에 못 이겨 스스로 삶을 마감하였다.

코르넬리아는 보석을 자랑하는 여인에게 자신의 두 아들이 보석이라고 말하였어요.
Cornelia told the woman who boasted about her jewels that her two sons were jewels.

그라쿠스 형제와 어머니 코르넬리아(오르세 미술관)
Brother Gracus and Their Mother Cornelia(Orsay Museum)

07 Political Changes in Rome

A Republic Government Is Created in Rome

Rome originated as a small city-state by the Tiber River in central Italy around the 8th century BC. In the late 6th century BC, Rome overthrew the monarchy and created a republican government. In the early days of the republican government, the Consul and the Senate were exclusively restricted to aristocrats only. Later, the growing clout of the commoners led to the creation of the Plebeian Assembly, through which commoners could elect tribunes.

In the 3rd century BC, Rome unified the Italian Peninsula. Rome went on to claim victory in a series of three wars, called the Punic Wars, and became the most powerful nation in the Mediterranean. Cheap crops streamed in from the occupied territories, and the aristocrats used slaves in their Latifundium, eventually depriving and driving off self employed farmers. The fall of these independent farmers translated into deepening conflicts between the aristocratic landowners and farmers.

The Gracchi brothers who served as tribunes tried to support these poor farmers by passing land reform and redistributing the aristocratic landholdings among them, but their efforts failed due to the objections of powerful landowners. After the failed land reform, Rome fell into chaos as warrior-statesmen continued to fight for political power.

....

◉ Why Did the Gracchi Brothers Try for Reform?

Tiberius Gracus, who became a tribune, was killed by the aristocrats while implementing policies for the benefit of independent farmers. Gaius Gracchus, who became a tribune after his brother, ended his life on his own because he could not overcome the threats of the aristocrats while implementing a policy of supplying grain to poor citizens at low prices.

공화정이 무너지고 황제가 로마를 다스리다

기원전 1세기 중엽에 갈리아 원정에서 큰 공을 세운 **카이사르**가 권력을 장악하였지만 공화정을 지키려는 원로원 귀족들과 브루투스에게 암살당하였다(기원전 44).

이후 카이사르의 양자였던 옥타비아누스가 안토니우스를 제압하고 모든 권력을 장악하였다. 그는 영토를 넓히고 번영을 주도하여 원로원으로부터 '아우구스투스(존엄한 자)'라는 칭호를 받았다(기원전 27).

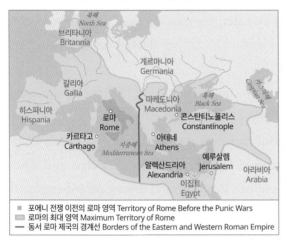

포에니 전쟁 이전의 로마 영역 Territory of Rome Before the Punic Wars
로마의 최대 영역 Maximum Territory of Rome
동서 로마 제국의 경계선 Borders of the Eastern and Western Roman Empire

로마 제국의 영역 Territory of the Roman Empire

이때부터 로마의 공화정은 사실상 끝나고 제정이 시작되었다. 이후 5현제로 불리는 5명의 현명한 황제들이 등장하면서 로마는 200여 년 동안 **팍스 로마나**(Pax Romana, 로마의 평화)라 불리는 전성기를 맞이하였다.

⚙ 5현제에는 누가 있나요?

5현제는 네르바, 트라야누스, 하드리아누스, 안토니우스 피우스, 마르쿠스 아우렐리우스이다. 이 시기에는 황제를 세습하지 않고, 가장 유능한 사람을 황제로 임명하였다. 특히 5현제의 마지막 황제였던 마르쿠스 아우렐리우스는 제국 동쪽과 도나우강 양쪽의 변경 방어에 힘썼으며, 스토아 철학에 조예가 깊어 전장의 참호 속에서 『명상록』을 저술하였다.

> 만물은 끊임없이 변화한다. 인간도 이 세상에 잠깐 지나가는 나그네에 불과하다. 우리는 철학이 인도하는 대로 자연의 본성에 맞는 생활을 해야 한다.

마르쿠스 아우렐리우스 기마상(이탈리아)
Equestrian Statue of Emperor Marcus Aurelius(Italy)

The Republic Gives Way to Emperors in the Rule of Rome

Around the mid-1st century BC, Julius Caesar seized power after winning the Gallic Wars, but he was assassinated by Roman senators and Brutus who tried to protect the republic(44 BC).

After his death, his adopted son Octavius overpowered Antonius and became the most powerful man in the Roman world. The Roman Senate conferred the name 'Augustus', which means 'the increaser' or 'venerable', upon Octavius(27 BC) in acknowledgement of his expansion of the Roman territory and the prosperity he brought.

Beginning from this time, the democratic Roman Republic transformed into the autocratic Roman Empire. Starting with the reign of Augustus, the Roman Empire enjoyed about 200 years of peace and stability called the Pax Romana(lit. Peace of Rome) under the reigns of the so-called 'Five Good Emperors'.

⊚ Who Were the Five Good Emperors?

The Five Good Emperors are Nerva, Trajan, Hadrian, Antoninus Pius, and Marcus Aurelius. During this period, the title of emperor was not inherited, but the most capable man was appointed as such. In particular, Marcus Aurelius, the last emperor of the Five Good Emperors, worked hard to defend the borders on both the eastern side of the empire and the Danube River, and because of his knowledge of Stoic philosophy, he wrote "*Meditations*" in the trenches of the battlefield.

All things are constantly changing. Humans are just strangers passing by in this world. We must live naturally, in harmony, as philosophy guides.

∞ 클레오파트라가 과연 세계를 바꾸었을까요?

로마의 권력자 카이사르에게는 폼페이우스라는 사위가 있었다. 폼페이우스는 아내가 죽자 귀족들과 제휴하고 장인 카이사르를 등졌다. 이에 카이사르는 "주사위는 던져졌다."라는 말과 함께 군대를 거느리고 루비콘강을 건너 로마로 진격하였다. 폼페이우스는 이집트로 도망갔으나 이집트 왕 프톨레마이오스의 부하에게 암살당하였다.

카이사르는 프톨레마이오스 왕의 누이이자 아내이며 공동 왕인 클레오파트라와 손을 잡고 프톨레마이오스 왕을 몰아냈다. 그러나 로마로 개선한 카이사르는 로마 공화정이 무너질 것을 우려한 자들에게 살해당하였다. 영국의 극작가 윌리엄 셰익스피어는 희곡 『줄리어스 시저』에서 암살을 도모한 귀족 사이에서 양아들 브루투스를 발견한 카이사르가 "브루투스, 너마저!"라고 말하며 쓰러졌다고 묘사하였다.

브루투스는 로마 시민들 앞에서 "나는 카이사르를 사랑했지만 로마를 더 사랑하였다."라고 연설하였다. 그러나 로마의 정치가 안토니우스가 "저들은 로마의 영웅을 비겁하게 죽인 암살자입니다."라고 말하며 카이사르의 주검과 유서를 공개해 민심을 흔들었다. 결국 브루투스 일파는 로마를 떠나 도망갔다.

안토니우스는 카이사르의 양자이자 후계자인 옥타비아누스와 유대 관계를 맺기 위해 그의 여동생 옥타비아와 결혼하였다. 하지만 클레오파트라에게 마음을 빼앗겨 옥타비아와 이혼하고 클레오파트라와 결혼하였다. 이후 옥타비아누스는 아그리파 장군에게 지휘를 맡겨 안토니우스와 클레오파트라의 연합군을 악티움 해전에서 물리쳤다.

클레오파트라와 카이사르 Cleopatra and Caesar

카이사르 Caesar
사위가 되어 감히 나를 배신하다니. 가만 두지 않겠어!
Dare to betray me as my son-in-law. I will make you regret it!

폼페이우스 Pompeius
장인 카이사르를 공격하여 로마의 권력을 차지할 거야.
I will attack father-in-law Caesar and take the power of Rome.

👓 Did Cleopatra Really Change the World?

Caesar, the ruler of Rome, had a son-in-law named Pompeius. When his wife died, Pompeius allied with the nobles and turned his back on his father-in-law Caesar. Then Caesar said, "The die has been cast" and he crossed the Rubicon River and advanced to Rome. Pompeius fled to Egypt, but was assassinated by Egyptian king Ptolemy's man.

Caesar joined hands with Cleopatra, the sister, wife, and co-ruler of Ptolemy, and drove him out. However, when Caesar returned to Rome, he was murdered by those who feared the collapse of the Roman Republic. English playwright William Shakespeare describes in his play "*The Tragedy of Julius Caesar*" that Caesar, who found his adopted son Brutus among the nobles who planned his assassination, fell down saying "Brutus, even you!"

Later, Brutus gave a memorial address in front of the Roman citizens, "I loved Caesar, but I loved Rome more". But Roman politician Antonius shook the heart of the people by saying, "They are assassins who cowardly killed a Roman heroes", revealing Caesar's body and will. Eventually, the faction of Brutus left Rome and ran away.

Antonius married Augustus's younger sister Octavia to bond with Caesar's adopted son and successor Augustus. However, he divorced Octavia and married Cleopatra because he was fascinated with her. Later, Augustus gave command to General Agrippa, defeating the allied forces of Antonius and Cleopatra in the Battle of Actium.

브루투스 Brutus
카이사르가 비록 내 양아버지일지라도 로마를 위해 그를 해칠 수밖에.
Even though Caesar is my stepfather, I have no choice but to kill him for Rome.

안토니우스 Antonius
브루투스는 로마의 영웅을 죽인 비겁한 암살자에 불과합니다.
Brutus is nothing more than a cowardly assassin who killed a Roman hero.

법률과 건축을 중심으로 여러 민족을 지배하다

로마 제국에는 다양한 민족과 종교가 분포하였다. 그래서 넓은 제국을 다스리는 데 필요한 건축과 법률 등 실용적인 문화가 발달하였다.

로마인들은 사람과 물자가 원활하게 이동할 수 있도록 정복지 곳곳에 도시를 세우고 도로로 연결하였다. 정복지에는 거대한 상하수도 시설을 마련하고, 공중목욕탕과 원형 경기장을 건설해 속주민에게 편의를 제공하고 기술적 우위를 선전하였다.

로마의 법률은 최초의 성문법_{문자로 적어 표현하고, 문서의 형식을 갖춘 법}인 12표법에서 로마 시민을 대상으로 하는 시민법으로 발전하였다. 시민법은 제국이 확장하는 과정에서 제국의 모든 민족에게 적용되는 만민법으로 확대되었다. 이에 따라 로마는 점령한 도시의 주민에게도 선거권 및 피선거권을 제외하고 로마인과 동등한 권리를 주었다. 이후 로마법은 유럽은 물론 세계 여러 나라 법률의 토대가 되었다.

◈ "모든 길은 로마로 통한다."라는 말은 무슨 의미인가요?

로마 제국은 이탈리아를 넘어 아프리카 일부와 에스파냐 지역까지 지배하였다. 그리고 도시에서 먼 지역까지 군대를 보내기 위하여 제국 구석구석에 도로를 건설하였다. 도로는 큰 바위를 바닥에 놓고 그 위에 그보다 작은 돌덩이를 깐 후 크고 납작한 포장용 돌로 덮는 방식으로 건설되었다. 이러한 길의 수가 워낙 많고 서로 이어져 있어 "모든 길은 로마로 통한다."라는 말이 나올 정도였다.

로마 공화정 시대에 감찰관이었던 아피우스 클라우디우스가 군사 목적으로 도로를 만들었어요. 고대 로마에서 가장 먼저 만들어진 이 도로의 일부는 오늘날에도 사용되고 있어요.

아피아 가도(이탈리아 민투르노)
Appian Way(Minturno, Italy)

Rome Rules Diverse Ethnic Groups with an Advanced Legal System and Architecture

The Roman Empire consisted of diverse ethnic groups and religions. As a result, they were able to advance the practical cultures such as law and architecture that were necessary to maintain such a massive empire.

Romans built cities and roads throughout occupied territory to facilitate easy transportation of people and goods. They installed large-scale water supply and sewage facilities in occupied lands, and also boasted of their advanced technology by building convenience facilities for citizens such as public bathing houses and amphitheaters.

The first written legislation of Roman law was called the 'Laws of the Twelve Tables' which later developed into civil law binding on all Roman citizens. The Laws of the Twelve Tables eventually evolved into the 'Law of Nations' that applied to all nations that belonged to the Roman Empire. Accordingly, citizens of cities occupied by the Roman Empire were given equal rights to Romans except for the rights to vote and run for election. Later on, Roman law became the foundation of legal systems of countries around the world, including continental Europe.

◉ What Does It Mean, "All Roads Lead to Rome"?

The Roman Empire ruled beyond Italy to parts of Africa and Spain. And roads were built to every corner of the empire to send troops to remote areas. The road was constructed by placing large rocks on the ground, placing smaller blocks of stones on top of them, and then covering that with large, flat paving stones. There are many such roads and they are connected to each other, so it was said that "All roads lead to Rome".

> Appius Claudius, a censor during the Roman Republic period, built roads for military purposes. Part of the Appian way, the earliest built in ancient Rome, is still in use today.

로마에 크리스트교가 확산되다

로마 제국의 지배를 받던 팔레스타인에서 예수가 **크리스트교**를 창시하였다. 예수는 유대교의 **선민사상** 신이 특정한 민족을 특별히 선택하였다고 믿는 사상 을 비판하고 평등과 사랑을 가르치다 십자가에 못 박혀 죽었다. 베드로를 비롯한 예수의 제자들과 바울은 제국 각지에 교회를 세우고 예수의 가르침을 전파하였다. 크리스트교는 차별받던 여성과 하층민에게 큰 호응을 얻었다.

크리스트교 신자들은 로마의 전통적인 신들과 황제 숭배를 우상 숭배로 여겨 거부하였다. 이에 로마는 크리스트교를 탄압하였지만 세력은 계속 확산되었다.

크리스트교의 확산 Spread of Christianity

제국의 안정과 황제권의 강화를 이루려 하였던 콘스탄티누스 대제는 313년 밀라노 칙령을 내려 크리스트교를 공인하였다. 392년에 테오도시우스 황제가 크리스트교를 국교로 인정한 이후 크리스트교는 유럽 문화의 중요한 기반이 되었다.

....

◉ 크리스트교를 탄압했던 로마 최초의 황제는 누구인가요?

64년 7월 로마에 대화재가 발생했다. 폭군이었던 제5대 황제 네로가 신도시를 만들기 위해 일부러 로마를 불태웠으며 그가 불타는 로마를 바라보며 시를 읊었다는 소문이 민중들 사이에 퍼졌다. 네로는 이러한 의혹을 잠재우기 위해 크리스트교도에게 책임을 씌워 화형에 처하였다. 그는 로마 제국 황제 중 최초로 크리스트교를 박해한 황제로 남게 되었다.

네로 황제(독일 글립토테크 미술관)
Emperor Nero(Ny Carlsberg Glyptotek, Germany)

Christianity Spreads in Rome

Christianity was founded by Jesus Christ who was born in Palestine which was under the rule of the Roman Empire. Jesus criticized Judaism's belief of 'Chosenness' and advocated peace and love until he was crucified by the Roman official Pontius Pilot. His disciples, including Peter and Paul, built churches throughout the empire and preached the teachings of Jesus. Christianity appealed greatly to women and the lower classes, who were discriminated against at the time.

Christians refused to worship the traditional Roman gods or to pay homage to the emperor because they considered them idols. Consequently, Rome persecuted Christians, but Christianity continued spreading nevertheless.

Constantine the Great, who attempted to stabilize the empire and strengthen royal authority, legalized the practice of Christianity through the proclamation of the Edict of Milan in 313. Then Emperor Theodosius established Christianity as the state religion in 392 and Christianity became an important foundation of the European culture.

Who Was the First Emperor of Rome who Oppressed Christianity?

In July 64, a fire broke out in Rome. Rumors spread among the people that the tyrant, the fifth emperor Nero, deliberately burned Rome to create a new city, and that he recited poetry while looking at the burning Rome. In order to quell this suspicion, Nero held the Christians accountable and burned them at the stake. And he remained the first Roman emperor to persecute Christianity.

II

세계 종교의 확산과 지역 문화의 형성

1. 불교 및 힌두교 문화의 형성과 확산
2. 동아시아 문화의 형성과 확산
3. 이슬람 문화의 형성과 확산
4. 크리스트교 문화의 형성과 확산

또 하나의 언어를 할 줄 아는 것은 두 번째 영혼을 갖는 것과 같다.
이 땅에 있었던 사람들의 문화를 받아들이기 위해 노력하라.

– 카롤루스 대제(742~814)

↓ 힌두교 사원에서 불교 사원으로 바뀐 앙코르 와트(캄보디아)
Angkor Wat(Cambodia) is converted from a Hindu temple to a
Buddhist temple.

II

Proliferation of Various Religions and Establishment of Regional Cultures

To have another language is to possess a second soul.

Try to embrace the culture of the people who have been on this earth.

– Charles the Great(742–814)

불교 및 힌두교 문화의 형성과 확산

01 인도의 정치 변화와 불교·힌두교 문화의 형성

불교가 등장하다

기원전 7세기 즈음 갠지스강 유역에서 많은 국가들이 성장하였고, 철제 무기의 등장으로 국가 간의 전쟁도 활발하게 일어났다. 이러한 상황에서 **크샤트리아 계급**의 권력이 강화되었고, 상업이 발달하면서 **바이샤 계급**의 영향력도 강화되었다. 이들은 형식적으로 변한 브라만교의 제사 의식과 카스트 제도에 따른 신분 차별을 반대하였다.

이러한 상황에서 **우파니샤드 철학**이 발달하였다. 우파니샤드 철학은 과거 행위의 축적인 업으로 말미암은 윤회의 구속에서 벗어나 인간 스스로 해탈에 이를 수 있다고 본다. 우파니샤드 철학을 바탕으로 기원전 6세기경 **석가모니** `'석가족 출신의 성자라는 뜻'`(고타마 싯다르타)가 불교를 창시하였다.

석가모니는 브라만교에서 주장하는 **윤회 사상**을 바탕으로 하면서도 인간의 평등을 강조하며 신분 차별적인 카스트 제도를 부정하였다. 불교는 크샤트리아와 바이샤 계급의 지지로 성장하였으며 이후 인도의 문화적 통합과 동아시아 문화권의 형성에 기여하였다.

💧 싯다르타가 불교를 창시하게 된 계기는 무엇인가요?

What Prompted Siddhartha to Create Buddhism?

싯다르타 기원전 624년 카필라바스투성(지금의 네팔 지방)에서 왕자로 태어났어요. 16살에 결혼해 아들을 낳고 평온한 삶을 살았지요. 그러던 어느 날 수레를 타고 가다가 몸과 마음의 고통으로 괴로워하며 살아가는 사람들을 보았어요. 이후 모든 부와 명예를 버리고 출가하였고, 오랜 수행 끝에 부다가야의 보리수 아래에서 깨달음을 얻었어요.

Siddhartha I was born in 624 BC as a prince in Kapilavastu castle(modern day Nepal). Married at the age of 16, I had a son and lived a peaceful life. One day, while riding a cart, I saw people suffering from pain in their body and mind. Afterwards, I abandoned all my wealth and honor, and after extensive training, I gained enlightenment under the bodhi tree of Bodh Gaya.

고행하는 석가모니(라호르 박물관)
Fasting Siddhartha(Lahore Museum)

Establishment and Spread of Buddhism and Hinduism-related Cultures

01 Political Changes in India and the Development of Buddhism and Hinduism-related Cultures

The Emergence of Buddhism

Around the 7th century BC, the Ganges River saw the birth of many empires, and wars among them became more dynamic as a result of the emergence of iron weapons. It was under this circumstance that the Kshatriyas gained stronger power, and the growth of commercial trade allowed the Vaishyas to grow its influence as well. They dissented from the Brahmin ceremonies for being so ritualistic and disliked the caste-based social status discrimination.

It was under this circumstance that the philosophy of the Upanishads began to develop. The philosophy as manifested in the Upanishads was about humans being able to release themselves from the cycle of death and rebirth and reach a state of cosmic bliss. From this philosophy came Buddhism, which was founded in the 6th century BC by Shakyamuni Buddha(Siddhartha Gautama).

Shakyamuni Buddha accepted the idea of reincarnation as advocated by Brahmanism but was critical of the caste system marked by social status discrimination. He instead promoted equality of all human beings. Buddhism kept growing with the support of the Kshatriyas and the Vaishyas, and greatly contributed to the development of the Eastern Asian cultural sphere and the integration of Indian cultures.

> 사르나트 유적은 석가모니가 최초로 설법을 시작한 곳으로, 불교 4대 성지 중 하나예요. Sarnath is the place where Shakyamuni first began preaching, and it is one of the four sacred places of Buddhism.

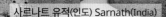
사르나트 유적(인도) Sarnath(India)

마우리아 왕조에서 상좌부 불교가 발전하다

기원전 4세기에 알렉산드로스가 인도의 서북부 일대에 침입하였다. 이에 자극을 받아 당시 **마우리아 왕조**의 찬드라굽타가 북인도를 정복하며 통일 왕조 탄생을 위한 발걸음을 내딛었다.

그 뒤 찬드라굽타의 손자인 **아소카왕**은 강력한 군대를 바탕으로 남부 지역을 제외한 모든 인도 지역을 정복하며 인도 최초의 통일 제국을 건설하였다. 아소카왕은 전국의 도로를 연결하고 지방에 관리를 파견하여 **중앙 집권제**를 정비하였다. 또한 전쟁의 참상을 깨닫고 불교에 귀의한 뒤 불교 교리로 왕국을 통치하려 하였다. 불교 경전을 정리하고 자신의 통치 방식과 불교의 교리를 새긴 석주도 전국 곳곳에 세웠다. 각지에 사원과 불탑을 건설하는 등 불교를 적극적으로 후원하였으며 동남아시아에 승려와 사절단 등을 파견하여 **상좌부 불교**를 전파하였다.

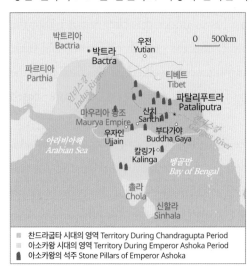

마우리아 왕조의 영역 Territory of the Maurya Empire

- 찬드라굽타 시대의 영역 Territory During Chandragupta Period
- 아소카왕 시대의 영역 Territory During Emperor Ashoka Period
- ▲ 아소카왕의 석주 Stone Pillars of Emperor Ashoka

....

◉ 아소카왕이 불교에 귀의한 이유는 무엇인가요?

아소카왕은 칼링가 왕국을 공격하여 승리를 거두었다. 적들의 시체가 즐비한 곳을 걸어가던 그는 얼마 후 알 수 없는 두려움과 후회에 사로잡혔다. 고통스럽게 죽어 가던 사람들을 떠올린 아소카왕은 힘으로 지배하던 통치 방식을 버리고 불교에 귀의하였다. 부처의 가르침을 적은 돌기둥도 곳곳에 세웠다. 또한 불교의 가르침에 따라 모든 생명체를 소중히 여기고 자비를 베풀어야 한다고 말하며, 인류 최초로 동물 학대 금지법을 만들고 동물병원을 지었다.

아소카왕 조각상
Statue of Emperor Ashoka

Development of Sthaviravada Buddhism in the Maurya Empire

In the 4th century BC, Alexander the Great invaded the northwestern part of India. In response, Chandragupta Maurya, the founder of the Maurya Empire, invaded and conquered northern India. This was his first step to building a unified empire.

Supported by extensive military power, his grandson, Emperor Ashoka, was able to conquer most of the Indian subcontinent, except for the southern provinces, and built the first unified empire in the history of India. He connected all roads throughout the empire and reformed the central government system by having viceroys govern the outlying domains. Upon realizing the misery of war, he converted to Buddhism and ruled his empire based on the Buddhist doctrine. He supported the research, composition, and development of Buddhist texts, and erected rocks and pillars where Buddhist teachings were inscribed throughout the empire. He also built a number of monasteries and stupas in various regions and enthusiastically supported the spread of the Sthaviravada school of Buddhism by sending missionaries to Southeast Asian countries.

◉ Why Did King Ashoka Come to Believe in Buddhism?

Emperor Ashoka attacked the Kingdom of Kalinga and won a victory. As he walked through the corpses of enemies, he was caught in unknown feelings of fear and regret. Reminiscent of those who were dying in pain, he abandoned the rule of power and turned to Buddhism. Stone pillars containing the teachings of the Buddha were erected in various places. In addition, according to the Buddhist teachings, he said that we should cherish all living things and show mercy. He legislated against animal cruelty and built an animal hospital for the first time in history.

쿠샨 왕조에서 대승 불교가 발전하다

마우리아 왕조는 아소카왕의 죽음 이후 급속도로 쇠약해지다 기원전 2세기경 멸망하였다. 이후 인도는 200여 년간 분열되었다. 그 가운데 이란 계통의 쿠샨족이 혼란을 수습하며 인도 북부 대부분을 차지하고 쿠샨 왕조를 세웠다.

카니슈카왕은 쿠샨 왕조의 전성기를 이끈 왕이다. 간다라 지방을 중심으로 중앙아시아에 이르는 대제국을 건설하였다. 또한 로마와 페르시아, 인도, 중국을 연결하는 중계 무역을 통해 경제적인 성장을 이룩하였다. 독실한 불교 신도였던 카니슈카왕은 이러한 경제력을 바탕으로 곳곳에 불교 사원과 탑을 건립하는 등 당시에 성립한 대승 불교를 전파하기 위해 노력하였다. 카니슈카왕의 노력으로 건축, 그림, 조각 등이 발전하여 수많은 사원과 석탑이 건립되었다.

쿠샨 왕조의 영역
Territory of the Kushan Dynasty

상좌부 불교와 대승 불교는 어떤 차이가 있나요?

마우리아 왕조의 아소카왕 시절에 유행하였던 상좌부 불교는 개인의 해탈을 강조하였고, 실론, 타이 등 동남아시아로 전파되었다. 아소카왕 시대에는 부처에 대한 인물상을 구체적으로 표현하지 않고 깨달음, 신성함을 상징하는 나무, 발바닥 등을 조각하거나 빈 공간으로 남겼다.

쿠샨 왕조의 카니슈카왕 시대에 유행하였던 대승 불교는 대중 구제를 중요시하였다. 이 시기에는 간다라 미술 양식에 따라 부처의 형상을 조각하기도 하였다. 대승 불교는 간다라 미술과 함께 한국, 중국, 일본 등 동아시아로 전파되었다.

Development of Mahayana Buddhism in the Kushan Dynasty

The Mauria Dynasty quickly declined after the death of Emperor Ashoka until its final fall in around the 2nd century BC. India remained divided for the next 200 years. Around this time, a tribe of Iranian origin called the Kushans put an end to the disorder when they expanded their territory into the northwest of the Indian subcontinent, establishing the Kushan Empire.

The Kushan Empire thrived during the reign of Emperor Kanishka who built a large empire whose territory covered much of Central Asia, centering on its capital in Gandara. He also achieved economic growth through transit trade linking to Rome, Persia, India, and China. Being a devout Buddhist with wealth, Emperor Kanishka built a number of temples and stupas and played an important role in the establishment and spread of Mahayana Buddhism. Emperor Kanishka is credited with the construction of numerous temples and stone stupas and the development of architecture, paintings, and sculptures.

....

What Is the Difference between Sthaviravada Buddhism and Mahayana Buddhism?

Sthaviravada Buddhism, which was popular during the period of Emperor Ashoka of the Mauria dynasty, emphasized individual liberation and spread to Southeast Asian countries such as Sri Lanka and Thailand. In the period of Emperor Ashoka, the figures of Buddha were not specifically expressed, and trees and the soles of the feet were sculpted or left as empty spaces, symbolizing enlightenment or sacredness.

Mahayana Buddhism, which was popular during the Kanishka period in the Kushan Dynasty, placed great importance on public relief. Buddha figures were also sculpted according to the Gandara art style. Mahayana Buddhism, along with Gandharan art, spread to East Asian countries such as Korea, China, and Japan.

굽타 왕조에서 힌두 문화가 꽃피다

쿠샨 왕조가 쇠약해지면서 4세기경 인도는 다시 여러 나라로 분열되었다. 굽타 왕조의 찬드라굽타 1세는 굽타 왕조 번영의 틀을 마련하였다. 굽타 왕조는 5세기 초 찬드라 굽타 2세 시기에 전성기를 맞이하여 벵골만에서 아라비아해까지 영토를 확장하였다. 또한 해상 무역을 통해 경제적인 번영을 이루었으며 문화와 예술이 발전하였다. 굽타 왕조 시기에는 브라만교를 바탕으로 불교와 다양한 민간 신앙이 결합한 힌두교가 형성되었다.

다신교인 힌두교는 브라만(창조의 신), 비슈누(유지의 신), 시바(파괴의 신)를 주된 신으로 믿었고, 『마누법전』에 힌두교도가 지켜야 할 규범을 담았다. 힌두교는 소속된 카스트에 따른 의무를 중시하였다. 힌두교에서는 신이 왕의 모습으로 세상에 나타났다고 주장하였다. 이에 굽타 왕조의 왕들은 왕권을 강화하기 위해 힌두교를 후원하였다.

굽타 왕조 시기는 예술, 종교, 건축 등 여러 분야에서 인도 고전 문화가 꽃핀 황금기였다. 미술에서는 **굽타 양식**이 나타났는데, 이는 간다라 미술과 인도 고유의 전통이 융합된 것이었다. **아잔타 석굴 벽화**는 이 시기를 대표하는 작품이다.

◎ 아잔타 석굴 속에는 무엇이 있나요?

1983년 유네스코 세계 문화유산으로 등재된 아잔타 석굴의 내부에서는 굽타 양식의 불상이나 벽화를 볼 수 있어요. 특히 아잔타 석굴 벽화의 보살 그림은 엷은 미소와 섬세하면서도 육감적인 표현이 돋보여 굽타 양식의 대표작으로 손꼽히지요.

아잔타 석굴 벽화의 연꽃을 든 보살 그림
Bodhisattva Painting with Lotus Flowers
on the Mural of Ajanta Cave

아잔타 석굴 외부 모습(인도)
Outside View of Ajanta Cave(India)

Hindu Culture Blooms in the Gupta Dynasty

India again became divided around the 4th century BC after the decline of the Kushan Dynasty. Chandragupta I, a king of the Gupta dynasty, united northern India and laid the foundation for the prosperity of the dynasty. The Gupta Dynasty flourished in the early-5th century during the reign of Chandragupta II, who expanded the territory to the Bay of Bengal and the Arabian Sea. The maritime trade provided the dynasty with economic prosperity and advanced culture and arts. During the Gupta Dynasty, Hinduism formed, combining Buddhism with various folk beliefs based on Brahmanism.

Hinduism is a polytheistic religion that believes in many gods and goddesses including Brahman, Vishnu, and Shiva. Important religious practice for Hinduism is described in the Hindu religious text called "The Code of Manu". Hinduism valued the duties of the caste to which it belonged. Hinduism claimed that God appeared to the world in the form of a king. Accordingly, the kings of the Gupta Dynasty supported Hinduism to strengthen their royal authority.

The Gupta Dynasty was the golden age of Indian classical culture in many fields such as art, religion, and architecture. Regarding art, the dynasty saw the emergence of the Gupta Style, which was a fusion of Gandharan art and traditional Indian art. One of the most widely-known artworks of this period are the murals found in the Ajanta Cave.

◉ What's in the Ajanta Cave?

Inside of the Ajanta Cave, which was designated as a UNESCO World Heritage Site in 1983, there are Gupta Style Buddha statues and murals. In particular, the Bodhisattva painting on the murals of the Ajanta Cave, with a thin smile and delicate yet sensual expressions, are considered representative works of the Gupta Style.

02 이슬람 세력의 인도 침입

인도 북부에 이슬람 왕조가 들어서다

6세기 중엽부터 굽타 왕조의 세력이 약해지면서 인도는 다시 분열되었다. 이러한 혼란을 틈타 8세기 무렵부터 이슬람 세력이 인도를 침입하기 시작하였다. 이슬람 세력은 11세기경 갠지스강 유역까지 세력을 확장하였다.

13세기 초에는 델리를 중심으로 이슬람 왕조가 세워졌다. 이후 약 300년 동안 인도 북부에는 다섯 이슬람 왕조가 잇따라 세워졌는데, 이들 왕조의 지배자는 술탄이라는 칭호를 사용하였다. 그래서 이 시기의 이슬람 왕조를 델리 술탄 왕조라고 부른다.

인도에 들어온 이슬람 세력은 초기에는 불교와 힌두교 사원을 파괴하기도 하였지만, 이후에는 이슬람교가 아니어도 인두세만 내면 기존의 종교를 믿는 것을 허용하였다. 카스트 제도에 불만을 품은 사람들은 평등을 내세우는 이슬람교로 개종하기도 하였다.

이슬람 세력이 들어온 북부 지방을 중심으로 힌두 문화와 이슬람 문화가 융합되는 현상도 나타났다. 힌두 문화 장식이 사용된 모스크가 만들어졌고, 힌두교와 이슬람교의 결혼식이나 장례식 절차가 비슷해지기도 하였다.

◉ **쿠트브 미나르는 어떤 탑일까요?**

쿠트브 미나르는 델리를 점령한 이슬람 세력이 승리를 기념하기 위해 세운 탑이에요. 인도에서 가장 높은 석조 탑으로 높이가 72.5m에 이르지요. 기둥에는 『쿠란』 구절이 적혀 있어요.

쿠트브 미나르 세부
Detail of Qutb Minar
ⓒMadan Inamdar

쿠트브 미나르 전경(인도 델리)
Paranomic View of Qutb Minar(Delhi, India)
ⓒRicha Bansal Agarwal

02 Islamic Forces Invade India

Islamic Empire Is Established in Northern India

India yet again became divided beginning in the mid-6th century as the Gupta Dynasty declined. In the disorder of the time, Islamic forces invaded India around the 8th century. By the 11th century, the Islamic forces expanded their territory to reach the basin of the Ganges River.

Around the early-13th century, the first Muslim dynasty was founded in the territory of Delhi. Over the next 300 years, five Muslim dynasties were established in northern India, and the rulers of these dynasties used the title of Sultan. For that reason, the five Muslim dynasties that emerged during this period are called the Delhi Sultanate.

In the beginning, the Islamic forces destroyed Buddhist and Hindu temples, but later allowed the Buddhists and Hindus to practice their religion as long as they agreed to pay a head tax. Since Islam was a religion that preached social equality, many people who were not happy with the current caste system converted to Islam.

This period saw the fusion of Hindu and Islamic cultures in the northern part of India, which was also under the occupation of Islamic forces. Islamic mosques that reflected the Hindu culture were built, and the procedures for ceremonies such as weddings and funerals became more similar between Hindus and Muslims.

⚬ **What Kind of Stupa Is Qutb Minar?**

Qutb Minar is a tower built to commemorate the victory of the Islamic forces who occupied Delhi. It is the tallest stone pagoda in India, reaching 72.5m in height. The phrase "*Quran*" is written on the pillar.

03 동남아시아의 정치 변화와 종교

인도차이나반도에서 여러 나라가 성장하다

미얀마에서는 11세기경 **파간 왕조**가 성립되었다. 파간 왕조는 인도 상좌부 불교의 영향을 받아 독자적인 문화를 발전시켰다. 13세기 말 파간 왕조가 원에 의해 멸망하면서 미얀마 지역은 분열되었다가 이후 **퉁구 왕조**로 발전하였다.

베트남 북부는 중국의 지배를 받다가 10세기경 독립하였다. 리 왕조는 국호를 '대월'로 정하고 중국으로부터 과거제를 수용하여 체제를 정비하고 불교를 보호하였다. 쩐 왕조 시대에는 몽골군의 침입을 격퇴하였으며, 『대월사기』를 편찬하고 한자를 기초로 한 **쯔놈 문자** 한자를 변형해 베트남어 발음을 표기한 문자를 만들어 민족의 정체성을 지키려 노력하였다.

베트남 남부에서는 2세기 말 인도 문화에 바탕을 둔 **참파**가 등장하였다. 참파는 해상 무역을 바탕으로 오랫동안 국가를 유지하였다.

타이 지역에서는 중국 남부로부터 이동해 온 타이족이 13세기에 **수코타이 왕국**을 건설하였다. 수코타이 왕국은 상좌부 불교를 받아들였으며 타이 문자를 만들어 독자적인 문화를 발전시켰다. 14세기 말에는 **아유타야 왕조**가 수코타이 왕국을 멸망시키고 타이 지역을 장악하였다.

⊚ **파간 왕조는 어떤 불교 유적을 남겼을까요?**

What Buddhist Relics Did the Pagan Empire Leave Behind?

파간 유적지는 캄보디아의 앙코르 와트, 인도네시아의 보로부두르와 함께 세계 3대 불교 유적지 중 하나예요. 11~13세기 사이에 약 5천여 개의 불탑이 파간 유적지에 세워졌어요. 파간 왕조 시기의 불탑은 약 2천여 개 남아 있지요.
The Pagan ruins are one of the world's three largest Buddhist sites, along with Angkor Wat in Cambodia and Borobudur in Indonesia. Between the 11th and 13th centuries, about 5,000 pagodas were built on the Pagan Ruins. About 2,000 pagodas from the Pagan dynasty remain.

파간의 불탑(미얀마)
The Temples of Pagan(Myanmar) ©Gerd Eichmann

03 Political Changes and Religions in Southeast Asia
Many Countries Emerge on the Indochinese Peninsula

In Myanmar, the Pagan Empire was established in the 11th century. The Pagan Empire developed its own unique culture under the influence of the Sthaviravada Buddhism of India. In the late-13th century, when the Pagan Empire fell to the Yuan Dynasty, Myanmar was divided and later developed into the Toungoo Dynasty.

The northern part of Vietnam was under the rule of China until it achieved its independence in the 10th century. Emperor Ly of the Ly Dynasty changed the name of the country to ʿDai Vietʾ, adopted and reformed the civil service exam system of the Chinese Song Dynasty, and supported the practice of Buddhism. During the Tran Dynasty, Dai Viet defeated the invading Mongols and the Vietnamese worked to keep their national identity by writing an official history text called *"Complete Annals of Dai Viet"* using their own writing script called Chu Nom that was based on Chinese characters.

Towards the end of the 2nd century, Southern Vietnam was occupied by the Champa Empire which had its roots in Indian culture. The Champa Empire, supported by a dynamic maritime trade, lasted for many years.

In Thailand, the Sukhothai kingdom was established by a Thai tribe that migrated from Southern China. The Sukhothai Empire accepted Sthaviravada Buddhism and developed its own unique culture with their own Thai script. Towards the end of the 14th century, the Ayutthaya Empire occupied Thailand after overthrowing the Sukhothai Empire.

캄보디아 지역에서 앙코르 왕조가 등장하다

1세기 무렵 메콩강 하류에서 부남이 성립되었다. 부남은 인도의 대승 불교를 수용하고, 해상 중계 무역으로 발전하다가 6세기경 진랍에 합병되었다. 이후 진랍은 남북으로 나뉘었다가 9세기경 수도를 앙코르로 이전하며 앙코르 왕조로 통일되었다.

앙코르 왕조는 힌두교와 불교의 영향을 받아 앙코르 톰과 앙코르 와트 앙코르는 '왕도(王都)', 와트는 '사원'을 뜻함를 건설하였다. 앙코르 와트는 본래 힌두교 사원으로 세워졌으나 후에 불교 사원으로 사용되었다.

......

⊚ 앙코르 와트는 힌두교 사원인가요, 불교 사원인가요?

앙코르 와트는 12세기 초 앙코르 왕조의 수리야바르만 2세가 힌두교의 주신 중 하나인 비슈누와 합일하기 위해 건립한 사원이다. 힌두교 사원이었지만 1300년대와 1400년대에 걸쳐 불교가 유행하면서 사원에 불상을 모셨다.

넓은 대지 위에 건물을 쌓고, 주위에는 연못을 파서 바다를 표현하였으며 히말라야의 봉우리를 상징하기 위해 건물 둘레에 벽을 쌓기도 하였다. 앙코르 와트 중앙의 높은 탑은 우주의 중심인 수미산을, 주위에 있는 4개의 탑은 주변의 봉우리들을 상징한다.

앙코르 왕조가 15세기경에 멸망하면서 앙코르 와트도 정글 속에 묻혀 버렸다가 1861년 프랑스 학자에 의해 알려지게 되었다. 유럽인은 앙코르 와트를 보고 '동양의 기적'이라 표현하였다.

앙코르 와트 전경(캄보디아)
Paranomic View of Angkor Wat(Cambodia) ⓒCharles J Sharp

Angkor Empire Is Established in Cambodia

Around the first century, the Funan Empire was established in the lower region of the Mekong River. The Funan Empire accepted Mahayana Buddhism and thrived via maritime trade until it was absorbed by the Chenla Empire in the 6th century. Later, the Chenla Empire was split into northern and southern regions until they were reunited when the Angkor Empire was established around the 9th century with its capital in Angkor.

Influenced by both Buddhism and Hinduism, the Angkor Empire constructed Angkor Thom and Angkor Wat. Angkor Wat was originally built as a Hindu temple, but later on, it was used as a Buddhist temple.

....

Is Angkor Wat a Hindu Temple or Buddhist Temple?

Angkor Wat was built in the early 12th century by King Suryavarman II of the Angkor Empire to unite with Vishnu, one of the Hindu gods. It was a Hindu temple, but as Buddhism became popular in the 1300s and 1400s, Buddha statues were enshrined in the temple.

Buildings were built on a large site, a pond was dug around it to represent the sea, and walls were built around the building to symbolize the Himalayan peaks. A high tower in the center symbolizes Mount Meru as the center of the universe, and four towers around it symbolize the surrounding peaks.

When the Angkor Empire fell in the 15th century, Angkor Wat was buried in the jungle and rediscovered by French scholars in 1861. The Europeans described it as a 'Miracle of the Orient.'

앙코르 와트(캄보디아) Angkor Wat(Cambodia)

동남아시아 섬 지역에서 여러 국가가 등장하다

동남아시아 섬 지역은 중국과 인도의 바닷길이 연결되는 곳 중심에 위치하여 중계 무역을 통해 발전하였다.

7세기경 수마트라섬에서는 **스리위자야**가 등장하여 믈라카 해협을 장악하고 동서 교역으로 번성하였다. 자와섬에서는 8세기경 **샤일렌드라 왕조**가 등장하였다. 샤일렌드라 왕조는 대승 불교를 받아들이고 **보로부두르 불탑**과 같은 불교 유적을 남기기도 하였다.

13세기 말에는 **마자파힛 왕조**가 등장하여 스리위자야를 무너뜨리고 인도네시아와 말레이반도를 지배하였다. 마자파힛 왕조는 자와 민족의 고유한 문화에 힌두교 문화를 융합하여 독자적인 문화를 발전시켰다.

◉ 보로부두르 불탑은 어떤 특징을 지니고 있나요?

보로부두르는 8~9세기에 만들어진 대승 불교 사원의 불탑이다. 산스크리트어로 '산 위의 절'을 의미하며, 세계 최대 규모의 불교 유적으로 알려져 있다.

보로부두르는 수많은 탑이 모여 하나의 거대한 탑을 이루도록 만들어졌다. 사원 벽면에는 각각 크기가 다른 조각들이 새겨져 있는데, 대부분 불교의 세계관과 철학에 대한 아름답고 흥미로운 이야기를 담고 있다. 그 내용은 불교 철학에서 말하는 인과응보, 석가모니의 일대기, 나무나 동물과 같은 자연, 평범한 사람들의 일상 등 매우 다양하여 하나의 거대한 이야기 책이라 할 수 있을 정도이다.

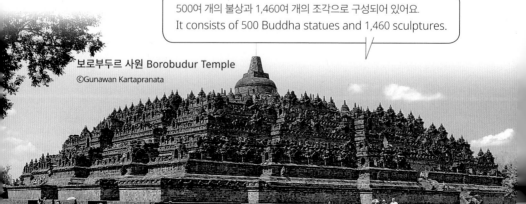

500여 개의 불상과 1,460여 개의 조각으로 구성되어 있어요.
It consists of 500 Buddha statues and 1,460 sculptures.

보로부두르 사원 Borobudur Temple
©Gunawan Kartapranata

Several Countries Emerge in the Southeast Asian Islands

The development of the area around the Southeast Asian islands was credited to maritime trade because the area was situated on the ocean midway between China and India.

Around the 7th century, the Srivijaya Empire was established on the island of Sumatra, extended its influence to control the Strait of Malacca, and thrived through maritime trade between west and east. On Java Island, the Shailendra Dynasty was established around the 8th century. The Shailendra Dynasty accepted Mahayana Buddhism and left certain Buddhist monuments such as the Borobudur Temple.

Towards the end of the 13th century, the Majapahit Empire emerged and overthrew the Srivijaya Dynasty to dominate Indonesia and the Malay Peninsula. The Majapahit Empire developed a unique culture through a fusion of Hindu culture and the traditional culture of the Java tribe.

⊚ **What Are the Characteristics of the Borobudur Temple?**

Borobudur is a stupa of a Mahayana Buddhist temple built in the 8th and 9th centuries. In Sanskrit, it means 'a temple on a mountain' and is known as the world's largest Buddhist relic.

Borobudur was made to form one huge stupa by gathering numerous pagodas. Sculptures of different sizes are engraved on the walls of the temple, most of which contain beautiful and interesting stories regarding the worldview and philosophy of Buddhism. Its contents are very diverse, such as retributive justice in Buddhist philosophy, the history of Shakyamuni, such as trees and animals, and the daily life of ordinary people, so it can be said to be a huge storybook.

보로부두르 사원의 석가모니불 Buddha Shakyamuni in the Borobudur ©CEphoto, Uwe Aranas

2

동아시아 문화의 형성과 확산

01 위·진·남북조 시대의 전개

북방 민족의 진출로 문화가 융합하다

중국은 한이 멸망한(220) 뒤 위·촉·오 세 나라로 분열되었다. 이후 진(晉)이 삼국을 통일하였으나 황실의 내분으로 혼란이 지속되었다. 이러한 상황을 틈타 5호로 대표되는 북방 민족은 화북 지역에 침입하여 여러 나라를 세웠다(5호 16국 시대).

이후 선비족이 세운 북위가 화북 지역을 통일하였다.

화북 지역을 빼앗긴 한족은 강남으로 이주하여 동진을 건국하였다. 동진이 멸망한 후 강남 지역에는 송·제·양·진이 잇달아 들어서 남조를 형성하였다. 이들은 북조의 왕조들과 대립하면서 남북조 시대를 이루었다.

남북조 시대에는 한족 문화와 북방 민족 문화가 어우러지며 새로운 변화가 나타났다. 북위의 효문제는 선비족의 풍습을 금지하고 한화 정책을 폈다. 또한 선비족과 한족의 혼인을 장려하여 민족 간의 융합을 더욱 촉진하였다.

위·진·남북조 시대의 전개
Development of Wei, Jin, and Northern and Southern

북위 효문제 한족의 언어와 의복을 사용하고 성도 한족식 성으로 바꾸도록 하라. 또한 북방 유목 민족과 한족 간의 혼인을 장려하여 두 민족을 통합할 것이다.
Emperor Xiaowen of Northern Wei Use the language and clothing of the Han, and use surnames in the Han style. Encourage marriage between the northern nomadic peoples and the Han tribe as well.

Formation and Proliferation of East Asian Culture

01 Development During the Wei, Jin, Southern and Northern Dynasty Periods

Northern Nomadic People Bring About the Fusion of Cultures

In China, the end of the Han Dynasty was followed by the division of China between the states of Wei, Shu, and Wu. These three kingdoms were united by the Jin Dynasty, but the tumultuous times continued due to internal conflict among members of the royal family. It was under this circumstance that five ethnic minorities in the northern area of China called the Five Barbarians invaded the northern territory of Jin and established more than a dozen states(Five Hus and Sixteen States Period). Later, the northern territory was unified by the Northern Wei Dynasty that was established by the Xianbei tribe.

After losing the northern territory, the Han tribe fled to the Jiangnan areas and established the East Jin Dynasty there. The fall of the East Jin Dynasty was succeeded by several dynasties such as Song, Qi, Liang, and Chen, all of which are grouped together and referred to as the Southern Dynasties. The period called the Northern and Southern Dynasties refers to the time when these southern dynasties fought with their counterparts in the north.

During the Northern and Southern Dynasties period, new changes occurred through the mix of the northern nomadic people's culture and the Chinese culture represented by the Han tribe. Emperor Xiaowen of Northern Wei banned the culture of the Xianbei tribe and promoted the Chinese culture instead. He also encouraged Xianbei and Han families to intermarry.

문벌 귀족 사회가 형성되고 불교와 도교가 발달하다

위 · 진 · 남북조 시대에는 중정관이 지방의 인재를 추천하면 중앙 정부가 관리로 임용하는 9품중정제가 실시되었다. 9품중정제는 본래 지방의 유능한 인재를 등용하기 위해 도입되었다. 하지만 호족을 비롯한 지배층이 9품중정제를 이용해 중앙 관직을 독점적으로 세습하여 문벌 귀족으로 성장하였다.

위 · 진 · 남북조 시대에 전쟁이 계속되어 사회가 불안해지자 사람들은 종교를 통해 정신적 위안을 얻고자 하였다. 이에 불교 · 도교 등 여러 종교가 융성하였다. 불교 승려들은 인도와 중국을 오가며 불경을 한문으로 번역하였다. 북조에서는 불교가 황실과 귀족의 보호를 받으며 융성하였고 윈강과 룽먼 등에 대규모 석굴 사원이 조성되었다. 위 · 진 · 남북조 시대의 불교는 고구려, 백제 등 한반도에도 전해졌다.

남조에서는 혼란스러운 정치에 참여하기보다는 죽림칠현처럼 속세를 떠나 자연과 함께 살고자 하는 청담 사상이 유행하였다. 청담 사상은 유교에 얽매이지 않고 개인의 자유로운 삶을 추구하여 중국의 문학과 종교 등에 큰 영향을 미쳤다. 또한 이 시기에는 노장사상과 민간 신앙이 결합하여 도교가 성립되었다.

💿 **죽림칠현은 어떤 사람들인가요?**

What Kind of People Are the Seven Sages of the Bamboo Grove?

죽림칠현은 위와 진의 정권 교체기에 부패한 정권에 등을 돌리고 죽림에 모여 청담(淸談)으로 세월을 보낸 7명의 선비를 말해요. 그들은 죽림에서 거리낌 없이 술을 마셨고 개인주의, 무정부주의, 도교 등에 빠져 있었다.

The Seven Sages of the Bamboo Grove refers to the seven scholars who spent years gathering and having wise conversation in the bamboo forest after turning their backs on the corrupt regime over the transitional period of Wei and Jin. They drank without hesitation in the bamboo forest and were immersed in individualism, anarchism, and Taoism.

죽림칠현도
The Seven Sages of the
Bamboo Grove

Formation of Aristocratic Society and the Development of Buddhism and Taoism

During the Wei, Jin, and the Northern and Southern Dynasties periods, government officials were recruited through the Nine Grades System of Officers and the candidates for the jobs were recommended by local government officials. The Nine Grades System was originally introduced to recruit talented people from regions outside the capital, but the ruling class, including powerful families, abused the system to monopolize high-level government jobs and pass them down to their descendants, thereby contributing to the growth of noble civilian families.

In response to the social unrest resulting from continuous wars during the Wei, Jin, and the Northern and Southern Dynasties periods, people turned to religion to find solace and comfort. The result was the proliferation of various religions including Buddhism and Taoism. Buddhist monks traveled between India and China and translated Buddhist scripts into Chinese. In the northern dynasties, Buddhism flourished with the support of royal and noble families, and massive Buddhist temples were constructed inside Yungang and Longmen Caves during this period. It was also during this period that Buddhism was introduced to the Goguryeo and Baekje dynasties in the Korean Peninsula.

In the southern dynasties, the popular school of thought was called Qingtan, which was about living in harmony with nature like the Seven Sages of the Bamboo Grove instead of living in the secular world and engaging in chaotic politics. The Qingtan school advocated a life of individuals that was free and unrestricted by Confucianism, and it left a great influence on Chinese literature and religion. It was also during this period that Taoism was born through the fusion of Lao Tzu's philosophy and folk beliefs.

02 수·당의 성립과 발전

수가 남북조를 통일하다

수는 중국을 다시 통일하여 약 370년 동안 이어진 위·진·남북조 시대를 마무리하였다(589). 수를 건국한 문제는 제도를 정비하여 강력한 중앙 집권 체제를 갖추었다. 중앙 통치 체제를 3성 6부로 구성하였고 북위 이래의 제도를 바탕으로 토지·조세·군사 제도를 마련하였다. 또한 시험을 거쳐 관리를 선발하는 과거제를 처음으로 실시하였다. 이 제도들은 당 율령의 기초가 되었다.

문제의 뒤를 이은 양제는 남북 지역을 연결하는 대운하를 완성하고 만리장성을 재건축하였다. 양제는 북쪽의 돌궐을 공격하는 등 영토 확장에도 적극적이었다. 그러나 대규모 토목 공사가 잦아져 백성들의 불만이 높아졌고 무리하게 추진한 고구려 원정도 실패하였다. 이에 곳곳에서 반란이 일어나 수는 건국 37년 만에 멸망하였다(618).

⚙ **수의 대운하 건설이 중국에 어떤 변화를 가져왔을까?**

위·진·남북조 시대에는 강남 지방이 개발되어 경제적 중심지로 거듭났다. 하지만 중국의 큰 강들은 대부분 서쪽에서 동쪽으로 흘러 남쪽의 물자를 북쪽으로 운송하기가 어려웠다. 이에 수는 남북 간의 원활한 물자 유통을 위해 대운하를 건설하였다.

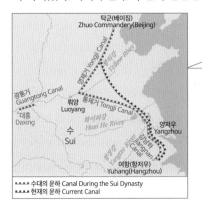

대운하는 남쪽의 항저우에서 북쪽의 베이징까지 이어졌고, 총길이는 1,515m에 달하였어요. 수의 대운하는 지금도 운행되고 있고, 중국의 경제 통합에 큰 역할을 하고 있어요.
The Grand Canal stretched from Hangzhou in the south to Beijing in the north, reaching a total length of 1,515m. It is still in operation and plays a large role in China's economic integration.

수의 대운하 Grand Canal of the Sui Dynasty

02 Formation and Growth of Sui and Tang Dynasties
Sui Unifies Northern and Southern Dynasties

The 370 years of Wei, Jin, and the Northern and Southern dynasties period came to an end when China was reunited by the Sui Dynasty (589). Emperor Wen, who founded Sui, undertook various reforms to build a strong centralized government system. He instituted the Three Departments and Six Ministries system for the central government, and reformed land, taxation, and military systems based on the systems that had been used since the northern dynasties period. He also introduced the civil service exam system for the first time to recruit government officials. All of these reforms became the foundations of the succeeding Tang dynasty.

Emperor Yang, who succeeded Emperor Wen, is credited with the construction of the Grand Canal that connected north and south and the reconstruction of the Great Wall. Emperor Yang aggressively expanded his territory by invading the Gokturk Empire to the north. But a series of massive construction projects resulted in numerous revolts by the people, and his disastrous expedition to Goguryeo ended in failure. Eventually, the Sui Empire came to an end just 37 years after its founding as the result of revolts by the people(618).

....

◉ How Has the Construction of the Grand Canal of the Sui Changed China?

During the Wei, Jin, and Nothern and Southern Dynasties periods, the Jangnan region was developed and transformed into a hub of economy. However, most of China's large rivers flow from west to east, making it difficult to transport goods from the south to the north. Accordingly, the Sui Dynasty built the Grand Canal for smooth distribution of goods between the two regions.

당이 대제국을 건설하다

수 말기의 혼란을 수습한 이연(고조)은 당을 세우고 장안을 수도로 삼았다 (618). 제2대 황제 태종은 수의 제도를 바탕으로 율령 체제를 정비하고 국가의 기틀을 확립하였다. 중앙 통치 조직을 3성 6부로 구성하였으며 과거제를 시행하였다. 균전제를 실시하여 농민에게 토지를 나누어 주었고 그 대신 조·용·조라는 세금을 걷었다. 또한 부병제를 시행하여 전쟁이 일어나면 농민들을 군인으로 동원하였다.

태종은 대외적으로 동돌궐을 복속시켰고, 뒤를 이은 고종은 서돌궐을 멸망시켜 돌궐 지역이 당의 세력권으로 흡수되었다. 태종은 고구려 원정에 실패하였으나, 고종은 신라와 동맹을 맺고 백제와 고구려를 멸망시켰다. 영토를 확장한 태종과 고종

은 중앙에서 관리를 파견하는 동시에 해당 지역의 왕을 지방관으로 임명하였다(기미 정책). 이로써 농경 지역과 유목 지역은 정치적·문화적으로 서로 영향을 받게 되었다.

수·당의 영역 Territory of Sui Dynasty and Tang Dynasty

🧭 **고구려 정벌 실패 전과 후의 당 태종은 어떤 입장 차이를 보였나요?**

(전) 첫째, 고구려의 연개소문이 신하된 자로서 그 왕을 죽였다. 나는 영류왕의 원한을 갚기 위해 연개소문을 쳐서 그 죄를 묻겠다. 둘째, 당의 신하국인 신라를 고구려가 거듭 공격하니 신라의 원수를 갚기 위해서 고구려를 공격하겠다.

당 태종
Taizong of Tang Dynasty

(후) 나의 자식들은 고구려를 공격하지 마라. 너희가 이길 수 있는 나라가 아니다. 고구려를 공격하다가 오히려 당이 위태로워질 것이다.

Tang Builds a Great Empire

Li Yuan(Gaozu) brought an end to the troubled Sui Dynasty and established the Tang Dynasty with its capital in Changan(618). His successor, Emperor Taizong, laid the groundwork for a nation by reforming government systems based on those of the previous Sui Dynasty. He built a central government structured on the Three Departments and Six Ministries system and installed the civil service examination system. He supported the Equal-field System to allocate land to peasants and gave them the option to pay tax either in grain, textile, or labor. He also carried on the Fubing System, in which peasants were mobilized and turned into soldiers in times of war.

Taizong externally subjugated the Eastern Gokturks. His successor, Gaozong, subjugated the Western Gokturks. The Gokturks region was thus absorbed into the sphere of influence of the Tang. Taizong's expedition to Goguryeo failed, but his successor, Gaozong, formed an alliance with Silla and brought down both Baekje and Goguryeo. Taizong and Gaojong, who expanded their territory, dispatched officials from the central government and appointed the king of the region as a provincial official. As a result, the agricultural and nomadic areas were influenced politically and culturally by each other.

◉ **What Was the Difference between Emperor Taejong's Position Before and After His Failure to Conquer Goguryeo?**

(Before) First, even though Yeon Gaesomun in Goguryeo was a servant, he killed the king. In order to pay for the resentment of the King Yeongnyu, I will attack him and ask forgiveness for the sin. Second, as Goguryeo repeatedly attacked Silla, a country under the Tang Dynasty's command, I will attack Goguryeo to avenge Silla's enemies.

(After) Do not attack Goguryeo. It is not a country that we can beat. Attacking Goguryeo would endanger the Tang Dynasty.

안·사의 난을 계기로 당이 쇠퇴하다

8세기 중엽에 이르러 당의 국력이 크게 약화되었다. 탈라스 전투에서 이슬람의 아바스 왕조에 패배하였고(751), 안·사의 난이 일어나면서 사회가 혼란스러워졌다.

안·사의 난 이후 중앙 관리들의 권력 다툼이 심해지면서 지방에서는 **절도사** 국경 지역의 행정과 국방을 담당하던 군대 지휘관들이 독립적인 세력을 구축하였다. 이어진 **황소의 난**(875) 소금 장수 황소가 주축이 되어 일으킨 농민 반란으로 당의 혼란은 더욱 극심해졌고, 결국 당은 절도사 주전충에 의해 멸망하였다(907).

⚫ 당 최고의 미인 양귀비는 안·사의 난에 어떤 영향을 주었나요?

당 현종은 며느리였던 양귀비의 아름다움에 반해 양귀비를 자신의 귀비로 책봉하였다. 양귀비의 사촌 오빠 양국충은 그 힘을 업고 승상이 되어 온갖 전횡을 일삼았다. 이에 절도사 출신 안녹산과 그의 부하 사사명이 반란을 일으켰다(안·사의 난).

현종은 반란을 피해 쓰촨으로 달아나려 하였지만, 그를 호위하던 고력사(현종의 환관)와 병사들이 나라를 위기에 빠뜨린 양귀비와 그 일족을 죽이지 않으면 현종을 모시고 가지 않겠다고 고집하였다. 안녹산의 군대에 쫓기던 현종은 병사들의 요구에 따라 양귀비를 내어 주고 말았다.

고력사와 병사들이 아름다운 양귀비를 차마 죽일 수 없어 일본으로 탈출시켰다는 설이 있어요. 일본 야마구치현에는 이 이야기를 뒷받침하는 사당과 무덤, 유물이 남아 있지요. 자신이 양귀비의 후손이라고 주장하며 족보를 들고 나타난 사람도 있었답니다.
There is a theory that the soldiers and Gao Lishi could not kill the beautiful Yang Guifei and extricated her to Japan. There are shrines, tombs, and relics that support this story in Yamaguchi Prefecture, Japan, and there were people who appeared with genealogy records, claiming to be her descendants.

양귀비 석상(중국 시안) Statue of Yang Guifei(Xian, China)

An Lushan Rebellion Deals a Critical Blow to Tang

By the mid-8th century, the Tang Dynasty experienced a significant decline in national power. In the Battle of Talas, Tang was defeated by the Islamic forces of the Abbasid Dynasty(751), and the nation became more chaotic due to the An Lushan Rebellion.

The conflict among the government officials intensified after the An Lushan Rebellion, and the regional military governors, called 'Jiedushi', used this chaos as an opportunity to grow their power. The following Huang Chao Agrarian Rebellion(875) dealt another blow to the Tang Dynasty until it was overthrown by a regional military governor, Zhu Quanzhong(907).

⊚ How Did Yang Guifei, the Greatest Beauty of Tang, Impact the An Lushan Rebellion?

Emperor Xuanzong of Tang fell in love with the beauty of Yang Guifei, his daughter-in-law, and proclaimed her the highest rank for imperial consorts. Her cousin, Yang Guozhong, used that power to become a chancellor and abused his authority. As a result, An Lushan, who was a Jiedushi, and his deputy, Shi Siming, rebelled(An Lushan Rebellion).

Emperor Xuanzong tried to flee to Sichuan to avoid the rebellion, but the Gao Lishi(the eunuch of Xuanzong) and the soldiers who escorted him insisted that they would not go with Xuanzong unless he killed Yang Guifei and her clan, who had put the country in crisis. Xuanzong, who was chased by An Lushan's army, gave in at the request of the soldiers.

귀족적이고 국제적인 문화가 발전하다

당은 귀족 중심 사회였으므로 당의 문화는 귀족적인 성격을 띠었다. 특히 귀족들의 취향에 맞는 문학, 서예, 회화 등이 발전하였다. 문학에서는 시가 발달하여 시인 이백, 백거이, 두보 등이 활약하였다.

중앙아시아까지 세력을 확장한 당은 비단길을 장악하고 바닷길을 활용하여 여러 나라와 교류하였다. 당의 수도인 장안 오늘날의 시안은 비단길의 시작점에 있어 세계 각국 사람들이 왕래하는 국제도시가 되었다.

장안 서쪽의 상설 국제 시장에서는 신라, 발해, 일본 등 주변국은 물론 서역의 상인들이 다양한 물품을 거래하였다. 그 영향으로 당의 문화는 국제적인 성격을 지니게 되었는데, 이는 당삼채에 잘 나타나 있다. 당에서는 서역풍 의복인 호복과 서역풍 음식인 호식이 유행하였고 서역 음악과 춤도 인기를 끌었다.

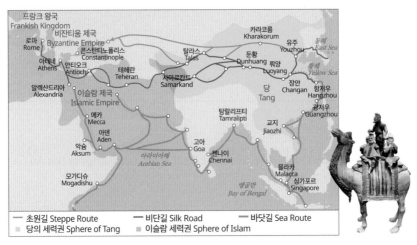

당의 국제 교류
International Exchange of Tang

서역인 악사를 태운 낙타 당삼채(중국 국가박물관)
Sancai Camel Carrying a Western Musician
(National Museum of China)

🌐 장안은 왜 국제도시로 불렸나요?

아시아의 여러 나라에서 시작된 길은 당의 수도인 장안으로 통하였다. 그 길을 이용하여 각국의 사절과 상인, 승려, 유학생들이 대거 당에 몰려들었다. 당은 외국인에게 관용을 베풀고, 외국인을 대상으로 한 빈공과를 설치하여 관직을 개방하였으며, 군인의 경우 누구라도 실력에 따라 장교가 되어 출세할 수 있는 길도 열어 두었다.

Development of Aristocratic and Internationalized Culture

Tang being an aristocratic society, its culture was characterized by being aristocratic in nature. In particular, it was a golden age of literature, calligraphy, paintings, and other interests that appealed to the tastes of aristocrats. In literature, poetry reached its zenith during this period with such notable poets as Li Bai, Bai Juyi and Du Fu.

Tang extended its influence as far as Central Asia, took control of the Silk Road, and traded with numerous countries through sea routes. Tang's capital, Changan(today's Xian), became an international city that attracted people from around the world because it was located at the head of the Silk Road.

Global marketplaces that opened throughout the year were situated in the west of the city where merchants from Silla, Balhae, Japan, and all other surrounding countries, as well as the Western Regions, came and traded a wide variety of goods. As a result, the Tang culture took on international characteristics, which is well manifested in a versatile type of decoration on Chinese pottery called Sancai. During the Tang period, western-style music, dance, as well as fashion and cuisine, called Hufu and Hushi, became widely popular.

◉ Why Was Changan Called an International City?

The paths that began in various Asian countries led to Changan, the capital of Tang. Using that path, envoys, merchants, monks, and international students from all over the world flocked to Tang. Tang was tolerant of foreigners, and opened up the offices by establishing the civil service exams for foreigners. In the case of soldiers, it also opened the way for any soldier to become an officer and succeed according to his ability.

다양한 종교가 유행하다

당과 외국의 교류가 활발해지면서 종교도 다양해졌다. 조로아스터교, 네스토리우스교(경교) 콘스탄티노폴리스의 대주교였던 네스토리우스가 만든 크리스트교의 일파, 이슬람교 등 외래 종교가 전해졌다. 한대에 들어온 불교는 토착화되어 여러 종파가 만들어졌고, 승려들이 인도에서 가져온 불교 경전이 번역되어 퍼지면서 불교는 더욱 발전하였다. 당의 고승덕이 높은 승려 현장은 인도에서 불교를 공부하고 돌아온 뒤 『대당서역기』라는 여행기를 남기기도 하였다.

유학에서는 공영달이 『오경정의』를 편찬하여 한대 이후의 훈고학을 정리하였으며, 도교는 황실의 특별 보호를 받으며 성장하였다.

....

🌀 『서유기』의 삼장 법사는 어떤 인물인가요?

당의 불교 발전에서 가장 많이 언급되는 인물은 현장이다. 현장은 629년 홀로 장안에서 출발하여 고생 끝에 인도에 도착하였다. 그리고 인도에서 10여 년 동안 경문을 배우고 연구한 후 645년에 불경 657부를 가지고 장안으로 돌아왔다.

현장은 인도에 다녀온 후 불경과 불상을 보관하기 위하여 대안탑을 건립하였다. 또한 자신의 경험을 바탕으로 『대당서역기』를 써서 서역과 인도 각국의 상황을 소개하였다. 현장이 중국 불교의 발전에 기여한 공이 워낙 커 훗날 그를 모델로 한 『서유기』라는 소설까지 탄생하였는데, 『서유기』의 삼장 법사가 바로 현장이다.

↓ 대안탑(중국 산시성 시안)
Giant Wild Goose Pagoda
(Xian, Shaanxi Province, China)
©Alex Kwok

현장 법사가 사막 한가운데서 길을 잃었을 때, 어디선가 기러기가 날아와 길을 인도해 주었어요. 이에 현장 법사가 중국으로 돌아와 보답하는 마음으로 탑을 세우고 '기러기탑(대안탑)'이라 이름 붙였다고 전해요.
When Xuanzang was lost in the middle of the desert, a goose flew in and led the way. It is reported that he returned to China and built a pagoda in repayment, and named it 'Goose Pagoda(Giant Wild Goose Pagoda)'.

→ 현장(복원, 도쿄국립박물관)
Xuanzang(Restored, Tokyo National Museum)

Diverse Religions Become Popular

Dynamic exchange with foreign countries translated into diversified religions. Some of the religions introduced to the dynasty during this period included Zoroastrianism, Nestorianism(a branch of Christianity) and Islam. Buddhism became more localized since it was introduced during the Han Dynasty, and gave birth to diverse religious orders. Buddhism proliferated further after the Buddhist monks translated Buddhist scriptures they brought from India. One of those monks was Xuanzang who wrote a travelogue titled *"The Great Tang Records on the Western Regions"* after he studied Buddhism in India.

With regard to Confucianism, Kong Yingda compiled with the *"Rectified Interpretation of the Five Classics"* which became the basis for all future exegesis of the Confucian classics that had been developed since the Han Dynasty, while Taoism flourished with special protection from the royal family.

....

🕉 Who Is Xuanzang Dharma Teacher of *"Journey to the West"*?

The person most often mentioned in the Buddhist development of Tang is Xuanzang. He left Changan alone in 629 and barely arrived in India with difficulty. After learning and studying the Buddhist scriptures for 10 years in India, he returned to Changan in 645 with 657 copies of Buddhist scriptures.

After visiting India, Xuanzang built the Giant Wild Goose Pagoda to store Buddhist scriptures and statues. Also, based on his own experience, he wrote *"The Great Tang Records on the Western Regions"* to introduce situations of the West and the countries in India. His contribution to the development of Buddhism in China was so great that a novel called *"Journey to the West"* was later created, which was modeled after him.

03 동아시아 문화권의 성립

동아시아 각국이 문화를 교류하다

세계 여러 나라와 교류하면서 당의 문화는 크게 발전하였다. 이에 동아시아 지역의 나라들은 당에 사신과 유학생을 보내 당의 선진 문물을 적극적으로 수용하였다. 당에 왕래하던 각국의 상인과 승려도 문화 전파에 크게 기여하였다.

문화를 교류하는 과정에서 동아시아 지역은 한자, 율령, 유교, 불교 등 공통적인 문화 요소를 가지게 되었다. 신라, 일본 등은 한자를 사용하였으며, 율령 체제를 도입하여 통치 체제를 정비하였다.

유교는 동아시아 국가들의 통치 이념이자 사회 윤리로 자리 잡았고, 불교 ^{대승 불교} 는 왕실의 권위를 높이고 학문과 예술이 발달하는 데 중요한 역할을 하였다. 이러한 문화적 유사성을 토대로 하여 중국, 한국, 일본, 베트남 등을 중심으로 동아시아 문화권이 형성되었다.

⊚ 동아시아의 공통적인 문화 요소는 무엇인가요?

한국, 중국, 일본, 베트남은 교통 표지판에 한자를 공통으로 사용하고 있다. 동아시아 4국에서는 유교가 퍼져 모두 공자를 모시는 문묘가 있다. 또한 수많은 불상은 이들 나라의 불교 문화가 발전하였음을 보여준다. 베트남은 지리적으로 동남아시아에 속하지만 오랫동안 중국의 영향을 받아 동아시아 지역과 같은 문화를 공유하였기 때문에 문화적으로는 동아시아 문화권으로 분류된다.

공묘 대성전(중국 산둥성)
Temple of Confucius, Qufu(Shandong, China)

하노이 공묘(베트남 하노이)
Temple of Literature, Hanoi(Vietnam)

03 Establishment of the East Asian Cultural Sphere
Cultural Exchanges Among East Asian Countries

The Tang culture bloomed while interacting with many countries around the world. East Asian countries sent their envoys and students to Tang to proactively learn and accept Tang's advanced civilization and culture. Merchants and monks who traveled in and out of Tang also made great contributions to the proliferation of the Tang culture.

During this process of cultural exchange, the East Asian regions began to share many cultural elements such as Chinese characters, the legal system, Confucianism, and Buddhism. Silla and Japan adopted and used Chinese characters and reformed their governmental systems by adopting Tang's legal system.

Confucianism became the ruling ideology and ethics in East Asian societies, while Buddhism played an important role in strengthening the authority of the royal families and advancing their academic standards and arts. This cultural assimilation resulted in the creation of the East Asian cultural sphere centering on China, Korea, Japan, and Vietnam.

········

@ **What are some common cultural elements in East Asia?**

Korea, China, Japan, and Vietnam use Chinese characters in common for traffic signs. In the four East Asian countries, Confucianism has spread, and all of them have tombs dedicated to Confucius. In addition, numerous Buddha statues show that the Buddhist culture of these countries has developed. Vietnam belongs to Southeast Asia geographically, but is culturally classified as an East Asian culture because it has long shared the same culture as the East Asian region under the influence of China.

04 고대 일본의 발전

야마토 정권이 중국, 한반도와 교류하다

기원전 3세기 무렵 일본에 한반도와 중국으로부터 청동기와 철기, 벼농사 기술이 전해졌다. 이 시기를 **야요이 시대**라고 한다. 이후 일본 각지에 여러 개의 작은 나라들이 세워졌다.

4세기에 **야마토 정권**이 등장하여 주변 소국을 통합해 나갔다. 야마토 정권은 규슈까지 세력을 확장하였다. 또한 중국의 남조, 수, 당, 한반도의 여러 나라와 교류하며 농업 기술과 직조 기술, 유교와 불교 등 선진 문물을 적극적으로 받아들였다. 이로써 불교를 중심으로 하는 **아스카 문화**^{일본 최초의 불교 문화}가 발전하였다. 6~7세기에 활동한 쇼토쿠 태자는 불교를 널리 보급하고 체제를 정비하여 국가 기틀을 마련하였다.

◎ **쇼토쿠 태자가 당에 모욕적인 국서를 보내게 된 배경은 무엇일까요?**

쇼토쿠 태자는 수의 양제에게 편지를 보내면서 일본은 '해가 뜨는 나라', 수는 '해가 지는 나라'라고 표현하였다. 이 편지를 받은 수 양제는 매우 불쾌해 하며 "야만국의 국서가 무례하구나. 다시는 상대하지 말라."라고 하였다. 그러나 고구려를 물리치려면 일본의 도움이 필요한 상황이었기 때문에 실제로 그렇게 하기는 어려웠다. 쇼토쿠 태자는 수의 상황을 알고 있었기에 적극적인 외교를 펴면서 대등한 관계를 지향했던 것이다.

> 해가 뜨는 나라의 천자가 해가 지는 나라의 천자에게 국서를 보냅니다. 건강하십니까?
> An emperor of the country where the sun rises sends a credential to an emperor of the country where the sun sets. Are you doing well?

쇼토쿠 태자와 두 아들 Crown Prince Shotoku and His Two Sons

04 Development of Ancient Japan

Yamato Clan Interacts with China and the Korean Peninsula

Around the third century BC, bronze and iron tools and rice farming were introduced to Japan from Korea and China. This period is called the Yayoi period. Soon after, several small states were established in various parts of Japan.

In the 4th century, the Yamato clan gained power and dominated the small surrounding states. The Yamato regime expanded its influence to Kyushu. The regime also interacted with various countries such as Sui, Tang, and Southern dynasties as well as the Korean peninsula, during which process it proactively accepted advanced civilization and culture such as farming and textile weaving. This resulted in the development of the Asuka culture which was based on Buddhism. In the 6th and 7th centuries especially, the Japanese Crown Prince Shotoku contributed to the foundation of a nation by passionately promoting Buddhism and successfully establishing a centralized government during his reign.

....

◉ What Was the Background Behind Crown Prince Shotoku's Sending of an Offensive Official Message to Tang?

Crown prince Shotoku wrote a credential to Emperor Yang of Sui Dynasty, describing Japan as 'the country where the sun rises' and the Sui Dynasty as 'the country where the sun sets'. Emperor Yang of Sui, who received this credential, was very unhappy and said, "The credential of this savage country is rude. Don't deal with them again." However, it was difficult to do that because he thought Sui Dynasty needed Japanese help to defeat Goguryeo. Crown prince Shotoku was aware of the situation in the Sui Dynasty, so he pursued an equal relationship while actively engaging in diplomacy with China.

중앙 집권 체제를 갖추고 일본이라는 국호를 사용하다

일본은 선진 기술과 문화를 받아들이고자 꾸준히 수와 당, 신라에 사신을 파견하였다. 당에는 7세기부터 9세기까지 여러 번 견당사 당으로 보낸 사신를 보냈다. 신라에도 668년부터 견신라사를 파견하였는데, 200명이 넘는 대규모 사신단을 보내기도 하였다.

7세기 중엽 일본에서는 다이카 개신이 이루어졌다(645). 그 결과 일본은 율령을 도입하여 통치 제도를 갖추고 국왕 중심의 중앙 집권 체제를 수립하였다. 7세기 후반부터는 왜가 아닌 일본이라는 국호를 사용하고 왕 대신 천황이라는 칭호를 사용하였다.

8세기 초에는 당의 장안성을 모방하여 헤이조쿄(나라)를 건설하고 수도로 삼았다. 이곳을 수도로 한 시기를 나라 시대라고 부른다. 나라 시대에는 불교문화가 융성하여 도다이사와 같은 거대한 불교 사원이 지어졌다. 『고사기』, 『일본서기』 등 일본의 역사서도 저술되었다.

⊘ 세계에서 가장 큰 목조 건축물은 무엇인가요?

세계에서 가장 큰 목조 건축물은 일본의 도다이사이다. 도다이사는 불교를 이용한 정치 통합을 원했던 쇼무 천황이 745년 발원하고 승려 로벤이 창건하였다. 752년 4월 점안식을 하였는데 이때 1만 명에 가까운 승려가 모여들었고 동아시아 여러 나라의 승려도 참여하는 등 국제적인 행사가 되었다.

> 금당 대불은 그 크기가 매우 커서 얼굴 길이만 5m나 된답니다. 그 옆의 보살상에는 금박을 입혔어요.
> The Great Buddha statue of the Todai-ji is very large, and its face is 5m long. The Bodhisattva statue next to it was overlaid with gold leaf.

도다이사의 대불전 대불(좌)과 보살상(우)
The Great Buddha(Left) and Bodhisattva Statue(Right) in the Todai-ji

도다이사(일본 나라, 에도 시대 재건)
Todai-ji(Nara, Japan, Reconstruction in the Edo Period)

Establishment of a Centralized Government System and the Use of an Official Name for the Country, Nihon

Japan continuously sent envoys to Sui, Tang, and Silla to learn advanced technology and culture. Between the 7th and 9th centuries, Japan sent Japanese missions to Tang called 'Kentoshi' several times. The missions were also sent to Silla beginning from 668, and there was a time when Japan sent a large group of over 200 missions.

Around the mid-7th century, Japan went through the Taika Reforms (645). As a result, Japan reorganized government structure by introducing the legal system, and established a centralized government centering on the emperor. Beginning from the late 7th century, Japan started using the name Nihon as the official name of the country and calling their kings emperors.

In the early 8th century, Japan built Heijo-kyo and made it the capital (Nara) by modeling it after Tang's capital Changan. The time when the city served as the capital is called the Nara period. Buddhism flourished during the Nara period, and large Buddhist temples such as Todai-ji were built. "*Kojiki* (Records of Ancient Matters)" and "*The Nihon Shoki* (The Chronicles of Japan)" were written during this period.

⊚ **What Is the Largest Wooden Structure in the World?**

The largest wooden structure in the world is Japan's Todai-ji. It was founded in 745 by Emperor Shomu, who wanted political integration using Buddhism, and was founded by monk Roben. In April 752, an instillation ceremony was held and nearly 10,000 monks gathered. Monks from various countries in East Asia participated and it was an international event.

헤이안 시대에 국풍 문화가 발전하다

귀족들의 권력 다툼이 심해지고 승려가 정치에 관여하는 등 중앙 정치가 혼란스러워지자 일본은 헤이안(교토)으로 다시 수도를 옮겼다(794). 이후 약 400년 동안을 헤이안 시대라고 한다. 천황은 수도를 옮겨 사회 혼란을 바로잡고자 하였으나 귀족과 외척의 정치 개입이 계속되었다. 천황의 권위는 약해졌고 지방의 귀족들은 장원을 늘려 나가며 세력을 키웠다. 귀족들은 늘어난 토지를 지키기 위해 무사를 고용하기 시작하였다.

헤이안 시대에 당이 쇠퇴하자 일본은 견당사 파견을 중지하였다. 이후 일본에서는 귀족 중심으로 고유한 문화가 발전하였는데, 이를 국풍 문화라 한다. 한자를 변형한 문자인 가나가 사용되기 시작하였고, 가나를 이용하여 생각과 감정을 표현하는 일본의 고유한 시인 와카가 만들어졌다.

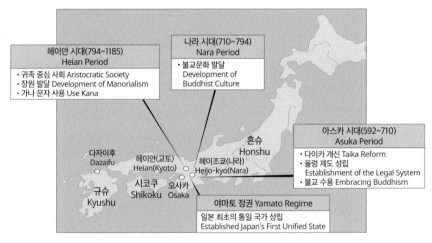

일본 고대 국가의 발전 Development of Ancient Japan

헤이안 시대의 별장을 사찰로 개축하였어요.
Byodoin is a villa in the Heian period that was converted into a temple.

뵤도인(일본 우지) Byodoin(Uji, Japan)

Development of Kokufu Bunka During the Heian Period

As the power struggle among aristocrats and growing influence of Buddhist temples disrupted the central government, Japan moved its capital again in 794, this time to Heian-kyo(Kyoto). The next four hundred years is called the Heian period. The emperor tried to bring order to society by moving the capital city, but the aristocrats and consort kin kept interfering in their politics. The authority of the emperor grew weaker while the regional aristocrats kept growing their influence and territory. These aristocrats began to hire warriors to protect their expanding manors.

During the Heian period, Japan stopped sending missions to Tang because Tang began to decline. Later on, Japan saw the birth of its own culture centering on the aristocracy, which came to be known as Kokufu Bunka(lit. original national culture). It was during this period Japan started using its own writing system called Kana, which was modified from the Chinese writing system. They also started expressing their emotions and thoughts in Kana in the form of Waka, which is Japan's unique form of poetry.

헤이안 시대에는 당에서 비단을 수입해 화려한 의복 문화가 발달하였어요.
During the Heian period, silk was imported from Tang and the colorful clothing culture developed.

헤이안 시대 귀족 여성의 전통 의상
Noble Women's Traditional Costumes in the Heian Period

이슬람 문화의 형성과 확산

01 이슬람 제국의 종교와 정치의 변화

무함마드가 이슬람교를 창시하다

대부분 사막으로 이루어진 아라비아반도에는 아랍인들이 살고 있었다. 대다수 아랍인들은 가축을 거느리며 유목 생활을 하였고, 간혹 비가 많이 내리는 지역에서는 농경이 발달하기도 하였다. 종교는 다신교많은 신의 존재를 인정하고 믿는 종교 형태였다.

6세기 무렵 사산 왕조 페르시아와 비잔티움 제국의 대립으로 기존의 교통로가 막히자 상인들은 아라비아반도 남쪽의 **홍해**를 교통로로 이용하였다. 이에 따라 홍해에 인접한 **메카**와 메디나와 같은 도시가 성장하였다.

하지만 상업에 종사하는 소수의 상인들만 부를 독점하였고, 일반 민중은 여전히 가난하였다. 또한 서로 다른 신을 섬기는 부족 사이에서 끊임없는 분쟁이 발생하였다.

이러한 사회적 혼란 속에서 메카의 상인이었던 **무함마드**가 크리스트교와 유대교의 영향을 받아 **이슬람교**를 창시하였다. 신 앞에서의 평등을 주장한 무함마드는 하층민들에게 환호를 받았지만 부유한 메카 상인들에게는 박해를 받았다.

그래서 무함마드는 그를 따르는 신도들과 함께 **메디나**예언자의 도시라는 뜻로 옮겨 갔다(622). 이 사건을 **헤지라**라고 한다. 메디나에서 세력을 키운 무함마드는 다시 돌아와 메카를 점령한 후 아라비아반도를 통일하였다(630).

◉ **무함마드는 알라에게 어떤 계시를 받았을까요?**

What Revelation Did Muhammad Receive from Allah?

알라 앞에서는 왕과 노예가 모두 평등하다. 알라를 믿고 바르게 행동하면 누구나 천국에 갈 수 있다.
In Allah, both kings and slaves are equal. Anyone can go to heaven if they believe in Allah and act properly.

천사 가브리엘의 계시를 받는 무함마드
Muhammad Receiving His First Revelation from the Angel Gabriel

The Formation and Proliferation of Islamic Culture

01 Religious and Political Changes of the Islamic Empire

Muhammad Establishes Islam

Arabs were a population inhabiting the Arabian Peninsula, which consisted mostly of desert. They were largely nomadic people herding livestock, but farming was also developed in a few regions that had occasional rain. They believed in multiple gods.

Around the 6th century, the Arab merchants developed new routes from the Arabian Peninsula up the coast of the Red Sea when routes that they used before were cut off due to the confrontation between the Sasanian Persian Empire and the Byzantine Empire. The result was the growth of cities close to the Red Sea, such as Mecca and Medina.

However, only a small number of merchants were able to build wealth, and most of the common people remained poor. They were also subjected to constant conflicts with other tribes who believed in different gods.

During this social unrest, Muhammad, a merchant in Mecca, founded Islam after being influenced by Christianity and Judaism. Muhammad was widely welcomed by the lower-class people because he claimed everybody was equal in God, but he was persecuted by rich merchants of Mecca.

So, he took his followers and moved to the city of Medina(622). His flight from Mecca to Medina is called Hegira. After building his influence in Medina, Muhammad returned and conquered Mecca, and eventually unified most of Arabia under a single religion(630).

이슬람 세계가 확대되고 우마이야 왕조가 성립하다

무함마드가 죽은 후 아랍인들은 후계자로 칼리프를 선출하였다. 칼리프는 이슬람교의 지도자인 동시에 정치적 권한과 군사적 권한도 행사하였다. 이슬람 세력은 이 시기에 사산 왕조 페르시아와 이집트 지역을 정복하여 대제국을 건설하였다.

이슬람 세력이 커지면서 칼리프 선출을 두고 내분이 발생하였고, 이로 인해 제4대 칼리프 알리가 살해되었다. 제1대 칼리프가 선출된 후부터 알리가 살해되는 시기까지를 정통 칼리프 시대(632~661)라고 한다.

시아 알리 알리를 따르는 사람들와 대립하던 시리아 총독 무아위야는 661년 다마스쿠스에 우마이야 왕조를 세웠다. 알리의 후손만이 칼리프에 오를 수 있다고 생각한 사람들은 이란 지역으로 피신하였다.

우마이야 왕조는 세력을 확대하여 서쪽으로는 이베리아반도를 점령하였고 동쪽으로는 파미르고원까지 이르러 중국의 당과 국경을 접하게 되었다. 그러나 우마이야 왕조는 아랍인이 아니면 이슬람교로 개종해도 세금을 걷는 등 아랍인 우대 정책을 펼쳐 정복지 주민의 불만을 샀다.

⊙ 수니파와 시아파는 어떻게 다른가요?

이슬람 창시자인 무함마드가 사망(632)한 후 그의 후계자 선정 방식을 놓고 이슬람교도가 충돌하며 수니파와 시아파로 분열되었다. 현재 전 세계 이슬람교도 가운데 수니파가 전체의 90%를 차지하는 다수파이고, 나머지 10%가 시아파이다.

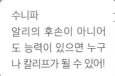

수니파
알리의 후손이 아니어도 능력이 있으면 누구나 칼리프가 될 수 있어!

시아파
오직 알리의 후손만 칼리프가 될 수 있다고!

Islamic World Expands and Umayyad Dynasty Is Established

After Muhammad's death, the Arabs chose a Caliphate to succeed him. A caliphate is an Islamic religious leader who had both political and military authority through the title of Caliph. The Islamic forces built a large empire during this period by conquering the Sasanian Persian Empire and Egypt.

The growing power of Islam resulted in growing internal conflict over the selection of caliphates, until it led to the assassination of the 4th caliph, Ali. The period between the selection of the 1st caliph and the assassination of the Shia Muslim caliph Ali is called the Rashidun Caliphate(632~661).

After the Shia Muslim Ali's death, the Governor of Syria Moiwaiya established the Umayyad Dynasty with its capital in Damascus in 661. Those who had believed that only Ali's descendants could become a caliph fled to Iranian regions.

The Umayyad Dynasty expanded its influence and occupied the Iberian Peninsula in Spain to the west and the Pamir Plateau to the east until it shared a border with Tang of China. However, the Umayyad Dynasty was criticized by people in the conquered regions for privileging Arabs, such as its policy of taxing non-Arabs even if they converted to Islam.

....

How Are Sunni and Shia Islam Different?

After the death of Islam founder Muhammad(632), Muslims clashed over how to choose his successor, splitting into Sunni and Shia Islam. Currently, Sunni are the majority of Muslims worldwide, accounting for 90%, and the remaining 10% are Shiites.

Sunni Islam	Shia Islam
Anyone competent can become a caliph even if they are not one of Ali's descendants!	Only Ali's descendants can become a caliphate!

아바스 왕조가 이슬람 제국의 번영을 이끌다

8세기에 무함마드의 일족인 아바스 가문은 시아파, 비아랍인 등과 협력하여 우마이야 왕조를 무너뜨리고 **아바스 왕조**를 건국하였다(750). 우마이야 왕조의 남은 세력은 이베리아반도의 코르도바에 **후우마이야 왕조**를 세웠다.

아바스 왕조의 수도 **바그다드**는 상업이 발전하자 경제와 문화의 중심 도시로 성장하였다. 아바스 왕조는 민족 차별 정책을 폐지하여 아랍인이 아니어도 이슬람교로 개종하면 세금을 감면해 주고 이란인과 튀르크인 노예도 병사로 기용하는 등 **관용 정책**을 폈다.

아바스 왕조는 **탈라스 전투**에서 당에 승리하여 동서 교역로를 장악하고 국제 무역으로 번영을 누렸다. 이후 지방에서 총독들이 점차 독립하면서 칼리프의 권력은 약화되었다.

북아프리카 지역에는 **파티마 왕조** ^{시아파 세력이 건국}가 들어섰는데, 이로 인하여 후우마이야 왕조의 군주까지 3인의 칼리프가 나타나면서 이슬람 세계는 분열되었다. 이후 아바스 왕조의 칼리프는 상징적으로 종교적인 권위만을 지니게 되었다.

⚜ **코르도바와 그라나다의 유적은 이슬람 세계의 역사와 어떤 관련이 있나요?**

> 코르도바 대모스크는 후우마이야 왕조를 세운 압두르라흐만 1세가 바그다드의 이슬람 사원에 뒤지지 않는 사원을 건설할 목적으로 785년에 짓기 시작하였어요.
> The Great Mosque of Cordoba was built in 785 by Abd al-Rahman I, the founder of the Caliphate of Cordoba, with the aim of constructing a mosque in Baghdad that was second to none.

코르도바 대모스크 전경과 내부(에스파냐 코르도바) Paranomic View and Interior of the Great Mosque of Cordoba(Cordoba, Spain) ©Toni Castillo Quero

Abbas Dynasty Leads Islamic Empire Prosperity

Descendants of Muhammad's uncle, al-Abbas, overthrew the Umayyad Caliphate with Shiites and non-Arabs and established the Abbasid Dynasty (750). The rest of the deposed Umayyad royal family established the Caliphate of Cordoba on the Iberian Peninsula with Cordoba as its capital.

The capital of the Abbasid Dynasty, Baghdad, grew into a hub of economy and culture through dynamic commercial activities. The dynasty embraced a tolerance policy in which people could receive tax breaks when they converted to Islam even if they were not Arabs, and Iranians and Turks were also allowed to be recruited as professional soldiers.

The Abbasid Dynasty defeated the Chinese Tang Dynasty at the Battle of Talas, dominated east-west trade routes, and enjoyed thriving prosperity via international trade. Later, the power of the caliph grew weaker as the regional rulers obtained their independence.

In North Africa, the Fatimid Dynasty was established, thereby dividing the Islamic community into three caliphates, including the caliphate of Cordoba. Later on, the caliph of the Abbasid Dynasty was symbolically recognized only for its religious authority.

....

🌀 How Do the Relics of Cordoba and Granada Relate to the History of the Islamic World?

알람브라 궁전은 에스파냐의 마지막 이슬람 왕조인 나스르 왕조가 13세기 후반 건립하였어요. 1492 년 카스티야 왕국의 이사벨 1세와 아라곤 왕국의 페르난도 2세가 나스르 왕조의 최후 거점인 그라나 다를 함락함으로써 이슬람 세력으로부터 이베리아반도를 탈환하는 레콩키스타가 종결되었지요. The Alhambra was built in the late 13th century by the Nasrid dynasty, Spain's last Islamic dynasty. In 1492, Isabella I of the Kingdom of Castile and Ferdinand II of the Kingdom of Aragon captured Granada, the last stronghold of the Nasrid dynasty. Thereby, the Reconquista of the Iberian Peninsula from Islamic forces was ended.

알람브라 궁전(에스파냐 그라나다) Alhambra(Granada, Spain)

👀 **탈라스 전투가 동서 문화 교류에 어떤 영향을 주었나요?**

아바스 왕조가 세력을 키워 나갈 무렵 중국에서는 당이 세력을 떨치고 있었다. 당은 서역과의 무역을 방해하던 유목 민족인 돌궐이 약해진 틈을 타서 서역으로 통하는 길목을 차지하였다. 이렇게 세력을 확대해 가던 당은 결국 아바스 왕조와 부딪혔다.

당에 쫓겨 서쪽으로 도망간 유목 민족들이 아바스 왕조에 복수를 부탁하였고, 아바스 왕조는 이를 구실로 군대를 보냈다. 당은 두 차례의 서역 원정에 성공한 고구려 출신 장수 고선지를 보냈다. 751년 탈라스강 유역에서 이슬람군과 당군은 닷새 동안 치열하게 싸웠다. 하지만 당과 연합하였던 돌궐군이 배신하면서 당군은 아바스 왕조의 군대에 크게 패하였다.

아바스 왕조가 탈라스 전투에서 승리하면서 비단길의 주도권이 이슬람 세력에게 넘어갔다. 게다가 포로로 잡힌 당의 병사에 의해 중국의 제지술이 이슬람 지역에 전파되었고, 이는 유럽에 전해져 르네상스에 영향을 주었다.

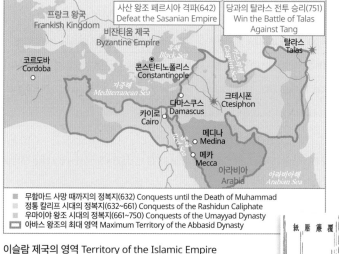

이슬람 제국의 영역 Territory of the Islamic Empire

탈라스 진투로 중국의 제지술이 이슬람에 전해졌어요
The Battle of Talas brought Chinese papermaking to Islam.

당의 제지 과정을 묘사한 그림
A Picture Depicting Tang's Papermaking Process

∞ How Did the Battle of Talas Affect East-West Cultural Exchanges?

By the time the Abbasid Dynasty grew in power, Tang was dominating China. Tang took the path leading to the West by exploiting a break in the weakening of the nomadic people who had obstructed trade with the West. Tang was expanding its power in this way and eventually collided with the Abbasid Dynasty.

The nomadic peoples who had fled to the west after being driven out by Tang asked the Abbasid Dynasty for revenge, and the Abbasid Dynasty sent troops under this pretext. Tang sent Go Seon-ji, a general from Goguryeo, who succeeded in two expeditions into the West. In 751, on the banks of the Talas River, the Tang forces fought army of Islam fiercely for five days. However, as the Turk troops, which had allied with Tang, betrayed Tang, Tang's army was soundly defeated by the army of the Abbasid Dynasty.

When the Abbasid Dynasty won the Battle of Talas, the supremacy of the Silk Road passed to the Islamic forces. In addition, Chinese papermaking techniques were spread to Islamic regions by captive Tang soldiers, which then spread to Europe and affected the Renaissance.

당대에는 중국의 도자기가 서역에 전파되었어요. At that time, Chinese ceramics were spread throughout the West.

격구는 말을 타거나 걸어 다니며 채로 공을 치던 무예예요. 페르시아에서 당을 거쳐 7세기경 우리나라에도 들어왔지요. Dakyu is a martial art in which people hit a ball while on horseback or walking. It was transmitted to Korea from Persia through Tang around the 7th century.

당의 도자기
Pottery of Tang
©Miguel Hermoso Cuesta

격구 경기를 표현한 당삼채 Sancai Expressing Dakyu ©VK Cheong

02 이슬람 문화의 확산

『쿠란』과 『하디스』를 통해 이슬람 문화권이 형성되다

이슬람 사회는 경전인 『쿠란』이 모든 일상생활의 규범이 되는 종교 중심의 사회였다. 『쿠란』은 구전으로 전해지다가 무함마드가 사망한 지 20여 년 후 아랍어로 작성되었다. 이슬람교에서는 알라의 뜻을 왜곡할까 봐 『쿠란』 번역을 엄격하게 금지하였다. 이 때문에 『쿠란』의 언어인 아랍어가 이슬람 문화의 바탕이 되었다. 이슬람 사회에서는 일부다처제를 허용하고, 돼지고기를 금기시하는 관습이 있는데, 이는 『쿠란』의 가르침에 따른 것이다.

『하디스』는 무함마드가 말하고, 행동하고, 다른 사람의 행위를 묵인한 내용을 기록한 책이다. 이슬람교는 『쿠란』과 더불어 『하디스』에 기록된 무함마드의 언행에 따라 행동하는 것을 원칙으로 한다. 이를 연구하는 과정에서 신학과 법학이 발달하였다.

⚗ 이슬람교도들이 지켜야 할 5가지 의무는 무엇인가요?

❶ '알라 외에 신은 없고, 무함마드는 그분의 사도다.'라는 신앙 증언이에요.

❷ 하루에 5번 카바 신전이 있는 메카를 향해 알라께 예배를 드려요.

❸ 이슬람 달력으로 9번째 달인 라마단에는 해가 떠 있는 동안 물을 포함해 어떤 음식도 먹지 않아요. 이 단식을 통해 세상의 유혹과 욕심으로부터 멀어져 올바르게 살 것을 다짐해요.

❹ 1년간 얻은 순이익의 2.5퍼센트를 무슬림 공동체의 가난한 사람들을 위해 헌금해요.

❺ 순례는 건강하고 경제적 여유가 있는 무슬림만 해요. 순례를 통해 이슬람교도들은 세상 모든 무슬림들은 형제이며 평등한 존재임을 느낀다고 해요.

02 Proliferation of Islamic Culture

Development of Islamic Culture Through the "*Quran*" and the "*Hadiths*"

Islamic society was a religion-centered society in which everything about their daily lives was based on its central religious text, the "*Quran*". The contents of the "*Quran*" had been passed down orally until they were written down in Arabic language 20 years after the death of Muhammad. Translating the "*Quran*" was strictly prohibited out of fear that the translation might distort the teachings of Allah. For that reason, the Arabic language used in the "*Quran*" became the foundation of the Islamic culture. In Islamic society, men were allowed to have many wives and eating pork was prohibited. All of the customs were based on the teachings of the "*Quran*".

"*Hadiths*" in Islam are records of the words, actions, and the silent approval of the Islamic prophet Muhammad. In principle, Muslims are required to follow the words and actions of Muhammad as recorded in "*Hadiths*" as well as in the "*Quran*". While researching these religious texts, Muslims were able to advance theology and law.

⚙ What Are the 5 Responsibilities Muslims Must Follow?

❶ A testimony of faith that 'There is no deity but God, Muhammad is the messenger of God'.

❷ Worship to Allah five times a day facing Mecca, where the Kaaba is located.

❸ During Ramadan, the ninth month of the Islamic calendar, Muslims do not eat or drink during the daytime. Through this fasting, Muslims promise not to fall into the temptations of the world, throw away their greed, and live properly.

❹ Muslims donate 2.5 percent of their annual net profit to the poor in Muslim communities.

❺ The pilgrimage is only for Muslims who are healthy and have financial resources. Through the pilgrimage, Muslims feel that all Muslims in the world are brothers and equal beings.

이슬람 상인이 세계 교류에 기여하다

이슬람 세계는 국가 차원에서 교통로를 정비하고 상업을 활성화하는 데 적극적이었다. 『쿠란』에도 상업에 관한 내용이 많이 나올 정도로 이슬람교는 상업을 긍정적으로 보았고, 자유로운 상업 활동을 보장해 주었다.

이슬람 상인들은 유럽, 아프리카, 아시아 등 세계 곳곳을 누비면서 동서 무역을 주도하였다. 비단길(실크로드)과 바닷길을 이용하여 인도, 동남아시아, 중국, 한반도까지 나아가 모피, 금 등 다양한 상품들을 거래하기도 하였다.

상업 활동과 함께 동서 문화 교류가 활발하게 이루어졌고 상인들의 교역로를 따라 이슬람교도 전파되었다. 아바스 왕조의 수도인 바그다드는 교역의 중심지로서 세계의 중심으로 불렸고, 인구가 100만 명을 넘었다.

🏅 『아라비안나이트』의 신드바드는 실존 인물일까요?

바그다드는 여러 이슬람 왕조의 수도이자 동서 교역의 요충지였다. 또한 페르시아 문학의 진수 『아라비안나이트』의 배경으로 등장하는 신비의 도시이기도 하다.

『아라비안나이트』는 원래 페르시아, 이집트, 인도의 전설적인 이야기를 담은 『1001일 밤의 이야기』라는 페르시아 책에서 유래하였다. 이 책에는 아바스 왕조 시대의 이야기부터 십자군을 물리친 이야기, 이집트의 이야기, 몽골에서 전래된 이야기까지 당시 세계의 다양한 이야기가 담겨 있다. 「알라딘과 요술 램프」와 「신드바드의 모험」, 「알리바바와 40인의 도적」도 『아라비안나이트』에 수록되어 있다.

『아라비안나이트』에 나오는 신드바드는 인도양을 항해하면서 다양한 모험을 하였는데, 사실 신드바드는 한 사람의 이름이 아니랍니다. 원래 '신드의 바람'을 뜻하는 말인데, 계절풍을 이용하여 교역에 나섰던 무역상들을 가리켜요.

Sinbad from "*Arabian Nights*" had various adventures while sailing the Indian Ocean. In fact, Sinbad is not one person's name. Originally, it means 'Sind's wind', referring to traders who used monsoon winds to trade.

『아라비안나이트』의 한 장면 A Scene from "*Arabian Nights*"

Islamic Merchants Contribute to Global Exchanges

In the Islamic world, people were passionate about improving transportation routes and promoting commercial activities. Islam positively affirmed commercialism as testified to by numerous verses regarding commercialism in the "*Quran*" and guaranteed free commercial activities as well.

Muslim merchants spearheaded East-West trade while traveling around the world including Europe, Africa, and Asia. They made inroads into India, Southeast Asia, China, and Korea through the Silk Road and Sea routes, and traded a wide variety of goods including fur and gold.

Along with their commercial activities came dynamic cultural exchange between the East and the West, and Islam was able to spread along the trading routes of these merchants. The capital of the Abbasid Dynasty, Baghdad, with its population of over 1 million people, became the central trade hub and was called the center of the world.

◉ Is Sinbad in "*Arabian Nights*" a Real Person?

Baghdad was the capital of several Islamic Empires and an important hub for east-west trade. It is also a mystical city that appears in the background of "*Arabian Nights*," the essence of Persian literature.

"*Arabian Nights*" originated from a Persian book called "*1001 Arabian Nights*", which contains legendary stories from Persia, Egypt, and India. This book contains various stories from around the world at that time, from the story of the Abbasid Dynasty to the story of defeating the Crusaders, the story of Egypt, and the story of Mongolia. The famous stories 'Aladdin's Wonderful Lamp', 'Sinbad's Adventures', and 'Ali Baba and the Forty Thieves' are also included in "*Arabian Nights*".

자연 과학이 발달하다

이슬람 세계에서는 인도와 그리스 과학을 종합한 자연 과학이 발달하였다. 천문학에서는 지구 구형설_{지구의 외형이 둥글다는 학설}을 설명하고 **태양력**을 만들었다. 연금술_{구리·납·주석 등으로 금·은을 제조하는 기술}을 연구하는 과정에서 화학 실험 방법과 합금 기술이 발전하였다.

의학이 발전하여 **인체 해부도**가 그려졌으며, 이슬람의 의학 서적은 중세 유럽의 대학 교재로 사용되기도 하였다. 또한 인도로부터 0의 개념을 받아들여 **아라비아 숫자**를 완성하였다. 이슬람 세계에서는 교역이 활발하여 그리스, 인도, 중국 등 다양한 문화가 융합되어 재구성되었다. 이러한 이슬람 문화는 유럽에 전해져 르네상스 문화의 바탕이 되었다.

◉ 이슬람의 자연 과학이 근대 과학에 어떤 영향을 미쳤나요?

사막이 많은 이슬람 지역에서는 달과 별에 의지하여 밤길을 가야 하였으므로 천문학이 발달하였다. 이슬람 과학자들은 아스트롤라베를 활용해 시간, 위도, 경도 등을 파악했는데, 이것이 유럽에 전해져 유럽의 항해술 발달에 영향을 주었다.

그들은 황금을 만들기 위한 연금술에도 관심을 가졌고, 이로 인해 화학이 발달하였다. 특히 이슬람 세계에서 증류법이 고안되었기 때문에 아랍어에서 유래한 알칼리, 알코올 등의 용어가 지금까지 사용되고 있다. 의학에서는 이븐시나가 저술한 의학서들이 유럽 의과 대학에서 17세기까지 교재로 사용되었다.

천문학 Astronomy	화학 Chemistry	의학 Medicine

이슬람의 천문학자들 Islamic Astronomers	이슬람의 증류 기술 Islamic Distillation Techniques	제왕 절개 수술 중인 이븐시나 Ibn Sina Doing a Cesarean Section

Development of Natural Sciences

The Islamic world saw the development of the natural sciences that combined Indian and Greek sciences. In astronomy, Muslim scholars explained that the Earth was a sphere and also created a solar calendar. While researching alchemy, they advanced chemical experimentation methods and alloy technology.

In addition, they drew human anatomy supported by advanced medical science and Medical books written by Muslim scholars were used as textbooks in colleges in Europe during the middle ages. They accepted the concept of zero from India and perfected the Arabic numeral. Since the Islamic society was dynamic with trade, they were able to blend diverse cultures from Greece, India, and China and restructure them. The resulting Islamic culture was introduced to Europe and became the foundation of Renaissance culture.

---

❷ How Did Islam's Natural Science Influence Modern Science?

In Islamic regions with vast deserts, astronomy developed because the moon and stars had to be relied on for travel at night. Islamic scientists were able to determine time, latitude, and longitude using astrolabes, which was passed down to Europe and influenced the development of European navigation.

They were also interested in alchemy stemming from the desire to gold, which led to the development of chemistry. In particular, since distillation was devised in the Islamic world, terms such as alkali and alcohol derived from Arabic are still used. In medicine, medical books written by Ibn Sina were used as textbooks in European medical schools until the 17th century.

이슬람 문화가 발달하다

이슬람 세계에서는 공상적인 시나 설화말로 전하여 온 이야기 문학이 발전하였다. 대표적인 작품으로는 『천일야화』라고도 불리는 『아라비안나이트』가 있다.

미술 분야에서는 화려한 세밀화가 유행하였는데, 이는 이슬람 전통 미술로 발전하였다. 이슬람의 대표적인 건축물은 이슬람 사원인 모스크이다. 모스크에는 둥근 돔과 뾰족한 탑이 있다. 내부는 아라베스크 무늬로 아름답게 장식되어 있다.

💠 **모스크에 신의 형상이 표현되지 않은 이유는 무엇일까요?**

이슬람교 사원인 모스크는 둥근 돔(지붕)과 뾰족한 탑으로 구성되어 있고, 아라베스크 무늬로 장식되어 있다.

『쿠란』의 율법에서는 성상 숭배를 금지하기 때문에 이슬람교도들은 종교와 관련된 인물을 그리거나 조각을 하지 않는다. 또한 식물, 꽃, 동물 등 살아 있는 것도 그리지 않는다. 이렇게 자연을 본뜨는 대신 아랍인들은 오로지 직선과 곡선만으로 도안을 만들어 모스크를 장식하였다. 이러한 무늬를 아라베스크라고 한다.

터키 이스탄불에 있는 모스크예요. 안쪽 벽면의 타일이 햇빛에 빛나 내부를 푸르게 하기에 '블루 모스크'라 부르기도 해요. 둥근 돔과 6개의 탑으로 이루어져 있어요.

술탄 아흐메트 사원
The Blue Mosque ©Joshua Davenport

이슬람교 예배를 드리는 모스크에서는 성상을 찾아볼 수 없어요. 대신 '아라베스크'라고 부르는 기하학적 무늬가 그려져 있지요. 뒤엉킨 식물 모양처럼 구불구불한 곡선은 조각이나 그림 못지않은 아름다움을 자랑해요.

아라베스크 무늬
Arabesque ©Patrickkringgenberg

Development of Islamic Culture

The Islamic world developed poems and tales based on imagination. One of the most well-known pieces of Islamic literature is "*One Thousand and One Nights*".

In art, the most popular type of painting was elaborate 'miniature painting' which evolved into a traditional Islamic art. The most iconic architecture style can be found in mosques, which refer to the place of worship for Muslims. Mosques are marked by a round dome shape, slim tower, and beautiful arabesque decorations.

....

🅰 Why Is the Image of God Not Represented in Mosques?

A Mosque consists of a round dome(roof) and pointed towers, and is decorated with arabesque patterns.

Because "*Quran*" law prohibits iconolatry, Muslims do not draw or sculpt religious figures. Also, they do not draw living things such as plants, flowers, or animals. Instead of imitating nature in this way, the Arabs decorated mosques by making designs using only straight lines and curves. This pattern is called arabesque.

This is a mosque in Istanbul, Turkey. It is also called the 'The Blue Mosque' because the tiles on the inner wall shine in sunlight and make the interior blue. It consists of a round dome and six towers.

There are no icons in mosques where Muslims worship. Instead, a geometric pattern called 'arabesque' is drawn. The meandering curves, like intricate plant shapes, are as beautiful as sculptures and paintings.

크리스트교 문화의 형성과 확산

01 서유럽 봉건 사회의 형성

게르만족의 이동으로 서로마 제국이 멸망하다

북유럽 지역에서 목축과 수렵을 하던 게르만족이 농경 생활을 하면서 인구가 늘었다. 경작할 토지가 부족해지자 게르만족은 점차 기름진 땅을 찾아 남쪽으로 이동하였다. 그들 중 일부는 로마 제국으로 들어가 소작인이나 용병이 되기도 하였다. 4세기 말에 아시아의 유목 민족인 **훈족**이 서쪽으로 이동하며 흑해 지역에 살던 게르만족을 압박하였다. **게르만족**은 서유럽과 지중해 연안, 아프리카 등지로 이동하여 여러 왕국을 세웠다. 이 과정에서 서로마 제국은 게르만족에 의해 멸망하였다(476).

- ■ 비잔티움 제국령 Realm of Byzantine Empire
- ■ 서로마 제국령 Realm of Western Roman Empire
- ■ 게르만족의 원래 거주지 Original Residence of the Germanic People

게르만족 왕국 대부분은 오래 지속되지 못하였지만 프랑크 왕국은 오랫동안 번성하였다. 프랑크족은 원래 살던 지역에서 가까운 서쪽으로 이동하여 새로운 곳에 쉽게 적응하였고, 크리스트교를 받아들여 로마 교회의 지지까지 받았다.

게르만족의 이동 Migration Period

◎ **프랑크족은 어떻게 크리스트교를 믿게 되었을까요?**

프랑크 왕국의 국왕 클로비스는 지략에 능한 사람이었다. 그는 프랑크족보다 인구수도 많고 문화도 앞선 로마인을 다스리기 위해 크리스트교를 받아들였다. 또한 크리스트교를 프랑크 왕국의 공식 종교로 채택하고, 자신의 신하 3천 명과 함께 세례를 받았다. 개종의 효과는 금세 나타났다. 프랑크 왕국이 갈리아 남부의 서고트족을 공격하자 크리스트교를 신봉하던 로마 원주민들이 그를 환영하였고, 서고트족은 이베리아반도에서 쫓겨났다.

세례를 받는 클로비스 1세 The Baptism of Clovis I

The Formation and Proliferation of Christian Culture

01 The Establishment of Western European Feudal Society

The Roman Empire Is Destroyed by Movement of the Germanic Tribe

Population increased in northern Europe when the Germanic tribes that used to raise livestock and hunt game started farming. When they encountered a farmland shortage problem, they moved south in search of fertile land. Some of them came to the Roman Empire and became tenant farmers or mercenaries. Towards the end of the 4th century, a nomadic people called the Huns moved westward and burdened the Germanic people who had settled in the Black Sea regions. These Germanic people moved to western Europe, the Mediterranean coast, Africa, and other regions and established several empires. During this period the Western Roman Empire was overthrown by the Germanic people(476).

Most Germanic kingdoms did not last, but the Kingdom of the Franks thrived for a long time. The Franks were able to adjust to their new environment quickly because they moved to regions that were not too far from their original settlements and received the support of the Roman Church after they converted to Christianity.

🏵 **How Did the Franks Come to Believe in Christianity?**

Clovis of Frankish Kingdom was a man of resource. He accepted Christianity to rule the Romans, who had a larger population and a more advanced culture than the Franks. He also adopted Christianity as the official religion of the Frankish Kingdom, and was baptized with 3,000 of his vassals. The effects of conversion quickly emerged. When the Frankish Kingdom attacked the Visigoths in Southern Gaul, the Roman natives who worshiped Christianity welcomed it, and the Visigoths were expelled from the Iberian Peninsula.

프랑크 왕국이 서유럽의 대부분을 차지하다

8세기 후반 프랑크 왕국의 **카롤루스 대제**는 활발하게 정복 활동을 벌여 이베리아반도와 브리튼 등을 제외한 서유럽 대부분을 차지하였다. 그는 정복한 지역에 교회를 세우고 크리스트교를 전파하였다. 교황은 카롤루스 대제의 공로를 인정하여 서로마 황제의 관을 수여하였다(800). 이로써 게르만족의 전통, 로마 문화, 크리스트교가 어우러져 중세 서유럽 문화의 기반이 형성되었다.

카롤루스 대제가 죽은 후 자손들 사이에서 영토 분쟁이 일어나 프랑크 왕국은 베르됭 조약과 메르센 조약을 통해 동프랑크·서프랑크·중프랑크로 분열되었다. 세 나라는 오늘날의 독일, 프랑스, 이탈리아의 기원이 되었다.

프랑크 왕국의 분열
Division of the Frankish Kingdom

....

💠 **카롤루스 대제상은 어떤 사람에게 수여되나요?**

카롤루스 대제상은 제2대 프랑크 왕국의 국왕이었던 카롤루스 대제를 기념하기 위해 1949년 창설되었다. 카롤루스 대제가 거주하였던 독일의 아헨시가 1950년부터 매년 유럽의 단합에 기여한 정치 지도자에게 수여하고 있다. 2002년에는 유럽 단일 통화인 유로화(貨)가 이 상을 수상하였다.

또 하나의 언어를 할 줄 아는 것은 두 번째 영혼을 갖는 것과 같다. 이 땅에 있었던 사람들의 문화를 받아들이기 위해 노력하라.

카롤루스 대제 동상(프랑스 파리)
Statue of Charles the Great(Paris, France)

The Kingdom of the Franks Occupies Most of Western Europe

In the late 8th century, the Kingdom of the Franks, Charles the Great, aggressively seized most of Western Europe, except for the Iberian Peninsula and Britain. He built schools and spread Christianity in his occupied lands. His great feats were recognized when he was crowned 'Emperor of the Romans' by Pope Leo III(800). Thus, the foundation was laid for the medieval Western European culture that embraced Germanic traditions, Roman culture, and Christianity.

Upon the death of Charles the Great, his descendants feuded over territory until the Kingdom of the Franks split into East Francia, Middle Francia, and West Francia through the Treaty of Verdun and Treaty of Meerssen. These three kingdoms became the origins of the three European countries that we know today as: Germany, France, and Italy.

◉ Who Can Be Awarded the Charlemagne Prize?

International Charlemagne Prize of Aachen was created in 1949 to commemorate the second king of the Frankish kingdom, Charles the Great. The German city of Aachen, where Carolus the Great lived, has annually awarded it to political leaders who have contributed to the unification of Europe since 1950. In 2002, the euro, the official single currency of the European Union, won this award.

> Knowing how to speak another language is like having a second soul. Try to embrace the culture of the people who have been on this earth.

주종 관계의 봉건제가 성립하다

9세기 중반에 프랑크 왕국이 분열된 이후 서유럽은 바이킹 및 마자르족과 이슬람 세력 등 이민족의 침입에 시달렸다. 각 지역의 세력가들은 혼란스러운 상황에서 생명과 재산을 지키고 지배권을 유지하기 위하여 자기보다 강한 기사를 주군으로 섬기고 충성을 맹세하였다. 주군은 그 대가로 봉신에게 **봉토**(토지)를 제공하였다.

토지를 매개로 한 주군과 봉신봉토를 받은 신하의 **주종 관계**는 쌍무적 계약 관계계약 당사자 양쪽이 서로 의무를 지는 것여서 한쪽이라도 의무를 지키지 않으면 계약은 파기될 수 있었다. 주종 관계는 왕과 제후부터 하급 기사에 이르기까지 단계적으로 이루어져 있었지만 한 기사가 여러 제후를 섬기거나 하나의 장원을 여러 영주가 다스리기도 하였다. 이처럼 봉토를 매개로 주종 관계를 이룬 지방 분권적인 중세 유럽의 사회 제도를 봉건제라고 한다.

봉신은 자신의 봉토에서는 주군의 간섭 없이 세금을 걷고 재판을 하는 등 독자적인 영향력을 행사하였다. 국왕도 자신이 직접 다스리는 지역에서만 통치권을 행사할 수 있었다.

마상 시합에 출전하는 중세 기사(메트로폴리탄 미술관)
A Medieval Knight Participating in a Tournament
(Metropolitan Museum of Art)

◉ 기사와 제후는 어떤 관계였나요?

당시 서유럽의 봉건적 주종 관계는 충효를 바탕으로 한 절대적인 것이 아니므로 기사가 포로가 되는 것은 수치스러운 일이 아니었다. 주군에게는 봉건 가신이 포로가 되면 몸값을 지급하고 빼 와야 할 의무가 있을 정도였다. 주군에게 봉토를 제공받은 봉신은 자신의 봉토에서 주군의 간섭 없이 농민에게 세금을 걷고 재판을 할 수 있었다.

이 그림은 주군과 봉신이 주종 관계의 의식을 행하는 모습이에요. 봉신은 주군에게 충성을 서약하는 선서를 하고, 영주는 어깨를 검으로 톡톡 두드리며 "그대에게 작위를 내리노라." 라고 선언하였어요.

서유럽의 봉건 제도
Feudalism of the Western Europe

Establishment of the Lord-Vassal Relationship and Feudalism

After the Kingdom of the Franks split in the mid-9th century, Western Europe was constantly invaded by foreign forces such as the Vikings, Magyars, and Muslims. To protect their lives and properties and maintain their power in the chaos of the time, regional rulers served a knight who was stronger than themselves as lord and swore allegiance. In return, the lords provided vassals with fiefs.

Their lord-vassal relationship over the fief was a bilateral contract which could be terminated if either one of the two parties failed to keep their obligations. The lord-vassal relationship was established on various levels from the king and the nobles to the lower-level knights. However, one knight served several lords or several lords ruled one manor. This decentralized social structure of medieval Europe marked by the lord-vassal relationship involving a fief is called feudalism.

The vassals exercised their own authority over taxes and jurisdiction without their lords' interference. Even the king was able to exercise his power only over the areas under his direct jurisdiction.

◎ What Was the Relationship between the Knights and Feudal Lords?

At that time, the feudal lord-vassal relationship in Western Europe was not absolute based on loyalty, so it was not a shame for a knight to become a prisoner. If the vassals became captive, the lord was obligated to pay the ransom and bring them back. The vassals were able to collect taxes from their fiefs and hold trials of peasants without interference from the lord.

This painting shows the lord and the vassal performing a ritual for the lord-vassal relationship. The vassal made an oath to pledge allegiance to the lord, and the lord tapped his shoulder with his sword and declared, "I present you with a knighthood".

농노, 영주에게 예속된 존재가 되다

봉신이 주군으로부터 받은 봉토는 자급자족하는 농촌 공동체의 형태를 띠었는데, 이를 장원이라고 한다. 기사들은 장원을 지배하는 영주가 되었다. 장원은 영주의 성, 교회, 촌락, 경작지 등으로 구성되었다. 경작지는 보통 영주 직영지 주인이 직접 경영하는 땅, 농민 보유지, 공유지 등으로 이루어져 있었다.

장원의 농민은 대부분 농노였다. 농노는 영주에게 예속되어 있어 영주의 허락 없이는 장원을 떠날 수 없었다. 하지만 고대의 노예와는 달리 집과 토지를 소유하거나 결혼하여 가정을 꾸릴 수 있었다. 농노는 영주에게 시설물에 대한 사용료는 물론 인두세, 사망세 등 각종 세금을 내고 부역을 제공해야 하였다.

◉ 중세 장원의 모습은 어떠했나요?

장원의 중심부에는 영주의 성과 교회가 있었다. 그 주변에는 방앗간, 제빵소 등 공공 시설물과 농민들이 사는 촌락이 있었다. 공공시설물은 영주의 소유였으므로 농노들은 이를 이용하려면 사용료를 내야 하였다. 비료가 발달하지 못하여 중세 유럽인들은 토지를 번갈아 가며 경작하는 삼포제 방식으로 농사를 지었다.

장원의 구조 Structure of Manor

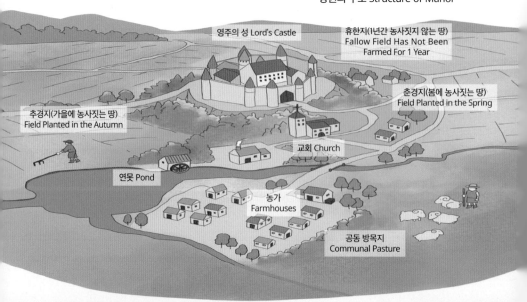

Serfs Belong to Their Lords

The fief given by the lord to the vassal took the form of a self sufficient rural community which they called a manor. Knights became lords of those manors. A manor consisted of the castle of the lord, the church, the village, and the farmland. There were three types of land within a manor: land under the direct control of the lord, land under the control of the farmer, and commonly shared land.

The majority of the farmers within a manor were serfs. Serfs belonged to their lords, and therefore could not leave the manors without the permission of the lord. But unlike ancient slaves, they could own a house and land, and they could also marry and have their own family. Serfs were obliged to pay taxes to their lords, such as the head tax, death tax, and facility tax, and were required to provide their services to their lords as well.

◉ What Did the Medieval Manor Look Like?

At the center of the manor was the castle of the lord and the church. Nearby there were public facilities such as blacksmiths, mills, and bakeries, and villages where farmers lived. Since public facilities were owned by the lord, the serfs had to pay fees to use them. Due to the lack of fertilizer development, Europeans in the middle ages cultivated the land by crop rotation under the Three-field system.

농노들은 '뿔 없는 소'에 비유될 정도로 힘들게 생활하였고, 돼지우리나 다름없는 헛간에서 살았어요. The serfs' lives were hard enough to be compared to a 'hornless cow' and they lived in barns that were like pigpens.

중세의 농노 A Medieval Serf

02 유럽 크리스트교 문화, 교회와 사회

교회가 분열하고 서유럽에서 교황권이 강화되다

로마 교회의 주교는 베드로의 후계자임을 내세우며 교황을 자처하였고, 그를 따르는 교회는 **로마 가톨릭교회**로 불렸다.

8세기에 들어 크리스트교 세력은 성상^{예수나 성모의 상(像)} 숭배 문제 때문에 동서로 분열하기 시작하였다. 당시 서유럽의 가톨릭교회는 게르만족에게 크리스트교를 포교하기 위해 성상을 사용하였으나 비잔티움 제국의 황제는 성상 숭배를 금지하였다. 결국 동서 교회는 로마를 중심으로 한 **로마 가톨릭교회**와 콘스탄티노폴리스를 중심으로 한 **그리스 정교**로 분리되었다.

교황은 비잔티움 제국 황제의 영향에서 벗어나기 위하여 프랑크 왕국과 유대를 강화하였다. 교회의 성직자는 국왕이나 제후로부터 토지를 받고 그 대가로 이들을 주군으로 섬겼다. 성직자가 봉건제에 편입됨에 따라 군주들에게는 성직자 임명권이 주어졌다.

교회가 세속화되면서 성직자가 결혼하거나 성직을 매매하는 등 부패하고 타락한 모습을 보였다. 이에 **클뤼니 수도원**을 중심으로 교회 개혁 운동이 일어났다. 수도사들은 기도를 하고 고전을 연구하면서 노동을 병행하는 청빈한 생활을 하였다.

🌀 **로마 교황과 비잔티움 제국 황제는 무엇 때문에 다투었을까요?**

What Did the Pope and the Emperor of the Byzantine Quarrel Over?

로마 교황
사람들이 글을 모르니 성상이나 그림으로 크리스트교를 믿게 해야 합니다.
The Pope
People don't know how to read, so we need to make them believe in Christianity with religious images or paintings.

비잔티움 제국 황제
겉모양만 갖춘 성상을 숭배하는 것보다 진실한 믿음이 더 중요합니다.
Emperor of the Byzantine Empire
Sincere faith is more important than worshiping only religious images.

02 European Christian Culture: The Church and Society
The Divided Church and the Growing Power of the Papacy in West Europe

The first bishop of the Roman Church assumed the position of the Pope, claiming that he was Christ's disciple Peter's successor, and the churches that followed him were called the Roman Catholic Church.

In the 8th century, the Eastern and the Western parts of the Church became divided over the issue surrounding iconoclasm. At that time, the Western part of the Church used religious images to propagate Christianity to the Germanic people, but the Byzantine emperors forbade the creation and veneration of religious images, claiming it as a form of idol worshipping. Eventually, the Eastern and the Western parts of the Church were divided into the Catholic Church centering on Rome and Greek Orthodoxy centering on Constantinople.

The Pope strengthened relations with the Frankish Kingdom to break free from the influence of the Byzantine emperors. The priests of the Church received land from the kings or nobles and served them as their lords in return. When the priests became part of the feudal system, the secular monarchs were given the right to appoint priests.

The secularization of the Church resulted in the corruption and decadence of the Church, such as seen in monks getting married and selling off their priesthood. Eventually, the situation led to a monastic reform movement centering on Cluny Abbey. The monks at the Abbey committed themselves to holy poverty, while praying, studying classics, and pursuing labor and other monastic endeavors.

교황이 황제를 굴복시키다

11세기 후반 교황과 황제가 성직자 임명권을 놓고 대립하였다. 교황 그레고리우스 7세가 국왕과 제후의 성직자 임명을 금지하자 신성 로마 제국의 황제인 **하인리히 4세**가 이를 거부하였다. 그러자 교황은 하인리치 4세를 파문^{가톨릭교회에서 신자의 자격을 박탈하는 것}하였다.

하인리히 4세는 교황을 폐위하려 하였으나 제후들이 반발하였다. 다급해진 하인리히 4세는 교황이 머물고 있는 이탈리아 북부의 카노사성으로 찾아가서 3일 동안 용서를 구한 끝에 겨우 파문을 면하였다(카노사의 굴욕, 1077).

이후 200여 년간 교황의 권한은 더욱 강화되었고 교황은 군주에게도 막강한 영향력을 행사하였다. 13세기에는 교황권이 절정에 이르러 '교황은 해, 황제는 달'이라는 말까지 생겨났다.

◈ **교황과 하인리히 4세의 싸움에서 누가 이겼나요?**

교황은 하인리히 4세를 사면해 주었지만 이후 하인리히 4세는 다시 지지자를 규합하여 교황과 재대결을 벌였다. 하인리히 4세는 새 교황을 선출하고, 곧바로 로마를 점령해 버렸다. 이에 그레고리우스 7세가 다시 하인리히 4세를 파문하였지만, 하인리히 4세가 이탈리아로 쳐들어가 교황을 폐위하였다. 이후 성직자 임명권은 교회가 갖되, 황제가 주교 선출에 직접 참여할 권리를 갖는 보름스 협약이 체결되었다(1122).

> 1076년 2월 교황 그레고리우스 7세는 하인리히 4세를 파문하였어요. 당시 교황은 황제에 대한 최종 결정을 논의하는 아우크스부르크 회의에 참석하기 위해 카노사에 머무르고 있었지요. 하인리히 4세는 추운 겨울 카노사에 찾아와 맨발로 3일간 교황에게 용서를 구하였어요.

카노사의 굴욕 Humiliation of Canossa

The Pope Brings the Emperor to His Knees

In the late 11th century, the Pope and the emperor confronted each other over the right to appoint priests. When Pope Gregory VII forbaded the monarchs and the feudal lords from appointing priests, Henry IV, the Emperor of the Holy Roman Empire, resisted the papal decree. Then the Pope excommunicated Henry IV.

Henry IV tried to demand Gregory's abdication, but he failed due to the objections of the feudal lords. The cornered Henry IV went to Canossa in the north of Italy where the Pope was staying, and waited for three days on his knees until his excommunication was finally lifted(Humiliation of Canossa, 1077).

For the next 200 years, the authority of the Church grew stronger than ever and had great influence over the secular kings. By the 13th century, the power of the Pope reached its zenith and gave birth to 'the Sun and Moon Allegory' that imaged spiritual authority as the Sun and all political secular authority as the Moon.

◉ Who Won the Conflict between the Pope and Henry IV?

The pope pardoned Henry IV, but after that Henry IV again rallied his supporters to challenge the pope. He elected a new Pope and immediately captured Rome. In response, Pope Gregory VII excommunicated Henry IV again, but Henry IV invaded Italy and deposed him. Afterwards, the Concordat of Worms was signed, giving the church the right to appoint priests, and the emperor the right to directly participate in the election of bishops(1122).

> In February 1076, Pope Gregory VII excommunicated Heinrich IV. At that time, the pope was staying in Canossa to attend an Augsburg conference to discuss the final decision on the emperor. King Heinrich IV visited Canossa during the cold winter and begged the Pope for forgiveness on bare feet for three days.

크리스트교가 중세인의 삶을 지배하다

중세 서유럽에서는 크리스트교가 사람들의 정신세계와 일상생활을 지배하였다. 사람들은 출생부터 죽음에 이르기까지 삶의 주요한 순간을 교회와 함께하였다. 태어나면 세례를 받아야 하였고, 죄를 지으면 성직자에게 고백해야 하였다.

또한 교회가 정한 달력에 맞추어 일하고 수확량의 10분의 1을 교회에 바쳤다. 풍년을 기원하는 풍습은 교회의 축제로 이어졌다. 교회는 기사의 활동에도 영향을 미쳐 교회의 축제일에는 기사들도 전투를 할 수 없었다.

크리스트교 사회에서 가장 무서운 형벌은 교회 공동체로부터 추방되는 것이었다. 중세 서유럽에서는 교회를 떠나서는 태어날 수도 죽을 수도 없었다.

⚫ 중세 시대의 사람들은 어떻게 살았을까요?

중세 유럽인은 교회와 성직자를 통해서만 구원을 받을 수 있다고 믿었다. 탄생, 혼인, 죽음 등 주요한 삶의 의식은 교회에 맡겼다. 중세의 성직자들은 고해성사와 결혼, 장례 등 일상생활에서 상당히 중요한 역할을 담당하였다. 교황은 사람들의 탄생과 죽음에 대한 정보를 파악하고 있었으므로 그 인구 정보를 이용하여 황제에게 영향력을 발휘할 수 있었다.

성직자 중에는 인간의 영혼 구제보다 농노들을 속여 부를 모으는 데 더 관심이 있는 이들도 많았다. 사제 중 일부는 의사나 변호사, 상인을 겸직하기도 하였다. 또한 술을 마시고 도박을 하거나 여자와 가정을 이룬 성직자도 있었다.

중세인 대다수는 글을 읽을 수 없었으므로 교리를 제대로 이해하지 못하였다. 성직자가 설교할 때는 떠들기 일쑤였고, 예배가 끝나면 끼리끼리 모여 술자리를 벌이기도 하였다.

결혼식은 반드시 교회에서 세금을 내고 성직자가 보는 앞에서 해야 했어요. 교회 밖에서의 결혼은 무효였지요.
Weddings must be done in front of the priest after paying taxes at the church. Marriage outside the church was invalid.

중세인의 결혼 Medieval Marriage

Christianism Rules the Life of Medieval People

In medieval Western Europe, Christianism dominated people's spiritual world and daily lives. The Church was involved in every important aspect of life from birth till death. People had to be baptized when they were born, and when they sinned, they had to confess their sins to a priest.

In addition, they worked according to the calendar given by the Church and gave the Church one-tenth of their harvests. The custom of praying for good harvests evolved into a festival of the Church. The Church also influenced the activity of knights, and knights were not allowed to engage in battles during Church festivals.

The most severe punishment in Christian society was to be expelled from the church community, excommunication. In medieval Western Europe, people could not be born or die away from the Church.

◉ How Did People Live in the Medieval Ages?

Medieval Europeans believed that salvation could only be achieved through churches and the priests. Major life ceremonies such as birth, marriage, and death were left to the church. Priests in the Medieval Ages played a very important role in daily life such as confession, marriage, and funeral. The Pope had information about people's birth and deaths, so he could use the demographics to influence the emperor.

However, there were also many priests who were more interested in collecting wealth by deceiving the serfs rather than saving souls. Some of the priests also served as doctors, lawyers, and merchants. There were also priests who drank alcohol, gambled, and had a family with a wife.

At that time, the majority of the people in the Medieval Ages could not read, so they did not understand the doctrines properly. When the priests preached, they often talked and after the worship service, they gathered together to have a drink.

크리스트교를 중심으로 중세 문화가 발전하다

중세 서유럽에서는 학문도 신학을 중심으로 발달하였다. 중세에는 거의 성직자만이 글을 읽고 쓸 수 있었으므로 학문과 교육은 크리스트교의 영향을 받았다. 이탈리아의 신학자 토마스 아퀴나스는 『신학대전』에서 신앙과 이성의 조화를 추구하는 스콜라 철학을 집대성하였다. 교육은 주로 수도원에 부속된 학교에서 이루어졌는데, 그중 일부는 훗날 대학으로 이어졌다.

건축도 교회를 중심으로 발달하였다. 10세기 말부터 둥근 천장과 반원형 아치를 특징으로 하는 로마네스크 양식의 성당이 만들어졌다. 12세기에는 천국으로 향하는 소망을 담은 높고 뾰족한 고딕 양식의 성당이 지어졌다. 고딕 성당의 높이가 높아진 후에는 커다란 창을 만들어 스테인드글라스로 장식하였다.

⚜ 로마네스크 양식과 고딕 양식은 어떻게 다른가요?
How Is Romanesque Style and Gothic Style Different?

'로마네스크'는 '로마의 영향을 받은 건축 양식'이라는 뜻의 프랑스어 '로망'에서 비롯되었어요. 피렌체 성당, 피사 대성당 등이 대표적이지요. 로마네스크 양식은 아치 형태가 특징이에요. 아치가 미는 힘을 견딜 수 있도록 기둥을 굵게 하고, 창문이 거의 없는 두꺼운 벽을 만들었지요. 그래서 성당 내부가 어둡습니다.

The Romanesque style comes from the French 'Roman', which means 'the style of architecture influenced by Rome'. Florence Cathedral and Pisa Cathedral are representative examples. Romanesque style is characterized by arches. The columns were thickened to withstand the force of the arch, and thick walls were made with few windows. That's why the interior of the cathedral is so dark.

로마네스크 양식의 피사 대성당
Romanesque-style Pisa Cathedral

Medieval Culture Develops Around Christianity

In medieval Western Europe, academic studies developed centering on theology. Christianity had great influence on academic studies and education because, in medieval times, almost all literate people were clergymen. The Italian theologian Thomas Aquinas wrote "*Summa Theologica*", and with this book, he culminated the Scholastic philosophy, which is about pursuing harmony between faith and reason. Education took place mostly in the institutions of learning attached to monasteries, which evolved into universities later on.

Architecture also developed around the Church. From the end of the 10th century, Romanesque cathedrals featuring vaults and Roman arches were constructed. In the 12th century, they constructed Gothic cathedrals marked by sharply pointed spires, which represented their focus on Heaven. As the heights of these Gothic cathedrals increased, they started using large expanses of stained glass for windows.

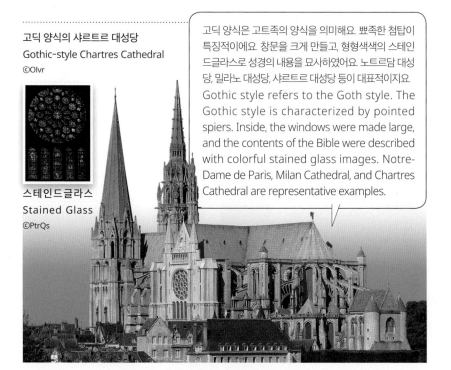

고딕 양식의 샤르트르 대성당
Gothic-style Chartres Cathedral
©Olvr

스테인드글라스
Stained Glass
©PtrQs

고딕 양식은 고트족의 양식을 의미해요. 뾰족한 첨탑이 특징적이에요. 창문을 크게 만들고, 형형색색의 스테인드글라스로 성경의 내용을 묘사하였어요. 노트르담 대성당, 밀라노 대성당, 샤르트르 대성당 등이 대표적이지요. Gothic style refers to the Goth style. The Gothic style is characterized by pointed spires. Inside, the windows were made large, and the contents of the Bible were described with colorful stained glass images. Notre-Dame de Paris, Milan Cathedral, and Chartres Cathedral are representative examples.

03 비잔티움 제국

로마 제국이 동서로 분열되다

로마 제국은 3세기 전반부터 급격히 흔들리기 시작하였다. 235년부터 약 50년 동안 여러 군인과 원로원 의원이 황제에 올라 정치가 혼란스러웠고, 게르만족과 사산 왕조 페르시아의 침입에 시달렸다. 군사비 증가로 세금 부담이 커져 도시와 상공업이 위축되었다.

군인 황제 시대의 혼란을 수습한 디오클레티아누스 황제는 효율적인 통치를 위해 거대한 제국을 4곳으로 나누고 2명의 황제와 2명의 부황제가 통치하도록 하였다.

4세기 초 콘스탄티누스 대제는 크리스트교를 공인하고 수도를 비잔티움(콘스탄티노폴리스)으로 옮겼다. 하지만 로마 제국의 혼란은 계속되었고 테오도시우스 황제가 죽은 후 제국은 동서로 분리되었다(395).

⚜ **콘스탄티누스 대제는 왜 크리스트교를 공인했을까요?**

콘스탄티누스 대제는 독자적인 황제권을 주장하는 막센티우스를 처단하기 위해 312년 출정하였다. 전세가 불리해져 큰 위기를 맞던 중 꿈에 나타난 그리스도의 계시를 받아 전쟁에서 승리하였다고 한다. 이듬해 콘스탄티누스 대제는 밀라노 칙령을 내려 크리스트교를 공인하였다. 그는 유일신 사상인 크리스트교를 이용하여 로마를 하나로 통합하고 황제권에 신성함을 부여하고자 하였다.

또한 그는 니케아 공회의에서 아타나시우스파의 삼위일체설을 정통으로 삼은 니케아 신조를 반포하였다(325). "하느님은 그분(아들)을 무에서 만들었다."라고 주장한 아리우스는 이단으로 몰렸다. 신은 진리에 대해 침묵하는데 인간이 회의에서 진리를 결정하였고, 이후 종교적 판단은 허락되지 않았다.

콘스탄티누스 개선문(이탈리아 로마) Arch of Constantine(Rome, Italy)

원로원은 콘스탄티누스의 승리를 기념하기 위하여 콘스탄티누스 개선문을 세웠어요. The Senate established the Arch of Constantine to commemorate Constantine's victory.

03 Byzantine Empire

The Roman Empire Splits into East and West

By the first half of the 3rd century, the Roman Empire started to crumble rapidly. Within a span of 50 years, beginning from the year 235, several soldiers and senators had ascended to the emperor's throne and confused politics, and the empire suffered the invasion of the Germanic tribes and the Sassanian Persian Dynasty. Increasing military expenses resulted in a mounting tax burden, consequently causing the decline of cities and commercial trade.

After Diocletian became the emperor, the age of the Barracks Emperors came to an end. In order to stabilize the empire, he instituted the 'rule of four', in which two Caesars and two emperors each ruled over a quarter-division of the empire.

Early in the 4th century, Constantine the Great legalized Christianity and moved the capital of the Roman Empire to the city of Constantinople. But the Roman Empire remained chaotic until it split into East and West upon the death of Theodosius the Great(395).

◉ Why Did Constantine the Great Legalize Christianity?

Constantine the Great entered the war in 312 to punish Maxentius, who claimed independent emperorship. It is said that he won the war by receiving the revelation of Jesus Christ in a dream while facing a great crisis. The following year, Constantine issued the Edict of Milan and recognized Christianity. He used monotheistic Christianity to unite Rome and confer sanctity on his authority as emperor.

He also proclaimed the Nicaean creed at the First Council of Nicaea, which orthodoxized the Atanasian Trinity(325). Arius, who claimed, "God created his son out of nothing", was driven to heresy. God is silent about truth, and humans decided it at the council, and religious judgments were not allowed thereafter.

비잔티움 제국, 천 년을 이어가다

서로마 제국은 게르만족의 침략으로 멸망하였지만 비잔티움 제국은 게르만족의 침입을 막아 내며 천 년 가까이 더 유지되었다.

비잔티움 제국은 유스티니아누스 대제 때 번성하였다. 그는 정복 활동을 펼쳐 이탈리아와 북아프리카 등 옛 로마 제국 영토의 상당 부분을 회복하였으며,『유스티니아누스 법전』을 편찬하고 성 소피아 성당을 재건하였다.

비잔티움 제국은 황제가 교회까지 지배하는 황제 중심의 국가였다. 수도인 콘스탄티노폴리스는 동서 무역의 중심지로서 당시 세계 최대 도시로 성장하였다.

11세기 이후 비잔티움 제국에서는 귀족과 교회가 대토지 소유를 늘려 자영 농민이 몰락하고 군사력이 약화되었다. 비잔티움 제국은 이슬람 세력의 거듭된 침입으로 영토가 줄어들었고 서유럽과 이슬람 세력의 전쟁 중에는 콘스탄티노폴리스를 내주기도 하였다. 결국 비잔티움 제국은 오스만 제국의 공격을 받아 멸망하였다 (1453).

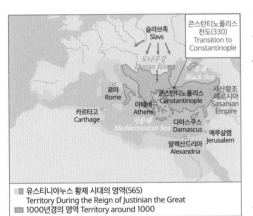

유스티니아누스 황제 시대의 영역(565)
Territory During the Reign of Justinian the Great
1000년경의 영역 Territory around 1000

비잔티움 제국의 영역
Territory of the Byzantine Empire

테오도라 황후와 시녀들
(이탈리아 산 비탈레 성당, 좌)
Empress Theodora and
Her Maids(Church of San
Vitale, Italy, Left)

유스티니아누스 대제
(이탈리아 산 비탈레 성당, 우)
Justinian the Great(Church of
San Vitale, Italy, Right) ©PetarM

The Thousand Year Byzantine Empire

While the Western Roman Empire was destroyed by the invading Germanic forces, Byzantine Empire prevented the invasion of the Germanic peoples and maintained itself for close to a thousand years.

The Byzantine Empire particularly flourished during the reign of Justinian the Great. He recovered much of the old Roman Empire, including North Africa, through aggressive expeditions, issued *"the Code of Justinian"*, and rebuilt the Church of Hagia Sophia.

The Byzantine Empire flourished under the power of Caesaropapism, a political system in which the head of the state is also the head of the church. The capital city of Constantinople grew into the largest city in the world at that time as it was the hub of east-west trade.

Beginning in the 11th century, aristocrats and churches in the Byzantine Empire kept increasing their shares of land, consequently resulting in the collapse of self-employed peasants and the weakening of military power. The Byzantine Empire was reduced to tatters due to the repeated invasions of Muslim forces, and the empire lost Constantinople during the Crusades. Eventually the Byzantine Empire was destroyed by the invading Ottoman Empire(1453).

유스티니아누스 대제의 왕관은 정치적 권위를, 후광은 종교적 권위를 상징해요. 황후 테오도라는 배우 출신이었는데, 민중의 심리를 잘 이해하고 결단력이 있어 황제를 적절히 보좌하였어요. The crown of Justinian the Great symbolizes political authority, and the halo symbolizes religious authority. Empress Theodora was a former actor, and she understood the psychology of the masses well and assisted the Emperor properly.

비잔티움 제국의 문화, 그리스 정교의 특징을 보이다

비잔티움 제국은 로마 문화를 유지하였지만 공용어를 라틴어에서 그리스어로 바꾸는 등 그리스 문화와 헬레니즘 문화도 받아들였다. 비잔티움 제국의 학자들은 그리스와 로마의 고전 문화를 활발하게 연구하였는데, 이는 서유럽에 전해져 르네상스가 일어나는 데 큰 영향을 미쳤다.

비잔티움 제국의 문화에는 그리스 정교의 특징이 잘 나타나 있다. 그리스 정교와 이슬람교 양식이 공존하는 성 소피아 성당은 비잔티움 양식의 대표적인 건축물이다. 비잔티움 문화는 그리스 정교의 보호자를 자처한 러시아를 비롯하여 슬라브족의 여러 나라에 전파되었다.

◉ 성 소피아 성당은 성당일까요, 모스크일까요?

현존하는 비잔티움 건축물 가운데 가장 유명한 것이 콘스탄티노폴리스에 세워진 성 소피아 성당이다. 성 소피아 성당은 유스티아누스 대제의 명령에 의해 세워졌다. 그리스 · 로마의 십자형 바실리카 양식으로 설계되었고, 중앙에 페르시아식 대형돔을 올렸다. 내부는 황금 바탕에 모자이크와 조각 등으로 장식하여 화려하고 장엄하다.

비잔티움 제국 멸망 이후 성 소피아 성당은 오스만 제국에 의해 모스크로 사용되다가, 1945년 2월 1일부터 터키 미술관으로 사용되었다. 그러다 2020년 박물관 지위가 취소되어 다시 모스크로 전환되었다.

4개의 첨탑은 오스만 제국이 이슬람 사원으로 이용하기 위해 추가로 세웠어요.
Four additional spiers were erected by the Ottoman Empire to use it as a mosque.

성 소피아 성당(터키 이스탄불)
Cathedral of Hagia Sophia(Istanbul, Turkey) ©ArildV

Byzantine Culture Reflects the Greek Orthodox Style

The Byzantine Empire preserved the Roman culture, but it also embraced Greek and Hellenistic cultures by taking such measures as changing its official language from Latin to Greek, among numerous other changes. The scholars of the Byzantine Empire proactively studied classic Roman and Greek, and their study results were introduced to Western Europe, greatly contributing to the rise of the Renaissance.

The culture of the Byzantine Empire is marked by the influence of the Greek Orthodox style. One of the most iconic Byzantine styles of architecture is the cathedral of Hagia Sophia, characterized by the influence of both the Greek Orthodox and Islamic styles. The Byzantine culture was introduced and spread to many Slav empires including Russia, a country that claims to be the protector of the Greek Orthodoxy.

◎ Is the Cathedral of Hagia Sophia a Cathedral or a Mosque?

One of the most famous existing buildings in the Byzantine Empire is the cathedral of Hagia Sophia built in Constantinople. It was built by order of Justinian the Great. It was designed in Greek and Roman cruciform basilica

style, and a large Persian dome was placed in the center. The interior is splendid and magnificent, decorated with mosaics and sculptures on golden backgrounds.

It was used as a mosque by the Ottoman Empire after the fall of the Byzantine Empire and as a Turkish art museum beginning on February 1, 1945. Later, in 2020, its status as a museum was canceled and it was converted back to a mosque.

성 소피아 성당 내부
Inside of the Cathedral of Hagia Sophia ©XtoF

04 중앙 집권 국가의 등장

서유럽과 이슬람 세력의 충돌로 교황 세력이 약화하다

아바스 왕조에 이어 이슬람 세계를 지배한 **셀주크 튀르크**는 11세기 중반 예루살렘을 점령하고 성지 순례를 금지하였다. 더 나아가 비잔티움 제국을 위협하자 비잔티움 제국의 황제는 로마 교황에게 도움을 요청하였다.

교황 우르바누스 2세는 클레르몽 공의회를 열어 예루살렘 탈환을 호소하였다. 교황의 호소에 서유럽의 국왕과 기사, 상인, 농민 등이 호응하여 서유럽과 이슬람 세력의 전쟁이 시작되었다(1096, **십자군 전쟁**).

서유럽 세력은 한때 **예루살렘**을 점령하였으나 얼마 못 가 이슬람 세력에게 빼앗겼다. 전쟁은 200여 년 가까이 지속되었으나 전쟁의 목적이 변질되어 제1차 원정을 제외하고 모두 실패로 끝났다. 그 결과 교회와 교황의 세력은 물론 전쟁에 참여하였던 봉건 영주와 기사의 세력도 약화되었다.

◈ **교황, 기사, 상인, 농민이 십자군 출정에 나선 이유는 무엇인가요?**

> **교황**
> 예루살렘을 이교도로부터 되찾고, 가톨릭교회와 교황권의 위세를 높이기 위해 전쟁을 독려하였습니다. 무엇보다 세력을 확대하여 그리스 정교를 가톨릭교회와 통합할 절호의 기회라고 생각하였습니다.

> **기사**
> 영토를 확장하고 부와 명예를 얻기 위해 전쟁에 참여하였습니다.

> **상인**
> 이슬람 상인들을 제거하여 지중해 무역권을 장악하기 위해 십자군에 경제적인 지원을 하였습니다.

> **농민**
> 전쟁에서 공을 세워 신분 상승을 하겠다는 목적으로 참전하였습니다.

04 Emergence of the Centralized Government

The Clash Between Western Europe and Islamic Groups Lead to a Weakening of Papal Power

In the mid-11th century, the Seljuk Turks, who dominated the Islamic world following the Abbasid Dynasty, occupied Jerusalem and banned pilgrimages to the Holy Land. When they went one step further and posed a threat to the Byzantine Empire, the Byzantine emperor turned to the Pope for help.

In response, Pope Urban II summoned the Council of Clermont and made a plea for the recapture of Jerusalem. The Pope's plea was met with a tremendous response from the kings, knights, merchants, and peasants of western Europe. This is how the Crusades began(1096).

They captured Jerusalem only to lose it again to the Islamic forces shortly thereafter. The Crusades lasted for nearly 200 years, but all of the wars failed except for the First Crusade because the initial goal kept changing. The result was a weakening of the powers of the Church and the Pope as well as the feudal lords and knights who participated in the wars.

⊚ **Why Did the Pope, Knights, Merchants, and Peasants Go on the Crusades?**

> **The Pope**
> I encouraged the Crusades to recover Jerusalem from pagans and to raise the prestige of the Catholic Church and the papacy. Above all, I thought it was an excellent opportunity to expand the power and integrate the Greek Orthodoxy with the Catholic Church.

Knights	Merchants	Peasants
I joined the war to expand my territory and gain wealth and honor.	I gave financial aid to the Crusades to get rid of Islamic merchants and take control of the Mediterranean trade.	I participated in the war with the aim of raising my status by contributing to the war.

도시가 발달하고 장원이 해체되다

서유럽에서는 11세기 이후 농업 생산량이 증가하여 잉여 생산물을 교환하기 위한 시장이 발달하였다. 이와 함께 상업과 수공업이 발달하면서 도시가 성장하였다. 특히 십자군 전쟁으로 동방과의 교역이 활발해져 이탈리아 항구 도시들이 번성하였다. 북유럽에서는 상공업 도시들이 한자 동맹을 맺어 무역을 주도하였다.

상인과 수공업자는 영주와 맞서거나 일정한 금액을 내고 도시의 자치권을 얻었고, 동업 조합인 길드를 조직하여 공동의 이익을 도모하였다. 상업이 발달하고 도시가 성장하면서 화폐가 널리 사용되었다. 농노들은 부역과 현물 대신 화폐로 세금을 내는 경우가 늘어 영주 직영지를 경작하는 부담에서 점차 벗어났다. 일부 영주들은 돈을 받고 농노를 해방하기도 하였다. 14세기 중엽에 유행한 흑사병 또한 장원의 붕괴를 촉진하였다.

....

🌀 **흑사병은 어떻게 장원제를 붕괴시켰을까요?**

흑사병 이후 노동력이 부족해지자 농촌과 도시의 노동자들은 이전보다 훨씬 높은 임금을 요구하였다. 농민들은 임금 인상 요구가 관철되지 않으면 더 좋은 조건을 찾아 이주하였다. 결국 봉건 영주들은 농민들의 요구를 수용할 수밖에 없었다.

유리한 조건을 찾아 이동한 농민 중 일부는 영주의 직영지를 임대하여 부농으로 성장하기도 하였다. 이로 인해 농노제가 쇠퇴하며 장원제도 붕괴되어 갔다.

페스트는 팔과 다리에 검은 반점이 나타나는 증상 때문에 '흑사병'으로 알려져 있어요. 흑사병으로 인해 유럽 인구의 3분의 1 이상이 사망하였어요.
Plague is known as the 'Black Death' due to the symptom of dark spots on the arms and legs. More than a third of Europe's population died from the Black Death.

흑사병을 묘사한 작품, 죽음의 승리(프라도 미술관)
A Work Depicting the Black Death, The Triumph of Death(Prado Museum)

Development of Cities and Dismantlement of Manorialism

As agricultural productivity started increasing after the 11th century, western Europe saw the development of markets for exchanging surplus agricultural products. Subsequent development of commercial and trading businesses led to the development of cities. In particular, the Italian port cities enjoyed a boom that became more dynamic than ever because of the merchants who moved east during the Crusades. In northern Europe, commercial and industrial cities joined the Hanseatic League, which dominated commercial activities.

Traders and merchants gained autonomy for cities by confronting the feudal lords or paying a fee and also sought to protect their mutual interests by organizing guilds. Development of cities and commercial activities helped currency to be widely used. Gradually, serfs were able to escape from the burden of having to cultivate land under the direct control of their lords because they were able to pay tax with currency instead of labor or commodities. Some feudal lords took the money and freed their serfs in exchange. The epidemic called the 'Black Death' that plagued Europe in the mid-14th century prompted the collapse of manors.

....

How Did the Black Death Prompt the Collapse of Manors?

After the Black Death, as the labor force became scarce, rural and urban workers demanded much higher wages than before. If the demand for a wage increase was not satisfied, farmers moved in search of better conditions. Eventually, the feudal lords were forced to accept the demands of the peasants.

Some of the farmers who moved in search of favorable conditions leased land directly managed by the lord and grew into wealthy farmers. As a result, the serf system declined and the manor system collapsed.

중앙 집권 국가가 등장하다

장원이 해체되면서 봉건 영주들의 힘이 약해지고, 화약과 대포가 사용되면서 기사 계급도 약화하였다. 상대적으로 왕권은 강화되어 14세기 초에는 로마의 교황청이 프랑스 아비뇽으로 옮겨져 프랑스 왕의 지배를 받기도 하였다(아비뇽 유수). 그리고 자유로운 경제 활동을 원하던 상공업자들이 국왕을 재정적으로 후원하여 중앙 집권 국가가 형성되기 시작하였다.

14세기 전반 프랑스의 왕위 계승 문제와 플랑드르 지방의 지배권을 둘러싸고 벌어진 **백년 전쟁**에서 프랑스는 영국을 상대로 승리하였다. 이후 영국에서는 왕위 계승권을 둘러싸고 **장미 전쟁**이 일어났다. 두 전쟁을 거치면서 영국과 프랑스에서는 봉건 질서가 흔들리고 중앙 집권 국가의 기틀이 더욱 다져졌다.

✿ 백년 전쟁은 정말 100년 동안 벌어졌을까요?

백년 전쟁은 양모 공업 지대인 플랑드르 지방에 대한 주도권과 프랑스의 왕위 계승 문제를 놓고 일어났다. 당시 영국의 왕은 에드워드 3세였는데, 그는 혈연관계로 볼 때 자신이 프랑스 왕이 되어야 한다며 프랑스 왕위 계승권을 주장하였다.

백년 전쟁은 1337년에 시작되어 1453년까지 100여 년에 걸쳐 진행되었는데, 전쟁이 100년간 계속된 것은 아니었고 그 기간에 휴전과 전투를 반복하였다. 백년 전쟁 동안 영국은 시종일관 우위를 점하였지만 잔 다르크가 등장하며 전세는 역전되었고, 결국 프랑스가 전쟁에서 승리를 거두었다.

잔 다르크
1412년 프랑스 동레미에서 농민의 딸로 태어났어요. 흰 갑옷을 입고 병사들 앞에서 직접 전투를 지휘했고 영국군을 무찔러 백년 전쟁을 승리로 이끌었지요. "프랑스를 구하라."라는 천사의 음성을 들었어요.

Joan of Arc
I was Born in 1412 in Dongremy, France as the daughter of a farmer. I wore white armor and commanded battles directly at the front of the soldiers, defeating British forces and leading France to a victory in the Hundred Years' War. I heard an angel say, "Save France".

Emergence of Centralized Government

The power of the feudal lords grew weaker after the dismantling of the manors, and the power of the knights grew weaker as well when soldiers started using gunpowder and cannons. Royal authority grew relatively stronger as the result and, in the early 14th century, even the popes were under the rule of the French kings when they took up residence at Avignon, France, after leaving Rome(Avignon Papacy). And when merchants and traders who wished to have free economic activities started supporting the kings financially, a strong centralized government began to form.

France fought with England and won the Hundred Years' War, a series of conflicts waged between the two countries over the control of Flanders, while in England, the Wars of the Roses were waged over the control of the throne. In the course of two wars, the feudal system in Britain and France began faltering, eventually making it possible for a centralized government to form.

....

◎ Did the Hundred Years' War Really Last over 100 Years?

The Hundred Years' War arose over the issue of leadership over Flanders, an industrial zone producing wool, and the succession of France to the throne. At the time, the king of England was Edward III, who insisted on succession to the French throne, saying that he should be king of France based on blood ties.

The Hundred Years' War began in 1337 and lasted over 100 years until 1453, but the war itself did not continually last for 100 years, and during that period, ceasefires and battles were repeated often. During the Hundred Years' War, Britain consistently maintained its dominance, but with the advent of Joan of Arc, the tide was reversed, and France eventually won.

05 르네상스와 종교 개혁

이탈리아에서 르네상스가 일어나다

14세기경 고대 로마의 문화유산이 많이 남아 있는 이탈리아에서는 지중해 무역으로 상공업과 도시가 발달하였다. 피렌체, 베네치아, 밀라노 등 도시 국가의 부호들과 통치자들이 고대 그리스와 로마의 문화를 연구하는 인문주의자들을 후원하면서 인간 중심의 문예 부흥 운동인 르네상스가 일어났다.

페트라르카는 인간적인 사랑을 아름다운 서정시로 표현하였고 보카치오는 『데카메론』에서 남녀 간의 사랑과 욕망을 솔직하게 표현하였다. 레오나르도 다빈치의 '모나리자', 라파엘로의 '아테네 학당', 미켈란젤로의 '다비드상' 등은 인체와 사물의 아름다움을 사실적으로 묘사한 걸작이다.

이탈리아에서 시작된 르네상스는 16세기 이후 알프스 이북으로 퍼져 나갔다. 북·서유럽에서는 봉건 사회의 관습과 교회의 권위가 여전히 남아 있었으므로 부패한 교회와 현실을 비판하는 경향이 강하였다. 네덜란드의 에라스뮈스는 『우신예찬』에서 성직자의 타락을 지적하였다. 영국의 토머스 모어는 『유토피아』에서 불평등한 사회 현실을 비판하면서 종교의 자유가 허락되고 재산을 함께 소유하는 이상 세계를 그렸다. 구텐베르크는 활판 인쇄술을 발명하여 새로운 지식과 사상의 보급에 크게 기여하였다.

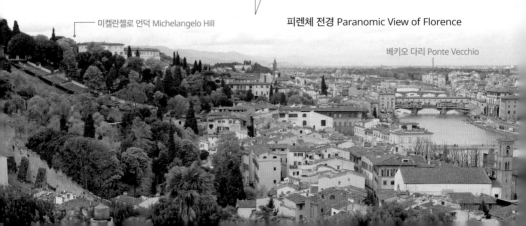

왼쪽에는 미켈란젤로 언덕이, 오른쪽에는 베키오 다리가 있어요.
On the left side of the picture is Michelangelo Hill and on the right is the Ponte Vecchio.

미켈란젤로 언덕 Michelangelo Hill

피렌체 전경 Paranomic View of Florence

베키오 다리 Ponte Vecchio

05 The Renaissance and Religious Reform

The Rise of the Renaissance in Italy

In the 14th century, trade in the Mediterranean helped cities and commercial businesses thrive in Italy, a country rich with the heritage of ancient Rome. Rulers and rich families from prosperous cities such as Milan, Florence, and Venice started supporting humanist scholars who researched the arts and literature from the days of ancient Greece and Rome, thereby reviving classical art and literature in a movement called the Renaissance.

For example, Francesco Petrarca wrote beautiful lyric poems about humanistic love, and Boccaccio wrote the *"Decameron"* in which he candidly described love and desire between men and women. Some of the important artworks from the Renaissance include Leonardo da Vinci's Mona Lisa, Raphael's The School of Athens, and Michelangelo's statue of David, all of which are masterpieces characterized by a realistic presentation of the beauty of humans and secular objects.

The Renaissance began in Italy and spread to the north of the Alps after the 16th century. In northern and western Europe, the movement produced works that criticized a corrupt church and reality since the customs of feudal society and the authority of the church still existed in the areas. Erasmus of the Netherlands criticized the decadence of priests and the corruption of the church in his book, *"In Praise of Folly"*. In *"Utopia"*, author Thomas Moore of England criticized the reality of an unfair society and described an ideal world where religious freedom and common wealth were guaranteed. In the meantime, Gutenberg invented the printing press and made a great contribution to the spread of new knowledge and thoughts.

종교 개혁으로 신교가 등장하다

　사회 개혁적인 북유럽의 르네상스는 부패한 성직자와 타락한 교회에 대한 비판으로 이어졌다. 이러한 상황에서 교황 레오 10세는 성 베드로 성당을 고치는 데 필요한 비용을 마련하기 위해 **면벌부** 죄를 면한다는 뜻으로 발행하는 증서를 판매하였다. 이에 독일의 신학자 **루터**는 교회와 교황의 잘못을 비판하는 **95개조 반박문**을 발표하였다(1517).

　루터의 주장은 많은 제후와 농민들에게 호응을 얻었고 인쇄술의 발달에 힘입어 독일 전역으로 퍼져 나갔다. 교황과 신성 로마 제국 황제가 루터를 탄압하였으나 독일의 제후들이 루터를 지지하여 루터파는 **아우크스부르크 화의**를 통해 종교의 자유를 얻었다.

　스위스에서는 **칼뱅**이 "인간의 구원은 이미 신에 의해 정해져 있다(예정설)."라고 주장하며, 현세의 직업에 충실해야 한다고 강조하였다. 칼뱅의 종교 개혁은 상공업에 종사하던 도시 시민의 지지를 받아 유럽 각지로 확산되었다.

⚙ 루터와 칼뱅은 왜 가톨릭을 비판하였을까요?

교황 레오 10세 금화를 헌금함에 넣어 딸랑거리는 소리가 나면 죽은 자의 영혼이 천국에 갑니다.

마틴 루터 인간에 대한 구원은 오직 믿음과 신의 은총으로 이루어집니다.

장 칼뱅 인간의 구원은 신에 의해 미리 정해져 있으므로 우리 모두 자신의 구원을 확신하고 자신의 직업에 충실해야 합니다.

Religious Reform Gives Birth to Protestantism

The reformative Northern Renaissance was also about criticizing clerical corruption and decadence. It was under this circumstance that Pope Leo X sold indulgences to raise the funds necessary to reconstruct St. Peter's Basilica. A German theologist, Martin Luther, made a list known as the '95 Theses' in which he criticized the misconduct of the Pope and the Church (1517).

Luther's claim was well received by peasants and wealthy families, and spread throughout Germany thanks to the new technology of the printing press. The Pope and the emperor tried to persecute Luther, but thanks to the support of the German feudal lords, he achieved religious freedom through the Augsburg Settlement.

In Switzerland, John Calvin claimed that since salvation was possible through the grace of God, people should be faithful to their work in this life(Predestination). Calvin's religious reform was supported by urban merchants and traders and spread throughout Europe.

....

◉ **Why Did Luther and Calvin Criticize Catholicism?**

> Pope Leo X When you put gold coins in the offering box and make a rattle, the souls of the dead go to heaven

> Martin Luther Salvation comes only through faith and divine grace.

> John Calvin Since salvation is ordained by God, we must all be sure of our own salvation and be faithful to our profession.

영국에서는 국교회가 성립하고 종교 개혁으로 종교 전쟁이 이어지다

영국에서는 헨리 8세가 로마 교황의 간섭에서 벗어나 영국 국교회를 성립하였다. 영국 국교회는 국왕이나 영주를 우두머리로 하는 교회 제도이다. 헨리 8세는 교황이 자신의 이혼을 허락하지 않자 수장법을 공포하여 스스로 영국 교회의 수장이 되었다. 종교 개혁으로 신교가 등장하면서 가톨릭교회의 권위는 점차 무너져 갔다.

종교 개혁으로 로마 가톨릭과 프로테스탄트(신교)가 대립하면서 프랑스에서는 위그노 전쟁이, 독일에서는 **30년 전쟁**이 일어났다. 30년 전쟁은 유럽에서 로마 가톨릭교회를 지지하는 국가들과 신교를 지지하는 국가들 사이에 벌어진 종교 전쟁이다. 800여만 명의 사망자를 낸 오랜 싸움 끝에 **베스트팔렌 조약**이 맺어졌다.

☉ 위그노 전쟁과 30년 전쟁은 어떤 종교적 자유를 가져왔나요?

위그노 전쟁(1562~1598)은 프랑스에서 위그노라 불리는 신교도들이 정부와 가톨릭교회에 저항하면서 일어난 종교 전쟁이다. 위그노 전쟁의 결과 낭트 칙령이 공포되어 위그노의 신앙적 자유가 부분적으로 허용되었다.

30년 전쟁(1618~1648)은 신성 로마 제국 황제가 신교도를 탄압하자 신교를 믿는 제후국들이 반란을 일으키면서 시작되었다. 종교 전쟁에서 시작된 30년 전쟁은 유럽의 여러 왕가들이 자신들의 이해관계에 따라 전쟁에 참여하면서 국제 전쟁으로 확대되었다. 전쟁 결과 베스트팔렌 조약(1648)이 체결되어 제후가 가톨릭, 루터파, 칼뱅파 중 선택하는 것이 허용되었다. 처음으로 프로이센이 왕국으로 등장하였고 네덜란드와 스위스가 독립을 인정받았다.

> 베스트팔렌 조약으로 황제와 교황의 권력이 약해졌는데, 이는 유럽의 근대화와 절대주의 국가 성립에 영향을 주었어요.
> The Treaty of Westphalia weakened the power of the emperor and the pope, which influenced the modernization of Europe and the establishment of an absolutist state.

베스트팔렌 조약(1648) Treaty of Westphalia(1648)

The Church of England Was Established and a Religious War Continued with the Reformation

In England, Henry VIII broke away from the Roman Catholic Church and established the Church of England instead. The Church of England is a church system with a king or lord as the head. When the Pope refused to allow his divorce, he promulgated the Act of Supremacy and became the head of the Church of England. The authority of the Roman Catholic Church gradually declined when religious reform resulted in the founding of Protestantism.

As Protestantism was born in the Reformation, a religious war broke out between Roman Catholicism and Protestantism. There was the Huguenot War in France and the 30 Years' War in Germany. The 30 Years' War was a religious war between the countries supporting the Roman Catholic Church and the countries supporting Protestantism. At the end of a long battle resulting in 8,000,000 deaths, the Treaty of Westphalia was signed.

<hr />

◈ What Were the Consequences of the Huguenots and the 30 Years' War?

The Huguenot War(1562-1598) was a religious war that took place in France when Protestants called Hugenonots resisted the government and the Catholic Church. As a result of the Huguenot War, the Edict of Nantes was promulgated, partially allowing the Huguenot's religious freedom.

The 30 Years' War(1618-1648) began when the Holy Roman Emperor oppressed the Protestants and the Protestant empires rebelled. The 30 Years' War, which began as a religious war, expanded into an international war as several European royal families participated in the war according to their interests. The war resulted in the Treaty of Westphalia(1648), allowing the feudal lords to choose between Catholic, Lutheran, and Calvinist. For the first time, Prussia appeared as a kingdom, and the Netherlands and Switzerland had their independence recognized.

◑◑ 헨리 8세는 왜 영국 국교회를 선포하였을까요?

키 190cm에 근육질 미남이었던 영국의 헨리 8세에게는 에스파냐 출신의 캐서린이라는 왕비가 있었다. 왕은 아들을 낳지 못하는 왕비를 내쫓고 싶었다. 하지만 이혼하려면 교황에게 동의를 받아야 하였는데, 교황은 교리를 내세우며 그의 이혼을 허락하지 않았다.

헨리 8세는 비록 교황일지라도 영국의 일에 간섭하는 것은 부당하다고 생각하였다. 결국 그는 가톨릭과 단절하고 수도원을 해산시켰다. 수도원의 땅을 몰수하였고 교황청으로 들어갈 돈은 왕실 재정에 사용하였다. 1534년 헨리 8세는 스스로 영국 국교회(성공회)의 수장이 되었음을 선포하였다.

영국 국교회의 수장이 된 헨리 8세는 곧바로 캐서린 왕비와 이혼하였다. 헨리 8세는 캐서린의 시녀 앤 불린에게 반하여 앤 불린과 결혼하였다. 하지만 그는 곧 앤 불린에게 싫증을 느껴 그녀가 친오빠와 근친상간하였다는 죄를 씌워 런던 탑에 감금하였고 2주 만에 처형하였다. 이후 헨리 8세는 4번 더 결혼을 하였다.

캐서린 헨리 8세와 정략결혼을 하여 딸 메리 1세를 낳았어요. 헨리 8세는 나의 시녀였던 앤 불린을 새 왕비로 맞아들이기 위해 자신이 교회의 수장이라고 선언하였어요.

헨리 8세 나의 통치 초기에 종교 개혁을 강력히 억압하였고 로마 교황청과 대립하였어요. 결국 캐서린과의 이혼 문제를 계기로 종교 개혁을 단행함으로써 6세기 이래 로마 가톨릭의 지배를 받던 영국 교회를 독립시켰습니다.

앤 불린 프랑스 루이 12세의 왕비 메리 튜더의 시녀였고, 헨리 8세의 왕비 캐서린의 시녀였어요. 1533년에는 헨리 8세와 결혼식을 올렸습니다. 그리고 메리 1세에 이어 여왕으로 즉위하는 엘리자베스 1세를 낳았어요.

∞ Why Did Henry VIII Proclaim the Church of England?

Henry VIII of England, 190 cm tall and muscular, had a queen named Catherine from Spain. The king wanted to expel the queen, who could not have a son. However, in order to divorce her, he had to obtain the consent of the Pope, who would not allow his divorce due to doctrine.

Henry VIII thought it was unfair for the pope to intervene in Britain's affairs, no matter who the pope was. Eventually he severed from Catholicism and disbanded the monastery. The monastic land was confiscated, and the money that would have gone into the Holy See was used to finance the royal family. In 1534, Henry VIII declared himself to be the supreme head of the Church of England.

The first thing Henry VIII did was to divorce Queen Catherine. Henry VIII fell in love with Catherine's maid Anne Boleyn, divorced Catherine and married Anne Boleyn. However, he soon became tired of Ann Boleyn, and charged her with incest with her brother and imprisoned her in the Tower of London. He then executed her two weeks later. After that, Henry VIII married four more times.

> Catherine I married Henry VIII and gave birth to a daughter, Mary I. Henry VIII declared that he was the head of the church in order to welcome the new queen, Anne Boleyn, who was my maid.

> Henry VIII In the early years of my reign, I strongly oppressed the Reformation and opposed the Vatican. Eventually, I started supporting the Reformation on the occasion of my divorce from Catherine and made the English Church, which had been dominated by Roman Catholicism since the 6th century, independent.

> Anne Boleyn I was the maid of Mary Tudor, Queen of Louis XII of France, and of Catherine, Queen of Henry VIII. In 1533, I married Henry VIII. I gave birth to Elizabeth I, who later became queen.

III

지역 세계의 교류와 변화

1. 몽골 제국과 문화 교류
2. 동아시아 지역 질서의 변화
3. 서아시아와 북아프리카 지역 질서의 변화
4. 신항로 개척과 유럽 지역 질서의 변화

인간은 태어날 때부터 자연권, 즉 생명, 자유, 재산의 권리를 가지고 있다.
국가가 시민의 자유를 침해하면 시민은 자신들의 안전을 위해
새로운 정부를 세울 수 있다.

– 존 로크(1632~1704)

III

Exchanges and Changes of the Regional Worlds

All individuals are born with naturable rights: life, liberty and property. If the state violates citizens' natural rights, the people can establish a new government for their own safety and security.

– John Locke(1632–1704)

← **발견 기념비(포르투갈 리스본)** | 대항해 시대를 열었던 포르투갈의 용감한 선원들과 후원자들을 기리기 위해 만든 기념비이다.
Monument to the Discoveries(Lisbon, Portugal) | This monument was erected to commemorate the brave sailors and their sponsors who opened the Portuguese Age of Discovery.

몽골 제국과 문화 교류

01 송의 발전과 교역의 확대

송이 문치주의를 실시하다

당이 멸망한 후 중국은 혼란에 빠졌다. 계속되는 전쟁으로 지배층이었던 문벌 귀족이 약화하고, 군인들과 지방의 신흥 지주 세력이 나타났다. 송이 중국을 통일하기 전까지 여러 나라가 생겨났다 사라졌는데, 이 시기를 **5대 10국 시대**라고 한다.

5대 10국의 혼란을 수습한 송 **태조**(조광윤)는 지방의 군대를 지휘하는 절도사 출신이었다. 그는 절도사 등의 무인 세력이 정치에 개입하는 것을 막기 위해 문인 관료를 우대하는 **문치주의**를 실시하였다.

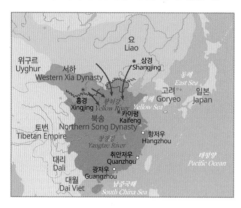

아울러 황제가 직접 과거 합격자의 등수를 매기는 **전시** 궁궐에서 주관한 시험를 주관하여 황제의 인사권을 강화하였다. 이러한 정책으로 송의 황제권이 강해졌다.

송의 건국과 거란의 남진
Founding of Song and Southward Advance of the Khitans

◉ 황제가 과거를 직접 주관한 이유는 무엇인가요?

송 태조는 문관들에게 영향력을 행사하기 위해 직접 시험을 주관하였다. 황제가 과거 시험의 주관자가 됨으로써 황제와 시험 합격자는 스승과 제자라는 특별한 관계를 맺게 되었다. 이로써 황제의 영향력이 강화되었다.

> 송 태조
> 군사력을 가진 절도사들이 언제 반란을 일으킬지 모른다.
> 국가 안정을 위해 문관 중심의 정치를 실시하겠다.

1

The Mongol Empire and Cultural Exchanges

01 Growth of the Song Dynasty and Expansion of Trade

Song Adopts Rule by Civil Officials

After the fall of the Tang Dynasty, China fell into turmoil. Continued wars weakened the ruling noble class, while soldiers and new landlords emerged as a new power group. A succession of dynasties rose and fell during what came to be known as the Five Dynasties and Ten Kingdoms period until Song came about and reunified China.

Emperor Taizu of Song was a former military governor who commanded a local army. He installed the 'rule by civil officials' policy and gave his preference to civil officials instead of military leaders to prevent military power including military governors getting involved in politics.

In addition, the emperor's personnel rights were strengthened by supervising the court exam called Dianshi in which the emperor directly ranks the passers of the civil service examination. These policies effectuated stronger royal authority.

⬙ Why Did the Emperor Directly Control the Civil Service Examination?

Emperor Taizu of Song personally conducted the civil service examination to take control of the civil officials. As the emperor became the organizer of the examination, the emperor and successful candidates had a special relationship of teacher and disciple which strengthened the emperor's influence.

> Emperor Taizu of Song
> Military governors with military power may revolt. I will practice politics centered on civil officials for national stability.

송이 북방 민족의 압박을 극복하기 위해 노력하다

송은 지나친 문치주의 정책을 펼쳐 군사력이 약해졌다. 이에 북방 민족의 지속적인 압박에 시달리며 막대한 양의 비단, 은, 차 등을 보내야 하였다.

한편 요는 발해를 멸망시키고 화베이 지방의 연운 16주를 차지한 후 송을 압박하였다. 송의 서북쪽에서는 서하가 비단길을 장악하여 동서 무역을 통해 이익을 얻었다. 세력을 넓힌 서하는 송에 대등한 관계를 요구하기도 하였다.

송은 요와 서하에 매년 많은 물자를 바치며 평화를 유지하였지만 재정은 나날이 어려워졌다. 이에 왕안석이 가난한 농민과 소상인을 보호하고 나라의 재정을 늘릴 수 있는 새로운 법을 만들어 위기에서 벗어나고자 하였다. 하지만 왕안석의 개혁은 보수파 관료들과 대지주들의 반대로 효과를 거두지 못하였다.

송 임안 천도(1132) Song Moved to Linan

12세기에는 여진족의 아구다가 부족을 통합해 금을 세웠다(1115). 송은 금과 연합하여 요를 멸망시켰으나, 금에 밀려 수도를 남쪽으로 옮기고 남송을 세웠다.

금과 남송
Jin Dynasty and the Southern
Song Dynasty

◎ 왕안석은 가난한 농민을 위해 무엇을 주장하였나요?

왕안석
봄·가을에 가난한 농민에게 낮은 이자로 돈과 곡식을 빌려줍시다. 그러면 높은 이자로 식량을 빌렸다가 빚을 지고 몰락하는 농민이 줄어들 것이오. 그리고 그동안 중간 상인들이 공물을 대신 내고 그 대가를 백성들에게 비싸게 받아 왔소. 이 고리를 끊으려면 지방에서 바친 공물을 운송할 때 관청이 통제하게 해야 하오.

Song Tries to Overcome the Threats of the Northern Tribes

Song's excessive focus on the 'rule by civil officials' policy took a toll on military power. As the result, Song was constantly harassed by nomads from Northern China and had to send them a massive amount of silk, silver, and tea to meet their demands.

Meanwhile, Liao brought down Balhae, took over the Sixteen Prefectures of the Yanyun area, and put pressure on Song. In the northwestern part of Song, the Western Xia Dynasty dominated the Silk Road and thrived on west-east trade. The Western Xia Dynasty kept growing its power and demanded that Song maintain an equal relationship with it.

Song maintained peace with Liao and Western Xia by paying them annual tributes, but it took a toll on their national revenue. Wang Anshi, tried to overcome the financial crisis by creating a new law designed to protect poor peasants and small merchants while improving the national revenue. But his reform policy did not return any results due to the objection of conservative bureaucrats and large landowners.

In the 12th century, a Jurchen tribal leader, Aguda, unified his people and founded the Jin Dynasty(1115). Song formed an alliance with Jurchen Jin and together they brought down the Liao Dynasty, but Jin turned on him after the victory. Consequently, Song was pushed by Jin to move the capital to the south and established the Southern Song Dynasty.

⦿ What Did Wang Anshi Claim for Poor Farmers?

Wang Anshi
Let's lend money and grain to poor farmers at low interest rates in spring and autumn. Then there will be fewer farmers who borrow food at high interest and fall into debt. And in the meantime, middlemen have paid tribute for the farmers and received a high price from them. To break this vicious circle, we must have the authorities control the transport of local tributes.

송대에 경제가 발전하고 해상 교역이 활발해지다

송이 5대 10국의 분열을 수습하고 통일을 이루자 상품 유통이 활발해졌다. 북송 (960~1127) 때에는 화폐 경제가 발달하여 동전이 널리 사용되었고 교자_{중국에서 가장} 오래된 지폐와 같은 지폐가 등장하였다.

남송(1127~1279) 때에는 화북 지역의 한족이 강남으로 이동하여 농토를 개발하였다. 그 결과 창장강 하류에서 2모작이나 3모작이 가능해졌고, 모내기와 비료를 사용하는 시비법도 발달하였다. 이에 서민들의 경제력이 향상되고 인구가 급격하게 증가하였다. 이 시기에는 상업과 수공업도 비약적으로 발전하였다. 상공업자는 동업 조합을 만들어 이익을 꾀하였고, 수공업자는 도자기 등을 만들었다.

송대에는 나침반의 발명과 지도 제작 기술에 힘입어 항해술이 발달하고 해상 교역이 활발하게 전개되었다. 대외 무역이 활발해지면서 항저우, 취안저우 등 국제 무역 도시가 성장하자 정부는 국제 무역항에 시박사를 설치하여 무역 사무를 맡아보게 하였다. 이러한 해상 교역을 통해 송의 비단, 도자기, 차 등이 세계 각지로 수출되었다.

....

🏵 **송대에 도시가 발달하게 된 배경은 무엇인가요?**

송대의 상인들은 생산된 작물과 상품들을 각지에 유통하였는데, 이로 인해 전국적인 규모의 시장이 형성되었다. 특히 북송의 카이펑과 남송의 항저우는 거대한 무역 도시로 성장하였다.

전문적인 이야기꾼 주변에 모인 사람들　　가게에 몰려 있는 사람들　　짐을 싣고 가는 낙타
People Gathered Around　　　　　　　　People in a Store　　　A Camel Carrying Luggages
a Professional Storyteller

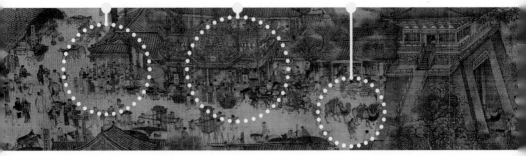

청명상하도(베이징 고궁박물원) Along the River During the Qingming Festival(The Palace Museum, Beijing)

Economic Development and Dynamic Maritime Trade of the Song Dynasty

When Song put an end to the chaos of the Five Dynasties and Ten Kingdoms period and unified China, the exchange of goods became more dynamic. During the Northern Song Dynasty(960-1127), the development of monetary economy brought about the wide circulation of coins, and the earliest form of paper notes, called Jiaozi, were also created and circulated.

During the Southern Song period(1127-1279), the Han tribe migrated from northern China to the Jiangnan region and cultivated farmland. As a result, farmers were able to grow two to three crops consecutively in the same field in a year in the lower Yangtze River region and also developed rice-planting and fertilizer application techniques. These developments resulted in an improved financial situation for ordinary people and a rapid increase in population. During this period, commerce and handcraft businesses boomed as well. Merchants and traders organized guilds to protect their interests and craftsmen made products such as pottery.

The invention of the compass and more advanced cartography technology effectuated advanced navigation skills and dynamic maritime trade. Increasing import and export activities gave rise to such hubs of international trade as Hangzhou and Quanzhou, and the government created and installed a Maritime Bureau called 'Shibosi' in the foreign trade ports to take charge of trade affairs. Through this maritime trade, such products as silk, ceramics, and tea were exported from Song to countries around the world.

◉ What Was the Background of the City's Development in the Song Dynasty?

The merchants of the Song Dynasty distributed the produced crops and products to various places, which created a nationwide market. In particular, Kaifeng in northern Song and Hangzhou in southern Song grew into huge trading cities.

문화와 과학 기술이 발달하다

경제의 발달로 도시가 성장하면서 서민들의 생활 수준과 사회적 지위도 높아졌다. 노래를 부르기 위해 구어체글에서 쓰는 말투가 아닌, 일상적인 대화에서 주로 쓰는 말투로 쓴 시를 뜻하는 사(詞), 연극에 해당하는 잡극, 구어체로 쓴 소설 등 서민 문화가 발전하였다.

유학에도 새로운 경향이 나타났다. 송대에는 인간의 심성과 우주의 원리를 탐구하려는 새로운 경향이 나타났는데, 주희가 이를 **주자학**(성리학)으로 집대성하였다. 역사책으로는 사마광이 편년체로 쓴 『**자치통감**』전국 시대부터 5대까지의 역사를 기록한 책이 유명하다. 송대에는 과학 기술도 획기적으로 발전하여 **나침반, 화약, 활판 인쇄술**이 발명되었다. 이 같은 발명품은 훗날 이슬람 세계를 거쳐 유럽에도 전해졌다.

◎ **나침반, 화약, 활판 인쇄술이 유럽에 어떤 영향을 미쳤나요?**

송대에 발명된 나침반은 이슬람 세계를 거쳐 유럽에 전해졌어요. 유럽인은 항해에 나침반을 이용하였고, 이는 신항로 개척으로 이어졌지요.
The compass invented in the Song Dynasty was passed on to Europe through the Islamic world. Europeans used compasses for sailing, which led to the pioneering of new routes.

나침반(복원 모형)
Compass(Restored Model)

처음에는 종이로 만든 용기에 화약을 넣고 던졌지만 이후에는 질려화구처럼 철로 만든 용기에 화약을 넣어 폭발물을 만들었어요. 화약은 유럽에 전파되어 기사 계급이 몰락하고 봉건제가 해체되는 데 영향을 미쳤어요.
At first, people put gunpowder in a paper container to make explosives. Later, explosives were made by putting gunpowder in iron containers like a firearm. Gunpowder spread to Europe and influenced the collapse of the knight class and the dissolution of feudalism.

질려화구(복원 모형)
Caltrop Bomb(Restored Model)

Development of Culture, Science and Technology

Economic development resulted in the growth of cities and the improvement of ordinary people's standard of living and social status. This period is also marked by the development of such pop culture as the ci-poetry written in spoken style for singing, a genre of drama called Zaju, and novels written in spoken style Chinese.

A new change happened in Confucian studies as well. During the Song Dynasty, a new tendency to explore human nature and the principles of the universe appeared, which the philosopher Zhu Xi compiled as Lixue(Neo-Confucianism). Notable history books written in this period include Sima Guang's "*ZizhiTongjian*(Comprehensive Mirror for Aid in Government)". During the Song period, science and technology made impressive advancements as well, such as those seen in the invention of the compass, gunpowder, and letterpress printing. These inventions were introduced to Europe via the Islamic world.

⚙ **How Did the Compass, Gunpowder, and Typography Affect Europe?**

한자가 새겨진 흙 도장을 원고에 따라 배열하고 인쇄하였어요. 나중에 분해하여 다른 원고를 찍을 수도 있었지요. 이러한 활판 인쇄술은 유럽에 전래되어 책의 대량 생산이 가능해졌답니다. 대표적으로 종교 개혁 때 루터의 입장을 발표한 발표문이나 각국의 언어로 쓰인 성경이 활판 인쇄술 덕분에 널리 퍼졌어요.

The clay stamps with Chinese characters were arranged and printed according to the manuscript. It was possible to disassemble them later and print another manuscript. This type of typography was introduced to Europe, making it possible to mass-produce books. Representatively, during the religious reform, Luther's statement and Bibles written in different languages became widespread thanks to the invention and proliferation of typography.

활자판(복원 모형)
A Typeboard(Restored Model)

02 몽골 제국 건설과 문화 교류

몽골이 유라시아에 걸친 제국을 형성하다

1206년 테무친은 몽골 부족을 통일한 후 족장 회의에서 **칭기즈 칸**으로 추대되었다. 칭기즈 칸의 군대는 서하와 금을 공략하고 중앙아시아의 나라들을 차례로 정복하였다. 후계자들은 고려를 침략하고 금을 멸망시켰으며 키예프 대공국과 서아시아의 아바스 왕조를 정복하여 오늘날의 러시아와 유럽 일부까지 지배하였다.

쿠빌라이 칸은 대도(베이징)에 수도를 정하고 나라 이름을 원이라고 하였다 (1271). 원은 남송을 멸망시키고 중국 전역을 지배하였다. 이로써 몽골족은 동아시아에서 유럽에 이르는 세계 최대 제국을 건설하였다.

⸺⸺⸺⸺⸺⸺⸺⸺⸺⸺⸺⸺⸺⸺⸺⸺⸺⸺⸺⸺⸺⸺⸺⸺⸺⸺⸺⸺⸺⸺⸺⸺⸺⸺⸺

⦿ 몽골 제국의 영토는 어느 정도였나요?

칭기즈 칸에 이어 두 번째 칸이 된 오고타이는 고려를 침략하였고, 1234년에는 금을 무너뜨렸다. 오고타이는 서남아시아와 유럽에 이르는 대제국을 세웠다. 세계의 절반을 차지한 몽골족은 오고타이한국, 차가타이한국, 킵차크한국, 일한국을 세웠고, 중국에는 대도를 도읍으로 하는 '원'을 수립하였다.

몽골 제국의 영역 Mongol Empire's Territory

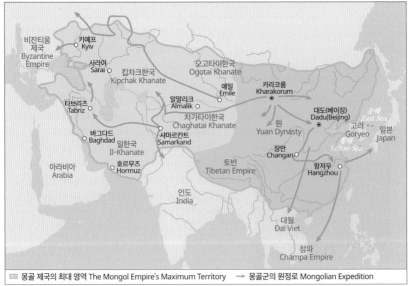

□ 몽골 제국의 최대 영역 The Mongol Empire's Maximum Territory → 몽골군의 원정로 Mongolian Expedition

02 Establishment of the Mongol Empire and Cultural Exchanges

Mongols Build an Empire Across Eurasia

In 1206, Temjin was elected as Genghis Khan at the chiefs' meeting after unifying the Mongol tribes. His troops invaded Western Xia and Jin and conquered Central Asian countries one after another. His successors invaded Goryeo, brought down Jin, and conquered Kievan Rus and the Abbasid Caliphate in West Asia until they dominated today's Russia and parts of Europe.

Kublai Khan established the Yuan Dynasty with its capital in Beijing (1271). Yuan brought down Southern Song and ruled all of China. With this feat, the Mongols were able to build the world's greatest empire whose territory reached from East Asia to Europe.

 How Large Was the Territory of the Mongol Empire?

Ogotai, the second khan after Genghis Khan, invaded Goryeo, and in 1234 destroyed Jin. He established a great empire spanning southwest Asia and Europe. The Mongols, who occupied half of the world, established Ogotai Khanate, Chaghatai Khanate, Kipchak Khanate, and Il-Khanate, and the Yuan Dynasty was established in China with Dadu as its capital.

칭기즈 칸
'칭기즈 칸'은 우주의 군주라는 뜻이에요. 1189년 몽골 씨족 연합의 우두머리로 추대되어 칭기즈 카이라는 칭호를 받았지요. 1204년에 몽골 초원을 통일한 뒤 세계 역사상 가장 넓은 제국을 건설하였어요.

Genghis Khan
'Genghis Khan' means the universal ruler. In 1189, I was elected as the head of the Mongolian Clan Federation, and received the title of Genghis Khan. After unifying the Mongolian grasslands in 1204, I built the largest empire in world history.

∞ 몽골은 어떻게 역사상 가장 넓은 제국을 세울 수 있었을까요?

몽골군은 각종 전술에 능하였고 뛰어난 지휘관도 많았다. 기마술, 역참제, 이동식 집 게르는 빠른 이동과 효율적인 전투를 가능하게 하였다. 회회포(回回砲)와 같은 뛰어난 무기도 전투에 큰 역할을 하였다.

능숙한 기마술과 가지고 다니기 쉬운 식량

몽골군은 말을 타고 빠르게 이동하였는데, 말 서너 필을 같이 몰다 말이 지치면 갈아탔다. 또한 몽골군은 말 위에서 작은 활을 자유자재로 사용하였다. 말에 올라탄 상태에서 몸을 뒤쪽으로 틀어 화살을 쏠 수도 있었다. 말은 비상시에는 식량으로도 활용되었다. 몽골군은 소고기나 양고기를 말린 전투 식량인 보르츠를 말안장에 넣고 다녔는데, 이것이 우리나라에 전해져 육포가 되었다고 한다.

몸을 뒤로 틀어 활을 쏘는 몽골 기병
A Mongolian Cavalry Turns His Body Backwards and Shoot Arrows

뛰어난 전략과 공성 무기

리그니츠 전투는 몽골의 전략이 성공한 대표적인 전투이다. 몽골의 유럽 원정군은 불가리아와 러시아 등을 정복한 후 폴란드를 침공하여 유럽 연합군과 리그니츠에서 전투를 벌였다(1241). 전투가 시작되자 몽골군은 힘에 부치는 듯 퇴각하기 시작하였다. 이에 유럽 연합군의 일부가 몽골군을 추격하였다. 하지만 이것은 함정이었다. 대기하고 있던 몽골군이 유럽 연합군을 포위한 후 맹렬한 공격을 가하였고 유럽 연합군은 큰 타격을 입었다.

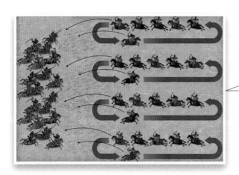

몽골군이 후퇴하는 것처럼 적을 유인하다가 교대로 화살을 쏘고 있어요. The Mongols lure the enemy out by looking as if they are retreating and then shoot arrows alternately.

몽골군의 전략
Srategy of the Mongols ⓒDick Gage

◷◷ **How Did the Mongol Empire Build the Largest Empire in History?**

The Mongols were good at various tactics and had many excellent commanders. Mounted combat, a wide network of messenger and postal stations, and mobile house Gers enabled fast movement and efficient combat. Outstanding weapons, such as Huihui trebuchet, also played a large role in battles.

Skillful Tactics of Horseback Riding and Easy to Carry Food

The Mongols moved quickly on horseback. They drove three or four horses together and changed when the horse was tired. Also, they used small bows freely when on a horse. While riding a horse, they could turn their body backwards and shoot arrows. Horses were also used as food in emergencies. They carried Borcha, which were dried beef or mutton, in their horse saddles. This food made its way to Korea and became beef jerky.

Excellent Strategy and Siege Weapons

The Battle of Liegnitz is a representative battle in which Mongolia's strategy was successful. After conquering Bulgaria and Russia, Mongolian expeditionary forces in Europe invaded Poland and fought against the European Allies in Liegnitz(1241). As the battle began, the Mongol forces began to retreat as if losing. As a result, some of the European Allied forces pursued the Mongolian army. But this was a trap. After the Mongols laying in wait surrounded the European Union forces, they launched a fierce attack and the European Union forces were severely damaged.

공성전에서 회회포를 사용하는 몽골군
Mongols Using Huihui Trebuchet in
Siege Warfare

원이 몽골 제일주의를 내세우다

원은 몽골 제일주의를 바탕으로 통치하였다. 중앙 정치는 중국의 제도를 따랐지만, 지방에는 몽골인 감찰관인 **다루가치**를 파견하여 다스렸다. 또한 몽골족과 그외 다른 민족을 4개의 계층으로 나누고 서로 다르게 대우하였다.

정치를 맡은 몽골인과 경제와 행정을 맡은 **색목인**은 지배 계급으로서 특권을 누렸다. 한인과 남인은 정치적·사회적으로 차별당하였는데, 특히 관리 선발이나 세금 부과에서 부당한 대우를 받았다.

쿠빌라이가 사망한 후 원에서는 황위 계승 분쟁이 끊이지 않았다. 또한 황실이 **라마교**를 맹신하며 사치에 빠져 심각한 재정 문제가 생겼다.

원은 경제 위기를 극복하기 위해 **교초**(원의 지폐)를 남발하였다. 그 결과 물가가 폭등하여 백성들의 불만이 커졌고 **홍건적의 난** 등 농민 반란이 일어나 원의 지배력은 급격히 약화되었다. 결국 주원장에 의해 몽골 세력은 북쪽으로 밀려났다.

··

🏵 **쿠빌라이 칸 때 원과 고려는 어떤 관계였나요?**

고려의 원종은 국가를 유지하고 풍속과 제도를 고치지 않는다는 조건으로 몽골의 쿠빌라이와 강화를 맺었다. 쿠빌라이는 자신의 딸과 고려의 태자 심(충렬왕)을 혼인시켜 원종과 사돈 관계를 맺기도 하였다. 이로써 원과 고려는 '부마국'이라는 특수한 관계를 형성하였다.

> 쿠빌라이 칸 의관은 본국(고려)의 풍속에 따르고, 모두 바꿀 필요가 없다. …… 짐(쿠빌라이 칸)은 천하를 경륜함에 있어 성의를 다하려고 애쓰니, 짐의 생각을 의심하고 두려워하지 말라.
> - 「고려사」
>
> Kublai Khan Attire depends on the customs of the country(Goryeo), and there is no need to change all of them. …… I(Kublai Khan) strive to be faithful in governing the world, so don't doubt and be afraid of my thoughts. - "History of Goryeo"

The Mongols Become the Ruling Class of the Yuan Dynasty

During the Yuan period, the Mongols made up the highest class and were always given preference over other ethnic groups. Yuan followed Chinese systems with regard to the central government, but local districts were ruled by Mongol overseers called Darugachi.

The Mongols and other ethnic groups were divided into four social classes with each class subjected to different treatment. Mongols who were in charge of politics and the Semus who were in charge of administration belonged to the ruling class and enjoyed special privileges. People from Northern China and the Southern Song Dynasty were discriminated against socially and politically and were subject to unfair treatment, particularly with regard to government official positions and taxation.

After Kublai Khan's death, disputes over succession to the throne continued in Yuan. In addition to Mongol rulers' blind favoritism of Lamaism, their indulgence in luxury created a serious financial problem.

Yuan overissued its paper money, called Jiaochao(silk note), to overcome its financial crisis. This resulted in skyrocketing inflation and growing complaints of the people until revolts by peasants, including the Red Turban Rebellion, caused the Yuan's ruling power to grow weaker. Eventually, the Mongols were pushed to the north by Zhu Yuanzhang.

....

How Was the Relationship between Yuan and Goryeo During the Period of Kublai Khan?

Wonjong of Goryeo signed a peace treaty with Kublai Kan of the Yuan Dynasty on the condition of maintaining the state and not modifying customs and institutions. Kublai Khan treated Goryeo specially by marrying his daughter to Prince Shim(King Chungnyeol of Goryeo) and establishing a relationship with Wonjong. As a result, Yuan and Goryeo established a special relationship called 'Son-in-law nation'.

유라시아 대륙이 연결되어 세계 문화 교류가 활성화되다

원대에는 초원길, 비단길, 바닷길을 이용한 동서 문명의 교류가 활발해졌다. 원은 광대한 제국의 교통망을 **역참제**로 관리하였다. 역참에서는 **패자**(통행증)를 가지고 있는 여행자에게 말과 마차, 식량, 숙소 등을 제공하며 여행을 도왔다. 역참 제도가 정비되면서 많은 상인과 여행가가 중국을 방문하였다. 이탈리아 상인 마르코 폴로는 원을 다녀간 후『**동방견문록**』을 남겼고, 모로코 출신 여행가 이븐 바투타도 중국을 방문하고『**여행기**』를 썼다.

원의 문화는 국제적이고 개방적이었다. 이슬람의 천문학과 수학 등이 전해진 후 이슬람 역법의 영향을 받아 **수시력**을 만들었고, **파스파 문자**를 만들어 몽골어와

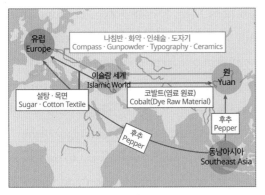

중국어를 표기하는 데 사용하였다. 라마교, 이슬람교, 크리스트교 등 다양한 종교도 들어왔다. 또한 송대의 발명품인 화약, 나침반, 인쇄술이 유럽에 전해져 신항로 개척과 종교 개혁에 영향을 주기도 하였다.

원대의 동서 문물 교류
Exchange between East and West Cultures During the Yuan Period

....

🌀 마르코 폴로는 원을 어떤 시각으로 보았나요?

육로와 수로가 모두 갖추어져 있고 교통은 사방으로 원활하게 통한다. 운하와 시내의 길은 매우 넓어서 배와 수레는 주민들에게 필요한 물건을 충분히 싣고 왕래한다. …… 다리는 높은 아치 형태로 매우 정교하게 축조되었다. 다리의 아치형 공간 아래로 돛대를 세운 배가 통과하고, 동시에 다리 위로는 수레와 말이 지나다닐 수 있다.
- 마르코 폴로,『동방견문록』

원의 복식을 한 마르코 폴로
Marco Polo in Yuan's Attire

United Eurasia Promotes a Global-scale Cultural Exchange

During the Yuan period, exchange between Eastern and Western civilizations became dynamic through the Silk Road, Sea Route, and Steppe Route. Yuan managed the transportation network of the expansive empire by installing an empire-wide network of messenger and postal stations called yizhan. Under this system, travelers who had an engraved metal pendant called 'paiza' were provided with horses, carriages, food, and shelter. The establishment of this network allowed numerous merchants and travelers to visit China. An Italian merchant named Marco Polo wrote "*The Travels of Marco Polo*" after visiting Yuan, and a Moroccan explorer called Ibn Battuta also wrote "*The Travels of Ibn Battuta*" after visiting China as well.

Yuan culture was open and global. Astronomy and mathematics were introduced to Yuan from the Islamic world, and Yuan was inspired by the Arabian calendar when it formulated a new Chinese calendar known as Shoushili. Yuan also formulated Phags-pa script and used it to write Mongol and Chinese text. A wide variety of religions were also introduced to Yuan, such as Lamaism, Islam, and Christianity. Various inventions from Song, such as gunpowder, the compass, and printing were introduced to Europe and influenced European exploration of new routes and religious reform.

....

◉ What Did Marco Polo Think of the Yuan Dynasty?

Both land routes and waterways are in place, and traffic goes smoothly in all directions. The canals and roads of downtowns are very wide, so boats and wagons come and go with enough goods for the residents. ······ The bridge is very elaborately constructed in the form of a high arch. Ships with masts can pass under the arched space of the bridge, while carts and horses can pass above the bridge.   - Marco Polo, "*The Travels of Marco Polo*"

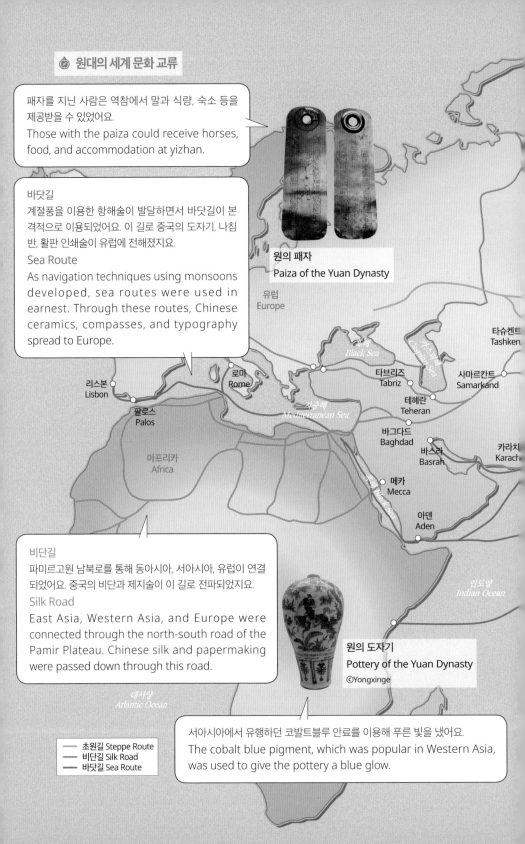

원대의 세계 문화 교류

패자를 지닌 사람은 역참에서 말과 식량, 숙소 등을 제공받을 수 있었어요.
Those with the paiza could receive horses, food, and accommodation at yizhan.

원의 패자
Paiza of the Yuan Dynasty

바닷길
계절풍을 이용한 항해술이 발달하면서 바닷길이 본격적으로 이용되었어요. 이 길로 중국의 도자기, 나침반, 활판 인쇄술이 유럽에 전해졌지요.
Sea Route
As navigation techniques using monsoons developed, sea routes were used in earnest. Through these routes, Chinese ceramics, compasses, and typography spread to Europe.

유럽
Europe

흑해
Black Sea

카스피해
Caspian Sea

타슈켄트
Tashken

타브리즈
Tabriz

사마르칸트
Samarkand

리스본
Lisbon

로마
Rome

테헤란
Teheran

팔로스
Palos

지중해
Mediterranean Sea

바그다드
Baghdad

바스라
Basrah

카라치
Karach

아프리카
Africa

홍해
Red Sea

메카
Mecca

아덴
Aden

인도양
Indian Ocean

비단길
파미르고원 남북로를 통해 동아시아, 서아시아, 유럽이 연결되었어요. 중국의 비단과 제지술이 이 길로 전파되었지요.
Silk Road
East Asia, Western Asia, and Europe were connected through the north-south road of the Pamir Plateau. Chinese silk and papermaking were passed down through this road.

원의 도자기
Pottery of the Yuan Dynasty
©Yongxinge

대서양
Atlantic Ocean

서아시아에서 유행하던 코발트블루 안료를 이용해 푸른 빛을 냈어요.
The cobalt blue pigment, which was popular in Western Asia, was used to give the pottery a blue glow.

초원길 Steppe Route
비단길 Silk Road
바닷길 Sea Route

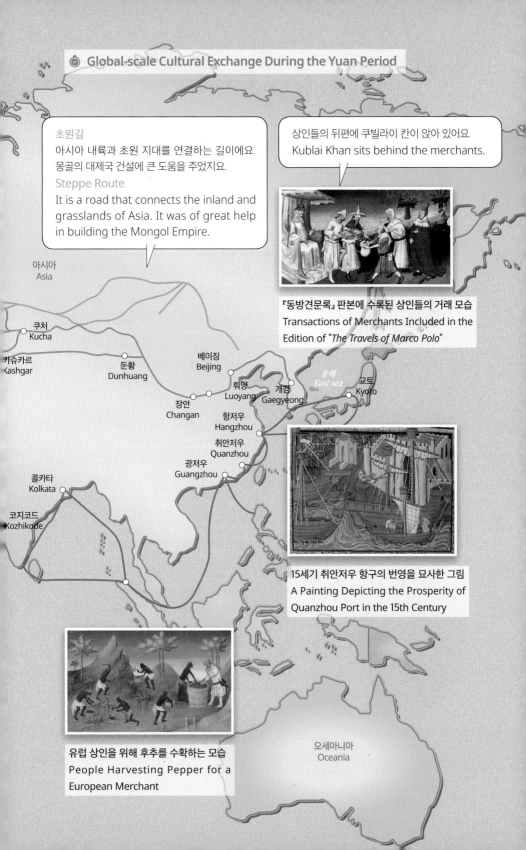

초원길
아시아 내륙과 초원 지대를 연결하는 길이에요.
몽골의 대제국 건설에 큰 도움을 주었지요.
Steppe Route
It is a road that connects the inland and
grasslands of Asia. It was of great help
in building the Mongol Empire.

상인들의 뒤편에 쿠빌라이 칸이 앉아 있어요.
Kublai Khan sits behind the merchants.

『동방견문록』 판본에 수록된 상인들의 거래 모습
Transactions of Merchants Included in the
Edition of "*The Travels of Marco Polo*"

아시아
Asia

쿠처
Kucha

카슈카르
Kashgar

둔황
Dunhuang

베이징
Beijing

뤄양
Luoyang

장안
Changan

개경
Gaegyeong

동해
East sea

교토
Kyoto

항저우
Hangzhou

취안저우
Quanzhou

광저우
Guangzhou

콜카타
Kolkata

코지코드
Kozhikode

15세기 취안저우 항구의 번영을 묘사한 그림
A Painting Depicting the Prosperity of
Quanzhou Port in the 15th Century

유럽 상인을 위해 후추를 수확하는 모습
People Harvesting Pepper for a
European Merchant

오세아니아
Oceania

동아시아 지역 질서의 변화

01 명 중심의 동아시아 질서

주원장이 명을 세우고 몽골을 몰아내다

원 황실 내의 권력 다툼과 부패로 사회가 혼란해진 가운데, 차별에 시달리던 한족은 곳곳에서 원의 지배에 저항하였다. 한족 농민 출신인 주원장(홍무제)은 **홍건적의 난**에 참여해 반란군을 이끌다가 난징을 수도로 삼아 **명**을 건국하였다(1368).

홍무제는 재상제를 폐지하여 행정 6부를 황제 직속으로 운영하고 권력을 가진 신하들을 대대적으로 숙청하는 등 모든 권력을 황제에게 집중시켰다.

또한 원의 잔재를 청산하기 위해 몽골의 풍속을 금지하고 과거제를 정비하였다. 홍무제는 향촌 조직을 정비하여 **이갑제** ^{명의 향촌 자치 행정 제도}를 실시하였다. 홍무제가 조카인 건문제에게 제위를 넘겨주자 영락제가 제위를 찬탈하였다.

💬 **영락제는 어떻게 황제가 되었나요?**

How Did the Yongle Emperor Become Emperor?

> 영락제
> 홍무제의 넷째 아들인 나는 연왕(燕王)으로 책봉된 후 베이징에 주둔하며 북원을 수비하는 역할을 하고 있었다. 그런데 홍무제가 나의 조카인 건문제를 후계자로 지명하였다. 건문제는 권력 안정을 위해 자신의 숙부들을 숙청하려고 하였고, 나는 건문제의 제위를 찬탈하여 황제로 즉위하였다(정난의 변).
> Yongle Emperor
> As Hongwu Emperor's fourth son, I was being rebuked as Prince of Yan, stationed in Beijing, and played a role in defending the Northern Yuan. By the way, Hongwu Emperor appointed my nephew, Jianwen Emperor, as his successor. Since he tried to purge his uncles for the stability of power, I was crowned emperor by usurping the throne of Jianwen Emperor(Jingnan Campaign).

2

Changing Regional Order of East Asia

01 East Asian Order Centering on Ming

Zhu Yuanzhang Establishes the Ming Dynasty and Drives Away the Mongols

As China's society turned chaotic because of rampant corruption from Yuan court officials and power struggles within the ruling class, the Han Chinese, who were suffering from discrimination, rebelled against the ruling Yuan in various parts of the land. Zhu Yuanzhang(the founder of the Ming Dynasty a.k.a. the Hongwu Emperor) was one of the Han Chinese rebels. Even though he grew up as a poor peasant, he moved up the ladder until he became the leader of the large Red Turban rebel army, made Nanjing his capital, and established the Ming Dynasty(1368).

The Hongwu Emperor abolished the Chancellor-in-Chief's post so that administrators of all six ministries of the government would report directly to the emperor. He also carried out a sweeping purge of those who had power to strengthen his own power.

Intending to eliminate all traces of the Yuan Dynasty, he banned Mongol customs and reorganized the civil service examination system that the Yuan Dynasty had abolished. The Hongwu Emperor overhauled the community organizations as well and introduced a kind of community self-monitoring system called Lijia. After Hongwu Emperor handed over the throne to his nephew Jianwen Emperor, Yongle Emperor usurped it.

> 영락제가 베이징으로 천도하면서 건설한 세계 최대 규모의 궁궐이에요.
> The Forbidden City is the world's largest palace, built by the Yongle Emperor when he moved to Beijing.

자금성(중국 베이징)
Forbidden City(Beijing, China)

명이 국제적인 위상을 드러내다

명은 제3대 황제인 **영락제** 때 전성기를 맞았다. 영락제는 베이징에 자금성을 건설하고 수도를 베이징으로 옮겼다. 유교 정치를 강화하기 위해 다양한 서적을 편찬하기도 하였다. 또한 영락제는 명의 위세를 과시하고 많은 나라들로부터 조공을 받기 위해 **정화**의 함대를 해외로 파견하였다.

정화의 함대는 1405년부터 1433년까지 7번에 걸쳐 원정에 나서 동남아시아, 인도, 아라비아, 아프리카 동부 연안 등 30여 개 나라에 진출하였다. 이는 화교외국에 사는 중국 사람가 세계 여러 지역에 진출하는 계기가 되었다.

한편 영락제 이후 명은 몽골족, 왜구 등의 침입에 시달리고, 환관이 권력을 장악하여 정치적으로도 혼란스러웠다. 명은 만주족의 침입을 방어하는 데 많은 재정을 소모하였다. 명 정부가 악화된 재정을 메꾸기 위해 많은 세금을 거두자 각지에서 농민 반란이 일어났다. 결국 명은 이자성 등이 이끌던 농민 반란으로 멸망하였다(1644).

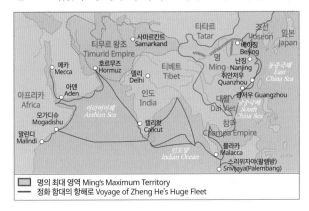

정화 함대의 항해로
Voyage of Zheng He's Huge Fleet

◉ 정화의 함대는 규모가 어느 정도였나요?

정화의 함대는 선원 2만 8천여 명, 배 62척으로 구성되었어요. 그중 가장 큰 배는 길이 138m, 폭 56m의 대형 함선이었지요. 1492년에 아메리카 대륙에 도착한 콜럼버스의 함대는 선원 88명, 배 3척으로 구성되어 있었어요. 그중 기함이자 가장 큰 배인 산타 마리아호의 크기는 길이 23m, 폭 7.5m였지요.

정화 함대의 함선(왼쪽)과 콜럼버스 함대의 산타 마리아호(오른쪽) 복원 모형

Ming Emerges as an International Superpower

Ming reached a golden age during the reign of the third emperor, known as the Yongle Emperor. The Yongle Emperor oversaw the construction of the Forbidden City and moved the capital from Nanjing to Beijing. He also commissioned scholars to write numerous books to strengthen Confucian politics. He sent admiral Zheng He's huge fleet overseas to demand tributes from many countries and to demonstrate the power of Ming.

Zheng He commanded seven expeditions between 1405 and 1433, and sailed to over 30 countries in Southeast Asia, India, Arabia, and the east coast of Africa. His expeditions provided an opportunity for the Chinese to make inroads into various regions of the world.

Meanwhile, after the period of the Yongle Emperor, Ming was raided by numerous foreign forces including the Mongols and Japanese pirates. The dynasty was also politically chaotic because eunuchs took the opportunity to seize power.

Ming spent a lot of money on defending against the invasion of the Manchus. As the Ming government collected a lot of taxes to make up for its deteriorating finances, peasant rebellions broke out in various places. Eventually, Ming collapsed in the aftermath of a rebellion led by Li Zicheng(1644).

How Big Was Zheng He's Fleet?

Admiral Zheng He's huge fleet is consisted of 28,000 sailors and 62 ships. The largest among them was a ship with a length of 138m and a width of 56m. Columbus' fleet, which arrived in the Americas in 1492, consisted of 88 sailors and 3 ships. Among them, the size of the flagship and largest ship, the Santa Maria, was 23m long and 7.5m wide.

Reconstruction of the Largest Ship of Zheng He's Huge Fleet(Left) and the Santa Maria of the Columbus Fleet(Right)

02 청 중심의 동아시아 질서

강력한 황제들이 청을 통치하다

명이 쇠약해질 무렵 **누르하치**(태조)는 만주족을 통합하여 **후금**을 건국하였다 (1616). 이어 태종은 나라 이름을 **청**으로 바꾸었다. 명이 멸망하자 청은 베이징을 점령하고 중국 전역을 지배해 나갔다. 이후 청은 약 130년간 유능한 황제들이 연 이어 등장하여 안정적으로 번성하였다.

강희제는 청의 중국 지배를 확실히 하였다. **삼번의 난**과 타이완의 반청 운동 등 각지에서 청에 반발하는 움직임이 일자 이를 진압하였다. 또한 러시아와 **네르친 스크 조약**을 맺어 청의 영역을 확실히 하였다(1689). **옹정제**는 황제권을 강화하 고, 새로운 화이사상을 제시하여 청의 중국 통치를 정당화하였다.

청은 **건륭제** 시기에 가장 넓은 영토를 확보하였다. 중국 본토와 만주, 타이완은 직할령이었고, 몽골, 티베트, 신장 등은 토착 지배자에게 어느 정도 자치를 허용하 는 번부로 삼았다.

◈ 전성기의 청과 현재의 중국 영토는 얼마나 다른가요?

청은 오늘날 중국 영토의 대부분을 확보하였다. 청은 강희제에 이어 즉위한 옹정제 와 건륭제 시기에 최전성기를 누렸는데, 이 시기를 '강건성세'라고 부른다. 130여 년에

달하는 긴 전성기를 누리는 동 안 청은 경제적·문화적으로 엄청난 발전을 이루었다. 청은 최대 전성기에 중국 북동부, 내 몽골, 외몽골, 신장과 티베트를 모두 차지하면서 현재의 중국 보다 더 넓은 영토를 차지하기 도 하였다.

명과 청, 오늘날의 영토 비교 Ming and Qing, Comparing Current Territory

02 East Asian Order Centering on Qing

Qing Ruled by Powerful Emperors

Just as Ming started to decline, Nurhaci(Taizu) united various Jurchen tribes(the later 'Manchus') and founded the Later Jin Dynasty(1616). Later, his successor Taijong changed the name of the dynasty to Qing. When Ming collapsed, Qing occupied Beijing and started ruling the entirety of Chinese territory. Later, Qing enjoyed 130 years of stability and prosperity under the reigns of powerful emperors.

By the reign of Kangxi Emperor, Qing secured China under its power. The Kangxi Emperor successfully suppressed various forces that challenged the dynasty, such as the Revolt of the Three Feudatories and Taiwan's anti-Qing movement. He also secured the Qing territory by signing a border agreement called the Treaty of Nerchinsk(1689) with Russia. The Yongzheng Emperor strengthened his royal authority and proposed a new Huayiguan to justify Qing's rule over China.

Qing secured its largest territory during the reign of the Qianlong Emperor. While mainland China, Manchu, and Taiwan were under the direct rule of the central government, Mongol, Tibet, and Xinjiang were feudatories where the residents had autonomy over their land.

⊚ How Different Is the Qing Dynasty in Its Heyday and the Current Chinese Territory?

Qing secured most of territory of China as we know it today. Qing enjoyed a heyday during the period of the Emperor Yongzheng and Qianlong, which was followed by the Kangxi Emperor. This period is called the 'High Qing era'. During this long heyday of over 130 years, Qing made tremendous economic and cultural advancements. In its heyday, Qing occupied all of China's northeastern regions, Inner Mongolia, Outer Mongolia, Xinjiang, and Tibet. It actually occupied a larger territory than it does today.

청이 한족 지배를 위해 회유책과 강경책을 쓰다

청은 만주족, 한족을 포함한 다양한 사람들이 거주하는 다민족 국가였다. 인구가 많지 않던 만주족은 한족을 지배하기 위해 회유책과 강경책을 적절히 혼용하였다. 한족을 등용하지 않던 원과는 달리 청에서는 한족 관리도 고위직에 임명될 수 있었다. 하지만 만주족의 풍습을 강요해 만주족의 옷을 입고 변발남자의 머리카락 중 앞부분만 깎고 뒷부분은 남겨 두어 길게 땋은 머리 모양을 하게 하였으며, 청을 비판하는 서적도 엄격하게 금지하였다.

청은 대내적으로는 만주족이 우위에 있는 정치 체제를 확립하고, 대외적으로는 주변국들과 조공·책봉 관계를 맺어 중국 중심의 동아시아 체제를 형성하였다.

청은 건륭제 때 최대의 번영을 이루었으나 건륭제 말기부터 쇠퇴하기 시작하였다. 인구가 급격히 증가하여 식량이 부족해지고 관리들의 부정부패가 끊이지 않아 백성들의 생활이 피폐해졌다. 그러자 큰 규모의 민란백련교의 난(1796~1804)이 일어났고, 청은 난을 진압하는 데 많은 물자와 군사력을 소모하였다. 청이 쇠약해지자 유럽의 국가들이 청을 넘보기 시작하였다.

◉ **문무를 겸비했던 강희제는 어떠한 정책을 폈나요?**

강희제(1654~1722)는 중국 역사상 가장 뛰어나다는 평가를 받는 황제 중 한 사람이다. 강희제는 수차례에 걸쳐 세금 감면을 시행하였는데, 그 결과 청의 인구가 비약적으로 증가하였다. 또한 남방을 6차례나 시찰하여 서민들의 생활을 살피고 한족들의 반감을 달랬다. 그는 청과 러시아의 국경을 정하는 네르친스크 조약을 맺기도 하였다.

강희제
재위 50주년을 기념하여 이후 태어나는 모든 남자들의 인두세를 받지 않겠다.
Kangxi Emperor
In commemoration of the 50th anniversary of my reign, all men born afterwards do not have to pay the poll tax.

Qing Turns to the Carrot and Stick Policy to Rule the Han Chinese

Qing was a multi-national dynasty inhabited by diverse ethnic groups including the Manchus and the Han Chinese. The Manchus, having a relatively small population, appropriately used both the carrot and the stick policies to contain the Hans. While the Yuan Dynasty did not recruit the Hans for government jobs, Qing allowed even the Hans to become high-level government officials. But they enforced nationalistic customs by requiring all men to cut their hair in the same hairstyle as the Manchus and wear Manchu clothing, and books that criticized Qing were strictly prohibited.

Internally, Qing established a governmental system wherein the Manchus were the ruling class, and externally, Qing established an investiture-tributary system with surrounding countries to build a Sinocentric East Asian world.

Qing reached its golden age during the reign of the Qianlong Emperor, but it was also during the last years of his reign that Qing started declining. A rapid increase in population resulted in a shortage of food, and on top of that, the endless corruption of government officials left people impoverished and devastated. Before long, people started to revolt, and Qing had to spend significant resources and military power to suppress the rebels. As Qing started to grow weaker, countries in Europe began to covet the dynasty.

💿 **What Kind of Policy Did the Kangxi Emperor, who Had both Literary and Martial Arts Experience, Pursue?**

The Kangxi Emperor(1654-1722) is one of the most prominent emperors in Chinese history. He implemented tax cuts several times, which resulted in a rapid increase in the Qing population. In addition, he visited the south six times to see the lives of the ordinary people and relieve the antipathy of the Hans. He also signed the Treaty of Nerchinsk, which established the border between Qing and Russia.

03 명·청의 경제와 문화

인구가 증가하고 상공업이 발달하다

명·청 시대에는 상공업이 발달하여 대상인들이 등장하였다. 또한 도자기, 면직업 같은 수공업이 발달하였다. 이 시기에는 의학이 발달하고 평화가 지속되어 인구가 늘었다. 인구 증가로 많은 식량이 필요해지자 창장강 중상류 지방이 새로운 곡창 지대로 개발되었다. 고구마, 옥수수, 땅콩 같은 외래 작물도 이 시기에 유입되었다.

명·청에서는 은이 화폐로 쓰였고, 세금도 은으로 냈다. 명은 **일조편법**을 시행해 토지세와 인두세를 은으로 납부하도록 하였다. 청은 **지정은제**를 실시해 인두세를 토지세에 병합하였다. 세계 각국이 중국의 비단, 도자기, 차, 예술품 등을 수입하는 대가로 은을 지급하여 중국에 은이 대량으로 유입되었다.

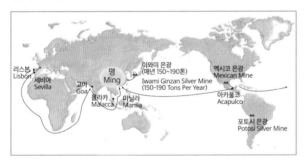

16~17세기 세계 은의 유통
Silver Circulation in the
16th-17th Century

🏵 **중국의 인구 증가가 지정은제와도 관련이 있었나요?**

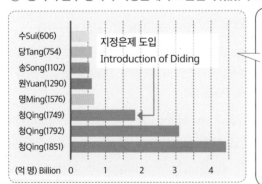

지정은제의 실시로 조세 부담이 줄어들면서 세금 때문에 호적을 올리지 않았던 사람들도 호구 등록을 하였어요. 그 결과 확인되지 않았던 인구가 드러났지요. 또한 인두세가 폐지되면서 세금 때문에 아이를 낳지 못하는 일이 없어졌어요. 그 결과 출생률이 증가하면서 중국의 인구가 급격히 늘어나게 되었답니다.

중국의 인구 변화(오금성, 『명·청 시대 사회경제사』, 2007)
Population Change of China(Oh Keum-sung, "*Socio-Economic History of Ming-Qing Times*")

03　Economy and Culture of Ming and Qing

Population Increase and the Development of Commerce

The Ming and Qing periods saw the birth of wealthy merchants due to the development of commerce. It was also during the same periods that handcraft businesses such as ceramics and textiles were developed, and the advanced medical science and long-lasting peace allowed the growth of population. Increased population translated into more food, and the middle and upper regions of the Yangtze River were developed and emerged as new granaries. At this time, people learned how to grow two crops in a year, and crops such as sweet potato, corn, and peanuts were introduced from foreign countries during the same period.

During the Ming and Qing periods, silver was used for money and people paid taxes in silver as well. The government enforced the 'Single Whip Law' which required people to pay land and poll taxes in silver. Qing reformed the tax policy and merged the land and poll taxes into one tax called 'Diding'. A massive amount of silver was flowing into China as countries around the world paid for the silk, ceramics, and tea that they imported from China in silver.

◉ **Was China's Population Growth Related to the Diding?**

As the tax burden was reduced with the implementation of the Diding (designated silver standard), even those who did not register in the civil registration due to taxes became registered as a household. As a result, the unconfirmed population was revealed. Also, with the abolition of the poll taxes, people are no longer prevented from having children because of the poll taxes. As the birth rate increased, China's population grew rapidly.

유학이 변하고 서민 문화가 발달하다

명·청 시대의 지배 계층은 **신사**였다. 이들은 전·현직 관리인 **신**(紳)과 학생이나 과거 합격자 등의 **사**(士)로 구성되었다. 신사는 유교적 소양을 갖춘 지식인 계층이었으며, 향촌의 여론을 주도하였다.

상공업이 발달하자 학문도 실용적인 방향으로 변화하였다. 명 중엽의 유학자 왕양명은 성리학이 이론적이고 형식적임을 비판하며 실천을 중시하는 **양명학**을 만들었다. 청대에는 경전을 실증적으로 연구하는 **고증학**이 발달하였다.

이 시기에는 서민들도 문화생활을 즐겼다. 역사 소설이나 기이한 이야기 등이 많이 유행하였는데,『수호전』,『삼국지연의』,『홍루몽』이 대표적이다. 소설을 출판하면서 인쇄술도 같이 발달하였다. 한편 청에서는 연극인 **경극**이 인기를 끌기도 하였다.

인물들 간의 사랑과 슬픔, 가문의 번성과 몰락을 그린 장편 소설이에요.
It is a full-length novel about love and sadness between characters, and the prosperity and fall of a family.

『홍루몽』삽화
Illustration of "*Dream of the Red Chamber*"

⚙ **양명학과 고증학의 차이점은 무엇인가요?**

왕양명(양명학)
마음이 곧 하늘이 부여한 이치이므로 아는 것을 실천하는 '지행합일'이 중요하다. 또한 인간은 본질적으로 평등하다.

고염무(고증학)
학문은 사회에서 쓸모 있는 지식을 탐구하는 것이다. 실증적으로 연구하여 증거를 구하고 사실을 밝히는 것이 중요하다.

Changes in Confucianism and Development of Popular Culture

During the Ming and Qing periods, a group called 'shenshi' constituted its elite class. They consisted of shen, who were current or former gentry or officials, and shi, who were scholars with Confucianism knowledge. They were the opinion leaders of the time and influenced rural communities.

The development of commerce shifted the focus of academic studies in a practical direction. A Neo-Confucian philosopher from the mid-Ming period, Wang Yangming, criticized the philosophy of Zhu Xi for being theoretical and systematic, and established a philosophical school named Yangmingism that focused more on action. In the Qing Dynasty, Kaozheng was developed and emphasized the importance of empirical research of classics.

During this period, the common people also enjoyed cultural life. Historical novels and strange stories such as "*Water Margin*", "*Romance of the Three Kingdoms*", and "*Dream of the Red Chamber*" were written and became popular during this period. Along with the popularity of novels came improved printing technology. In Qing, a form of Chinese opera called Peking opera became popular.

．．

◉ What Is the Difference between Yangmingism and Kaozheng?

Wang Yangming(Yangmingism)
Since the mind is the reason given by the heavens, it is important to practice what you know. Also, humans are essentially equal.

Gu Yanwu(Kaozheng)
Science is the search for useful knowledge in society. It is important to empirically research to seek evidence and reveal the facts.

04 무사가 지배하던 시대의 일본

무사 정권이 시작되다

10세기경 일본에서는 사회의 혼란으로 **무사**가 등장하였다. 무사들은 궁정, 귀족 사택, 사원, 신사의 경비를 맡았고 무사단을 조직하였으며, 귀족들의 권력 투쟁에 가담해 힘을 키웠다. 12세기 말 **미나모토노 요리토모**가 가마쿠라에 **막부** 전쟁터에서 지휘관이 머물던 집무실. 점차 무사 정권을 지칭하는 용어로 쓰임를 세우고 일본의 최고 실권자가 되었다.

이후 **쇼군**(장군)이 정치적 실권을 행사하는 일본 특유의 봉건제가 발달하였다. 무사 정권 시대는 약 700년간 지속되었다.

14세기 초반에는 **아시카가 다카우지**가 교토의 **무로마치**에 막부를 열었다. 15세기 중반부터는 무사들이 세력을 다투는 **전국 시대**가 이어져 사회가 혼란하였다.

무로마치 막부 때 아시카가 요시미쓰 장군의 별장이었어요. 그가 죽은 뒤 유언에 따라 선종 사찰로 바뀌었지요.
Kinkaku-ji was a villa of general Ashikaga Yoshimitsu. After he died, it was converted into a Zen temple by his son, according to his wishes.

긴카쿠지(금각사, 金閣寺)(일본 교토) Kinkaku-ji(Kyoto, Japan)

⚙ 전국 시대의 대표적 인물들은 어떤 특징이 있었나요?

일본 소설『대망』에는 전국 시대 지도자를 구분하는 방법으로 자주 인용되는 '울지 않는 두견새'에 대한 교훈이 있다. 오다 노부나가는 빠른 의사결정과 과감한 결단, 도요토미 히데요시는 꾀와 노력, 도쿠가와 이에야스는 인내심을 보여준다.

오다 노부다가
울지 않으면 죽일 터이다,
두견새야.

도요토미 히데요시
울지 않으면 울려 보이마,
두견새야.

도쿠가와 이에야스
울지 않으면 울 때까지 기다리마, 두견새야.

04 Japan During the Period of Rule by Warriors

The Beginning of the Warrior Government

The 10th century saw the emergence of warriors called samurai in Japan. They were in charge of guarding the royal court, estates held by noble families, Buddhist temples, or Shinto shrines, and they built their power by participating in the power struggle of the noble classes. Towards the end of the 12th century, Minamotono Yoritomo established the Shogunate in Kamakura and became the most powerful ruler in Japan.

For almost 700 years after that, a feudal system in which the shogun (general) exercised political power developed. The era of the Warrior Government lasted about 700 years.

In the early 14th century, Ashikaga Takauji established his own shogunate in Muromachi, Kyoto. Then, followed the Sengoku period beginning in the mid-15th century that was marked by political intrigue, social upheaval and extended warfare among samurai occurred.

⊚ **What Were the Characteristics Attributed to the Representative Characters of the Sengoku Period?**

In the Japanese novel "*Tokugawa Ieyasu*", there is a lesson about 'a little cuckoo that does not cry', which is often cited as a way to distinguish leaders. It can be said that Oda Nobunaga talks about quick and bold decisions, Toyotomi Hideyoshi talks about wits and hard work, and Tokugawa Ieyasu talks about patience.

Oda Nobunaga	Toyotomi Hideyoshi	Tokugawa Ieyasu
I will kill you if you don't cry.	If you do not cry, I will make you cry.	If you do not cry, I will wait until you cry.

일본을 통일한 도요토미 히데요시가 임진왜란을 일으키다

도요토미 히데요시는 100여 년 동안 계속된 전국 시대를 끝내고 일본을 통일하였다(1590). 도요토미 히데요시는 무사를 지배 계급으로 정하고 신분 이동을 금지하였으며 농민이 가지고 있는 도검을 몰수하는 등 사회 질서를 정비하였다.

도요토미 히데요시는 영토를 확장하고 무사들에게 줄 봉토를 확보하기 위해 조선을 침략하였다(임진왜란, 1592~1598). 전쟁 중에 도요토미 히데요시는 병사하였고 일본은 조선에서 패배하여 물러났다.

⊚ 일본이 임진왜란을 일으킬 수 있었던 배경은 무엇인가요?

일본은 17세기에 세계 은 생산량의 1/3을 차지하였는데, 이와미 은광은 볼리비아의 포토시 은광에 이어 세계 제2의 은 생산지로 꼽혔다. 이는 조선이 개발하고도 활용하지 못한 연은 분리법을 일본이 이용함으로써 가능하였다.

이와미 은광은 1584년 도요토미 히데요시에게 넘어갔는데, 여기서 생산된 은이 군자금으로 쓰였다. 임진왜란 때 일본이 무려 30만 대군을 일으킬 수 있었던 것도 은이 있어 가능하였다. 당시 히데요시는 "만약 명을 정복하면 일왕은 베이징에 앉히고 나는 닝보(은 무역 중심지, 현재의 저장성)로 가겠다."라고 하였다.

> 나는 나라를 다스리는 일은 내부에 맡기고, 몸소 조선에 들어가 그 군대를 선봉으로 삼아 명으로 들어갈 것이다. 그리하여 요동에서 곧장 베이징을 습격해서 그 나라를 차지하고 땅을 제군에게 나누어 줄 것이다.
> - 『일본외사』

도요토미 히데요시
Toyotomi Hideyoshi

도요토미 히데요시가 축성한 오사카성(일본 오사카)
Osaka Castle Built by Toyotomi Hideyoshi(Osaka, Japan)

Toyotomi Hideyoshi Unites Japan and Invades Korea

Toyotomi Hideyoshi put an end to the Sengoku period that lasted about a hundred years and unified Japan(1590). Toyotomi Hideyoshi carried out social reforms and made samurai the ruling class, banned social mobility, and confiscated swords owned by farmers.

Toyotomi Hideyoshi launched a war against Joseon in order to expand the territory and secure the fiefs for the warriors(Imjinwaeran, 1592–1598). During the war, Toyotomi Hideyoshi died of illness, and Japan was defeated by Joseon.

What Was the Background Behind the Japanese Invasion of the Joseon?

Japan accounted for one-third of the worlds silver production in the 17th century, and the Iwami Ginzan Silver Mine was ranked as the world's second largest silver production area after the Potosi Silver Mine in Bolivia. This was made possible by Japan's use of a Lead-silver separation method that was developed and turned away by Joseon.

Iwami Ginzan Silver Mine was passed on to Toyotomi Hideyoshi in 1584, and the silver produced there was used for military funding. It was possible because of silver that Japan was able to raise a whopping 300,000 troops during the Imjinwaeran. At the time, Hideyoshi said, "If I conquer Ming, I will leave Beijing to the Emperor and go to Ningbo(silver trading hub, now Zhejiang)."

I will entrust the task of governing the country to the inner circle, and personally go into Joseon and use the army as the spearhead and enter Ming. So, I will attack Beijing directly from Liaodong, take over the country, and distribute the land to my lads.   - "Nihon Gaishi"

도쿠가와 이에야스가 에도에 막부를 열다

도요토미 히데요시가 사망하자 **도쿠가와 이에야스**가 쇼군이 되어 오늘날의 도쿄인 **에도**에 막부를 세웠다(1603). 도쿠가와 이에야스는 쇼군이 중앙과 직할지를 다스리고 **다이묘**(영주)에게 영지를 주어 지방을 다스리게 하는 막번 체제를 구성하였다.

도쿠가와 이에야스는 다양한 방식으로 다이묘를 통제하였다. 반역의 기미가 보이면 다이묘를 교체할 수 있는 제도와 **산킨고타이 제도**를 시행하였다. 산킨고타이 제도는 지방의 다이묘가 에도와 영지를 오가며 생활하도록 한 것인데, 이로 인하여 여관, 상점 등이 늘어나 상업 활동이 활발해졌다.

에도 시대에는 '조닌'이라는 상인 계층이 성장하여 서민적이고 도시적인 **조닌 문화**가 발달하였다. 또한 대중 연극 **가부키** 서민의 애환과 사회 현실 비판 등을 다룬 일본 전통극가 유행하였고, 목판화인 우키요에, 꽃꽂이, 정원 장식 등의 예술도 발달하였다.

....

🏵 산킨고타이 제도가 무엇인가요?

산킨고타이 제도는 다이묘들이 일정 기간 수도인 에도에 머물러 근무하고, 영지로 내려갈 때는 가족들을 에도에 인질로 두고 가는 제도였다. 산킨고타이 제도를 통해 에도 막부는 다이묘들이 대규모 수행원을 이끌고 에도로 오게 하였다. 이로 인해 다이묘들이 번(행정 구역)의 재정을 소진하게 되었고, 빈곤해진 다이묘들은 막부에 도전할 수 없었다. 이 제도 덕분에 평화가 유지되었다.

도쿠가와 이에야스
다이묘의 가족들을 모두 에도에 살게 하라. 그리고 다이묘들이 반년이나 1년에 한 번 에도에 올라와 가족과 함께 지낼 수 있게 하라.
Tokugawa Ieyasu
Let all daimyos' families live in Edo. And let the daimyo come up to Edo once a year or half a year to stay with their families.

Tokugawa Ieyasu Establishes a Shogunate in Edo

When Toyotomi Hideyoshi died, Tokugawa Ieyasu became the Shogun and established a shogunate in Edo, today's Tokyo(1603). Tokugawa Ieyasu is credited with the establishment of 'bakuhantaisei', in which the shogun had direct control only over the central government and the land that was under his jurisdiction while the rest was dominated by the Daimyo (feudal lords).

Tokugawa Ieyasu controlled the daimyo in various ways. He established a policy called Sankin-Kotai that mandated daimyos to alternate living in their domain and in Edo so that he could replace daimyos at any time if treason was suspected. When the local daimyos had to travel between their domains and Edo due to Sankin-Kotai, it created a business boom with an increasing number of inns and stores.

It also gave rise to the folksy and urban Chonin culture centering on the merchant class. Some of the popular cultures that emerged and developed during this period include the classical Japanese dance-drama Kabuki, the art of woodblock print called Ukiyo-e, flower arrangement, and garden decoration.

에도 성에 모인 다이묘 일행들
Scenes of the Attendance of Daimyos at Edo Castle

What Is the Sankin-Kotai?

Sankin-Kotai was a system where daimyo stayed and worked in Edo for a certain period of time, leaving their families as hostages in Edo when going down to their territory. Through this system, the Edo shogunate led daimyo to Edo with large numbers of attendants. This caused the daimyo to run out of money in the county(administrative district) so that the poor daimyo could not challenge the shogunate. Peace was maintained thanks to this system.

05 동아시아의 교류와 화이관의 변화

해금 정책과 조공 무역을 실시하다

명은 왜구의 침입이 극심해지자 엄격한 해금 정책으로 바다를 통제하였다. 민간인의 무역을 금지하였고 조공 무역만 허용하였다. 하지만 외국 물건에 대한 수요 증가로 밀무역이 성행하자 명은 16세기 후반부터 부분적인 대외 무역을 허용하였다. 청도 초기에는 해금 정책을 폈지만 이후 일부 항구를 열어 세계 각국과 교류하였다.

동아시아 각국은 명과의 조공 무역을 통해 명 중심의 동아시아 질서 속에서 왕권의 안정과 국제적 지위를 확보하는 등 실리 외교를 펼쳤다. 조선도 명과 매년 사절을 교환하였으며, 명의 앞선 문화를 받아들이고 물품을 교역하였다.

....

◉ 명의 해금 정책은 어떤 결과를 초래하였나요?

명은 해금 정책을 펴며 외부와의 교역을 통제하였다. 그러자 대항해 시대의 주역인 포르투갈, 스페인, 네덜란드 등이 중국이 포기한 바다에 들어가 중계 무역으로 막대한 이득을 챙겼다. 반면 해금 정책으로 명에서는 밀무역이 성행하였고 왜구가 약탈을 일삼았다. 이러한 상황에서 포르투갈은 1552년 광저우만 일대의 왜구와 밀무역 상선들을 토벌하였는데, 그 대가로 마카오에 무역 거점을 확보하였다. 이후 네덜란드, 영국 등이 중국과 교역하였다. 영국은 중국, 인도 등과 교역하여 자본을 축적하였고 산업 혁명에 성공하였다. 결국 영국은 청에 무역 확대를 요구하며 아편 전쟁을 일으켰고 전쟁에서 승리하였다. 그 결과 청은 홍콩을 영국에 할양하였다.

▨ 왜구 침탈 지역 Area the Japanese Raiders Invaded

왜구의 침입 Invasion of Japanese Raiders

05 Exchange in East Asia and Changed Sino-Centrism

Introduction of the Seafaring Prohibition Policy and the Tribute Trade

When the situation became worse due to the constant attacks by Japanese pirates, the Ming dynasty enforced a series of policies called Haijin to take control of the ocean. Ming restricted private maritime trading and foreign trade was limited only to tribute missions. But when the demand for foreign products resulted in rampant smuggling activities, Ming partially allowed foreign trade beginning in the late 16th century. In the early days of Qing, it enforced the haijin policies, but later, it opened ports and traded with countries around the world.

East Asian countries engaged in practical diplomacy in which they sought to ensure the stabilization of royal authority and their international status within the East Asian order centering on Ming through tributary trade with Ming. Joseon exchanged envoys with Ming each year, and Joseon accepted Ming's advanced culture and interacted with it by exchanging goods.

✪ What Are the Consequences of the Hajin Policies?

Ming took control of trade with the outside world by implementing the hajin policy. Then, Portugal, Spain, and the Netherlands, the leaders of the era of voyage, entered the sea that China had given up and made huge profits from the intermediate trade. On the other hand, smuggling was prevalent in Ming due to the hajin policy, and Japanese raiders looted the area. Under these circumstances, Portugal subjugated Japanese raiders and smugglers in the Guangzhou Bay area in 1552. In return, Portugal established a trading hub in Macau. Later, the Netherlands and the United Kingdom traded with China. The UK accumulated capital by trading with China and India and succeeded in the Industrial Revolution. In the end, Britain started the Opium War, demanding that Qing expand its trade, and won. As a result, Qing ceded Hong Kong to England.

동아시아에 자국 중심의 화이관이 나타나다

동아시아 각국은 명이라는 문화의 중심지가 사라지자 자국 중심의 **화이관**을 새로이 설정하였다. 청이 중국 전역을 지배하자 조선은 진정한 유교 문화가 살아 있는 곳은 조선뿐이라는 화이관을 지니게 되었다. 이를 조선 중화 의식이라고 한다.

명·청 교체 이후 일본의 에도 막부는 청과 국교 관계를 맺지 않고 독립적인 세계를 만들어 나갔다. **에도 막부**는 정통성을 확보하고 청과의 대등한 관계를 내세우기 위해 독자적인 화이관을 내세웠다. 이는 **메이지 유신** 이후 천황 중심의 국가 체제를 뒷받침하는 이론적 토대가 되었다.

◈ 청에 대한 조선의 인식은 어떻게 변화하였나요?

두 차례의 호란 이후 조선에서는 청에 대한 적대감이 커졌다. 이에 임진왜란 때 우리를 도와준 명에 대하여 의리를 지키고 청에 복수하자는 북벌론이 전개되었다. 효종은 어려운 국가 재정에도 불구하고 적극적으로 북벌을 추진하였지만 군비 확충이 쉽지 않았고 민생에 어려움만을 안겨 주었다.

17세기 말 청의 국력이 크게 신장하자 조선은 청과 관계를 개선할 수밖에 없었다. 조선은 청에 연행사를 파견하고 물자도 교역하였다. 이 과정에서 청의 발달한 문물을 수용하자는 북학론이 대두하였다. 이를 통해 북학파는 조선의 문물을 발전시키고자 하였다.

박지원 청에 가보니 수레와 선박을 통한 물자의 유통이 원활했습니다. 조선도 상공업 진흥을 위해 수레와 선박을 사용하고 화폐를 널리 유통시켜야 합니다.
Park Ji-won When I went to Qing, the distribution of goods over land and sea was smooth. Vehicles and ships should be used to promote the commerce and industry of Joseon, and currency should be widely circulated.

박제가 재화는 우물과 같지요. 길어서 쓰면 물이 계속 솟아나오지만 쓰지 않으면 물이 마릅니다. 소비를 권장하여 생산을 늘려야 합니다. 또한 청과 교류하고 물품을 교역해야 합니다.
Park Je-ga Goods are like wells. If you use the water by pulling it out, the water will keep coming out, but if you don't use it, the water will dry out. Joseon should encourage consumption to increase production. It also should exchange and trade with Qing.

East Asian Countries Redefine and Establish Their Own Idea of Sino-Centrism

When the center of culture was gone with the fall of the Ming Dynasty, East Asian countries redefined Sino-centrism from their own perspectives. When the Qing Dynasty was established and ruled all Chinese territory, Joseon embraced the Sino-centric view in which it perceived Joseon as the only state that kept authentic Confucianism alive.

Even as China was going through a transition from the Ming to the Qing dynasty, the Edo Shogunate in Japan was building its own independent world without establishing diplomatic ties with the Qing Dynasty. Intending to ensure the legitimacy of the Edo Shogunate and maintain an equal relationship with Qing, Japan adopted its own Sino-centric view. This worldview became the theoretical foundation of the emperor-centered government system after the Meiji Reform.

◉ How Did Joseon's Perception of Qing Change?

Having suffered serious damage during the two invasions by the Chinese, anti-Qing sentiment grew strong in Joseon. Accordingly, a northern expedition campaign was developed to keep the loyalty to Ming, who helped us during the Imjinwaeran, and take revenge against the Qing. In spite of the difficult national finances, King Hyojong actively promoted the Northern Campaign, it was not easy to expand armaments, and it only caused difficulties in the lives of the people.

At the end of the 17th century, Joseon had no other choice but to improve relationships with Qing, which by then had grown into a super power. Joseon started making exchanges with Qing by sending missions periodically and traded goods. In this process, the 'Northern Learning' movement to accept Qing's developed civilization emerged. Through the Northern Learning, Bukhakpa(pro-Northern scholars) tried to develop Joseon's civilization.

동아시아에 유럽 문화가 전래되다

명·청 시대에는 서양의 상인들과 선교사들이 중국에서 활동하면서 서양의 문화를 소개하였다. 특히 선교사 마테오 리치가 중국 지식인과 함께 제작한 「곤여만국전도」는 중국이 세상의 중심이라고 생각하였던 중국인들에게 큰 충격을 주었다.

일본에서는 에도 막부가 선교사들의 활동을 금지하고 사무역을 통제하는 해금(쇄국) 정책을 펼쳤다. 하지만 네덜란드와 중국 상인에게는 나가사키항에서의 무역을 허용하였다. 네덜란드 상인을 통해 서양의 의학·조선술·천문학 등이 일본에 전해졌는데, 이를 토대로 난학이 발전하였다.

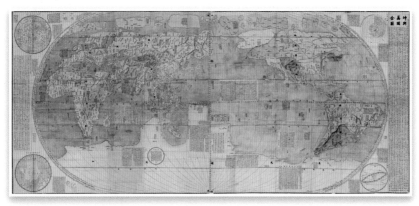

「곤여만국전도」(일본 도호쿠대학교)
'*Kunyu Wanguo Quanty*(A Map of the Myriad Countries of the World)'(Tohoku University, Japan)

◎ 난학이 일본의 근대화를 어떻게 이끌었을까요?

에도 시대에는 네덜란드를 '화란'이라고 불렀고, 네덜란드를 통해 일본에 전해진 서양의 학문을 '난학'이라 하였다. 1771년 스기타 겐파쿠는 네덜란드어로 된 해부학 책을 번역하여 『해체신서』를 완성하였다. 초기에는 의학 중심이었던 난학이 점차 여러 학문으로 다양화되었다.

이렇게 발전한 난학으로 양학(洋學)의 토대가 마련되었다. 학자들이 서구의 자본과 기술, 역사, 철학 등에 주목하면서 폐쇄적인 막부 사회를 비판하고 합리적인 정신을 갖추자는 분위기가 형성되기도 하였다. 훗날 탈아론(脫亞論)을 주장한 일본 개화기의 계몽가 후쿠자와 유키치 역시 청년 시절 난학 연구에 몰두했던 것으로 알려져 있다.

Introduction of European Culture to East Asia

During the Ming and Qing periods, merchants and missionaries from the West introduced western cultures while residing in China. A map titled 'Kunyu Wanguo Quantu', created by the Catholic missionary Matteo Ricci and Chinese intellectuals, shocked the Chinese who had thought China was the center of the world.

The Edo Shogunate in Japan prohibited missionaries and restricted maritime trade with strict sea ban policies. However, the Dutch and Chinese merchants were permitted to trade with the Japanese at Nagasaki Harbor. Western medicine, shipbuilding, and astronomy were introduced to Japan through Dutch merchants, and 'Rangaku' was able to develop based on these.

How Did Rangaku Lead the Modernization of Japan?

During the Edo period, the Netherlands was called 'Holland', and the Western learning that was passed down to Japan through the Netherlands was called 'Rangaku'. In 1771, Sugita Genpaku translated an anatomy book in Dutch and then completed the "*Kaitai Shinsho*". Rangaku, which mainly dealt with medicine, gradually diversified into various studies.

With the development of Rangaku, the foundation of Western learning was laid. As scholars paid attention to Western capital, technology, history, and philosophy, an atmosphere was formed that criticized the closed shogunate society and desired a more reasonable path. It is known that Yukichi Fukuzawa, an enlightened thinker during the Japanese enlightenment period, was also immersed in the study of Rangaku in the days of his youth.

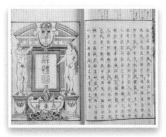

『해체신서』 *"Kaitai Shinsho"*

서아시아와 북아프리카 지역 질서의 변화

01 서아시아와 북아프리카를 이끈 이슬람 왕조

셀주크 튀르크, 이슬람 세계의 지배자가 되다

중앙아시아의 유목 민족이었던 **셀주크 튀르크**는 서아시아로 이동하며 이슬람 교를 받아들였다. 이들은 11세기경 아바스 왕조의 수도인 바그다드를 점령하여 칼리프로부터 정치적 지배자인 **술탄** 칭호를 받고 이슬람 세계의 새로운 지배자로 등장하였다.

셀주크 튀르크의 영역 Territory of the Seljuk Turks

셀주크 튀르크는 서아시아와 중앙아시아 지역을 점령하고 비잔티움 제국을 압박하였다. 하지만 예루살렘 정복으로 크리스트교 세계의 공격을 받았고 왕위 계승 문제로 내부 분열이 일어나 국력이 약해졌다. 13세기 중반에는 몽골군의 침입으로 쇠퇴하였다.

◉ 셀주크 튀르크와 오스만 튀르크는 어떻게 생겨났을까요?

중앙아시아의 초원 지대에서 살았던 유목 민족에는 훈족, 튀르크족, 몽골족 등이 있다. 훈족이 4세기 말 서쪽으로 이동하면서 게르만족의 대이동이 시작되었다.

6세기 경 부민 카간의 지도하에 돌궐이 몽골 초원의 강자로서 유연을 계승(552)하여 중앙아시아에서 급속히 영토를 확장하였다. 터키 공화국은 552년을 건국의 해로 본다.

튀르크는 초원 지대를 통일하였지만, 곧 서튀르크와 동튀르크로 분열되었다. 서튀르크는 비잔티움 제국과 교류하며 계속 발전하였는데, 그중 일부는 서쪽으로 계속 이동하여 이후 셀주크 튀르크와 오스만 튀르크를 세웠다. 현재까지도 튀르크족은 중앙아시아 및 서아시아의 주류 민족으로 살아가고 있다.

Changes in the Regional Order in West Asia and North Africa

01 Islamic Empire, the Leader of West Asia and North Africa

The Seljuk Turk Empire Becomes the Ruler of the Islamic World

The Seljuk Turks were originally a nomadic tribe inhabiting Central Asia, but they converted to Islam when they moved to Western Asia. Around the 11th century, they occupied Baghdad, the capital city of the Abbasid Dynasty, and received the title of Sultan, which means rulership, from the caliph and emerged as the new rulers of the Islamic world.

The Seljuk Turks occupied Western and Central Asian regions and posed a threat to the Byzantine Empire. But their power grew weaker after they took control of Jerusalem and were attacked by Christian forces because of it. They also faced decline due to internal conflicts over the throne. Eventually, they were overthrown by the invading Mongols in the mid-13th century.

How Did the Seljuk Turks and the Ottoman Turks Come About?

The nomadic tribes that lived in the grasslands of Central Asia include the Huns, Turks, and Mongols. As the Huns moved westward in the late 4th century, the Germanic migration began.

Under the leadership of Bumin Qaghan the First Turkic Khaganate succeeded the Rouran Khaganate as the hegemonic power of the Mongolian Plateau(552) and rapidly expanded its territories in Central Asia. The Republic of Turkey considers 552 the year of its founding.

The Turks unified the grasslands, but soon split into West Turk and East Turk. Western Gokturks continued to develop through exchanges with the Byzantine Empire. Some of them continued to move west, later establishing the Seljuk Turks and the Ottoman Turks. To this day, the Turks still live as the mainstream people of Central and Western Asia.

다양한 이슬람 왕조가 발전하다

13세기 중반 칭기즈 칸의 손자인 **훌라구**는 바그다드를 점령하고 아바스 왕조를 멸망시켰다. 이후 현재의 이란 지역을 기반으로 **일한국**을 건국하고 이슬람교를 받아들였다. 이들은 중계 무역의 이득을 누리며 이슬람과 페르시아의 문화를 바탕으로 번영을 누렸으나 내부 분열로 쇠퇴하다가 멸망하였다.

14세기 후반 칭기즈 칸의 후손이라 주장한 티무르가 등장하여 서아시아와 중앙아시아에 걸친 **티무르 왕조**를 건설하였다. 티무르 왕조의 수도인 **사마르칸트**는 동서 교역로의 중심에 위치하여 중계 무역으로 번영하였다. 하지만 티무르 왕조는 티무르가 명 원정 도중 사망한 후 점차 약화되어 멸망하였다.

16세기 초 이란 지역에서는 페르시아 문화를 기반으로 한 **사파비 왕조**가 건국되었다. 사파비 왕조는 시아파 이슬람을 믿으며 수니파 이슬람 국가들과 경쟁하였다. 또한 상업을 장려한 사파비 왕조는 막대한 경제력으로 수도 **이스파한**을 건설하였는데, 왕조의 전성기에 이스파한은 '세계의 절반'이라 불리며 번영하였다.

티무르 왕조의 최대 영역
Timur Empire's Maximum Territory
티무르의 진출 방향
Direction of the Timur's Expansion

티무르 왕조의 영역 Area of the Timur Empire

....

💧 **티무르가 사마르칸트를 수도로 정한 이유는 무엇일까요?**

Why Did Timur Make Samarkand the Capital?

중앙아시아에서 가장 오랜 역사를 지닌 도시 중 하나인 사마르칸트를 수도로 삼겠다. 고대부터 무역으로 번영한 사마르칸트는 천문학을 비롯한 다양한 학문이 발달하였고 문화 역시 최고 수준에 도달하였다.
I will make Samarkand, one of the oldest cities in Central Asia, as its capital. Samarkand, which has flourished in trade since ancient times, has been a city flush with various studies, including astronomy. The city's culture reached its zenith.

두개골을 토대로 복원한 티무르 흉상
Timur Bust Restored from a Skull ©Shakko

Emergence of Diverse Islamic Empires

In the mid-13th century, Genghis Khan's grandson, Hulagu Khan, captured Baghdad and brought down the Abbasid Dynasty. Later, he founded the Il-Khan Dynasty based in today's Iran and converted to Islam. The Il-Khan Dynasty was built on a mix of Islamic and Persian cultures, and it thrived on profits from intermediate trade until it declined and came to an end due to internal conflict.

In the late 14th century, Timur, who considered himself a true descendant of Genghis Khan, founded the Timur Empire, whose territory covered Western Asia and Central Asia. Its capital city, Samarkand, thrived on the trade that passed through the city because it was located in the middle of the west-east trading route. But the Timur Dynasty gradually weakened after Timur was killed during an expedition to Ming and eventually collapsed.

In the early 16th century, the Safavid Dynasty was founded in Persia, a land that is now called Iran. The Safavid Dynasty established Shia Islam as the official religion and competed with Sunni Islamic empires. The Safavid Dynasty encouraged commerce and built its capital in Isfahan, which flourished so greatly that during its peak, the city was called 'half of the world'.

레기스탄 광장에는 사원과 마드라사(이슬람 신학교)가 있어요.
In Registan Square, there are mosques and madrasas(Islamic institutions of learning).

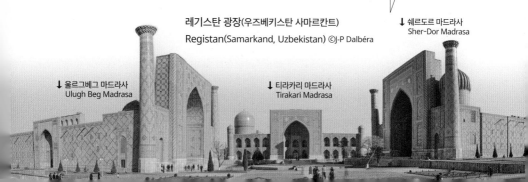

레기스탄 광장(우즈베키스탄 사마르칸트)
Registan(Samarkand, Uzbekistan) ©J-P Dalbéra

↓ 쉐르도르 마드라사
Sher-Dor Madrasa

↓ 울르그베그 마드라사
Ulugh Beg Madrasa

↓ 티라카리 마드라사
Tirakari Madrasa

이집트 지역에 강력한 이슬람 왕조들이 들어서다

7세기 중반 비잔티움 제국의 지배하에 있던 이집트 지역은 이슬람에 의해 점령되었다. 10세기 후반에는 **파티마 왕조** 현재의 튀니지 지역에서 건국가 이집트 지역을 점령하였다. 파티마 왕조는 시아파 이슬람을 신봉하여 수니파의 아바스 왕조와 경쟁하며 번영을 구가하였다. 하지만 종교 탄압으로 인한 내부 분열과 반란으로 쇠퇴하기 시작하여 12세기 후반 쿠르드족 쿠르디스탄 지방에 사는 유목 민족 출신 장군인 **살라딘**에 의해 멸망하였다.

살라딘은 노예 출신 군인들인 맘루크를 이용하여 **아이유브 왕조**를 건국한 후 예루살렘을 정복하였다. 이를 계기로 서유럽과 아이유브 왕조가 충돌하였다(제3차 십자군 전쟁). 하지만 아이유브 왕조는 맘루크에 지나치게 의존하다 결국 맘루크의 반란으로 멸망하였다.

맘루크 왕조는 북아프리카로 진출하려는 몽골군을 격퇴하였고 크리스트교 세

력과의 전쟁에서도 승리하였다. 몽골에 의해 아바스 왕조가 멸망한 후 칼리프는 맘루크 왕조로 이주하였고 맘루크 왕조는 이슬람 세계의 보호자 역할을 하며 번영을 누렸다. 하지만 16세기 맘루크 왕조를 포함한 북아프리카의 왕조들은 대부분 오스만 제국에 의해 점령당하였다.

맘루크 왕조의 영역 Territory of the Mamluk Dynasty

....

◉ 정복자 살라딘이 유럽인들에게 너그러운 사람이라는 칭송을 받은 이유는 무엇인가요?

살라딘
나는 이슬람 세계와 십자군의 싸움에서 예루살렘을 되찾았다. 예루살렘 정복 후에도 크리스트 교도들을 풀어 주었고, 크리스트 교도들에 대한 폭행이나 학살 등을 철저히 금지하였다. 이 때문에 나는 유럽 사람들로부터 '자비롭고 너그러운 사람'이라는 칭송을 받기도 하였다.

Powerful Islamic Empires Establish in Egypt

Egypt was part of the Byzantine Empire until it was conquered by Muslims in the mid-7th century. Then in the late 10th century, it was occupied by the Fatimid Caliphate. The Fatimid Caliphate was part of the Shia dynasty and enjoyed prosperity while competing with the Sunni Abbasid Caliphate. However, it started declining due to religious persecution, internal conflict, and rebellions until it was brought to an end by a Kurdish warrior named Saladin in the late 12th century.

Saladin founded the Ayyubid Dynasty by using slave soldiers called 'Mamluks' and occupied Jerusalem, which led to collusion between West Europe and the Ayyubid Dynasty(The third Crusade). But the Ayyubid Dynasty depended on the Mamluks too much and came to an end when the Mamluks rebelled against it.

The Mamluk Dynasty defeated the Mongols who were trying to invade North Africa and also expelled Christian forces after winning in the crusade as well. After the Abbasid Caliphate was brought down by the Mongols, its caliph moved to the Mamluk Dynasty during the time when the Mamluk Dynasty enjoyed prosperity as protector of the Islamic world. But most of the northern African dynasties, including the Mamluk, were conquered by the Ottoman Empire in the 16th century.

....

◉ Why Was Saladin Hailed as a Generous Man after the Conquest of Jerusalem?

> Saladin
> In the battle between the Islamic world and the Crusades, I reclaimed Jerusalem. Even after the conquest of Jerusalem, I released the Christians and strictly prohibited assault or massacre against the Christians. So I was praised by Europeans as 'the most generous man of all time'.

02 오스만 제국의 성립과 발전

오스만, 제국으로 성장하다

몽골의 침입으로 셀주크 튀르크가 약화되고 이후 오스만족이 소아시아 지역에 나라를 건국하였다(1299). 오스만 제국은 영토를 확장하며 발전을 거듭하였지만 티무르 왕조와의 전쟁 앙카라 전투(1402)에 패해 큰 위기에 빠지기도 하였다. 하지만 다시 부흥하여 1453년 콘스탄티노폴리스를 점령하고 비잔티움 제국을 정복하였다. 오스만 제국은 콘스탄티노폴리스를 수도로 삼고 이스탄불이라고 불렀다.

이후 오스만 제국은 이집트를 점령하였고, 오스만 제국의 술탄은 칼리프의 칭호까지 이어받아 **술탄·칼리프** 세습 군주·이슬람 국가의 최고 종교 지도자라 불리며 이슬람 세계

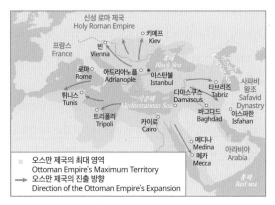

의 정치와 종교를 지배하였다. 오스만 제국은 유럽 및 아프리카, 중앙아시아 지역으로 세력을 넓히며 대제국을 건설하였다.

오스만 제국의 영역
Territory of the Ottoman Empire

◉ **오스만 제국이 콘스탄티노폴리스를 점령할 수 있었던 이유는 무엇인가요?**

오스만 제국의 제7대 술탄이었던 메흐메트 2세는 1453년에 비잔티움 제국의 콘스탄티노폴리스를 공격하였다. 하지만 천혜의 요새인 이 도시를 공략하기는 쉽지 않았다.

오스만 제국은 비잔티움 군대의 허를 찌르기 위해 수십 마리의 소를 이용하여 72척의 배를 언덕 반대편으로 옮겼고, 헝가리 기술자가 만든 8m에 달하는 대포 등을 이용하였다. 결국 두 달 만에 비잔티움 제국의 천년 수도인 콘스탄티노폴리스는 오스만 제국에 점령당하였다.

콘스탄티노폴리스 공격을 준비하는 메흐메트 2세
Mehmed Ⅱ Prepares for an Assault on Constantinople

02 Establishment and Growth of the Ottoman Empire

The Ottomans Build a Great Empire

When the Seljuk Turks grew weaker after being invaded by the Mongols, the Ottoman tribe established an empire in the Asia Minor region(1299). The Ottoman Empire occupied the Anatolian Peninsula and continued growing its influence, but it also experienced a crisis after being defeated in a war against the Timur Empire. It subsequently experienced a revival, occupied Constantinople in 1453, and went on to conquer the Byzantine Empire. The Ottoman Empire made Constantinople its capital city and renamed it to Istanbul.

After occupying Egypt, the Ottoman Empire received the title of Caliph and dominated the politics and religion of the Islamic world as both their Sultan and Caliph. The Ottomans built a great empire by expanding their power to Europe, Africa, and Central Asia.

◉ Why Was the Ottoman Empire Able to Conquer Constantinopole?

Mehmet II, the seventh sultan of the Ottoman Empire, attacked Constantinopole in the Byzantine Empire in 1453. However, it was not easy to attack this city, a heavenly fortress.

The Ottoman Empire transported 72 ships to the other side of the hill by using dozens of cattle to catch the Byzantine army off guard, and used 8 m of artillery made by Hungarian engineers. In the end, within two months, Constantinopole, the millennium capital of the Byzantine Empire, was occupied by the Ottoman Empire.

술레이만 1세, 제국의 전성기를 이끌다

오스만 제국은 술레이만 1세 때 전성기를 맞이하였다. 그는 헝가리를 정복하고 당시 유럽의 가장 강력한 세력이었던 합스부르크가의 오스트리아 빈을 포위 공격하였다. 또한 로마 교황과 에스파냐 등의 연합 함대를 격파하여 지중해의 해상권을 장악하였고, 이를 바탕으로 동서 무역을 독점하여 전성기를 누렸다.

오스만 제국은 1571년 **레판토 해전**에서 에스파냐에 패하였지만 영향력은 계속 유지되어 이스탄불은 국제 무역의 중심 도시 역할을 수행하였다.

오스만 제국은 17세기 말에 다시 한번 빈을 포위 공격하였지만 실패하였고, 관료와 군인들의 부패로 점차 쇠퇴의 길로 접어들었다. 오스만 제국이 흔들리자 서양 세력이 침입하기 시작하였다.

레판토 해전(런던 국립해양박물관)
Battle of Lepanto(National
Maritime Museum, London)

🧭 **오스만 제국이 강대국이 될 수 있었던 이유는 무엇인가요?**

오스만 제국은 다른 민족과 종교를 포용하였다. 비이슬람교도라도 인두세만 납부하면 밀레트라는 종교 자치 공동체를 구성하여 생활할 수 있었다. 또한 비이슬람교도 및 노예 중에서도 능력이 뛰어나면 중요한 관직에 등용하였다.

한편 오스만 제국은 정복지의 크리스트교도 청소년들을 뽑아 이슬람교도로 개종하게 한 후 예니체리(술탄의 친위 부대)나 관료로 육성하였다. 이러한 청년 징병 제도를 '데브쉬르메'라고 한다. 예니체리는 제국의 핵심 부대로 활약하며 막강한 권력을 얻기도 하였다.

Suleiman I and the Golden Age of the Ottoman Empire

The Ottoman Empire was in its golden age during the reign of Suleiman I. He conquered Hungary and went on to attack and lay siege to the capital of the Habsburg Empire, Vienna. He also dominated the seas around the Mediterranean by defeating the allied fleet of Spain and the papacy, which allowed his empire to prosper by monopolizing east–west trade.

He was defeated at a naval engagement with Spain known as Battle of Lepanto in 1571, but the influence of the Ottoman Empire was still so great that its capital city, Istanbul, became the hub of international trade.

The Ottoman Empire once again besieged Vienna at the end of the 17th century but failed, and the corruption of bureaucrats and soldiers gradually led to a decline. As the Ottoman Empire began declining, Western forces invaded.

사람의 운명을 결정하는 것은 출신과 신분이 아니고 바로 능력입니다.
It is not the origin and status that determines a person's fate, but the ability.

예니체리 Janissary

🔘 What Made the Ottoman Empire a Powerful Nation?

The Ottoman Empire embraced other people and religions. Even non–Muslims could live in a religious autonomous community called a Millet by paying poll taxes. In addition, among non–Muslims and slaves, if they were capable, they were appointed to important offices.

Meanwhile, the Ottoman Empire recruited Christian youths from conquered lands to convert them to Muslims and raised them as Janissary(Sultan's guards) or bureaucrats. This youth conscription system was called 'Devshirme'. Janissary served as the core unit of the empire and gained great power.

다양성을 바탕으로 문화를 발전시키다

오스만 제국은 정복지의 주민에게 이슬람교로 개종할 것을 강요하지 않았다. 대신 인두세를 납부하면 각자의 종교 공동체를 만들어 자치를 할 수 있도록 허용하였다. 또한 튀르크족이 아니어도 능력에 따라 중요한 관직에 임명하는 등 개방적이고 관용적인 정책을 실시하였다. 이에 오스만 제국에는 다양한 민족과 종교가 공존하였다.

이러한 정책의 영향을 받아 이슬람, 튀르크, 페르시아, 비잔티움 문화가 융합된 오스만 튀르크 문화가 발달하였다. 수도인 이스탄불에서는 다양한 종교와 민족들이 어우러져 술탄 아흐메트 사원이 건설되는 등 문화적 발전이 이루어졌다.

오스만 제국은 아시아, 유럽, 아프리카 세 대륙을 연결하는 무역의 요충지에 위치하였다. 이에 따라 오스만 제국은 바다뿐만 아니라 육지에서도 중심지 역할을 하며 동서 무역을 주도하였다. 오스만 제국의 수도인 이스탄불은 항상 각지에서 온 상인과 물자들로 가득하였고, 이 때문에 바자르 _{페르시아어로 '시장'을 뜻하는 단어로, 흔히 이슬람 세계의 시장을 지칭함}는 세계의 시장이라 불리기도 하였다.

15세기 후반부터 19세기 중엽까지 술탄이 살았던 궁전이에요. 현재는 박물관으로 운영되고 있어요.
This is the palace where the Sultan lived from the late 15th century to the middle of the 19th century. Currently, it operates as a museum.

6세기 중반 유스티니아누스 황제 때 조성된 성당이에요. 오스만 제국의 정복 이후에는 내부 장식을 바꾸고 4개의 첨탑을 세워 모스크로 활용하였지요.
It is a cathedral built during Justinian the Great's reign in the mid-6th century. After the conquest of the Ottoman Empire, the interior decoration was changed and four spiers were built so it could be used as a mosque.

❶ 톱카프 궁전 Topkapi Palace Museum
©Faraways

❷ 성 소피아 성당 Cathedral of Hagia Sophia ©Robster1983

The Development of Cultures that Embraced Diverse Religions and Ethnic Groups

Even though the Ottoman Empire was a Muslim dynasty, people were free to create and run their own religious communities as long as they paid the poll tax. Its open, tolerant policy allowed even non-Turkic people to be appointed to important government jobs depending on their capabilities. Accordingly, the Ottoman Empire was a melting pot of diverse ethnic groups and religions.

These policies contributed to the development of the Ottoman-Turkic culture that was fused with the Islamic, Persian, and Byzantine cultures. Its capital city of Istanbul also saw the development of cultures that embraced diverse religions and ethnic groups, such as can be seen in the construction of the Sultan Ahmed Mosque.

The Ottoman Empire was located at the heart of the trade route that connected the three continents of Asia, Europe, and Africa. As a result, the Ottoman Empire was able to spearhead east-west trade while playing a central role not only in the sea but also on the land trade routes. The capital city of Istanbul was constantly bustling with merchants and goods from various regions, and the Grand Bazaar in the city was called the market of the world.

터키에서 가장 아름다운 건축물로 손꼽히는 모스크입니다. 성 소피아 성당을 기본으로 삼아 건축하였지요. 일반적으로 모스크에는 4개의 첨탑이 있는데 블루 모스크에는 6개의 첨탑이 있어요.

It is one of the most beautiful buildings in Turkey. It was built on the basis of the Church of Hagia Sophia. Typically, there are 4 spires in a mosque, but there are 6 spiers in the Blue Mosque.

❸ 술탄 아흐메트 사원(블루 모스크) Sultan Ahmed Mosque(The Blue Mosque)

이스탄불 전경(Panoramic View of Istanbul)

4

신항로 개척과 유럽 지역 질서의 변화

01 신항로 개척과 유럽 지역 질서의 변화

유럽이 새로운 항로 개척에 나서다

지중해 무역이 활발해지면서 **향신료**, 도자기, 비단 등이 유럽에서 크게 인기를 끌었다. 하지만 이러한 물품은 이탈리아 상인과 이슬람 상인이 독점하여 비싼 가격에 거래되었다. 이에 유럽인들은 동방과 직접 교역을 하여 많은 이익을 남기고자 하였다. 당시 유럽에서는 지리학과 천문학의 보급으로 **항해술**이 발달하였고 **나침반**이 항해에 이용되면서 먼 거리 항해가 가능하였다. 또한 마르코 폴로가 쓴 『**동방견문록**』이 유럽인들의 호기심을 자극하였다.

지중해 서쪽에 위치하여 향신료 무역에서 소외되었던 포르투갈과 에스파냐는 국가가 나서서 신항로 개척을 지원하였다. 포르투갈의 후원을 받은 **바르톨로메우 디아스**는 아프리카 남쪽 끝의 희망봉까지 가는 데 성공하였고(1488), 에스파냐의 후원을 받은 **콜럼버스**는 대서양을 건너 아메리카 대륙의 서인도 제도에 도착하였다(1492). 포르투갈 항해가인 **바스쿠 다 가마**는 희망봉을 돌아 인도의 캘리컷에 도착하였다(1498). **마젤란**이 이끄는 에스파냐 함대는 태평양을 가로질러 세계 일주에 성공하였다(1522).

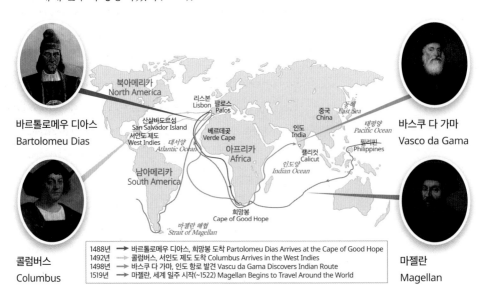

바르톨로메우 디아스
Bartolomeu Dias

바스쿠 다 가마
Vasco da Gama

콜럼버스
Columbus

마젤란
Magellan

1488년	→	바르톨로메우 디아스, 희망봉 도착 Partolomeu Dias Arrives at the Cape of Good Hope
1492년	⇢	콜럼버스, 서인도 제도 도착 Columbus Arrives in the West Indies
1498년	→	바스쿠 다 가마, 인도 항로 발견 Vascu da Gama Discovers Indian Route
1519년	→	마젤란, 세계 일주 시작(~1522) Magellan Begins to Travel Around the World

Discovery of New Routes and the Changing Order of European Regions

01 Discovery of New Routes and the Changing Order of European Regions

Europe Sets off on the Journey to Discover New Routes

Dynamic Mediterranean trade made spices, pottery, and silk widely popular in Europe. But these items were traded at high prices because they were monopolized by Italian and Muslim merchants. Therefore, the Europeans wished to trade them directly with Eastern countries and make a profit from them. At the time, long voyages were made possible due to advanced geographic and astronomical knowledge and the use of the compass, all of which resulted in the further development of navigation skills. On top of that, Marco Polo's book "*The Travels of Marco Polo*" was enough to make Europeans curious about Far Eastern countries.

Portugal and Spain were two countries that were excluded from spice trading because they were located in the west of the Atlantic Ocean. These two countries took the lead in the exploration of new sea routes. Portugal supported Bartolomeu Dias who successfully established a sea route and arrived at the Cape of Good Hope in South Africa(1488), while Spain supported Christopher Columbus, who completed voyages across the Atlantic Ocean and arrived at the West Indies in America as well(1492). A Portuguese explorer named Vasco da Gama sailed around the Cape of Good Hope in Africa and reached Calicut, India(1498). Ferdinand Magellan and his Spanish fleet sailed across the Pacific Ocean, and his successful circumnavigation of the world proved that world was round(1522).

신항로 개척을 계기로 대서양 삼각 무역이 형성되다

신항로가 개척되면서 유럽의 무역 중심지가 지중해에서 대서양으로 이동하였다. 이로 인해 지중해 연안의 이탈리아 도시 국가들과 오스만 제국이 쇠퇴하고, 포르투갈과 에스파냐는 번영을 누렸다. 무역의 형태는 아메리카 토착 문명 정복을 계기로 변하였다. 에스파냐의 코르테스가 멕시코고원의 아스테카 제국을 정복하고, 피사로는 안데스산맥 일대의 잉카 제국을 정복하였다.

원주민들은 금 · 은 채굴과 사탕수수 · 담배 재배에 동원되어 착취당하였다. 게다가 천연두, 홍역 등 전염병이 퍼져 면역력이 없던 수많은 원주민이 사망하였다. 이에 유럽 상인들은 아프리카에서 무기나 면제품과 교환한 노예를 아메리카에 팔아 부족한 노동력을 제공하였다.

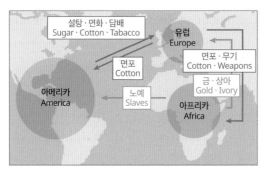

아메리카에서는 설탕, 담배, 감자 등을 유럽으로 들여와 막대한 이익을 남겼다. 그 결과 유럽, 아프리카, 아메리카를 연결하는 대서양 삼각 무역이 형성되었다.

대서양 삼각 무역 Atlantic Triangular Trading System

··

⚙ 대서양 삼각 무역으로 아메리카와 아프리카는 어떻게 변화하였나요?

아메리카 대륙에서 금과 은만을 가져가던 유럽인들은 더 많은 이득을 얻기 위해 다른 대륙의 특산품들을 아메리카 대륙에 옮겨 심어 거대한 농장을 건설하였다. 그리고 노동력을 충당하기 위해 아프리카에서 노예들을 데려왔다. 그러자 아프리카 대륙에서는 노예 유출로 노동 인구가 급감하여 생산성이 떨어졌고, 다른 부족을 노예로 팔아넘기기 위해 부족 간 전쟁이 빈번하게 일어났다. 한편 아메리카 대륙 역시 사탕수수, 담배 등 상품 작물 위주의 농업에 치중하여 경제의 해외 의존도가 높아졌다.

노예 무역선에 실린 아프리카 노예 African Slaves who Had to Endure Long Voyages Trapped in Slave Ships

Discovery of New Routes Creates the Atlantic Triangular Trade

After the establishment of new sea routes, the center of European trade moved from the Mediterranean to the Atlantic. This resulted in the decline of the Italian cities on the shores off the Mediterranean and the Ottoman Empire, and the prosperity of Portugal and Spain. The trade situation took a turn in the aftermath of the American conquests. The Spanish conquistador Hernan Cortes overthrew the Aztec Empire in Mexico, while a Spanish conquistador, Francisco Pizzaro Gonzalez, conquered the Inca Empire.

The natives of the conquered empires were mobilized and exploited to mine gold and silver or to grow sugar cane and tobacco. Countless natives also died after contracting contagious diseases such as smallpox and measles, to which they had no immunity. European merchants responded to the shortage of labor forces that followed by bringing in goods such as weapons and cotton to Africa in exchange for slaves and selling them to America.

Merchants made great profits by exporting the sugar, tobacco, potatoes, and other goods to Europe. The result was the establishment of the Atlantic Triangular Trading System that connected Europe, Africa, and America.

....

⊚ How Were the America and Africa Changed by the Atlantic Triangular Trading System?

Europeans, who only took gold and silver from the Americas, built huge farms by transferring specialties from other continents to the Americas to gain even more profit. Slaves were brought from Africa to the Americas to cover the labor force. Then, on the African continent, the labor force fell sharply due to the outflow of slaves, resulting in a decrease in productivity, and frequent wars between tribes to sell other tribes as slaves. Meanwhile, the Americas also focused on the production of commodity crops such as sugar cane and tobacco, and the economy's dependence on foreign countries increased.

신항로 개척 이후 유럽이 가격 혁명과 상업 혁명을 겪다

신항로 개척 이후 동방의 향신료, 비단, 차 등이 유럽 지역에 대량으로 수입되고 아메리카 대륙의 담배, 감자, 옥수수 등의 작물이 들어오면서 유럽인의 생활은 크게 변화하였다. 그리고 아메리카로부터 막대한 양의 금과 은이 유입되어 유럽의 물가도 크게 올랐다. 이러한 **가격 혁명**으로 제조업과 상업이 성장하였지만, 임금을 받던 노동자와 토지세를 화폐로 받던 귀족은 몰락하였다.

아프리카와 아시아로부터 값싼 원료가 들어오고 해외 시장이 확대되면서 상공업과 금융업도 비약적으로 발전하였다. 이에 힘입어 주식회사와 같은 근대적 기업이 나타나면서 근대 자본주의가 발달하였다. 이를 **상업 혁명**이라고 한다.

🌀 아메리카에서 유럽으로 전래된 작물은 무엇인가요?

감자 감자는 초창기에 항해 식량이나 가축 사료로 활용되었어요. 저온에서도 잘 자라고 단기간에 많은 수확이 가능하였기 때문에 급속도로 전 유럽에 전파되었지요.

감자 먹는 사람들(고흐) The Potato Eaters(Gogh)

카카오 카카오는 초콜릿의 원료예요. 코르테스가 아스테카인들이 카카오를 갈아 만들어서 즐기던 음료를 맛보고 유럽에 소개하였어요. 이것이 에스파냐의 귀족과 부유층을 중심으로 확산되다가 17세기 중반에는 유럽 전역으로 퍼졌어요.

카카오 열매를 들고 있는 아스테카인 조각상 Aztec Statue Holding a Cacao Bean

옥수수 1492년 아메리카 사람들이 옥수수를 재배하는 것을 본 콜럼버스가 옥수수 종자를 에스파냐로 가지고 가서 유럽에서도 재배하기 시작하였어요. 옥수수는 짧은 기간에 수확이 가능하고, 토질, 수질의 영향을 덜 받으며 별다른 관리 없이도 잘 자랐기 때문에 유럽인들의 사랑을 받았지요.

아스테카의 옥수수 재배 안내서 Aztec Maize Agriculture as Depicted in the Florentine Codex

마추픽추(페루) Machu Picchu(Peru)

Discovery of New Routes Lead to Price and Commercial Revolution in Europe

The new routes brought about significant changes to the lives of Europeans because massive amounts of spices, silk, and tea were imported and crops such as tobacco, potatoes, and corn were introduced from the American continent. Europe also experienced serious inflation because a massive amount of silver and gold also came in from America. This Price evolution helped manufacturing and commercial industries grow but it brought down the noble class who used to collect land tax in currency and the labor class who used to live on wages.

Cheap materials coming from Africa and Asia along with expanding markets overseas resulted in the remarkable growth in commerce and financial services. This development was followed by the emergence of a modern form for companies such as corporations and modern capitalism. This series of changes is called the Commercial revolution.

⊚ What Crops Were Brought to Europe from America?

Potatoes Potatoes were initially used as food for sailors and livestock. They grew well at low temperatures and workers were able to harvest a lot in a short period of time, so they spread rapidly throughout Europe.

Cacao Cacao is the raw material of chocolate. Hernan Cortes tasted a drink that the Aztec people made by grinding cacao and introduced it to Europe. This spread among the nobles and wealthy people in Spain, and then spread throughout Europe in the mid-17th century.

Corn In 1492, Columbus saw the Americans grow corn and brought corn seeds to Spain. He started growing them in Europe. Corn was loved by Europeans because it could be harvested in a short period of time and it grows well without any special management regardless of soil and water quality.

02 유럽 지역 질서의 변화
절대 왕정이 등장하다

16~18세기 유럽에서는 봉건 영주가 몰락하고 중앙 집권적인 통일 국가가 등장하면서 절대 왕정이 출현하였다. 국왕은 신에게서 권력을 받았다는 **왕권신수설**을 내세워 절대적인 권력을 행사하였다.

절대 군주는 명령을 충실하게 이행할 수 있는 **관료**와 언제나 동원할 수 있는 **상비군**을 두었다. 이를 유지하는 데 필요한 막대한 비용은 상공 시민 계층의 세금과 재정적 지원으로 충당하였다. 절대 군주는 상공 시민 계층의 지지를 얻기 위해 수입을 줄이고, 국내의 상공업을 육성하는 **중상주의 정책**을 실시하였다. 이러한 국왕의 상업 활동 지원에 힘입어 성장한 상공 시민 계층은 절대 왕정의 지지 기반이 되었다.

절대 군주
Absolute Monarch

경제 정책
Economic Policy

관료제
Bureaucracy

상비군
Standing Army

정치 이론
Political Theory

중상주의
Mercantilism

왕권신수설
Divine Right of Kings

균형 관계
Balanced Relationship

신흥 시민 세력
Emerging Civic Forces

봉건 세력
Feudal Forces

> 절대 군주는 상공 시민 계층의 지원과 관료제, 상비군에 힘입어 강력한 왕권을 행사할 수 있었어요.
> Absolute monarchs were able to exercise powerful royal authority thanks to the support of the commerce and civil class, the bureaucracy, and the standing army.

절대 왕정의 구조
The Structure of the Absolute Monarchy

◉ 프랑스의 루이 14세는 어떻게 왕권을 강화하였나요?
How Did Louis XIV Strengthen the Kingship?

> 루이 14세 화려한 베르사유 궁전을 지어 왕실의 권위를 과시하였고, 콜베르를 등용하여 중상주의 정책을 추진하였어요. 또한 상비군을 키워 프랑스를 유럽 최강의 나라로 만들었지요.
> Louis XIV I built the splendid Palace of Versailles to show off the authority of the royal family and appointed Colbert to promote mercantilism. Also, by training a standing army, France became the strongest country in Europe.

02 Changes in the Regional Order in Europe

Emergence of an Absolute Monarchy

The period between the 16th and 18th centuries saw the collapse of the feudal lord class and the emergence of unified nations and the concept of the absolute monarchy. Monarchs in Europe exercised absolute power under the doctrine of 'the divine right of kings', which was stated a monarch derived the right to rule directly from the will of God.

Absolute monarchs had bureaucrats who would faithfully fulfill their commands and standing armies who were ready for war at any time. The enormous expenses necessary to maintain them came from the taxes and financial support of commercial and individual citizen groups. Absolute monarchs carried out mercantilist policies to cut back import in order to win the support of those commercial and citizen groups and also to promote domestic commerce. Kings' support for businesses resulted in the growth of those private individuals and businesses, which in turn became a faithful support group for the absolute monarchy.

> 베르사유 궁전은 원래 루이 13세가 지은 사냥용 별장이었으나 루이 14세의 명령으로 대정원을 조성히고 건물 전체를 증축하여 지금의 모습을 갖추었어요.
> Originally, the Palace of Versailles was a hunting lodge built by Louis XIII, but under Louis XIV's order, the grand garden was built and the entire building was expanded to become what it is now.

베르사유 궁전(프랑스 베르사유) Palace of Versailles(Versailles, France)

각국에서 절대 왕정이 성립하다

서유럽에서는 에스파냐가 가장 먼저 절대 왕정을 이루었다. 에스파냐는 신대륙에서 들여온 금과 은을 이용하여 국력을 키우고 대서양 무역의 주도권을 잡았다. 영국에서는 엘리자베스 1세가 동인도 회사를 설립하여 아시아에 진출하고, 북아메리카에 식민지를 건설하였다. 프랑스는 해외 식민지를 확보하고 중상주의 정책으로 상공업을 발전시켰다.

동유럽에서는 도시와 상공업의 발달이 미약하여 농노제가 유지되는 곳이 많았다. 그 때문에 상공 시민 계층이 성장하지 못하여 봉건 귀족이 세력을 유지할 수 있었다. 17세기 중엽에 이르러 동유럽에서도 서유럽의 번영에 자극받은 계몽 군주들이 나타나 절대 왕정을 수립하였다.

◉ 엘리자베스 1세는 왜 펠리페 2세의 청혼을 거절하였나요?

엘리자베스 1세는 헨리 8세와 두 번째 왕비인 앤 불린 사이에서 태어났다. 헨리 8세가 죽자 이복동생인 에드워드 6세가 9살에 왕좌에 올랐다. 그가 병에 걸려 일찍 죽자 헨리 8세와 첫 번째 왕비 캐서린 사이에서 태어난 메리 1세가 왕위에 올랐다. 메리 1세는 에스파냐의 국왕 펠리페 2세와 결혼하였다. 엘리자베스는 이복언니인 메리 1세에게 언제 죽임을 당할지 몰라 늘 불안에 시달렸다. 1558년 '피의 메리'라고 불리던 메리 1세가 난소암으로 죽자, 엘리자베스 1세가 왕위에 올랐다.

메리 1세와 결혼했던 펠리페 2세는 개신교 신자인 엘리자베스 1세가 가톨릭을 탄압하지 못하게 하려고 처제였던 엘리자베스 1세에게 청혼하였다. 하지만 엘리자베스 1세는 "나는 영국과 결혼하였다."라고 말하며 거절하였다. 이후 평생을 독신으로 지내서 '처녀 여왕'이라 불렸다.

> 엘리자베스 1세 펠리페 2세의 무적함대를 격파하여 해상권을 장악하였고, 중상주의 정책을 추진하여 모직물 공업 등 국내 산업을 발전시켰어요. 또한 식민지 경영을 위해 동인도 회사를 설립하여 훗날 영국이 대영 제국으로 발전하는 데 필요한 기반을 만들었어요.

Establishment of Absolute Monarchs in Various Countries

In 16th century Western Europe, Spain became the first to see the emergence of an absolute monarchy and attained hegemony in the Atlantic trade. In England, Elizabeth I established the East India Company to advance into Asia and colonized North America. France developed commerce with mercantilist policies.

In Eastern Europe, the serf system remained in many countries due to the slow development of cities and commerce. As a result, the feudal nobles were able to maintain their power because the private individuals and businesses were not growing. It was only around the mid-17th century that absolute monarchy could be established with the emergence of enlightened despots inspired by the prosperity of Western Europe.

⊛ Why Did Queen Elizabeth I Turn Down the Proposal of Philip II?

Elizabeth I was the daughter of Henry VIII and Queen Anne Boleyn. When Henry VIII died, his half-brother Edward VI ascended to the throne at the age of nine. Upon his early death from illness, Mary I, the daughter of Henry VIII and first Queen Catherine, took the throne. Mary I married Philip II of Spain. Elizabeth was always in a state of anxiety because she didn't know when she would be killed by her half-sister Mary I. In 1558, when Mary I, called Mary of Blood, died of ovarian cancer, Elizabeth I ascended to the throne.

Philip II proposed to his sister-in-law, Elizabeth I, to prevent Elizabeth I, a Protestant, from suppressing Catholicism. But she refused, saying, "I'm married to England." After that, she remained single for the rest of her life, so she was called the 'Virgin Queen'.

> Elizabeth I By defeating the invincible fleet of Philip II, I seized the maritime power and promoted mercantile policies to develop domestic industries such as the wool industry. I also founded the East India Company, which became the basis of the British Empire.

∞ 동유럽에서 절대 왕정을 수립한 계몽 군주는 누구인가요?

마리아 테레지아
나는 신성 로마 제국 황제의 제위를 계승하던 합스부르크 왕가의 여제였어요. 카를 6세가 죽고 대부분의 영토를 상속받았지요. 각 국이 이에 반발하여 오스트리아 왕위 계승 전쟁이 일어났어요. 이 때 프로이센에 슐레지엔을 내주었는데 후에 슐레지엔을 회복하려고 7년 전쟁을 일으켰지만 실패하였어요.

표트르 대제
적극적으로 서유럽의 제도와 문물을 받아들여 러시아의 근대화를 추진하였어요. 스웨덴과의 전쟁에서 승리하여 발트해를 확보하였고 상트페테르부르크를 건설하여 서유럽으로 나가는 통로를 마련하였지요.

프리드리히 2세
나는 '국가 제1의 하인'을 자처하며 관료제와 상비군을 마련하고 산업을 육성하였어요. 그 결과 프로이센은 여러 나라로 나뉘어 있던 독일에서 가장 강력한 국가로 성장하였지요.

상수시 궁전은 베르사유 궁전을 본떠 지은 궁전이에요. 어린 시절부터 프랑스식 교육을 받으며 자란 프리드리히 2세의 개인적 취향이 반영되어 있어요.
The Sanssouci Palace is a palace modeled after the Palace of Versailles. It reflects the personal taste of Friedrich II, who was educated in French style since childhood.

프로이센 상수시 궁전(독일 포츠담)
Sanssouci Palace of Prussia(Potsdam, Germany) ©Sven Scharr

🔎 Who Is the Enlightened Monarch who Established the Absolute Monarchy in Eastern Europe?

Maria Theresia
I was the empress of the Habsburg royal family who succeeded to the throne of the Holy Roman Emperor. After Charles VI died, I inherited most of the territory. Several countries opposed it, and the war for succession to the Austrian throne broke out. At this time, Schlesien was handed over to Prussia. I later fought a seven-year war to recover Schlesien, but failed.

Peter the Great
I actively embraced Western European institutions and cultures and promoted the modernization of Russia. By winning the war with Sweden, the Baltic Sea was secured, and Saint Petersburg was built to provide a pathway to Western Europe.

Friedrich II
I declared myself 'the first servant of the state'. I established a bureaucracy and a standing army, and fostered industry. As a result, Prussia grew into the most powerful country in Germany, which was divided into several countries at the time.

쇤부른 궁전은 오스트리아 합스부르크 왕가의 여름 궁전이에요. 어린 모차르트가 마리아 테레지아 앞에서 피아노 연주를 한 곳으로도 유명하지요.
The Schonbrunn Palace is a summer palace of the Habsburg family in Austria. The Schonbrunn Palace is also famous as the place where young Mozart played the piano in front of Maria Theresa.

합스부르크 왕가의 쇤브룬 궁전(오스트리아 빈)
Schonbrunn Palace of the Habsburg family(Vienna, Austria) ©Thomas Wolf

03 17, 18세기의 유럽 문화

과학 혁명이 전개되다

르네상스 시기부터 싹트기 시작한 근대 과학은 16~17세기에 **과학 혁명**이라고 불릴 정도로 눈부신 발전을 이루었다. **코페르니쿠스**는 지구가 태양의 주위를 돈다고 주장하였고, 갈릴레이는 망원경으로 천체를 관찰하여 코페르니쿠스의 주장을 증명하였다.

뉴턴은 **만유인력** 모든 물체 사이에는 서로 끌어당기는 힘이 있음**의 법칙**을 발견하여 근대적 우주관을 확립하는 데 기여하였다. 하비가 혈액 순환의 원리를 발표하고 제너가 종두법 천연두를 예방하기 위하여 백신을 인체의 피부에 접종하는 방법을 발견하는 등 의학 분야에서도 큰 진전이 이루어졌다.

◉ **뉴턴은 어떻게 사과를 보고 중력을 생각해 냈을까요?**

17~18세기 커피하우스는 과학자, 신학자, 법조인 등 여러 지식인들이 모여 자유롭게 대화를 나누는 곳이었다. 뉴턴은 커피하우스에서 '중력의 역제곱 법칙과 타원형 궤도'에 대해 토론하였고, 그 후 몇 년 동안 이 문제에 깊이 파고들었다.

어느 날 뉴턴은 사과나무 아래에서 생각에 잠겼다. '돌을 실에 매달아 돌리면 돌이 실의 궤도를 벗어나지 않고 원운동을 한다. 그렇다면 달은 어떻게 지구 주위를 돌며 원운동을 하는 것일까?' 이때 뉴턴의 머리 위로 사과 하나가 떨어졌다. 순간 뉴턴은 사과를 지구로 떨어뜨린 힘이 달을 지구의 궤도에 붙들고 있다는 사실을 깨달았다. 뉴턴은 이렇게 만유인력의 법칙을 발견하였고, 그 내용을 책으로 출간하였다.

경제학의 아버지로 불리는 애덤 스미스의 『국부론』 역시 커피하우스에서 탄생했어요(1776). 그는 주로 런던의 '브리티시 커피하우스'란 곳에서 글을 썼다고 해요.

17세기 영국의 커피하우스 전경(영국 박물관)
Interior of a London Coffee-house, 17th Century(The British Museum)

03 European Culture in the 17 and 18th Centuries

Dawning of the Scientific Revolution

Modern science began budding from the Renaissance period and made such remarkable strides in the 17th century that it was called the Scientific Revolution. It was during this time that Nicolaus Copernicus posited the idea of a heliocentric solar system in which the planets orbit the sun and Galileo Galilei observed the universe with a telescope, proving that Copernicus was right.

Newton discovered the law of universal gravity and contributed to the establishment of modern cosmology. Remarkable achievements were made in medical science as well, such as William Harvey's discovery of systematic circulation and Edward Jenner's discovery of vaccination.

⊚ How Did Newton Discover Gravity When He Saw the Apple?

In the 17th and 18th centuries, coffee houses were a place where scientists, theologians, legal professionals, and other intellectuals gathered and chatted freely. Newton discussed the 'the Law of Gravity and the Elliptical Orbit' at a coffee house, and in the years that followed, he dug deeper into this problem.

One day Newton contemplated this under an apple tree. 'When a stone is hung on a thread, it moves in a circular motion without going out of the orbit of the thread. Then, how does the moon move around the earth in a circular motion?' At this time, an apple fell on Newton's head. Instantly Newton realized that the force that dropped the apple to Earth was holding the Moon in Earth's orbit. Newton thus discovered the law of universal gravitation and published it in a book.

Adam Smith's *"The Wealth of Nations"* was also born in a coffee house(1776). It is said that he mainly wrote in a place called 'British Coffee House' in London.

근대 철학과 계몽사상이 발달하다

과학 혁명으로 근대 철학도 발달하였다. 17세기에 데카르트는 신과 분리된 인간의 이성을 강조하여 **합리론** 진정한 앎은 태어날 때부터 주어진 이성에 의하여 얻어진다는 주장 의 토대를 닦았다. 18세기에 로크는 인간의 경험과 감각을 지식의 원천으로 여기는 **경험론**을 주장하였다.

새로운 우주관은 자연법을 토대로 한 사회 계약설과 이성에 의한 인류의 진보를 믿는 계몽사상의 토대가 되었다. 로크의 **사회 계약설**은 다른 계몽사상가들에게 큰 영향을 주었다. 대표적인 계몽사상가로는 삼권 분립을 주장한 **몽테스키외**와 국민 주권설 나라의 주권이 국민에게 있다는 설 을 제시한 **루소**가 있다. 이들의 사상은 미국 혁명과 프랑스 혁명의 사상적 토대가 되었다.

🎯 계몽사상가들은 어떤 주장을 하였나요?

존 로크 인간은 태어날 때부터 자연권, 즉 생명, 자유, 재산에 대한 권리를 지니고 있습니다. 국가가 시민의 자유를 침해하면 시민은 자신들의 안전을 위해 새로운 정부를 세울 수 있습니다.

몽테스키외 권력이 집중되면 시민은 자유로울 수 없습니다. 온건한 정부를 형성하기 위해서는 권력을 법률로 규제하고, 조정하여야 합니다. 각각의 권력에 합당한 역할을 부여하여 다른 권력의 월권을 견제해야 합니다.

장 자크 루소 인간의 권리는 자연에서 오는 것이 아니기 때문에 합의에 근거해야 합니다. 국민은 자신들의 권리를 공동체 전체에 양도합니다. 하지만 국가는 대리자일 뿐이고 주권은 국민에게 있습니다.

Development of Modern Philosophies and Enlightenment Ideology

Along with the scientific revolution came the development of modern philosophies. In the 17th century, Rene Descartes laid the groundwork for Rationalism by understanding the use of reason that was independent from God. In the 18th century, John Locke advocated Empiricism that involved the claim that all knowledge came from experience and senses.

New worldviews became the foundation for such ideas as the social contract that was founded upon natural law and enlightenment believed that rational thoughts could lead to human improvement. Locke's Idea of social contract influenced other enlightenment philosophers. Some of the leading enlightenment philosophers included Montesquieu, who advocated the idea of dividing government power into three branches, and Jean-Jacques Rousseau, who advocated the concept of popular sovereignty. These ideas became the ideological foundation of the American Revolution and the French Revolution.

⊘ What Did the Enlightenment Philosophers Argue?

John Locke All individuals are born with natural rights: life, liberty, and property. If the state violates citizens' natural rights, the people can establish a new government for their own safety and security.

Montesquieu If power is concentrated, the people cannot be free. To form a moderate government, power must be regulated and adjusted by law. Each power should be given a reasonable role to keep the other power from overstepping its authority.

Jean-Jacques Rousseau Human rights do not come from nature, so they should be based on consensus. The people hand over their rights to the whole community. However, the state is only an agent and sovereignty lies with the people.

유럽 예술이 화려하고 섬세해지다

17세기 유럽에서는 절대 왕정의 영향으로 **바로크 양식**의 호화로운 건축물과 그림이 만들어졌다. 건축에서는 **베르사유 궁전**이 대표적이고 회화에서는 렘브란트의 작품이 유명하다. 18세기부터는 경쾌하고 섬세한 **로코코 양식**이 유행하였다. 화가들은 주로 귀족과 부자의 향락적인 생활을 묘사하였다.

음악에서도 바흐와 헨델 등에 의해 **바로크 음악**이 절정을 이루었다. 이후 모차르트와 베토벤이 **고전 음악**을 완성하였다. **고전주의 문학**도 유행하였는데, 프랑스의 라퐁텐, 독일의 괴테가 대표적이다.

⚜ 바로크 양식과 로코코 양식은 어떤 차이가 있나요?

바로크는 '일그러진 진주'를 뜻하는 포르투갈어 '바로코'에서 나온 말이에요. 17세기에 절대 왕정의 후원을 받으며 발전한 바로크 미술은 궁전과 교회의 양식에서 나타났어요. 주로 왕이나 귀족의 초상화 또는 종교적인 의미를 담은 작품들로 제작되었지요.

바로크 양식의 베르사유 궁전 내부(프랑스 베르사유)
Interior of the Palace of Versailles in Baroque Style(Versailles, France) ©Myrabella

로코코는 귀족의 분수 등을 꾸밀 때 쓰던 조개나 바위를 뜻하는 프랑스어 '로카이유'에서 나온 말이에요. 로코코 미술은 18세기 무렵 전성기를 구가하였는데, 섬세함과 우아함이 특징이지요. 특히 루이 14세 때부터 화려한 궁전 문화를 추구하던 귀족들의 취향을 반영하여 발달하였어요.

로코코 양식의 상수시 궁전 내부(독일 포츠담)
Interior of the Sanssouci Palace in Rococo Style(Potsdam, Germany) ©Bgabel

European Artwork Becomes Ornate and Elaborate

In 17th century Europe, highly ornate and extravagant Baroque style architecture and artworks were created under the influence of absolute monarchs. A few examples include the Palace of Versailles in architecture and paintings by Rembrandt in art. Beginning in the 18th century, the elaborate but graceful and light Rococo style was in vogue. Artists of this period mostly painted the hedonistic lifestyles of the wealthy and noble.

Baroque music reached its zenith as well in such composers as Bach and Handel. Later on, Mozart and Beethoven perfected Classical music. Classical literature was also popular during this era, with leading writers from the era including the French poet Jean de La Fontaine and the German writer Johann Wolfgang von Goethe.

What Is the Difference between Baroque Style and Rococo Style?

Baroque comes from the Portuguese 'Barroco' which means 'coarse and uneven'. Baroque art, which developed in the 17th century under the support of the absolute monarchy, is characterized in the style of palaces and churches. Mainly, portraits of kings or nobles, or works with religious meanings were produced.

Rococo comes from the French word 'Rocaille', which means shells or rocks used to decorate noble fountains. Rococo art was in its heyday around the 18th century, and is characterized by delicacy and elegance. In particular, it was developed by reflecting the tastes of nobles who pursued a splendid palace culture from the time of Louis XIV.

IV

제국주의 침략과 국민 국가 건설 운동

앞 시대는 영웅 혁명의 시대였지만, 지금은 국민 혁명의 시대이다.

이른바 국민 혁명이라는 것은 한 나라의 백성이

모두 자유·평등·우애의 정신을 가지는 것이다.

- 『민보』

IV

Imperialist Invasions and Nation-state Building Movements

1. Nation-state System in Europe and America
2. Industrialization and Imperialism of Europe
3. Establishment of Nation-states in West Asia and India
4. Nation-state Movement in East Asia

The previous era was the era of the heroic revolution, but now is the era of the national revolution. The so-called national revolution means that all the people of a country have a spirit of freedom, equality, and friendship.

– "*The People's Report*"

베르사유 궁전(프랑스 베르사유)
Palace of Versailles(Versailles, France)

유럽과 아메리카의 국민 국가 체제

01 영국의 시민 혁명

찰스 1세, 권리 청원을 승인하다

16세기 영국에서 장원제가 무너지면서 자영 농민층이 형성되고, 새로운 지주 계급인 젠트리가 등장하였다. 젠트리는 상인, 제조업자 등 시민 계급과 함께 의회(하원)의 다수를 차지하였다. 젠트리와 시민 계급 중에는 신교를 받아들인 청교도가 많았다.

엘리자베스 1세의 뒤를 이어 왕위에 오른 제임스 1세는 왕권신수설을 내세우며 청교도를 탄압하였다. 그 뒤를 이은 찰스 1세도 의회의 동의 없이 세금을 걷고 전제 정치 _{국가의 권력을 오로지 개인이 제약하는 정치}를 강화하였다. 이에 의회는 '의회의 동의 없이 과세할 수 없다.'라는 내용을 담은 권리 청원을 제출하였다(1628). 찰스 1세는 이를 승인하였으나 이듬해 의회를 해산하였다.

🧭 영국 입헌 정치의 기초는 언제 마련되었나요?

1215년 존 왕은 프랑스에 잃어버린 영국 영토를 되찾기 위해 무리하게 세금을 거두었다. 그러자 귀족 세력이 반란을 일으켰고, 이에 굴복한 존 왕은 귀족의 자문을 거쳐야만 세금을 거둘 수 있다는 내용이 담긴 마그나 카르타(대헌장)에 서명하였다.

마그나 카르타의 39조에는 자유민의 권리를 인정한다는 내용이 담겨 있었다. 그러나 당시의 자유민이란 성직자, 귀족을 의미했다. 17세기에 이르러 왕권과 의회가 대립하게 되면서 마그나 카르타는 왕의 절대 권력을 제한하는 근거로 주목받게 되었고 근대 헌법의 토대가 되었다.

마그나 카르타에 서명하는 존 왕
King John Signs the Magna Carta

마그나 카르타(영국 국립도서관)
Magna Carta(British Library)

Nation-state System in Europe and America

01 Civil Revolutions of England

Charles I Approved a Petition of Right

The end of manorialism in England in the 16th century gave rise to a group of self-sustained peasants and a new class of landowners called gentry. Gentry provided the bulk of the members of the English parliament along with merchants, manufacturers, and citizens. Many of the members of the gentry and commoner classes were Puritans who accepted Protestantism as their religion.

James I, who succeeded Elizabeth I, asserted the doctrine of the divine right of kings and persecuted Puritans. His successor Charles I also assumed a despotic government and collected taxes without receiving the approval of Parliament. The English Parliament sent King Charles I a Petition of Right that included their demand for no taxation without the consent of Parliament (1628). Charles I approved it but dismissed Parliament the following year.

When Was the Foundation of British Constitutional Government Laid?

In 1215, King John forced people to collect taxes to reclaim lost British territory to France. As the nobles rebelled, King John surrendered and signed the Magna Carta(the Great Charter of Freedoms), which states that he can only collect taxes after consulting with the nobles.

Article 39 of the Magna Carta states that it recognizes the rights of free people. At that time, free citizens meant only priests and nobles. Later, in the 17th century, when the kingship and the parliament confronted each other, the Magna Carta was noted as the basis for limiting the absolute power of the king and became the foundation of the modern constitution.

청교도 혁명으로 공화국이 수립되다

1640년에 스코틀랜드에서 반란이 일어나자 찰스 1세는 전쟁 비용을 마련하기 위해 다시 의회를 소집하였다. 이때 의회가 국왕을 비판하고 과세를 승인하지 않자 국왕은 의회를 무력으로 탄압하였다. 그러자 왕을 지지하는 왕당파와 의회를 지지하는 의회파 사이에 내전이 일어났다. 이 내전에서 청교도인 크롬웰이 이끄는 의회파가 승리하였다.

의회는 찰스 1세를 처형하고 공화국을 세웠다(청교도 혁명, 1642~1649). 크롬웰이 발표한 항해법으로 영국은 네덜란드와의 해상권 경쟁에서 우위를 점하였다. 항해법은 유럽 내에서 영국으로 수입되는 상품은 영국이나 생산국의 선박만이 수송할 수 있고, 유럽 외의 지역에서 영국으로 수입되는 상품은 영국 선박만이 수송할 수 있도록 규정한 법이다. 크롬웰은 항해법을 제정하여 무역을 발전시켰지만, 청교도 윤리를 강요하는 등 독재를 하여 국민의 반감을 샀다.

....

◉ 독재자를 없앤 크롬웰은 어떤 정치를 하였나요?

1653년 크롬웰은 군대의 지지를 바탕으로 의회를 해산하고 잉글랜드, 스코틀랜드, 아일랜드 등 세 나라를 통치하는 호국경 자리에 올랐다. 최고 통치자가 된 크롬웰은 모든 군사권을 장악하고, 독재 체제를 구축하였다. 크롬웰이 청교도 법령에 입각하여 성탄절을 금지하는 등 엄격한 종교적 원칙을 적용하자 민중의 불만이 높아졌다. 결국 크롬웰 사망 이후 왕정이 복고되었다.

> 던바 전투(1650)에서 크롬웰이 이끈 철기군은 의회파에 반발한 스코틀랜드 군대를 진압하는 데 성공하였어요.
> At the Battle of Dunbar(1650), Cromwell's Ironsides succeeded in subduing the Scottish army against Parliamentarians.

던바 전투에서의 크롬웰(테이트 브리튼)
Cromwell at the Battle of Dunbar(Tate Britain)

Puritan Revolution Leads to the Establishment of the Republic

When the Scots rebelled, Charles I had to recall Parliament again in 1640 to raise money for a war. But when Parliament criticized the king and refused to approve his request for taxes to fund a war, the king forced the dissolution of Parliament. This political conflict was elevated into a civil war between the Royalists who supported the king and the Parliamentarians who supported Parliament. The Parliamentarians won the war under the leadership of a Puritan named Oliver Cromwell.

Parliament executed Charles I and established the republican Commonwealth(English Civil War, 1642-1649). Due to the Navigation Act enacted by Cromwell, England gained the upper hand in their maritime competition with the Netherlands. The Navigation Act stipulated that goods imported from Europe into England can only be transported by ships of England or a producing country, and goods imported from outside Europe into England can only be transported by British ships. Cromwell was credited with the development of trade by enacting the Navigation Act, but the people resented him for his dictatorial policies and strict imposition of Puritan ethics.

◉ **What Kind of Politics Did Cromwell Engage in after Getting Rid of the Dictator?**

In 1653, with the support of the military, Cromwell disbanded Parliament and became the Lord Protector governing three countries: England, Scotland, and Ireland. As he became the highest ruler, he seized all military power and established a dictatorship. Cromwell applied strict religious principles, such as prohibiting Christmas, in accordance with the Puritans Act, and dissatisfaction within the populace increased. The monarchy was eventually restored after Cromwell's death.

명예혁명으로 입헌 군주제가 확립되다

크롬웰이 죽은 후 의회는 찰스 2세를 왕으로 세워 왕정을 부활시켰다. 그러나 찰스 2세와 그 뒤를 이은 제임스 2세는 의회를 무시하며 전제 정치를 강화하였다. 이에 맞서 의회는 제임스 2세를 폐위하고 그의 딸 **메리 2세**와 메리의 남편 **윌리엄 3세**를 공동 왕으로 추대하였다. 이 과정에서 유혈 사태가 거의 발생하지 않았기 때문에 이를 **명예혁명**(1688)이라고 한다.

의회는 메리 2세와 윌리엄 3세에게 왕의 권력을 제한하는 **권리 장전**을 승인받았다. 이로써 영국은 전제 정치가 무너지고 의회 중심의 **입헌 군주제** 군주의 권력이 헌법에 의하여 일정한 제약을 받는 정치 체제 국가가 되었다.

18세기 초에는 **내각 책임제**가 시작되었다. 이때부터 '왕은 군림하나 통치하지 않는다.'라는 영국의 전통이 만들어졌다.

....

☯ 폐위 당한 왕의 딸과 사위는 어떻게 공동 왕이 되었나요?

찰스 2세의 동생이었던 제임스 2세는 가톨릭을 부활시키고 강력한 전제 정치를 펼쳤다. 이에 의회는 제임스 2세를 폐위하고 신교도였던 그의 딸 메리 2세와 메리의 남편 윌리엄 3세를 공동 왕으로 추대하였다.

영국 의회의 요구에 따라 메리와 윌리엄 부부는 대규모 군대를 앞세워 런던으로 들어왔다. 자신의 딸과 사위가 여러 귀족의 환영을 받으며 입성하자 제임스 2세는 프랑스로 도피하였다. 메리 2세와 윌리엄 3세는 국왕이 의회의 동의 없이 권력을 남용할 수 없다는 내용의 권리 장전을 승인하였는데, 이는 영국 의회 정치 발달의 기초가 되었다.

> 국왕이 의회의 동의 없이 법의 효력을 정지하거나 집행을 막는 것은 위법이다. 국왕이 의회의 승인 없이 세금을 징수하는 것도 위법이다. It is against the law for the king to suspend the law or prevent it from being enforced without the consent of Parliament. It is also against the law for the king to collect taxes without Parliamentary approval.

권리 장전을 승인하는 메리 2세와 윌리엄 3세(런던 국립초상화미술관)
Mary II and William III approved the English Bill of Rights(National Portrait Gallery, London)

Glorious Revolution Leads to the Establishment of Constitutional Monarchy

After Cromwell's death, Charles II came to the throne and restored the monarchy. Charles II and his successor James II ignored Parliament and ruled through despotism. In response, Parliament deposed James II and replaced him with his daughter Mary II and her husband William III as co-rulers. Since this all happened without shedding blood, this chain of events is called the Glorious Revolution(1688).

Parliament made Mary II and William III sign the English Bill of Rights, which restricted the authority of the king, into law. With this, England ended despotism and established a Constitutional monarchy.

England adopted the principle of Parliamentary Sovereignty in the early-18th century. It was the beginning of the English tradition that is summed up as 'The king reigns, but he does not rule'.

◉ How Did the Deposed King's Daughter and Son-in-law Become Co-rulers?

James II, the younger brother of Charles II, revived Catholicism and ruled under absolute despotism. In response, Parliament attempted to depose James II and tried to place his daughter Mary II, who was a Protestant, and Mary's husband William III as co-rulers.

At the request of the British Parliament, Mary and William III came to London with a large contingent of troops. James II fled to France when his daughter and son-in-law were welcomed by several nobles. Mary II and William III approved the English Bill of Rights stating that the king cannot abuse power without the consent of Parliament, which became the basis for the political development of Parliament in England.

02 미국 혁명과 미국의 발전

영국이 아메리카에 무리하게 과세하다

17세기 무렵부터 종교의 자유를 원한 청교도와 경제적 이득을 얻으려는 영국인들이 북아메리카로 이주하기 시작하였다. 18세기 초 북아메리카 동부 연안에는 13개의 영국 식민지가 건설되었고, 식민지 주민들은 독자적인 의회를 만들어 자치를 누렸다.

18세기 후반 영국은 프랑스와 **7년 전쟁** 슐레지엔 영유를 둘러싸고 오스트리아와 프로이센을 중심으로 벌어진 전쟁을 벌여 재정이 악화된 상태였다. 전쟁에서 승리한 영국은 재정 부담을 해결하기 위하여 새로운 세금을 걷으려 하였다. 식민지에서 수입하는 설탕, 차, 종이 등에 **관세**를 부과하였고, 인지세법을 제정하여 모든 인쇄물에 **인지**를 붙이게 하였다. 식민지 주민들은 영국 의회에 자신들의 대표가 참석하지 않았으므로 '대표 없는 곳에 과세할 수 없다.'라며 반발하였다.

영국은 차에 대한 세금을 제외하고 모든 세금을 폐지하였으나 반발은 계속되었다. 이러한 상황에서 식민지 주민들이 보스턴 항구에 정박 중인 영국 동인도 회사의 선박을 습격하여 차 상자를 모두 바다에 던져 버리는 **보스턴 차 사건**이 일어났다(1773).

◉ 아메리카노 커피와 보스턴 차 사건은 어떤 관련이 있을까요?

보스턴 차 사건 The Destruction of Tea at Boston Harbor

아메리카노의 유행은 '보스턴 차 사건'과 관련이 있어요. 당시 미국인들은 차를 즐겨 마셨는데, 영국 정부가 중상주의 정책을 강화하면서 수입 차에 과중한 세금을 부과하기 시작하였어요. 미국인들은 이에 반발하여 수입 차 불매 운동을 하였지요. 차 대신 진한 에스프레소에 물을 타서 묽게 만든 커피를 많이 마시게 되면서 아메리카노가 유행하게 되었어요.

02 American Revolution and the Development of the United States

England Imposes Heavy Taxes on American Colonies

Beginning in the 17th century, Puritans who wanted religious freedom and English who wanted economic opportunities migrated to North America. In the early 18th century, there were 13 British colonies along the East Coast of North America, and the settlers of these colonies established their own assembly and enjoyed autonomy.

In the late-18th century, England was experiencing a financial crunch in the wake of the Seven Year War with France. England won the war, but the government tried to impose new taxes as a solution to the ensuing financial problems. The English government began imposing tariffs on sugar, tea, and paper that were imported by the colonies, and enacted the colonial stamp law to tax all printed materials. The American colonists resisted the law claiming, 'No taxation without representation' because they were not represented in the English Parliament.

The English government abolished all taxes except the tax imposed on tea, but their resistance continued. It was under these circumstances that the American colonists attacked British commercial ships that were anchored in Boston Harbor and dumped all the chests of tea the ships were carrying in the harbor. This incident is known as the Boston Tea Party(1773).

 What Is the Relationship between Americanos and the Boston Tea Party?

The trend of Americanos is related to the 'Boston Tea Party'. At that time, Americans enjoyed drinking tea, but as the British government strengthened mercantilist policies, it began to impose heavy taxes on imported tea. Americans opposed this and boycotted imported tea. Instead of tea, they drank a lot of coffee made by adding water to a strong espresso, which influenced the rise in popularity of Americanos.

독립 전쟁에서 승리하고 최초의 민주 공화국이 수립되다

보스턴 차 사건 이후 영국의 탄압이 강화되자 식민지 대표들은 대륙 회의를 열어 영국에 맞서기로 결의하였다. 1775년 보스턴 근교의 **렉싱턴**에서 영국군과 식민지의 민병대가 충돌하면서 독립 전쟁이 시작되었다. 13개 주 식민지 대표들은 다시 대륙 회의를 열어 조지 워싱턴을 총사령관으로 임명하고 **독립 선언서**를 발표하였다(1776). 독립군은 영국군에 비해 열세였지만 프랑스, 에스파냐 등의 지원을 받아 전쟁에서 승리하였다. 이후 **파리 조약**을 통해 북아메리카의 13개 주가 독립하게 되었다(1783).

독립 후 13개 주의 대표들은 필라델피아에서 삼권 분립을 규정한 연방 헌법을 제정하였다. 이 헌법에 따라 세계 최초의 민주 공화국인 아메리카 합중국이 탄생하였고, 조지 워싱턴이 초대 대통령으로 선출되었다(1789).

미국 혁명은 독립운동의 성격을 지니고 있지만 자유와 평등의 이념을 실현하고자 한 시민 혁명이기도 하였다. 또한 프랑스 혁명을 비롯한 유럽의 시민 혁명과 라틴 아메리카의 독립 운동에 큰 영향을 끼쳤다.

🎖 미국 독립 선언서에는 어떤 내용이 있나요?
What's in the Declaration of Independence?

모든 인간은 평등하게 태어났고, 생명, 자유, 행복을 추구할 권리를 신으로부터 부여받았습니다. 이러한 권리를 확보하기 위해 정부를 수립하였으며, 정부의 정당한 권력은 국민의 동의에서 발생합니다. 정부가 이러한 목적을 파괴할 때에 국민은 언제든지 그 정부를 바꾸거나 없애고 민중의 안전과 행복을 가져올 수 있는 정부를 조직할 수 있습니다.

미국 초대 대통령 조지 워싱턴
George Washington, the First President of the United States

Victory in the War of Independence and Establishment of the First Democratic Republic

When the British government beefed up its oppression of the American colonies in the aftermath of the Boston Tea Party, delegates of all colonies came together at the Continental Conference and decided to resist Britain. In 1775, the first military engagement of the American Revolutionary War took place in Lexington between the British military and the colonial militia. The delegates of the 13 colonies held another continental conference, chose George Washington as the Commander-in- Chief of the Continental Army, and drafted the Declaration of Independence(1776). The colonial militias were outnumbered by the British forces but they eventually won the war with the support of France and Spain. Afterwards, 13 states in North America became independent through the Treaty of Paris(1783).

After declaring independence, delegates of the 13 colonies came together at the Constitutional Convention that took place in Philadelphia and adopted a federal constitution that mandated the separation of powers. With this constitution, the United States of America was established as the world's first democratic republic, and George Washington was elected as the first president(1798).

The American Revolution had the nature of an independence movement, but it was also a citizen revolution aiming to achieve freedom and equality. It also had great influence on the French Revolution as well as civil revolutions in Europe and independence movements in Latin America.

> George Washington All human beings were born equal and given the right to pursue life, freedom, and happiness by God. The government was established to secure these rights, and the legitimate power of the government arises from the consent of the people. Whenever a government destroys this purpose, the people have the right to change or eliminate it and organize a government that can ensure people's safety and happiness.

남북 전쟁 이후 세계 최대의 공업국으로 성장하다

독립 이후 미국에서는 서부 개척이 활발하게 전개되어 1840년대 말에는 영토가 태평양 연안에까지 이르렀다. 서부 개척과 함께 산업화도 빠르게 진행되었다. 공업화가 진행된 북부에서는 자유로운 임금 노동에 기초한 **상공업**이 발달하였다. 반면 남부에서는 노예를 이용하여 목화를 재배하는 **대농장 경영**이 발달하였다. 이러한 상황에서 노예제 확대에 반대한 **링컨**이 대통령에 당선되자 남부의 여러 주가 연방을 탈퇴하고 북부를 공격하면서 **남북 전쟁**이 일어났다(1861).

전쟁 초기에는 남부가 우세하였지만 링컨이 **노예 해방 선언**을 발표한 이후 전세는 인구와 공업 생산력에서 앞선 북부에 유리하게 전개되었다. 결국 남북 전쟁은 북부의 승리로 끝났다. 전쟁 피해를 복구하며 미국에서도 산업화가 본격적으로 진행되었다. 특히 1869년 완성된 **대륙 횡단 철도**는 미국의 경제 발전에 큰 기여를 하였다. 이후 미국은 풍부한 지하자원과 노동력을 바탕으로 19세기 후반 세계 최대의 공업국으로 성장하였다.

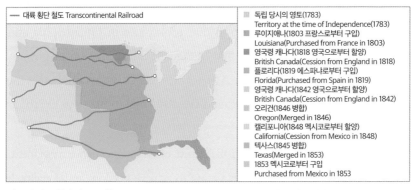

▬▬ 대륙 횡단 철도 Transcontinental Railroad	▦ 독립 당시의 영토(1783) Territory at the time of Independence(1783)
	▦ 루이지애나(1803 프랑스로부터 구입) Louisiana(Purchased from France in 1803)
	▦ 영국령 캐나다(1818 영국으로부터 할양) British Canada(Cession from England in 1818)
	▦ 플로리다(1819 에스파냐로부터 구입) Florida(Purchased from Spain in 1819)
	▦ 영국령 캐나다(1842 영국으로부터 할양) British Canada(Cession from England in 1842)
	▦ 오리건(1846 병합) Oregon(Merged in 1846)
	▦ 캘리포니아(1848 멕시코로부터 할양) California(Cession from Mexico in 1848)
	▦ 텍사스(1845 병합) Texas(Merged in 1853)
	▦ 1853 멕시코로부터 구입 Purchased from Mexico in 1853

미국의 영토 확장과 주요 철도 Territory Expansion and Major Railroads of the US

◉ 대륙 횡단 철도는 미국에 어떤 변화를 일으켰나요?

100여 개의 화물칸을 매단 열차가 미국 캘리포니아의 모하비 사막을 지나고 있어요. 대륙 횡단 철도가 완성되어 물자를 빠른 속도로 이동할 수 있었고 태평양 연안이 급속도로 발전하였습니다.

오늘날의 대륙 횡단 철도 Current Transcontinental Railroad

The US Becomes the World's Largest Industrial Country in the Aftermath of the Civil War

After achieving independence, Americans began to probe further west, and by the end of the 1840s, the American territory reached as far as the Pacific Ocean. Along with the westward expansion came rapid industrialization. In the industrializing northern American states, commerce based on free wage labor developed. On the other hand, the southern states had vast cotton plantations kept productive through slavery. When the abolitionist Lincoln was elected as the president, several southern states seceded from the Union. The American Civil War broke out when southern states attacked the northern states(1861).

In the beginning, the southern states were winning, but after Lincoln declared the abolition of slavery(Emancipation Proclamation), the war took a turn to favor the northern states, which were superior in terms of population and industrial productivity. Eventually, the Civil War came to an end with the victory of the northern states. The industrial revolution moved into full swing while the country was still recovering from the damages of the war. The Transcontinental railroad that was built in 1869 made a particular contribution to the economic development of the United States. Supported by rich natural resources and labor, the United States grew into the world's largest industrial country in the late 19th century.

⦿ What Changes Did the Transcontinental Railway Make in the United States?

A train carrying more than 100 cargo compartments is passing through the Mojave Desert in California, USA. The transcontinental railroad was completed so that supplies could be moved at a rapid pace. This allowed the Pacific coast to develop rapidly.

03 프랑스 혁명과 나폴레옹 시대

구제도의 모순이 곪아 터지다

프랑스 혁명은 **구제도의 모순**에서 비롯되었다. 소수에 불과한 제1 신분인 **성직자**와 제2 신분인 **귀족**은 막대한 토지를 소유하면서도 세금은 거의 내지 않았다. 하지만 인구의 대부분을 차지하는 제3 신분인 **평민**은 각종 세금과 부역을 부담하면서도 정치에는 참여하지 못하였다.

제3 신분 중에서 상공업의 발달로 부를 축적한 시민 계급인 **부르주아지**는 구제도의 모순을 비판하기 시작하였다. 이들은 계몽사상과 미국 혁명의 영향을 받아 구제도의 모순을 해결하고 평등한 사회를 건설하고자 하였다.

프랑스의 재정은 왕실의 사치와 미국 혁명 지원으로 바닥났다. 이를 해결하기 위해 루이 16세는 **삼부회**를 소집하였다. 삼부회에서 제3 신분은 신분별 투표 대신 대표 머릿수에 따른 투표를 주장하였지만 받아들여지지 않자 따로 **국민 의회**를 구성하였다. 이들은 베르사유 궁전의 테니스 코트에 모여 새로운 헌법이 제정될 때까지 해산하지 않겠다고 선언하였다(**테니스코트의 서약**). 왕이 국민 의회를 무력으로 탄압하려 하자 파리 시민은 **바스티유 감옥**을 습격하였고, 혁명의 불길은 프랑스 전체로 퍼져 나갔다(1789).

⚙ **프랑스 구제도의 모순은 무엇을 야기하였나요?**
What Did the Contradictions of the French Old System Cause?

프랑스 구제도의 모순을 표현한 풍자화
Satirical Painting Expressing the Contradictions of the Old System

노인은 평민을, 노인의 등에 올라탄 이들은 성직자와 귀족을 상징해요. 프랑스 혁명은 일하지 않는 사람과 죽도록 일하는 사람이 정해져 있는 구제도의 모순에서 비롯되었어요.
The old man symbolizes the commoners, and the man on the old man's back symbolizes the clergymen and nobles. The French Revolution originated from the contradiction of the old system in which people who do not work and those who work till death are set.

03 The French Revolution and the Era of Napoleon

Contradictions of the Old System Reach a Tipping Point

The French Revolution was triggered by the contradictions of the old system. A small number of clergymen and nobles enjoyed the privilege of being the highest and the second highest classes in society, but they paid almost no taxes. The commoners, who were the third class and accounted for almost the entire population, had to shoulder the heavy burden of working and paying taxes, but were not allowed to participate in politics.

Among the people who belonged to the third class, the Bourgeoisie class, who became wealthy due to the development of commerce started criticizing the old system. Influenced by the enlightenment movement and the American Revolution, they wanted to find a solution to the contradictions of the old system and build an equal society.

The national revenue of the French government was in ruins because of the exuberant lifestyle of the royal family and the government's support of the American Revolution. To solve this financial problem, King Louis XVI summoned the Estates General. In the Estates General, the Third Estate wanted the vote to be based on the number of members instead of a body where each estate would get one vote as proposed by the king. When their demand was not accepted, they formed a National Assembly. They assembled in the tennis court of the Palace of Versailles and swore an oath not to separate until the constitution of the kingdom was established(Tennis Court Oath). When the king tried to persecute them with force, the Paris citizens raided the Bastille. The revolution spread like wildfire throughout France(1789) from that point on.

혁명이 과격화하다

국민 의회는 혼란을 바로잡기 위해 봉건제 폐지를 선언하고, 프랑스 혁명의 기본 정신이 담긴 인간과 시민의 권리 선언(인권 선언)을 발표하였다. 이어서 입헌 군주제를 규정한 헌법을 제정하고, 새로운 헌법에 따라 입법 의회를 구성하였다.

프랑스 혁명이 자국으로 파급되는 것을 두려워한 오스트리아, 프로이센 등이 혁명에 간섭하자 입법 의회가 오스트리아에 선전 포고하였다. 초기에는 프랑스 군이 패전을 거듭하였으나 전국에서 의용군이 일어나 전세가 역전되었다. 그러나 전쟁과 물가 상승으로 생활이 어려워진 파리 민중들이 왕궁을 습격하였다. 이에 급진파가 정권을 장악하고 입법 의회 대신 국민 공회를 구성하였다.

국민 공회는 공화정을 선포하고(1792) 이듬해 루이 16세를 처형하였다. 이에 놀란 영국, 오스트리아 등이 동맹을 맺고 프랑스를 공격하였다. 거듭된 전쟁으로 물가 폭등, 생필품 부족이 심해지자 혁명에 반대하는 운동이 일어났다. 로베스피에르가 중심이 된 급진파는 전쟁을 치르기 위해 징병제를 실시하고 반대파를 무차별 처형하는 공포 정치를 시행하였다. 가혹한 공포 정치에 시민들의 불만이 커지자 온건파가 쿠데타를 일으켜 로베스피에르를 처형하였다. 이후 5명의 총재가 이끄는 총재 정부가 구성되었으나 혼란은 지속되었다.

🌀 **삼색기는 무엇에서 유래되었나요?**

분노한 파리 시민들이 파란색과 빨간색 장식을 두르고 바스티유 감옥을 습격해 갇혀 있던 사람들을 풀어주었다. 여기에서 삼색기가 유래하였다.

자유, 평등, 우애(삼색기에서 파랑은 자유, 하양은 평등, 빨강은 우애를 상징)를 위하여 가자 앞으로!
Let's go for liberty, equality, fraternity(blue, white, red in the tricolor)!

바스티유 감옥 습격(프랑스 국립도서관) The Storming of the Bastille(National Library of France)

Revolution Turns Radical

In order to contain the chaos, the National Assembly declared the abolition of feudalism and announced the Declaration of the Rights of Man and of the Citizen(Bill of Rights). They wrote a constitution that included an article about a system of constitutional monarchy, and the Legislative Assembly was formed in accordance with the new constitution.

Concerned about the French Revolution spreading to their countries, Austria and Prussia interfered in the revolution, to which the Legislative Assembly responded by declaring war. In the beginning, the French army kept losing battles, but the nationwide rise of righteous armies turned the tables. Having suffered from war and inflation, the impoverished Paris citizens raided the palace. Soon the Parisian militant radicals seized power and formed the National Convention to replace the Legislative Assembly.

The National Convention declared France a republic(1792) and the following year Louise XVI was executed. Shocked at this turn of events, England and Austria forged an alliance and attacked France. When the continuous wars created inflation and a serious shortage of daily commodities, some of the people joined the anti-revolution movement. The radical group under the leadership of Maximilien Robespierre conscripted soldiers to fight in the war and mercilessly persecuted political rivals during the 'Reign of Terror'. When the citizens revolted against the cruelty of the Reign of Terror, a group of soft-liners conducted a coup and executed Robespierre. They then created a five-person executive body called the Directory, but the chaotic situation continued.

....

◉ What Did the Tricolor Come from?

Paris citizens dressed in blue and red decorations attacked the Bastille prison in anger and freed the prisoners. The tricolor originated from this event.

나폴레옹이 프랑스 혁명 이념을 전파하다

총재 정부의 혼란이 지속되자 오스트리아와의 전쟁에서 큰 공을 세우고 이탈리아와 이집트 원정에서 승리하여 국민적 영웅이 된 **나폴레옹**이 쿠데타를 일으켜 정권을 장악하고 **통령** 정부를 수립하였다(1799). 제1 통령이 된 나폴레옹은 중앙 집권적 행정 제도와 국민 교육 제도를 마련하고, 자유와 평등의 프랑스 혁명 정신을 반영한 『**나폴레옹 법전**』을 편찬하였다. 내정 개혁 추진으로 국민의 지지를 얻은 나폴레옹은 1804년 국민 투표를 통해 황제가 되었다.

이후 나폴레옹은 오스트리아, 프로이센 등을 물리치고 유럽 대부분을 장악하였다. 하지만 영국과의 해전에서는 패하였고 이에 영국과 유럽 대륙의 통상을 금지하는 **대륙 봉쇄령**을 내렸다. 러시아가 대륙 봉쇄령을 어기고 영국과 무역을 계속하자 나폴레옹이 러시아 원정에 나섰지만, 러시아의 후퇴 전략과 추위로 참패하였다. 이 틈을 타서 유럽 국가들이 동맹을 맺고 프랑스를 공격하여 나폴레옹 군대를 무너뜨렸다.

나폴레옹은 정복 전쟁 과정에서 유럽 전역에 프랑스 혁명 이념을 전파하였고, 혁명 정신은 유럽 각국의 자유주의와 민족주의 운동을 촉진하였다.

나폴레옹 시기의 유럽
Europe During the Napoleonic Period

....

🌀 나폴레옹은 영웅인가요, 폭군인가요?

헤겔 멀리서 나폴레옹이 말을 타고 진군하는 것을 보았습니다. 그때 내가 본 것은 말을 타고 진군하는 '세계 정신'이었지요.

베토벤 나는 나폴레옹을 위해 교향곡 「영웅」을 작곡하였지요. 하지만 공화정을 무너뜨리고 황제에 오른 것을 보니 그는 '모든 인간 위에 군림하는 폭군'이나 다름없어요.

Napoleon Spreads the Spirit of the French Revolution

While the unrest continued during the rule of the Directory, Napoleon emerged as the people's hero when he returned from his expeditions to Italy and Egypt and a big victory in the war with Austria. Eventually, he instigated a coup, seized power, and established the Consulate(1799). Napoleon became the first Consulate of France, established a centralized government administration structure and educational system for the people, and commissioned four eminent jurists to write the "*Napoleonic Code*" that reflected the spirit of liberty and equality of the French Revolution. His internal reform policies won the approval of the people and he proclaimed himself emperor in 1804.

Napoleon then defeated Austria, Prussia, and dominated most of Europe. However, when he was defeated by England in a sea battle, he issued the Continental Blockade to ban all trade with England and continental Europe. When Russia ignored the blockade and continued trading with England, Napoleon set out on an expedition to Russia, but was crushed due to the cold and Russia's retreat strategy. European countries took this as an opportunity to sign an alliance, attacked France, and brought down Napoleon's army.

Napoleon spread the spirit of the French Revolution throughout Europe during his conquests, and the spirit of revolution gave impetus to liberalistic and democratic movements.

🧭 Is Napoleon a Hero or a Tyrant?

> Hegel In the distance, I saw Napoleon marching on horseback. What I saw at that time was the 'World Spirit' advancing on horseback.

> Beethoven I wrote the Symphony No. 3 Eroica for Napoleon. However, seeing that he broke the Republic and became an emperor, he is nothing but a 'Tyrant who reigns over all human beings'.

04 자유주의와 민족주의의 확산

빈 체제가 성립되고 자유주의가 확산되다

유럽 여러 나라의 지도자들은 나폴레옹 전쟁의 전후 처리를 위해 오스트리아 수도 빈에 모여 논의하였다. 오스트리아의 **메테르니히**가 주도한 빈 회의에서 유럽 각국은 정치 체제와 영토를 프랑스 혁명 이전으로 돌리는 데 합의하였다(1815).

복고주의 과거의 정치, 사상, 제도 등을 회복하여 옛 체제로 되돌아가려는 태도를 내세운 **빈 체제**가 성립됨으로써 유럽에서는 옛 왕조가 대부분 부활하였다. 빈 회의 결과 프랑스에 부르봉 왕조가 들어섰다. 그러나 샤를 10세가 의회를 해산하고 자유주의 운동을 탄압하자 파리 시민들이 **7월 혁명**을 일으켜 샤를 10세를 몰아내고 루이 필리프를 왕으로 추대하여 **입헌 군주정**을 수립하였다(1830).

루이 필리프의 왕정에 불만을 품고 있던 공화주의자들은 1832년 6월 봉기를 일으켰지만 실패로 끝났다. 프랑스의 새로운 왕정은 산업 혁명으로 시민과 노동자 세력이 성장하는 상황에는 아랑곳하지 않고 여전히 일정한 재산이 있는 시민에게만 선거권을 주었다. 이에 중하층 시민과 노동자들은 선거권 확대를 요구하며 **2월 혁명**을 일으켜 루이 필리프를 몰아내고 공화정을 세웠다(1848). 2월 혁명의 영향으로 오스트리아에서 **3월 혁명**이 일어나 메테르니히가 추방되고 빈 체제는 무너졌다.

민중을 이끄는 자유의 여신(루브르 박물관)
Liberty Leading the People(Louvre)

외젠 들라크루아가 7월 혁명을 기념하기 위해 1830년에 그린 낭만주의 화풍의 그림입니다. 자유의 여신이 한손에는 삼색기를 들고 다른 손에는 총검을 휘두르며 민중을 이끌고 있어요.
This is a painting of romanticism drawn by Eugène Delacroix in 1830 to celebrate the July Revolution. The goddess of liberty is leading the people with a tricolor flag in one hand and a bayonet in the other.

04 Spread of Liberalism and Nationalism

Establishment of the Vienna System and Spread of Liberalism

Ambassadors of European states came together in the capital city of Austria, Vienna, and discussed the post-war state of the world after the Napoleonic Wars. In this meeting known as the Congress of Vienna chaired by Austrian statesman Klemens von Metternich, the European states agreed to return the political structure and territories of Europe to the days before the French Revolution(1815).

With the establishment of the reactionary Vienna System, most of the old monarchies came back in Europe. As a result of the Congress of Vienna, the House of Bourbon was restored in France. When the French Bourbon monarch Charles X dismissed Parliament and persecuted liberalist movements, the citizens revolted against him in the July Revolution, overthrew King Charles X, brought Louis Philippe I to the throne, and established a Constitutional monarchy(1830).

The Republicans who were not happy about Louis Philippe's constitutional monarchy initiated a rebellion in June 1832, but it failed. The new monarchy of France cared less about the situation occurring in which the power of the citizenry and working classes were growing as the result of the industrial revolution and gave voting rights only to a small percentage of citizens who qualified in terms of their wealth. Popular discontent finally resulted in the February Revolution by the lower-middle class citizens and the workers who demanded an enlarged voting base. The rebels overthrew Louis Philippe and established a republic government(1848). In the aftermath of the February Revolution, the March Revolution that broke out in Austria and Metternich was dismissed, thus ending the Vienna System.

이탈리아에 통일 왕국이 건설되다

프랑스 혁명과 나폴레옹 전쟁의 영향으로 유럽 각국에 민족의 독립을 요구하는 **민족주의** 민족의 독립과 통일을 가장 중시하는 사상가 확산되었다. 민족주의는 분열되어 있던 이탈리아와 독일 지역의 통일 운동에 영향을 미쳤다.

19세기 후반까지 이탈리아는 여러 나라로 나뉘어 있었고 북부 이탈리아는 오스트리아의 지배를 받고 있었다. **사르데냐** 왕국의 재상 **카보우르**는 산업을 육성하고 군대를 개편하는 개혁을 단행하였고, 오스트리아와 전쟁을 벌여 북부와 중부 이탈리아를 통합하였다. 이후 의용대를 거느린 **가리발디**가 시칠리아와 나폴리 등 이탈리아 남부를 점령하여 사르데냐 왕에게 바치면서 **이탈리아 왕국**이 수립되었다(1861). 이탈리아 왕국은 베네치아와 교황령을 차례로 병합하여 이탈리아의 통일을 이루었다(1870).

....

🏛 비토리오 에마누엘레 2세 기념관은 어떤 건축물인가요?

에마누엘레 2세는 카보우르를 재상으로 기용하여 이탈리아 통일의 대업을 이루었고, 이를 기념하기 위해 거대한 기념관을 세웠다. 건물과 계단, 거대한 에마누엘레 기마상, 두 빅토리아 여신상 등은 모두 하얀 대리석으로 만들어졌다. 기념관 안에는 이탈리아 통일 박물관과 제1차 세계 대전 때 숨진 무명 용사의 무덤이 있다.

이 기념관은 독특한 외형 때문에 '타자기' 또는 '웨딩케이크'라는 별명을 지니고 있다. 카피톨리누스 언덕의 일부와 중세풍 동네 하나를 완전히 철거하여 세웠기 때문에 주변 유적과 조화를 이루지 않는다는 평을 듣기도 한다.

비토리오 에마누엘레 2세 기념관(이탈리아 로마)
Monumentto a Vittorio Emanuele II(Rome, Italy)

A Unified Kingdom Is Established in Italy

The French Revolution and the Napoleonic Wars played a key role in the birth and spread of nationalism across other countries and triggered a wave of national independence movements. Nationalism influenced the unification movement in Germany and Italy, which were divided.

Until the early 19th century, Italy was divided into several states, and northern Italy was under the rule of Austria. Cavour, the premier of the Kingdom of Sardinia, carried out sweeping reforms to overhaul the military and promote industry and succeeded in unifying northern and central Italy after winning a war with Austria. Then the leader of a militia group, Giuseppe Garibaldi, conquered Sicily and Naples and handed them over to King Victor Emmanuel II of Sardinia. Thus, the Kingdom of Italy was born(1861). After Victor Emmanuel II took over Venetia and Rome, Italy was finally united under one crown(1870).

....

◉ What Kind of Building Is the Vittorio Emanuele II Memorial?

Emanuele II established the great achievement of the unification of Italy by appointing Chancellor Cavour. A huge memorial hall was built to commemorate this. Buildings and staircases, huge mounted statues of Emanuele II, and the two Victorian goddesses are all made of white marble. Inside the memorial hall are the Italian Museum of Unification and the tombs of unknown soldiers who died in World War I.

The memorial hall is nicknamed 'typewriter' or 'wedding cake' because of its unique appearance. Some say that it does not harmonize with the surrounding ruins because part of the Capitolinus Hill and a medieval neighborhood were completely demolished to built it.

독일에 통일 왕국이 건설되다

독일도 오랫동안 여러 국가와 도시로 나뉘어 있었다. 그러다 1834년 프로이센을 중심으로 독일 내에서 관세를 없애는 **관세 동맹**이 체결되면서 통일을 위한 경제적 기반이 마련되었다.

이후 프로이센의 재상 **비스마르크**는 **철혈 정책**을 내세워 군비를 확장하고 강력한 군대를 육성하였다. 이를 바탕으로 프로이센은 통일을 방해하던 오스트리아를 물리치고 북독일 연방을 결성하였다. 프랑스와의 전쟁에서도 승리하여 **독일 제국**을 수립하였다(1871).

2월 혁명 이후 프랑스에서는 나폴레옹의 조카인 루이 나폴레옹이 대통령으로 선출되었다. 루이 나폴레옹은 쿠데타를 통해 황제에 즉위하여 자신을 **나폴레옹 3세**로 칭하였다. 하지만 프로이센과의 전쟁에서 패배하면서 프랑스의 제정은 다시 붕괴하였다.

독일 제국의 경계(1871)
Border of the German Empire

러시아
Russia

프로이센
Preussen

베를린
Berlin

알자스·로렌
Alsace-Lorraine

남독일 연방
Commonwealth of Southern Germany

프랑스
France

스위스
Switzerland

오스트리아 제국
Austrian Empire

사보아
Savoy

베네치아
Venice

토리노
Torino

제노바
Genoa

피렌체
Florence

교황령
Papal States

나폴리
Napoli

사르데냐 왕국
Kingdom of Sardinia

가리발디의 원정대
Garibaldi's Expedition

지중해
Mediterranean Sea

팔레르모
Palermo

시칠리아
Sicily

- ■ 1815년의 프로이센 Prussia in 1815
- ■ 1859년 사르데냐 영토 Territory of Sardinia in 1859
- ■ 1860년 프랑스에 할양한 영토 Territory Ceded to France in 1860
- ■ 1861년 이탈리아 왕국 Kingdom of Italy in 1861
- ■ 1866년 병합 지역 Region Merged in 1866
- ■ 1870년 병합 지역 Region Merged in 1870
- □ 북독일 연방 North German Confederation
- ■ 1871년 병합 지역 Region Merged in 1871
- ■ 남독일 연방 Southern German Confederation

독일과 이탈리아의 통일 Unification of Germany and Italy

◉ 프로이센은 철혈 정책으로 무엇을 얻었나요?

철혈 정책에서 철은 병기를, 혈은 병력을 의미한다. 비스마르크는 독일의 통일이 병기와 병력에 의해서만 해결될 수 있다고 생각하였다. 이에 자유주의자들의 반대를 무릅쓰고 군비를 증강하였다. 프로이센은 철혈 정책을 바탕으로 강력한 군대를 육성한 후 프랑스와의 전쟁에서 승리하였다.

군비가 큰 부담이 될지라도 우리에게 유익하다면 열정을 다해 몸에 지녀야 합니다. 우리가 당면한 과제를 수행하기 위해 주목해야 할 것은 프로이센의 자유주의가 아니라 군비입니다. 연설이나 다수결이 아니라 철과 피로써만 문제가 해결됩니다.　　　　- 비스마르크, 1862년 의회 연설

비스마르크 Bismarck ©Loescher, P. & Petsch

A Unified Empire Is Established in Germany

Germany was also divided into several states. In 1834, the German Customs Union was formed under Prussian leadership to manage tariffs and economic policies within their territories, thereby laying the groundwork for national unification.

Later, a Prussian, Otto von Bismarck, expanded armaments and built stronger military forces under his infamous Blood and Iron policy. Supported by this military power, Prussia defeated Austria, which had been preventing unification, and established the North German Confederation. The Prussian army went on to defeat France and finally established the German Empire(1871).

In France, Napoleon's nephew Louis Napoleon Bonaparte was elected President of the Second Republic after the February Revolution. Louis Napoleon became the emperor through a coup and called himself Napoleon III. However, the empire quickly declined after losing a war with Prussia.

....

🌀 What Did Prussia Gain from Its Blood and Iron Policy?

In the Blood and Iron policy, iron means weaponry and blood means military strength. Bismarck thought that German unification could only be resolved by means of weapons and troops. In response, despite opposition from the liberals, armaments were increased. Prussia won the war with France after fostering a strong army based on this Blood and Iron policy.

> Even if armaments can be a huge burden, if it is good for us, we must keep it with all our passion. It is the armaments, not Prussian liberalism, that we should pay attention to in order to carry out the task at hand. Only iron and blood solve the problem, not speech or majority vote.
>
> - Bismarck, Speech at the Parliament in 1862

05 라틴 아메리카의 독립
라틴 아메리카 국가들이 독립하다

16세기 이후 에스파냐와 포르투갈은 라틴 아메리카를 지배하면서 막대한 금과 은을 약탈하고 식민지인들을 착취하였다. 미국 혁명과 프랑스 혁명에 영향을 받은 식민지들은 나폴레옹 전쟁으로 유럽이 혼란해진 틈을 타서 독립 운동을 벌였다.

1804년 **아이티**가 흑인 노예들의 혁명으로 가장 먼저 프랑스로부터 독립하였다. 이어서 에스파냐인의 후손인 **크리오요** 아메리카에서 태어난 백인을 일컫는 말가 본국의 차별 대우와 부당함에 맞서 독립 운동에 나섰다. 라틴 아메리카 북부에서는 **볼리바르**의 활약에 힘입어 베네수엘라, 콜롬비아, 에콰도르, 볼리비아 등이 에스파냐로부터 독립하였다. 멕시코는 **이달고 신부** 등의 독립 투쟁에 힘입어 1821년에 에스파냐로부터 독립하였다. 이듬해에는 브라질이 포르투갈로부터 독립하였다. 라틴 아메리카 남부에서는 **산마르틴**이 혁명군을 양성하여 에스파냐군을 물리치고 아르헨티나, 칠레 등을 독립시켰다.

유럽 국가들은 라틴 아메리카의 독립 운동을 탄압하려 하였다. 하지만 영국이 새로운 상품 시장을 확보하기 위해 독립을 지원하고 미국이 아메리카에 대한 유럽의 간섭을 배격하는 **먼로 선언**을 발표하면서 라틴 아메리카의 독립은 계속되었다.

라틴 아메리카의 독립 Independence of Latin America

- 에스파냐령 Spanish Territory
- 포르투갈령 Portuguese Territory
- 영국령 British Territory
- 프랑스령 French Territory
- 네덜란드령 Dutch Territory

볼리바르
베네수엘라, 콜롬비아, 에콰도르를 합한 대콜롬비아 공화국을 수립하였어요. 이어 페루를 해방하고, 볼리비아 공화국을 세웠지요.

05 Independence of Latin America

Independence of Latin American Countries

Since the 16th century, Spain and Portugal plundered a massive amount of gold and silver and had exploited colonists during their colonization of Latin America. Inspired by the American Revolution and French Revolution, these colonists joined the independence movement while Europe was in a state of unrest because of the Napoleonic Wars.

Haiti was the first to become independent from France in 1804 as a result of the Haitian Revolution brought about by Haitian slaves against the French colonial rulers. Soon after, Latin Americans of Spanish roots, the Criollos, launched an independence movement against Spain in protest of their unfair treatment. In the northern part of the Latin Americas, Simon Bolivar contributed to the liberation of Venezuela, Colombia, Ecuador, Bolivia and other countries from Spanish rule. In Mexico, a Roman Catholic priest, Miguel Hidalgo, and others struggled and successfully achieved independence from Spain in 1821. In the following year, Brazil became independent from Portugal. In southern Latin America, José de San Martín led his revolutionary army, defeated the Spanish forces, and liberated Argentina and Chile.

European countries tried to suppress the independence movements of Latin America. But the Latin Americans were able to continue to fight for their independence because England supported their independence to secure new markets for their products, and the United States also supported them with the declaration of the Monroe Doctrine regarding opposition to European colonialism in the Americas.

> Bolivar
> I united Venezuela, Colombia, and Ecuador to establish Greater Colombia.
> Then I liberated Peru and established the Republic of Bolivia.

👓 바이러스가 아메리카의 지도를 바꾸다

 콜럼버스가 신대륙을 발견한 이후 유럽인들은 아메리카 원주민들에게 천연두, 홍역, 결핵, 장티푸스 등 전염병을 퍼뜨렸다. 아메리카 원주민들은 유럽인의 전염병에 면역력이 없었으므로 대다수가 죽음을 맞았다. 천연두는 스페인 군대가 아스테카 제국과 잉카 제국을 정복하는 데 중요한 변수로 작용하기도 했다.

 아프리카로부터 흑인 노예들이 신대륙으로 끌려오면서 황열병도 유입되었다. 1791년 아이티 혁명이 일어나자 나폴레옹은 혁명군을 진압하기 위해 3만여 명의 병력을 파견했다. 아프리카에서 온 흑인들은 황열병에 면역이 형성돼 있었으나 프랑스 군인들은 면역이 형성되어 있지 않아 황열병으로 대부분 사망하였다. 1804년 아이티는 프랑스로부터 독립하였다.

 프랑스는 여러 전쟁과 황열병으로 타격을 입었고 미시시피강 유역의 루이지애나를 미국에 단돈 1500만 달러에 팔아야 했다. 미국은 스페인 점령지였던 미국 서부까지 확보하여 강대국의 기틀을 마련하였다.

 미국은 황열병 덕분에 파나마 운하도 확보하였다. 수에즈 운하를 건설한 경험이 있던 프랑스의 레셉스가 1881년 파나마 운하를 건설하기 시작하였다. 하지만 3만여 명의 노동자들이 말라리아와 황열병으로 죽어갔고 공사는 중단되었다.

 1900년 미국의 리드가 이끄는 연구팀이 황열병을 옮기는 모기가 알을 낳을 수 없도록 고인 물을 없앴고 말라리아와 황열병은 줄어들었다. 미국은 1914년 파나마 운하를 완공하였고 막대한 경제적 이득을 얻었다.

흑인 노예 출신인 투생 루베르튀르는 나폴레옹에 맞서 흑인 노예들의 독립 운동을 이끌다가 옥사하였어요. 결국 프랑스 군대는 황열병에 시달리다 아이티의 독립 운동을 막지 못했고 루이지애나까지 미국에 팔아야 했지요.
Toussaint Louverture, a black slave, died in prison while leading the independence movement of black slaves against Napoleon. Eventually, the French army suffered from yellow fever and, unable to stop Haiti's independence movement, had to sell Louisiana to the United States.

투생 루베르튀르 Toussaint Louverture

∞ Viruses Changed the Map of America

After Columbus discovered the New World, Europeans spread infectious diseases such as smallpox, measles, tuberculosis, and typhoid among Native Americans. Native Americans were not immune to European infectious diseases, and many were killed. Smallpox served as an important variable for the Spanish army in their conquest of the Aztec and Inca empires.

Yellow fever was introduced when black slaves from Africa were brought to the New World. When the Haitian Revolution broke out in 1791, Napoleon sent more than 30,000 troops to quell the revolutionary forces. Black people from Africa were immune to yellow fever, but French soldiers died from it because they were not. In 1804, Haiti gained independence from France.

France was hit by wars and yellow fever, and had to sell Louisiana in the Mississippi basin to the United States for just 15 million dollars. The United States secured the western part of the United States, which was occupied by Spain, and laid the foundations to become a great power.

The United States also secured the Panama Canal thanks to yellow fever. French Lesseps, who had experience in constructing the Suez Canal, began constructing the Panama Canal in 1881. However, more than 30,000 workers died of malaria and yellow fever, and the construction was halted.

In 1900, a medical team led by Walter Reed in the U.S. removed the stagnant water so that mosquitoes carrying yellow fever could not lay eggs, and the occurrence of malaria and yellow fever were subsequently reduced. The United States completed the Panama Canal in 1914 and gained enormous economic benefits.

2

유럽의 산업화와 제국주의

01 산업 혁명

영국에서 산업 혁명이 시작되다

영국에서는 명예혁명 이후 안정된 의회 정치 체제가 확립되어 비교적 자유로운 경제 활동이 보장되어 있었다. 이러한 정치적 안정과 중산층의 활발한 경제 활동에 힘입어 18세기 후반 영국에서 가장 먼저 **산업 혁명**이 시작되었다.

영국은 일찍부터 **모직물 공업**이 발달하여 상당한 자본과 기술을 축적하였고 공업 발전에 필요한 석탄과 철 등의 지하자원도 풍부하였다. 게다가 **인클로저 운동**
_{영국의 지주들이 미개간지와 공유지에 울타리를 쳐서 자신의 소유지로 만든 운동}으로 토지를 잃고 도시로 유입된 농민이 많아 노동력도 풍부하였다. 영국의 넓은 식민지는 원료를 공급하고 생산된 상품을 소비하는 역할을 하였다.

산업 혁명은 **면직물 공업**이 발달하면서 본격적으로 시작되었다. 면직물은 모직물에 비해 가볍고 세탁하기 쉬워 세계 시장에서 수요가 폭발적으로 늘었다. 면직물의 수요가 늘자 실을 뽑는 **방적기**와 천을 짜는 **방직기**가 잇따라 발명되었다. 특히 **제임스 와트**가 개량한 **증기 기관**이 동력으로 사용되면서 면직물 생산이 크게 늘었다. 이로써 면직물 공업은 가내 수공업에서 벗어나 공장제 기계 공업의 형태를 띠게 되었다.

제니 방적기를 이용해 동시에 16가닥의 실을 뽑아낼 수 있게 되었어요.
Using the spinning Jenny, it was possible to pull out 16 threads at the same time.

와트는 증기 기관을 개량하여 전보다 적은 비용으로 더욱 강한 동력을 공급할 수 있었어요.
James Watt improved the steam engine to provide more power for less cost than before.

하그리브스의 제니 방적기
Hargreaves' Spinning Jenny

제임스 와트의 증기 기관 개량
James Watt's Steam Engine ©Nicolás Pérez

Industrialization and Imperialism of Europe

01 Industrial Revolution

Industrial Revolution Kicks off in England

In Britain, relatively free economic activitiy was guaranteed after a stable parliamentary political system was established in the aftermath of the Glorious Revolution. Supported by this political stability and dynamic economic activities of the middle class, Britain was able to get a head start on the Industrial revolution in the late 18th century.

England had accumulated wealth and technology thanks to its advanced woolen industry and also being blessed with rich natural resources such as coal and iron that were necessary for industrial development. In addition, the country had a rich labor force because many peasants moved into cities after losing their farmland due to the Enclosure Movement. The extensive territory that England had colonized supplied resources to England, and it also became its consumer market for the goods manufactured and exported by England.

The Industrial Revolution picked up with the development of the cotton industry. Since cotton fabrics were lighter and easier to wash compared to wool fabrics, there was a big demand for cotton throughout the world. The increasing demand for cotton fabrics was followed by the invention of spindles and weaving machinery. The production of cotton fabrics skyrocketed when the textile industry started using the improved steam engine invented by James Watt as their source power. Eventually, the cotton industry was able to grow from a cottage industry into the factory system.

산업 혁명이 전 세계로 확산하다

영국의 산업 혁명은 제철 및 석탄 공업으로 이어졌고 원료와 상품을 수송하기 위한 새로운 교통수단도 나타났다. 스티븐슨은 증기 기관차를 실용화하고 미국의 풀턴은 증기선을 만들어 상업적으로 이용하는 데 성공하였다. 또한 미국의 모스가 유선 전신을, 벨이 전화기를 발명하여 소식을 빠르게 전할 수 있게 되었다.

산업 혁명은 유럽 각지로 확산되었다. 19세기 전반 벨기에에서는 석탄이 풍부해 광업이 발전하였고, 프랑스에서는 석탄이 생산되는 북동부 지역을 중심으로 산업화가 이루어졌다. 독일은 통일을 이룬 후부터 정부 주도 아래 중화학 공업 분야를 중심으로 산업화를 추진하였다. 미국은 광대한 영토와 풍부한 지하자원을 바탕으로 중화학 공업을 발전시켰다. 러시아는 시베리아 철도를 부설하고, 광산업과 석유 산업을 중심으로 발전하였다. 일본도 메이지 유신 이후 산업화에 성공하면서 강국으로 부상하였다.

🧭 80일간의 세계 일주는 어떻게 가능하였나요?

쥘 베른이 쓴 소설 『80일간의 세계 일주』의 주인공 필리어스 포그는 80일 만에 세계 일주를 하겠다는 내기를 하고 1873년 세계 일주에 나섰어요. 포그 일행은 런던에서 출발한 후 증기 기관차와 증기선을 이용하여 샌프란시스코에 도착하였지요. 대륙 횡단 열차로 뉴욕에 갔으며, 증기선을 타고 대서양을 건너 80일 만에 런던에 도착하였어요. 포그는 세계 일주 중에 날짜 변경선을 통과하여 하루를 벌게 되었고, 결국 내기에서 이겼어요.

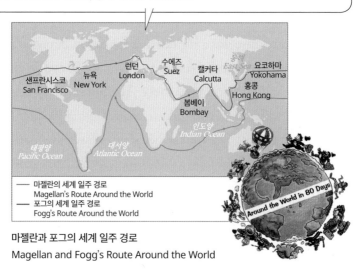

마젤란과 포그의 세계 일주 경로
Magellan and Fogg's Route Around the World

Industrial Revolution Spreads Throughout the World

The industrial revolution that started in England spread from cotton to the iron and coal industries and triggered the development of new means of transportation which were necessary to transport raw materials and manufactured goods. Robert Stephenson invented an early steam locomotive and an American engineer, Robert Fulton, developed a commercially successful steamboat. Fast communication was made possible as well thanks to Morse code invented by the American inventor Samuel F. B. Morse and the practical telephone was invented by the Scottish scientist Alexander Graham Bell.

The industrial revolution spread throughout Europe. By the early 19th century, Belgium saw the development of a mining industry, and in France, industrialization kicked off in the northeast part of the country where coal was being produced. In the case of Germany, the government-led industrialization began centering on the heavy chemical industry soon after the unification of the country. The United States saw the growth of a heavy chemical industry supported by its vast territory and rich natural resources, while Russia constructed the Trans-Siberian Railway and saw the growth of mining and petroleum industries. Japan also achieved successful industrialization after the Meiji Reform and emerged as a super power.

◉ How Was It Possible to Travel Around the World in 80 Days?

Phileas Fogg, the protagonist of Jules Verne's novel "*Around the World in 80 Days*", set out to travel around the world in 1873 with a bet that he would travel around the world in 80 days. After leaving London, Fogg and his companions arrived in San Francisco by steam locomotive and steamship. They went to New York by transcontinental train, and arrived in London, after 80 days, by acrossing the Atlantic in a steamboat. Fogg saved a day by crossing the date line during his trip around of the world and won the bet.

02 국제 경제 질서의 변화

산업 혁명으로 자본주의 체제가 자리 잡다

공장제 기계 공업의 발달에 힘입어 산업 자본가는 많은 임금 노동자를 고용하여 상품을 대량으로 생산하였다. 대량 생산된 상품들은 새로운 교통수단으로 전 세계에 운반되어 사람들은 전보다 풍요로운 삶을 누리게 되었다.

공장이 들어선 지역은 공업 도시로 변하였고, 산업화로 몰락한 수공업자와 농민이 일자리를 찾아 도시로 몰리면서 도시의 인구는 크게 증가하였다. 생산 수단과 자본을 갖지 못한 노동자는 자본가에게 고용되어 임금을 받으며 살아갔다.

그 과정에서 생산과 소비가 시장에 의해 결정되는 **자본주의 경제 체제**가 자리를 잡았다. 애덤 스미스는 자본가가 정부의 간섭 없이 시장에서 자유롭게 이윤을 추구하는 **자유방임주의**를 주장하여 자본주의 체제를 이론적으로 뒷받침하였다.

◉ **산업 혁명은 모든 사람에게 편리함을 안겨 주었을까요?**

산업 혁명으로 도시에 많은 공장이 생겨나면서 도시의 규모가 커졌다. 기계를 이용한 대량 생산으로 물자가 풍부해지고, 도시 간 이동이 자유로워지면서 생활이 편리해졌다.

반면 도시에 인구 과밀 현상이 나타나면서 노동자들의 거주지 문제가 심각해졌고 저임금, 장시간 노동, 아동 노동 문제 등이 발생하였다.

혁신적인 발명품들이 런던 만국 박람회에 전시되었어요.

많은 인구가 도시로 유입되면서 주거 환경과 위생 상태가 매우 나빠졌어요.

화려하게 장식된 수정궁 Ornately Decorated Interior of Crystal Palace

런던의 빈민가 London Slums

02 Changing Economic Order of the World

Industrial Revolution Gives Rise to Capitalism

Supported by the development of a factory system, industrial capitalists could mass produce products by hiring more factory workers. New means of transportation were used to transport the mass produced merchandise throughout the world, thereby allowing people to enjoy a more enriched life than ever before.

The areas that housed factories turned into industrial cities, and cities experienced a sharp increase of population due to the influx of artisans and peasants who lost their livelihood because of the industrialization. Workers who did not have the capital and means of production were employed by capitalists and lived on wages.

During this period, the capitalist economic system emerged in which production and consumption were determined by the market. Adam Smith provided the theoretical foundation for the capitalist system by advocating the principle of Laissez-faire, in which capitalists have the freedom to pursue profits in the market without government intervention.

....

❷ Did the Industrial Revolution Bring Convenience to Everyone?

As the industrial revolution created many factories in the city, the scale of cities increased. Mass production using machinery has made life more convenient as supplies have become plentiful and movement between cities has become freer.

On the other hand, due to overpopulation in cities the problem of residences for poor workers became serious and problems such as low wages, long working hours, and child labor occurred.

Innovative inventions were exhibited at the Great Exhibition in London.	As a large number of people entered the city, the living environment and sanitation conditions became very poor.

자본주의의 대안을 모색하다

노동 문제와 빈부 격차 등 자본주의의 문제점이 심화되자 이를 해결하기 위한 방안으로 사회주의가 등장하였다. 생시몽, 오언 등은 자본가와 노동자가 협력하여 빈부격차가 없는 이상 사회를 건설해야 한다고 주장하였다.

마르크스와 엥겔스는 이들의 주장이 실현 가능성이 없는 공상적 사회주의라고 비판하였다. 마르크스는 산업 자본가가 생산 수단을 독점하고 끝없이 이윤을 추구해 자본주의의 문제점이 생겼으므로 노동자들이 혁명을 일으켜 자본가들을 타도해야 평등한 사회를 이룩할 수 있다고 주장하였다. 마르크스주의는 20세기 초 러시아 혁명에 큰 영향을 미쳤다.

🏵 마르크스는 세계사에 어떤 영향을 끼쳤나요?

마르크스는 젊은 시절 프로이센에서 기자 생활을 하였다. 그가 쓴 기사가 당국의 검열을 받게 되자 그는 프랑스로 망명하였다. 마르크스는 낭비벽이 심해 아버지 유산을 다 팔고 귀족 딸이었던 부인이 물려받은 유산도 다 팔아버렸다. 그의 어머니는 그가 『자본론』으로 유명해지자 "자기 자본도 못 챙긴 놈이 무슨 자본론을 말하냐."라고 푸념했다고 한다.

프랑스에서도 쫓겨난 마르크스는 벨기에의 브뤼셀로 가서 공산당을 창당하였으나, 이것이 문제가 되어 영국으로 가게 되었다. 영국에서 마르크스는 엥겔스의 도움을 받아 『공산당 선언』(1848)과 『자본론』(1867)을 출간하였다.

마르크스 사후 소련이라는 공산 국가가 탄생하였다. 공산주의 국가들은 획일성과 비효율성으로 자본주의 국가들에 뒤처졌지만, 마르크스주의는 사회적 의무에 대한 각성을 불러일으켰다는 긍정적인 면도 있다.

> 노동자들이 혁명에서 잃을 것은 쇠사슬뿐이고 얻을 것은 세상이다. 만국의 노동자여, 단결하라! - 마르크스, 『공산당선언』
> The proletarians of the world have nothing to lose but their chains. They have a world to win. Workers of the world, unite!
> - Karl Marx, "*The Communist Manifesto*"

카를 마르크스 Karl Heinrich Marx

Search for the Alternative to Capitalism

Problems associated with capitalism such as the labor issues and the growing gap between the rich and the poor gave birth to Socialism as a solution to these problems. Henri de Saint-Simon, Robert Owen, and other socialists argued that a society should be built as long as there is no gap between the rich and the poor through cooperation between capitalists and workers.

Karl Marx and Friedrich Engels criticized their claims as being utopian socialism. Marx claimed proletarian revolution should happen in all capitalist societies in order to ensure equality for all because the capitalist problems were the result of industrial capitalists who monopolized the means of products and endlessly pursued profits. His idea, called Marxism, had a great influence on the Russian Revolution in the early 20th century.

🌐 How Did Karl Marx Influence World in History?

Marx was a journalist in Prussia in his youth. When his article was censored by the authorities, he defected to France. Marx was so wasteful that he used up all the inheritance left by his father and all the inheritance of his wife, who was a daughter of a noble family. Marx's mother said that when he became famous for "*capitalism*", she complained, "How can a man who couldn't even keep his own capital talk about capitalism?"

Marx, who was soon expelled from France, went to Brussels, Belgium, and founded the Communist Party. This caused him to have to go to England. In England, Marx, with the help of Friedrich Engels, published "*The Communist Manifesto*" (1848) and "*Das Kapital*" (1867).

After Marx's death, the Soviet Union, a communist country, was born. Communist countries lag behind capitalist countries because of their uniformity and inefficiency, but there is also a positive side to Marxism that has evoked an awakening of social obligations.

03 제국주의 침략과 식민지 경쟁

제국주의가 등장하다

19세기 후반 서양 열강은 자국의 자본주의 체제를 유지 · 발전시키기 위해 값싼 원료 공급지와 자국 상품 판매 시장 및 국내 잉여 자본 투자 시장이 필요하였다. 이에 서양 열강은 군사력을 앞세워 약소민족을 식민지화하는 적극적인 대외 팽창 정책을 추진하였다. 이를 **제국주의**라고 부른다. 제국주의 열강은 지하자원과 노동력이 풍부한 아프리카와 아시아 등지에 진출하여 광대한 지역을 차지하였다.

서양 열강은 식민지 개척에 대한 자신들의 행위를 정당화하기 위해 **사회 진화론** 허버트 스펜서가 다윈이 주장한 자연 도태와 적자생존의 법칙을 사회 발전에 적용하여 설명한 이론을 내세워 식민지 침략을 사상적으로 뒷받침하였다. 사회 진화론은 인종주의와도 연결되어 백인종이 황인종이나 흑인종보다 우월하다는 인종적 우월 의식이 강화되었다. 이를 이용해 강대국이 약소국을 지배하는 것을 정당화하기도 하였다.

🌐 **세실 로즈는 어떻게 제국주의에 앞장서게 되었나요?**

세실 로즈는 아프리카에서 다이아몬드를 채굴하여 부를 축적하였다. 이를 바탕으로 케이프타운의 총독이 되었고, 적극적인 대외 팽창 정책을 펼쳤다.

나는 어제 런던에서 열린 실업자 집회에 가서 그들의 목소리를 들었다. 거기에서 빵을 달라는 절규나 다름없는 거친 연설을 들었다. 그리고 제국주의의 필요성을 더욱 확신하였다. …… 우리 정치가는 대영 제국의 4,000만 인구를 내란으로부터 지키고, 과잉 인구를 수용할 방법을 찾아야 한다. 이를 위해 새로운 영토를 개척하고, 공장이나 광산에서 생산한 상품의 판로를 만들어 내야만 한다. 그들이 내란을 원하지 않는다면 그들은 제국주의자가 되어야만 한다.

세실 로즈의 제국주의를 그린 풍자화
Satirical Painting of Cecil Rhodes' Imperialism

03 Imperialist Invasions and Race for Colonization

Emergence of Imperialism

In the late 19th century, the Western powers needed sources that would supply inexpensive raw materials as well as markets to sell their products in and invest their surplus capital. So, the Western powers pushed forward with aggressive foreign expansion policies which included using their military forces to colonize weak nations. This is called imperialism. The imperialist powers made inroads into Asia and Africa, which were rich with a labor force and natural resources, and occupied vast territories.

The Western powers justified their acts of colonial invation with the theory of social evolution. The theory of social evolution was connected with racial supremacy, and together, these ideologies strengthened their belief in racial superiority in which they believed the white race was superior to other races. They used this belief to justifiy powerful nations dominating weaker ones.

⸺⸺⸺⸺⸺⸺⸺⸺⸺⸺⸺⸺⸺⸺⸺⸺⸺⸺

⊚ How Did Cecil Rhodes Take the Lead in Imperialism?

Cecil Rhodes accumulated wealth by mining diamonds in Africa. Based on this, he became governor of Cape Town and implemented aggressive foreign expansion policies.

> Yesterday I went to a rally of unemployed people in London and heard their voices. There, I heard rough speech, like a scream, asking for bread. Then, I was more convinced of the need for imperialism. ⸺⸺ Politicians must find a way to protect 40 million people of British Empire from a civil war and accommodate the overpopulation. To do this, we must explore new territories and create a market for goods produced in factories and mines. If people don't want civil war, they have to be imperialists.

제국주의 국가들이 아프리카를 분할하다

리빙스턴, 스탠리 등의 탐험으로 아프리카의 내륙 사정이 유럽에 알려지기 시작하면서 유럽의 제국주의 열강은 앞다투어 아프리카로 진출하였다. 영국은 이집트 수에즈 운하의 관리권을 차지하고 이집트를 보호국화하였다. 또한 케이프 식민지를 합병하여 남아프리카 연방을 조직하였다. 이후 카이로, 케이프타운, 콜카타를 연결하는 팽창 정책을 추진하였다(3C 정책).

프랑스는 알제리를 정복한 후 사하라 사막 일대를 장악하고 튀니지를 보호령으로 만들었다. 이후 마다가스카르를 차지하고 이를 연결하려는 **횡단 정책** 아프리카를 동서로 연결을 추진하였다. 결국 프랑스는 아프리카를 남북으로 연결하는 종단 정책을 추진하던 영국과 수단의 파쇼다에서 충돌하였다(**파쇼다 사건**, 1898). 하지만 당사국 간의 합의로 전쟁으로까지 번지지는 않았다.

뒤늦게 식민지 경쟁에 뛰어든 독일은 베를린, 바그다드, 이스탄불을 잇는 정책을 추진하였다(3B 정책). 독일의 세력 확장은 영국은 물론 남하 정책을 펼치던 러시아를 자극하였다.

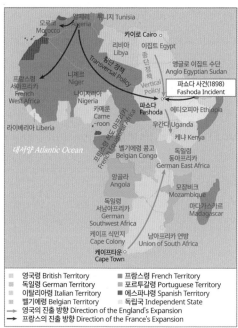

열강의 아프리카 분할
African Division by the Western Powers

◉ 벨기에 초콜릿이 유명한 이유는 무엇인가요?

> 콩고 지역을 식민지로 지배한 벨기에는 그곳에서 들여온 코코아로 초콜릿을 만들었어요. 그 과정에서 많은 토착민이 희생당하였지요. 콩고 민주 공화국은 1960년에 벨기에로부터 독립하였지만 지금도 초콜릿은 벨기에를 대표하는 상품 중 하나입니다.

Imperialist States Divide Africa

When explorers such as Henry Stanley and David Livingston introduced the situations of continental Africa to the world, European imperialist powers jumped into a race to colonize Africa. England seized control over the Suez Canal in Egypt and declared Egypt its protectorate. England went on to establish the Union of South Africa by taking over the Cape Colony. Since then, an expansion policy linking Cairo, Cape Town, and Kolkata has been implemented(3C policy).

After conquering Algeria, France took control of the Sahara Desert and took Tunisia under a protective decree. Afterwards, the government implemented a transversal policy to occupy Madagascar and link it. Tension over the imperial territorial disputes between Britain and France climaxed in their clash in Fashoda, Sudan(Fashoda Incident, 1898), but it did not escalate into war.

Germany, which belatedly entered the colonial race, pushed for policies linking Berlin, Baghdad, and Istanbul(3B policy). Germany's expansion of power stimulated not only Britain but also Russia, which has pursued a southward policy.

⚜ **Why Is Belgian Chocolate So Famous?**

Belgium, which ruled the Congo region as a colony, made chocolate with cocoa from it. Meanwhile, many of the indigenous people were sacrificed. The Democratic Republic of Congo became independent from Belgium in 1960, but chocolate is still one of Belgium's leading commodities.

벨기에 브뤼셀의 초콜릿 상점
A Chocolate Shop in Brussels, Belgium

제국주의 국가들이 아시아와 태평양 지역을 분할하다

영국은 17세기 전반에 **동인도 회사** 아시아 무역에 대한 독점권을 특허받은 회사를 앞세워 인도 무역을 주도하였다. 플라시 전투(1757)에서 프랑스를 물리친 후에는 무굴 제국 황제로부터 **벵골 지역**의 통치권을 인정받았다. 이후 영국은 인도 대부분의 지역을 점령하였다. 영국은 인도인들에게 **목화**와 **아편** 재배를 강요하였고, 영국의 값싼 면직물을 인도에 대량으로 들여와 인도의 면직물 공업을 무너뜨렸다. 이어서 영국은 태평양 지역으로도 진출하여 오스트레일리아와 뉴질랜드를 영국의 자치령으로 삼았다.

한편 인도에서 밀려난 **프랑스**는 베트남, 캄보디아 등 인도차이나 지역으로 진출하였다. 네덜란드도 동인도 회사를 앞세워 인도네시아를 차지하는 등 동남아시아 대부분이 유럽의 식민지가 되었다.

미국은 에스파냐와의 전쟁에서 승리한 후 에스파냐의 식민지였던 쿠바와 필리핀을 차지하였다. 또한 괌과 하와이 제도를 차지하여 태평양으로 세력을 확장하고 **파나마 운하**까지 장악하였다. 독일은 비스마르크 제도와 마셜 제도 등을 점령하였고, 러시아도 남하 정책 과정에서 오스만 제국을 압박하는 등 식민지 확보를 위한 제국주의 열강의 경쟁은 더욱 치열해졌다.

제국주의 국가들이 분할한 아시아와 태평양 지역
Asia and Pacific Regions Divided by Imperialist Powers

Imperialist States Divide Asia and the Pacific Region

In the first half of the 17th century, Britain established the East India Company and dominated trade with India. After defeating France in the Battle of Plassey(1757), Britain was acknowledged for its control over Bengal by the Mughal emperor, thereby occupying almost all of India. Britain forced India to grow cotton and opium, but India's cotton industry struggled because India became the largest importer of cheap British cotton textiles. Britain went on to invade the Pacific region and absorbed Australia and New Zealand under its dominion.

After losing India to Britain, France turned its eyes to the Indochinese peninsula and occupied Vietnam and Cambodia. The Netherlands also established its own Dutch East India Company and colonized Indonesia. By now, almost the whole of southeastern Asia had become colonized by Europe.

In the case of the United States, it defeated Spain in the Spanish–American War and took over Cuba and the Philippines, which used to belong to Spain. The United States expanded its influence to the Pacific regions by colonizing Guam and Hawaii and gained control of the Panama Canal as well. Germany annexed the Bismarck Archipelago and the Marshall Islands, and Russia posed a devastating threat to the Ottoman Empire with its Southward Invasive Policy. The race among these imperialist powers to expand their colonies continued growing in intensity.

3

서아시아와 인도의 국민 국가 건설 운동

01 서아시아의 국민 국가 건설 운동

오스만 제국, 국민 국가 건설을 위해 탄지마트를 실시하다

18세기 들어 오스만 제국을 둘러싼 서구 열강의 압박이 심해졌다. 19세기에는 그리스가 오스만 제국으로부터 독립하였고, 세르비아와 이집트 등도 자치권을 획득하였다.

나라 안팎으로 위기를 맞이한 오스만 제국은 위기에서 벗어나기 위해 **탄지마트** 터키어로 '개선'이라는 뜻(1839~1876)라는 근대적 개혁을 실시하였다. 이에 따라 근대적인 군대 양성, 행정 개편, 신교육제 도입을 추진하였다. **미드하트 파샤**는 의회를 개설하여 근대적 헌법인 미드하트 헌법을 제정하였다. 그러나 오스만 제국의 개혁은 보수 세력의 반대와 **러시아·튀르크 전쟁**에서 오스만 제국이 패배하면서 좌절되었다. 미드하트 헌법이 폐기되고 전제 정치가 강화되었으나 청년 튀르크당이 무장봉기를 통해 정권을 장악하고 헌법을 부활하였다. 하지만 제1차 세계 대전에서 오스만 제국이 패하자 청년 튀르크당은 해체되었다.

오스만 제국의 쇠퇴 Decline of the Ottoman Empire

⚙ **미드하트 파샤가 추구한 개혁의 목표는 무엇인가요?**

미드하트 파샤
미드하트 헌법은 아시아 최초의 헌법입니다. 국민의 기본권 보장, 의회 설립, 내각의 권한 강화 등을 이루기 위해 입헌 정치를 도입하고자 하였지요.

Establishment of Nation-states in West Asia and India

01 Nation-state movement in West Asia

Ottoman Empire Launches Tanzimat to Establish a Nation-State

During the 18th century, the Ottoman Empire was under serious threat by the Western powers. Then in the 19th century, the Ottoman Empire lost Greece when Greece became an independent country and also lost Serbia and Egypt when they gained autonomy.

The Ottoman Empire tried to overcome the crises it faced from within and without by pushing forward with a series of modernization reforms called Tanzimat(1839–1876), which included reconstitution of the Ottoman Modern Army, overhauling the administration, and the introduction of a new educational system. During the late Tanzimat period, one of the leading statesmen, Midhat Pasha, founded the Ottoman Parliament and led the Ottoman constitutional movement. But all these reform efforts wound up fruitless because of objections by the conservatives and defeat in the Russo-Turkish War. When the Ottoman constitution was suspended and the dictatorship was strengthened, the Young Turks took over the regime through an armed uprising and revived the Constitution. Ultimately, the Young Turks was disbanded when the Ottoman Empire lost in World War I.

◉ **What Were the Goals of the Reforms Midhat Pasha Pursued?**

> Midhat Pasha
> The Ottoman Constitution of 1876 was the first constitution in Asia. I tried to introduce constitutional politics to ensure the basic rights of the people, establish parliament, and strengthen the power of the Cabinet.

이란에서 입헌 혁명이 일어나고 아라비아에서 와하브 운동이 일어나다

18세기 말 이란을 통일한 **카자르 왕조**는 러시아와 영국의 침략으로 많은 영토와 이권을 빼앗겼다. 카자르 왕조가 주요 수출품인 담배에 관한 독점권을 영국에 넘겨주자 상인과 이슬람교 지도자를 중심으로 담배 이권 수호 운동이 전개되었다. 그 결과 담배에 대한 이권은 회수하였으나 영국에 막대한 손해 배상금을 지급하게 되었다.

1906년에는 카자르 왕조의 전제 정치에 반대하는 **입헌 혁명**이 일어나 헌법이 제정되고 의회가 설립되었다. 그러나 입헌 혁명은 영국과 러시아의 간섭으로 실패하였고 영국과 러시아의 분할 협정으로 남부는 영국, 북부는 러시아가 점령하며 영토의 상당 부분을 상실하였다. 이란은 반식민지 상태로 전락하였다.

이러한 상황에서 18세기 **압둘 와하브**가 아라비아에 와하브 왕국을 세웠다. 18세기 이후 오스만 제국의 지배가 약화되면서 유럽 열강들이 아랍 세계에 침입하기 시작하였다. 이에 이븐 압둘 와하브는 이슬람교의 근본 교리와 경전인 『쿠란』으로 돌아가자는 **와하브 운동**을 일으켰다. 이 운동은 오스만 제국에 반대하는 민족 운동으로 발전하여 아랍인의 민족의식을 일깨웠다.

19세기 초에는 아랍 고전을 연구하는 아랍 문화 부흥 운동과 계몽 운동이 일어났다. 이러한 민족 운동은 오늘날 아랍 민족주의의 기반이 되었다.

사우디아라비아의 국기는 와하브 운동 당시 쓰였던 깃발을 바탕으로 만들어졌어요. 국기에는 아랍어로 "알라 외에는 다른 신이 없고, 무함마드는 알라의 사도이다."라는 『쿠란』의 구절이 쓰여 있어요.
The flag of Saudi Arabia is based on the flag used during the Wahhabism movement. On the flag, there is an Arabic phrase from the "*Quran*", "There is no other god than Allah, and Muhammad is the apostle of Allah."

사우디아라비아 국기 Flag of Saudi Arabia

Constitutional Revolution in Iran and Wahhabism Movement in Arabia

The Qajar dynasty, which unified Iran at the end of the 18th century, lost significant territory and interest due to invasion by Russia and Britain. When the king granted Britain the exclusive right to grow, sell, and export tobacco, which was their main export item, merchants and Muslim leaders took the lead in revolts against the tobacco concession. The tobacco protests resulted in the cancellation of the concession, but the Qajar government had to pay a large sum in compensation to Britain.

In 1906, the Constitutional Revolution took place in protest of the dictatorship of the Qajar Dynasty, and it led to the establishment of a parliament and constitution. But the revolution failed in the end due to the intervention of Britain and Russia. The split agreement between the United Kingdom and Russia resulted in British occupation in the south and Russian occupation in the north. Iran lost much of its territory and fell into a semi-colonial state.

In this situation Abdul Wahab founded the Wahab Kingdom in Arabia in the 18th century. As the power of the Ottoman Empire weakened after the 18th century, European powers began to invade the Arab world. A religious leader from Central Arabia named Muhammad ibnAbd al-Wahhab started the Wahhabism movement and advocated the return to the "*Quran*" and the practices of the Prophet. This movement evolved into the Arab nationalistic movements against the Ottoman Empire and awakened the Arabs' national consciousness.

The early 19th century saw the enlightenment movement and the Arab Renaissance characterized by a return to classical literature. These nationalistic movements became the foundation of today's Arab nationalism.

이집트가 독립 운동을 전개하다

오스만 제국으로부터 이집트 통치를 위임받은 **무함마드 알리**는 근대적 군대를 창설하고 산업을 장려하였다. 또한 조세와 토지 제도를 개혁하였으며 교육과 행정을 개편하는 등 적극적인 근대화 정책을 실시하였다. 이러한 개혁의 성과를 바탕으로 이집트는 그리스 독립 전쟁 때 오스만 제국을 지원해 자치를 획득하였다. 이후 **수에즈 운하**를 건설하는 과정에서 영국과 프랑스의 자금을 빌리면서 경제적 종속이 심화되었고 결국 영국에 수에즈 운하 관리권을 넘겨주게 되었다. 이에 맞서 **아라비 파샤**의 군부 세력은 '이집트인을 위한 이집트'를 내세운 반영 운동을 일으켰으나 영국은 이 운동을 진압하고 이집트를 보호국으로 삼았다.

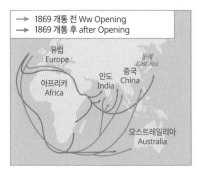

수에즈 운하 개통 후 항로의 변화 Change of Route after Opening of Suez Canal

---

◎ 수에즈 운하 건설은 이집트에 어떤 영향을 주었나요?

수에즈 운하는 아시아와 아프리카 두 대륙의 경계인 이집트의 시나이반도 서쪽에 건설된 운하이다. 이집트가 재정난을 해소하기 위하여 건설을 추진하였고, 19세기 중반 이집트 총독이었던 사이드 파샤가 프랑스의 레셉스에게 수에즈 운하 건설 특허권을 주었다.

10여 년의 공사 끝에 1869년 수에즈 운하가 완성되었다. 그러나 프랑스 등으로부터 막대한 빚을 얻어 공사를 진행하였다. 운하가 완성되자 빚 대신 발행한 주식을 사들인 영국이 수에즈 운하의 경영권을 차지하였다. 결국 수에즈 운하에서 나오는 수입은 프랑스와 영국 등 다른 나라가 가져가게 되었다. 게다가 영국은 수에즈 운하 경영을 핑계로 이집트의 정치에 간섭하였고, 결국 이집트를 보호국으로 삼았다.

오늘날의 수에즈 운하 Current Suez Canal ©2020 Enterprise Ventures LLC

Independence Movement Rises in Egypt

When appointed as the new governor of Egypt by the Ottoman sultan, Muhammad Ali promoted industry and built a modern military. He also reformed the tax and land system, overhauled education and administration, and carried out a series of modernization policies. As a result of his reforms, Egypt was able to support the Ottoman Empire during the Greek War of Independence and was granted autonomy from the Ottomans. Later on, Egypt borrowed money from Britain and France for the construction of the Suez Canal, and became heavily indebted to them as a result. Eventually, Egypt had to sell their majority stake in the Suez Canal to Britain to satisfy its debt obligations. The Egyptian military forces led by Colonel Ahmed Arabi Pasha revolted against this concession shouting the slogan 'Egypt for Egyptians' but Britain suppressed their nationalist liberation movement and declared Egypt a protectorate.

....

◉ How Did the Construction of the Suez Canal Affect Egypt?

The Suez Canal was built on the west side of the Sinai Peninsula in Egypt, the border between Asia and Africa. Egypt promoted construction to alleviate its financial crisis, and in the mid-19th century, Egypt's governor Said Pasha granted Lesseps, who was a French diplomat, a patent for the construction of the Suez Canal.

After 10 years of construction, the Suez Canal was completed in 1869. However, the construction was undertaken with huge amounts of loans from France. When the canal was completed, the UK, which bought stocks issued instead of taking on debt, took over the management of the Suez Canal. Eventually, the income from the Suez Canal was taken by other countries such as France and England. Moreover, Britain intervened in Egyptian politics under the pretext of managing the Suez Canal, and eventually made Egypt a protectorate.

02 무굴 제국의 성립과 발전

무굴 제국, 인도를 정복하다

13세기부터 인도 북부 지방에서 델리 술탄 왕조 시대가 시작되었다. 16세기 초 티무르 왕조의 후손인 **바부르**가 중앙아시아에서 인도로 진출하여 델리 술탄 왕조를 무너뜨리고 이슬람교 국가인 **무굴 제국**을 세웠다. 이후 **아크바르 황제**는 북인도 및 아프가니스탄 지역까지 정복하여 대제국을 건설하였다. 아크바르는 힌두교도에게 걷던 인두세를 폐지하고, 스스로 힌두교도와 결혼하였다. 또한 힌두교도를 고위 관리에 등용하는 등 종교 관용적인 정책으로 사회의 안정을 이루었다.

무굴 제국은 **아우랑제브 황제** 때 남부 인도 대부분을 정복하여 영토를 크게 확장하였다. 하지만 아우랑제브는 **이슬람 제일주의**를 내세워 인두세를 부활시켰고, 힌두교 사원을 파괴하는 등 탄압을 가하였다. 이에 힌두교도와 시크교도 등이 각지에서 반란을 일으켜 무굴 제국은 점차 쇠퇴하기 시작하였다.

- 아크바르 황제 시대의 영역
  Territory During Akbar the Great Period
- 아우랑제브 황제 시대의 최대 영역
  Maximum Territory During Aurangzeb Period

무굴 제국의 영역 Territory of the Mughal Empire

🔎 **아크바르 황제와 아우랑제브 황제의 종교 정책은 어떻게 달랐나요?**

아크바르 황제
지금까지 나는 나와 신앙이 다른 사람들을 박해하여 나와 같게 만들려고 하였으며, 그것을 신에 대한 귀의라고 생각하였다. 그러나 강제로 개종시킨 사람에게서 어떻게 성실한 신앙생활을 기대할 수 있을까?

아우랑제브 황제
나는 이슬람만을 위한 통치자가 될 것이다. 이슬람교를 믿지 않는 자들에게는 종교의 자유에 대한 대가인 인두세를 다시 부과할 것이다.

02 Establishment and Growth of the Mughal Empire

Mughal Empire Occupies India

Beginning in the 13th century, the northern part of India was under the rule of the Delhi Sultans. Then in the early 16th century, Babur, a direct descent of Emperor Timor, made inroads from Central Asia to India, brought down the Delhi Sultanate, and founded the Islamic Mughal Empire. Later on, Akbar the Great built a great empire by expanding its territory to North India and as far as Afghanistan. Akbar stopped collecting poll tax from the Hindus and married a Hindu himself. He brought order to society by enforcing religious tolerance policies, such as recruiting Hindus to bureaucracy.

The Mughal Empire conquered most of southern India during Emperor Aurangzeb's rule and greatly expanded its territory. But Aurangzeb being a Muslim supremacist, persecuted Hindus by reviving the poll tax and destroying Hindu temples. Subsequently, the Mughal Empire started to decline because the Hindus and the Sikhs began to revolt throughout the empire.

⊚ How Was the Religious Policy of Akbar the Great and Emperor Aurangzeb Different?

Akbar the Great
Until now, I have tried to persecute people of different faiths with me and make them the same as me, and have considered it a devotion to God. But how can I expect a devout life of faith from someone who has been forcibly converted?

Emperor Aurangzeb
I will be a ruler only for Islam. Those who do not believe in Islam will be charged again with the poll tax, which is the price of religious freedom.

무굴 제국, 인도 이슬람 문화를 꽃피우다

무굴 제국에서는 힌두교를 바탕으로 한 인도의 전통문화와 페르시아, 튀르크, 아랍의 영향을 받은 이슬람 문화의 융화가 이루어져 **인도 이슬람 문화**가 발전하였다.

종교에서는 힌두교와 이슬람교의 융합을 통해 탄생한 시크교가 발전하였다. 언어에서는 힌두어, 페르시아어, 아랍어 등을 혼합하여 만든 **우르두어** ^{현재 파키스탄과 인도의 공용어 가운데 하나}를 공용어로 사용하였다. 건축 분야에서는 인도와 이슬람의 양식을 조화롭게 반영한 **아그라성**과 **타지마할**을 건설하였다.

무굴 제국은 농업과 상공업의 발전을 토대로 하여 중국, 동남아시아, 서아시아, 유럽을 잇는 대외 무역을 통해서 많은 부를 축적하였다. 무굴 제국의 대표적 수출품인 **면직물**은 동남아시아, 서아시아뿐만 아니라 유럽에서도 인기였다. 그 밖에 후추 등 향신료도 유럽에 수출하였다.

◉ 타지마할은 누가 만들었나요?

샤자한은 15세 때 14세의 뭄타즈 마할을 만나 결혼하였다. 샤자한에게는 여러 명의 부인이 있었지만 그의 애정은 오로지 뭄타즈 마할에게만 향하였다. 그런데 뭄타즈 마할이 14번째 아이를 낳는 도중 사망하였고, 샤자한은 뭄타즈 마할을 기리기 위해 타지마할을 짓기 시작하였다. 매일 2만 명의 인부와 1,000마리의 코끼리가 동원된 타지마할은 완공되기까지 22년이 걸렸다.

타지마할 Taj Mahal

Mughal Empire Blooms the Indo-Islamic Culture

In the Mughal Empire, the fusion of the Hindu-based traditional Indian culture and the Islamic culture influenced by Persia, the Turks, and the Arabs gave birth to the Indo-Islamic culture.

In terms of religion, the empire saw the establishment of a new religion called Sikhism through the fusion of Hinduism and Islam. Regarding language, the empire created and commonly used Urdu, which was a mix of Arabic, Hindi, and Persian languages. Regarding architecture, the Agra Fort and the Taj Mahal were built during this period by harmoniously blending the Indian and Islamic styles.

The Mughal Empire, supported by advanced farming and commerce built wealth through international trade with China, Southeast Asia, West Asia, and Europe. Cotton textiles from the Mughal Empire were exported and became popular in Southeast Asia and West Asia, as well as in Europe. In addition, spices such as pepper were also exported to Europe.

⚫ Who Built the Taj Mahal?

Shah Jahan met 14-year-old Mumtaz Mahal at the age of 15 and married. He had several wives, but his affection was directed only toward Mumtaz Mahal. However, while giving birth to her 14th child, Mumtaz Mahal died, and Shah Jahan began to build the Taj Mahal in honor of Mumtaz Mahal. The Taj Mahal took 22 years to complete with 20,000 workers and 1,000 elephants working every day.

> 훗날 샤자한은 아들 아우랑제브에게 제위를 찬탈당하고 아그라성에 유폐되어 2.5km 떨어져 있는 타지마할을 바라보며 여생을 마쳤어요.
> Later, Shah Jahan was usurped by his son Aurangzeb and confined to Agra Fort, ending his life looking at the Taj Mahal 2.5 km away.

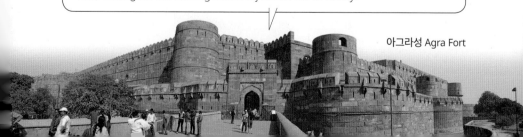

아그라성 Agra Fort

03 인도의 국민 국가 건설 운동

영국이 인도를 침략하다

무굴 제국은 17세기 말부터 잦은 정복 전쟁과 지방 세력의 반란 등으로 점차 쇠퇴하였다. 이러한 상황에서 서양 열강들이 인도에 본격적으로 침입하기 시작하였다. 영국은 **동인도 회사**를 앞세워 인도 지방 세력을 장악하였고, 프랑스도 동인도 회사를 설립하고 인도에 진출하였다. 이후 영국은 **플라시 전투**에서 프랑스와 벵골 연합군을 물리쳐 **벵골** 지역의 통치권을 장악하였고, 대인도 무역을 독점하였다. 이후 인도는 영국의 원료 공급지이자 상품 시장이 되었으며 식민 통치를 받고 착취를 당하였다.

이러한 영국인들의 횡포에 대한 불만이 고조되었고, 종교적인 갈등까지 더해져 동인도 회사의 용병인 세포이^{페르시아어로 '병사'라는 뜻으로, 인도에서 채용된 현지 용병을 부르는 명칭들}이 항쟁을 일으켰다(세포이의 항쟁). 이들은 한때 델리를 점령하였으나 영국 동인도 회사의 무력 진압으로 실패하고 말았다.

세포이의 항쟁은 인도 최초의 대규모 민족 운동으로 인도인의 민족의식을 각성시켰다. 또한 영국의 태도가 변화하는 계기가 되어 영국은 무굴 제국 황제를 폐위하고 **인도 통치 개선법**을 제정하였다. 그리고 동인도 회사를 해체하고 영국령 인도 제국을 성립해 영국 빅토리아 여왕이 인도 제국 황제를 겸임하였다.

....

🅰 세포이가 항쟁을 일으킨 원인은 무엇인가요?

Why Did the Sepoys Initiate the Mutiny?

동인도 회사에서 지급한 탄약 주머니에 소와 돼지의 기름이 칠해져 있다는 소문이 돌았어요. 힌두교도는 소를 신성시하고 이슬람교도는 돼지를 부정하다고 생각하였어요. 그래서 힌두교와 이슬람교를 믿는 세포이들이 반발하였지요.

Rumor has it that the ammunition bags provided by the East India company were coated with cow and pig oil. Hindus think of cows as sacred and Muslims believe pigs are unclean. These rumors triggered the mutiny of the Sepoys, who believed in Hinduism and Islam.

탄약통의 구조와 세포이의 모습
The Structure of the Cartridge
and the Appearance of Sepoy

03 Nation-state Movement in India

England Invades India

The Mughal Empire gradually declined after the end of the 17th century due to the frequent conquest wars and insurrections by local forces. It was under this circumstance the Western powers began to invade India in full force. Britain established the East India Company and began to take control over cities in India, and France established its own East India Company and advanced to India. Britain and France engaged in a Battle of Plassey over the control of Bengal. In this battle, Britain defeated the French and Mughal forces in Bengal, took control over the Bengal region and monopolized trade with India. Now, India became the supplier of raw materials while at the same time a market for their products, and was subsequently exploited under British colonial rule.

The growing resentment against Britain's tyranny on top of religious conflict blew up into a rebellion called the Sepoy Mutiny, so named because it was led by the Sepoys, the native soldiers serving under the British. The Sepoys captured Delhi but lost it to Britain again soon after, and the rebellion ended a failure when the East India Company brought in military forces to crack down on it.

The Sepoy Mutiny was significant because it was the first large-scale nationalist movement in India and awakened national consciousness in Indians. In the wake of the rebellion, the British changed their stance on India. Britain dethroned the Mughal Empire and passed the Government of India Act. The East India Company was closed down, and Queen Victoria of the United Kingdom was declared sovereign, placing a representative from London there, known as the Governor-General.

❶ 탄약주머니 Ammunition Bag ❷ 화약 Gunpowder ❸ 총알 Bullet

인도 국민 회의가 국민 국가 건설 운동을 전개하다

인도인들의 민족 운동이 확대되자 영국은 인도인들을 회유하여 식민 지배를 원활히 하고자 하였다. 이에 지식인, 관리, 민족 자본가, 지주 등이 **인도 국민 회의**를 결성하였다(1885).

인도 국민 회의는 초기에는 영국의 인도 지배를 인정하면서 자치를 주장하였다. 그러나 영국이 **벵골 분할령**을 발표하자 반영 운동을 전개하였다. 인도 국민 회의는 틸라크를 중심으로 콜카타 대회를 열어 자치 획득(스와라지), 국산품 애용(스와데시), 영국 상품 불매, 국민 교육의 4대 강령을 채택하는 등 반영 운동을 전개하였다. 결국 영국은 벵골 분할령을 취소하고 명목상 인도인의 자치를 인정하였다.

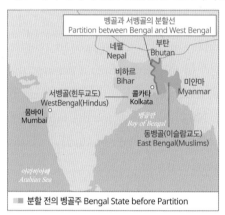

벵골과 서벵골의 분할선
Partition between Bengal and West Bengal

네팔 Nepal
부탄 Bhutan
비하르 Bihar
미얀마 Myanmar
서벵골(힌두교도) WestBengal(Hindus)
콜카타 Kolkata
뭄바이 Mumbai
벵골만 Bay of Bengal
동벵골(이슬람교도) East Bengal(Muslims)
아라비아해 Arabian Sea

■ 분할 전의 벵골주 Bengal State before Partition

벵골 분할령 Partition of Bengal

◉ **벵골 분할령에 인도인들은 어떻게 대응하였나요?**

1905년 인도 총독은 벵골주가 면적이 넓고 인구가 많아 한 사람의 장관이 다스리기에 힘들다는 명분으로 동벵골과 서벵골로 나누어 통치하겠다고 발표하였다. 인도인들은 영국이 힌두교와 이슬람교도의 분열을 꾀하기 위해 벵골 분할령을 발표하였음을 깨닫고, 반영 운동을 시작하였다. 이러한 상황에서 인도 국민 회의의 지도자가 된 간디는 인도의 완전 독립을 목표로 비폭력·불복종 운동을 전개하였다. 인도 국민 회의를 중심으로 한 인도의 반영 운동이 전국적으로 확산되자, 영국은 벵골 분할령을 취소하고 명목상 인도인의 자치권을 인정하였다.

인도인은 자기 손으로 자기 옷을 만드세요. 영국 상품과 직물은 인도를 가난하게 만듭니다.
Indians have to make their own clothes.
British goods and textiles make India poor.

물레를 돌리는 간디 Mahatma Gandhi Spinning the Wheel

Indian National Congress Launches Nation-state Building Movement

As the national movement expanded among the Indians, Britain sought conciliation with them for more efficient colonial rule in India. In response, Indian intellectuals, officials, national capitalists, and landowners formed the Indian National Congress in 1885.

In the beginning, the members of the Indian National Congress acknowledged Britain's domination of India while calling for autonomy. But when Britain declared the Partition of Bengal, it triggered Anti-British movements under the leadership of the Indian National Congress. At its Calcutta Session, led by Talik as a part of their anti-British campaign, the Congress passed four resolutions that included self-government(Swaraj), revival of domestic products(Swadeshi), a boycott of British products, and national education. In the end, Britain canceled the Partition of Bengal and granted nominal sovereignty to India.

◉ How Did Indians Respond to the Partition of Bengal?

In 1905, the Viceroy of India announced that the state of Bengal would be divided into East Bengal and West Bengal on the grounds that it would be difficult for a single minister to rule because of its large area and population. Indians realized that the British had announced the Partition of Bengal in an attempt to separate Hindus and Muslims, and which triggered anti-British movements. In this situation, Gandhi, who became the leader of the Indian National Congress, launched a non-violence and disobedience movement aiming for complete independence of India. As the anti-British movements centered on the Indian National Congress spread across the country, England canceled the Partition of Bengal and nominally recognized Indians' autonomy.

④

동아시아의 국민 국가 건설 운동

01 중국의 국민 국가 건설

아편 전쟁으로 불평등 조약이 체결되다

청은 18세기 중반 이후 광저우에서 특허 상인인 **공행**을 통한 무역만 허용하고 있었다. 영국은 청의 차와 비단 등을 구입하면서 무역 적자가 늘어나자 인도에서 생산한 아편을 청에 밀수출하였다. 이로 인해 청에서는 대량의 은이 유출되고 아편으로 인한 사회 문제가 발생하였다. 청은 **임칙서**를 광저우로 보내 아편을 몰수하고 아편 밀무역을 단속하였다. 그러자 영국은 군함을 파견하여 전쟁을 일으켰다(**제1차 아편 전쟁**).

영국에 패한 청은 영국과 불평등 조약인 **난징 조약**을 체결하여 영국에 홍콩을 할양하고 5개 항구를 개항하였다. 영국은 난징 조약이 체결된 후에도 무역량이 크게 늘지 않자 애로호 사건을 빌미로 프랑스와 연합하여 청을 공격하였다(**제2차 아편 전쟁**).

전쟁에서 패한 청은 **텐진 조약**과 **베이징 조약**을 체결하여 10개 항구를 추가로 개항하고 외교관의 베이징 주재와 크리스트교 포교를 허용하였다.

아편 전쟁의 전개 Unfolding of the Opium War

초기 무역(18세기)
Early Trade(18th Century)

삼각 무역(19세기)
Triangle Trade(19th Century)

---

④

Nation-state Movement in East Asia

01 Establishment of Nation-state in China

Opium Wars Result in Unequal Treaties

Since the mid‒18th century, the Qing Dynasty had allowed import and export in Guangzhou only through a guild of Chinese merchants called Cohong. When increasing the importation of tea and silks from Qing resulted in growing trade imbalance, Britain found the solution by exporting opium grown in India and selling it to Qing. Consequently, Qing was faced with numerous problems associated with the opium epidemic as well as the massive drainage of silver. Qing tried to solve the problems by sending Viceroy Lin Zexu to Guangzhou to confiscate opium and crack down on the contraband trade in opium. Britain protested by sending a military fleet to China, and a conflict ensued(First Opium War).

After being defeated by Britain, Qing was forced to sign the unequal Treaty of Nanjing, which ceded Hong Kong Island to Britain and made Qing open five trade ports to foreign merchants. When the treaty did not result in increased trade with Qing, Britain used an incident that involved its ship named the Arrow as an excuse to declare war and fight against Qing along with France(Second Opium War).

This time, the war concluded with the Treaty of Tianjin and the Treaty of Beijing, which allowed opening of an additional ten ports for

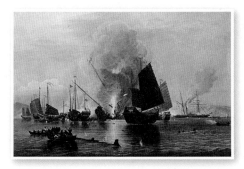

trade, diplomats to establish legations and live in Beijing, and freedom of movement for Christian missionaries.

제1차 아편 전쟁 The First Opium War

태평천국 운동이 일어나다

아편 전쟁을 계기로 청 왕조의 권위가 추락하였고 배상금 지급으로 농민의 조세 부담이 가중되었다. 이때 **홍수전**은 크리스트교 신앙을 바탕으로 상제회를 조직하고 청 왕조 타도와 한족 국가 부흥을 주장하며 **태평천국 운동**을 일으켰다 (1851).

태평천국군은 토지의 균등 분배, 남녀평등을 주장하였고, 변발 · 전족 · 아편 흡연 · 축첩 등을 금지하였다. 태평천국은 난징을 중심으로 기세를 올렸으나 내

부의 분열로 점차 세력이 약화되었고, 증국번과 이홍장 등을 비롯한 지방의 한인 지주 · 신사와 관료들이 조직한 의용군 및 서양 군대의 공격을 받아 멸망하였다 (1864).

난징에 입성하는 태평천국군
The Taiping Rebels Entering Nanjing

◉ 여성의 발이 자라지 못하도록 한 풍습이 있었던 이유는 무엇인가요?

태평천국군은 난징을 점령하여 도읍으로 정한 후 토지, 사회, 행정, 군사 제도를 발표하고 이상사회를 실현하고자 하였다. 이들은 특히 전족의 폐지를 주장하였다. 전족은 중국 여성들이 어린 시절에 발을 천으로 감싸고 묶어 자라지 못하게 만드는 풍습이었다. 당시 작은 발은 미인의 조건이었고, 발이 큰 여성은 결혼하기 힘들 정도였다. 송대에 시작된 전족은 명과 청에서 유행하였는데, 청대에 전족 금지령이 내려졌지만 쉽게 사라지지 않았다.

전족 풍습은 전족을 금지한 태평천국 운동, 신해혁명 이후에 일어난 여성 운동 등을 겪으며 점차 줄어들어 현재는 거의 사라졌다.

전족을 한 여성 A Woman with Foot Binding

Taiping Rebellion in China

The authority of the Qing Dynasty tumbled in the aftermath of the opium wars and when the liability of tax on farmers increased because of the reparations. It was around this time when, influenced by Christian teachings, Hong Xiuquan raised the Taiping Rebellion, which was about supporting the overthrow of the Qing dynasty and the revival of the Chinese Han tribe(1851).

The Taiping rebels prescribed an ideal society of sharing land and equality for men and women, and banned the Chinese queue hairstyle, foot-binding, inhaling opium, and polygamy. The Taiping rebels captured Nanjing and seemed to be successful in the beginning, but they grew weaker due to internal conflicts until they were driven out when attacked by the Western troops and militias organized by the Han landlords and bureaucrats, including Zeng Guofan and Li Hongzhang(1864).

⊜ Why Was There a Custom that Prevented Women's Feet from Growing?

After the Taiping rebels occupied Nanjing and designated it as the capital, they announced land, society, administration, and military systems to realize an ideal society. The Taiping rebels particularly insisted on the abolition of foot-binding. Food-binding is a custom that has persisted among Chinese women to artificially tie their feet and make them smaller. Small feet were a condition of beauty at the time, and women with large feet even had difficulty marrying. Foot-binding began in the Song Dynasty and became popular in the Ming and Qing dynasties. During the Qing Dynasty, a foot-binding ban was imposed, but it did not disappear.

Foot-binding gradually declined after the Taiping Rebellion banned it and the women's movement that took place after the Xinhai Revolution, and has now almost completely disappeared.

양무운동과 변법자강 운동이 추진되다

청은 아편 전쟁과 태평천국 운동을 통해 개혁의 필요성을 인식하였다. 그래서 태평천국 운동 진압에 앞장선 **증국번**, **이홍장** 등 한인 출신 관료들의 주도하에 서양의 과학 기술을 받아들여 부국강병을 이루려는 **양무운동**을 전개하였다.

청은 근대적 공장 설립, 군수 공업 육성, 서양식 육·해군 창설, 신식 학교 설립 등의 개혁을 추구하였지만 의식이나 제도의 개혁 없이 진행되었고, 정부의 체계적인 계획도 부족하였다. 결국 **청·일 전쟁**에서 패하며 양무운동은 한계를 드러냈다.

청·일 전쟁 이후 열강의 이권 침탈이 심해지면서 중국인들의 위기의식이 높아졌다. 이에 강유웨이, **량치차오** 등 개혁적 성향의 지식인들이 광서제의 호응을 얻어 입헌 군주제 도입, 과거제 개혁, 신교육 실시 등 근대적인 개혁을 추진하였다(**변법자강 운동**). 그러나 변법자강 운동은 서태후 등 보수파의 반발로 실패하였다.

⚫ 양무운동과 변법자강 운동은 어떤 차이가 있나요?

What Is the Difference between Self-Strengthening Movement and the Hundred Days' Reform?

이홍장 서양식 기계는 농경이나 직포, 인쇄, 도자기 제조 등의 용구를 모두 제조할 수 있고 …… 위기를 안정으로 돌리고 허약함을 강력함으로 바꾸는 길은 기계를 모방하여 제조하는 데서 비롯됩니다.
Li Hongzhang Western-style machines can manufacture all tools such as farming, woven fabric, printing, and pottery manufacturing. …… The way to turn crisis into stability and transform weakness into power comes from imitating machinery and manufacturing.

량치차오 변화해서는 안 된다고 말하는 사람들은 옛것을 지키자는 말만 되풀이한다. 기존의 관행만을 따라가면서 제도가 서서히 무너지는 것을 바라만 본다. 그들에게는 아무런 생각도 없고 바꿔 보려는 움직임도 없다.
Liang Qichao Those who say we shouldn't change only repeat their words to keep the old ones. They only follow existing practices and watch the system slowly collapse. They have no thoughts and no moves to change.

Self-Strengthening Movement and the Hundred Days' Reform

The opium wars and the Taiping Movement made Qing realize the need for reform. So began the Self-Strengthening Movement designed to build a strong nation by learning Western science and technology under the leadership of the Han Chinese officials such as Zeng Guofan and Li Hongzhang who took the lead in quelling the Taiping Movement.

Qing pushed forward with sweeping reforms that included the construction of modern factories, promotion of a military supply industry, creation of a Western style army and navy, and the founding of modern schools. But the movement was unsuccessful due to a lack of Qing support and also because it was not supported by reforms to consciousness and systems. The limits of the Self-Strengthening Movement were proven when Qing was defeated in the Sino-Japanese War.

After losing the Sino-Japanese War, Chinese people's sense of crisis continued growing due to the increasing aggression of super powers. In response, a movement that came to be known as 'the Hundred Days' Reform' was undertaken by the Guangzu Emperor and his progressive intellectual supporters such as Kang Youwei and Liang Qichao to modernize the country through the reformed civil service examination system and modernized educational system, all based on a constitutional monarchy structure. But the movement was unsuccessful due to objections by conservative bureaucrats and Empress Dowager Cixi.

이홍장은 난징에 기기국을 세워 대포와 화약을 생산하였어요.
Li Hongzhang set up a bureau of the machinery in Nanjing to produce cannons and gunpowder.

양무운동 때 만들어진 금릉 기기국
Jinling Arsenal Established During the Self-Strengthening Movement

의화단이 외세의 침략에 저항하다

개항 후 열강의 이권 침탈이 심화되고 크리스트교가 확산되자 이에 저항하는 운동이 일어났다. 의화단은 '부청멸양'청을 도와 외세를 몰아냄을 주장하며 교회와 철도를 파괴하고 베이징의 외국 공관을 습격하였다. 청은 의화단을 이용하여 서구 열강을 몰아내려 하였다.

제국주의 열강은 청 정부가 의화단 진압에 대한 열의도 없고 그만한 통치력도 없다고 비난하면서 직접 출병하기로 결정하였다. 영국, 독일, 러시아, 일본 등 8개국 연합군에 의해 의화단은 진압되었고 열강이 베이징을 점령하면서 배상금 지급과 외국 군대의 베이징 주둔을 인정하는 신축 조약이 체결되었다. 이로 인해 청은 더욱 위기에 처하였다.

....

🏵 의화단이 교회와 철도를 파괴한 이유는 무엇인가요?

청·일 전쟁 이후 독일이 산둥 지역을 점령하자 농민과 노동자들은 서양 세력에 대한 반감을 갖게 되었다. 철도가 부설되면서 전통 마을이 파괴되었고, 로마 가톨릭교회의 선교사들을 통해 천주교가 빠르게 확산되었다.

산둥 지역의 농민과 노동자들은 서양 열강에 대항하는 의화단 운동을 전개하였다. 의화단은 전선과 철도 등을 서구 열강의 침략 도구로 여겨 파괴하였고, 교회를 불태우고 선교사를 살해하였다. 또한 외국 공사관을 포위하여 습격하는 등 과격한 반외세 투쟁을 전개하였다.

> 서양 세력을 몰아내자! 철도를 파괴하자!
> Let's drive out the foreign forces!
> Let's destroy the railway!

당시 프랑스 신문 기사에 실린 의화단의 모습
The Yihequan in a French Newspaper Article at that time

The Yihequan Resists the Invading Foreign Forces

The growing threat of economic plundering by foreign powers and spreading Christian presence that followed the opening of trade ports gave rise to rebellions. A Chinese secret society known as the Yihequan rebelled by destroying church buildings and railroads and raiding foreign legations in Beijing under the slogan 'Support the Qing government and exterminate the foreigners'. The Qing Dynasty tried to drive out foreign forces by using this militia group.

The imperialist powers decided to launch troops directly, accusing the Qing government of having no enthusiasm for suppressing the Yihequan and a lack of governance. The Yihequan was eventually suppressed and Beijing was recaptured by an allied force of eight countries that included England, Germany, Russia, and Japan. The rebellion concluded with the signing of the Boxer Protocol(Xinchou Treaty) that required Qing to award indemnities to the victorious foreign powers and allow the stationing of foreign troops in Beijing. This incident placed Qing into an even deeper state of crisis.

◉ Why Did the Yihequan Destroy Churches and Railways?

When Germany occupied Shandong after the Sino-Japanese War, peasants and workers became resentful to foreign powers. With the construction of the railway, the traditional village was destroyed, and Catholicism quickly spread through the missionaries of the Roman Catholic Church.

Farmers and workers in the Shandong region launched the Boxer Rebellion against Western powers. The Yihequan destroyed the electric wires and railroads, considering them as a tool for invasion by Western powers, and burned the churches and killed the missionaries. In addition, they also developed a radical anti-foreign struggle, such as raiding the foreign legation.

신해혁명으로 중화민국이 탄생하다

의화단 운동의 실패 이후 보수 세력은 신식 군대 편성, 과거제 폐지 등 근대화 정책을 추진하였다. 또한 입헌 군주제로의 전환을 준비하기도 하였다. 그러나 청의 지배에 반대하는 운동은 계속 일어났다. **쑨원**은 **삼민주의** 민족적 독립, 정치적 민주주의, 경제적 균등를 내세우며 도쿄에서 중국 동맹회를 결성하였고, 공화 정부를 세울 것을 주장하면서 여러 차례 무장봉기를 시도하였다.

이 와중에 청이 재정난을 타개하기 위해 민영 철도의 국유화를 추진하자 이에 반대하는 운동이 일어났다. 이때 우창에서 일어난 무장봉기를 시작으로 혁명이 전국으로 확산되었다(**신해혁명**, 1911).

혁명파는 쑨원을 임시 대총통으로 선출하고 중화민국을 수립하였다. 청은 **위안스카이**에게 혁명 진압을 맡겼으나 혁명군과 타협한 위안스카이가 청 황제를 퇴위시키고 중화민국 대총통에 취임하였다. 이후 위안스카이는 태도를 바꾸어 혁명파를 탄압하고 제정의 부활을 시도하였으나 사망하였다. 위안스카이 사망 이후 군벌 세력이 각 지역을 분할·지배하면서 중국은 혼란한 상황에 빠져들었다.

한편 제1차 세계 대전 중 일본은 독일이 가지고 있던 중국에서의 이권을 빼앗기 위해 중국에 '21개조 요구'를 강요하였다(1915). 중국은 전후에 열린 파리 강화 회의에서 21개조 요구의 취소와 산둥반도 반환을 요구하였으나 받아들여지지 않았다. 이에 3·1 운동에 영향을 받은 베이징 학생들이 반일본·반군벌 민족 운동을 일으켰다(5·4 운동, 1919). 상인과 노동자가 가세하면서 시위는 대규모 민족 운동으로 발전하였다.

선통제 퇴위(1912. 2. 12.)
Abdication of Puyi

위안스카이 제2대 임시 대총통 취임
(1912. 3. 10.)
Yuan Shikai Inaugurated as the
Second Provisional President

쑨원 임시 대총통 취임
중화민국 성립(1912. 1. 1.)
Sun Yat-sen
Inaugurated as the
Provisional President
Established Republic of
China

우창 봉기(1911. 10. 10.)
Wuchang Uprising

동해
East Sea

황해
Yellow Sea

베이징 Beijing
시안 Xian
청두 Chengdu
충칭 Chongqing
우창 Wuchang
난징 Nanjing
광저우 Guangzhou

■ 혁명이 발생한 지역 Areas Where the Revolution Took Place
■ 혁명에 호응한 지역 Areas that Responded to the Revolution
■ 청의 세력 지역 Realm of Qing
■ 주요 혁명 봉기지 Major Revolutionary Uprisings

신해혁명의 전개 과정
Progress of the Xinhai Revolution

Xinhai Revolution Gives Birth to the Republic of China

After the failed rebellion by the Yihequan, the Chinese conservatives carried out modernization projects such as the organization of a modern military and the abolishment of the civil service examination system. But the anti-Qing movement continued. Sun Yat-sen advocated the Three People's Principles, organized a secret underground resistance movement named Tongmenghui in Tokyo, Japan, and attempted armed rebellion several times on his quest for a republic government.

While this was going on, the Qing government planned to nationalize local railway development projects and transfer control to foreign banks. This plan was met with protests that started with an armed protest in Wuchang before spreading throughout the nation(Xinhai Revolution, 1911).

Later, the revolutionists appointed Sun Yat-sen as the first provisional president. Qing tried to quell the rebellions by dispatching Yuan Shikai, but he negotiated with the revolutionists, deposed the last Qing Emperor and became the first president of the Republic of China himself. However, he suddenly changed his political stance, suppressed the revolutionists, and attempted the revival of the monarchy. After the death of Yuan Shikai, China fractured into many regions controlled by warlords and again fell back into chaos.

Meanwhile, during World War I, Japan attempted to force China to acquiesce to its 'Twenty-One Demands' to deprive Germany of its interests in China(1915). When this request was approved at the Paris Peace Conference in the post-war period, the Chinese, centered on Beijing students who were influenced by the March 1st Movement, instigated anti-Japanese and anti-war national movements(5·4 movement, 1919). As merchants and workers joined these movements, it developed into a single large-scale nationalist movement.

02 일본의 국민 국가 건설

개항 후 근대적 개혁을 추진하다

미국의 페리 제독이 군함을 이끌고 무력으로 일본에 개항을 강요하자 일본은 미·일 화친 조약을 체결하였다(1854). 이어 미·일 수호 통상 조약을 체결하여 미국에 영사 재판권, 협정 관세 등을 인정하였다(1858).

미국과의 불평등 조약이 체결된 이후 하급 무사를 중심으로 서양 세력을 배척하고 막부 정권에 대항하는 움직임이 일어났다. 이러한 상황에서 조슈번이 중심이 되어 막부 타도 운동이 전개되었고, 그 결과 메이지 정부가 수립되었다.

메이지 정부는 지방 분권적인 막부와는 달리 중앙 집권 체제 수립과 부국강병을 위한 개혁에 힘썼다. 에도의 이름을 도쿄로 고쳐 수도로 삼고, 막번 체제를 폐지하였다. 의무 교육제를 도입하고 유학생과 사절단을 서양에 파견하였으며 신분제를 개혁하였다. 징병제를 실시하여 근대식 군대를 정비하기도 하였다. 또한 서양의 기술을 도입하고 우편, 철도, 은행과 상공업 육성에 힘을 기울여 적극적인 경제 발전을 추진하였다.

메이지 정부는 국민 국가 체제를 수립하기 위해 1889년에 메이지 헌법을 제정해 입헌제에 바탕을 둔 근대적 국가의 제도적 기반을 마련하였다.

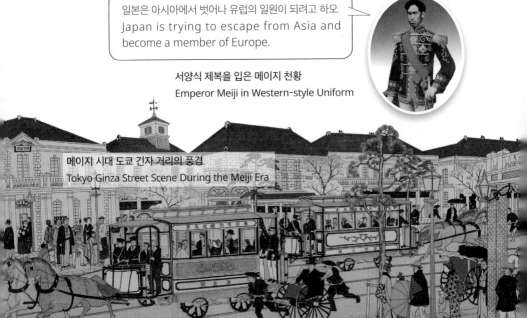

일본은 아시아에서 벗어나 유럽의 일원이 되려고 하오.
Japan is trying to escape from Asia and become a member of Europe.

서양식 제복을 입은 메이지 천황
Emperor Meiji in Western-style Uniform

메이지 시대 도쿄 긴자 거리의 풍경
Tokyo Ginza Street Scene During the Meiji Era

02 Establishment of Nation-state in Japan

Port Opening Followed by Modernization Reforms

Commodore Matthew Perry of the United States Navy sailed into Tokyo Harbor with a squadron of steamers and vessels, demanded the opening of Japanese ports to U.S. merchant ships, and successfully signed the Convention of Kanagawa(1854). This was followed by the Treaty of Amity and Commerce which granted the US consular jurisdiction and fixed low import–export duties(1858).

The unequal treaties with the US were met with anti–foreign powers movements and resistance to the Shogunate government among the low–level warriors. It was under this situation that a movement to overthrow the Shogunate broke out in the allied forces of the Chosu Domain, which resulted in the establishment of the Meiji government.

Unlike the decentralized Shogunate, the Meiji government carried out reforms to build a centralized government system, strong military, and overall powerful nation. The Meiji government changed the name of the capital city from Edo to Tokyo and dismantled the old feudal regime known as bakufu. The government also introduced universal education, sent students and delegates for Western learning, and overhauled the social class system. A conscription system was implemented to improve the modern army as well. And the Western learning policy designed to develop the economy by promoting commerce, industry, and finance businesses as well as the spread of railroads and modern postal networks.

The Meiji government promulgated the Meiji Constitution in 1889 in order to establish a nation–state system, thereby laying the groundwork for a modern state built upon a constitution.

일본이 제국주의의 길로 들어서다

근대적 국민 국가의 기틀을 닦는 데 성공한 일본은 동아시아에 대해 제국주의적 침략을 벌였다. 일본은 내부의 혼란을 무마하고 국내외의 모순을 해결하기 위해 류큐를 합병하고 조선으로의 진출을 모색하였다. 조선 지배를 놓고 청과 대립하던 일본은 청·일 전쟁을 일으켜 승리하고 시모노세키 조약을 체결하였다.

이후 한반도와 만주를 둘러싸고 러시아와의 대립이 심화되자 러·일 전쟁을 일으켜 승리하고 포츠머스 조약을 체결하였다. 이를 통해 대한 제국에 대한 영향력을 더욱 강화하였으며 만주의 이권을 인정받았다. 1910년에는 대한 제국을 식민지로 삼으며 본격적으로 제국주의 열강의 대열에 합류하였다.

⊙ 후쿠자와 유키치는 왜 중국과 한국을 나쁜 친구로 여겼나요?

메이지 유신 추진 과정에서 특권을 상실한 무사 계급이 불만을 품자, 일본 정부는 조선을 정벌하자는 '정한론'으로 관심을 돌리려 하였다. 정한론의 이론적 바탕이 된 것은 일본 메이지 시대의 계몽사상가인 후쿠자와 유키치의 '탈아론(脫亞論, 아시아를 벗어나자는 주장)'이었다.

후쿠자와 유키치는 1860년에 함장의 심부름꾼으로서 배를 타고 미국에 다녀왔고 1862년에는 막부 사절단을 따라 유럽에 다녀왔다. 서구 열강의 발달된 문명을 접하고 큰 충격을 받은 후쿠자와 유키치는 이를 일본에 전하고자 하였다. 그는 서양 문명에 대한 경험을 바탕으로 『지지신보』에서 탈아론을 주장하였다.

> 서구인들은 언제나 일본, 중국, 조선을 같은 문화를 가진 비슷한 나라들이라고 생각하는데, 이는 일본에 걸림돌이 될 뿐이다. …… 우리는 아시아의 나쁜 친구들을 멀리해야 한다.
> Westerners always think of Japan, China, and Joseon as similar countries with the same culture, which is only an obstacle for Japan. …… Japan has to stay away from bad Asian friends.

일본 지폐에 새겨진 후쿠자와 유키치
Fukuzawa Yukichi on Japanese Banknote

Japan Takes the Path to Imperialism

After building the foundation for a modernized nation-state, Japan launched imperialistic invasions throughout East Asia. Japan annexed the Ryukyu Kingdom and started looking for a chance to invade Joseon to deflect the focus away from the national chaos in order to resolve internal and external problems. Before going to war with Qing, Japan had been in conflict with Qing over the occupation of Joseon. After winning this Sino-Japanese War, Japan signed the Treaty of Shimonoseki with the Qing Dynasty.

Later on, when the tension continued to grow with Russia over the Korean peninsula and Manchuria, Japan went to war with Russia and won the Russo-Japanese War, resulting in the signing of the Treaty of Portsmouth with Russia. Through these victories, Japan expanded its influence over the Daehan Empire and affirmed its dominance in Manchuria. In 1910, Japan colonized the Daehan Empire, joining the race for colonization, and began competing with other imperialist powers.

❷ Why Did Fukuzawa Yukichi Regard China and Korea as Bad Friends?

When the warriors, who lost their privileges in the process of promoting the Meiji Restoration became dissatisfied, the Japanese government tried to turn its attention to the 'Seikanron(Advocacy of a punitive expedition to Korea)' to conquer Joseon. The theoretical basis of Seikanron is 'Datsu-A Ron(Argument for Leaving Asia)' by Fukuzawa Yukichi, an enlightenment thinker during the Meiji era in Japan.

Fukuzawa Yukichi traveled to the United States by ship in 1860 as the captain's messenger and followed a shogunate delegation to Europe in 1862. As he was shocked by the advanced civilization of the Western powers, he tried to convey this to Japan. Based on his experience with Western civilization, he insisted on the theory of 'Datsu-A Ron' in *"Jiji Shinpo"*.

03 한국의 국민 국가 건설

강화도 조약이 체결되다

19세기 서양 열강은 조선에도 개항을 요구하였지만 조선은 이를 거부하였다. 프랑스와 미국이 조선의 개항을 요구하며 각각 병인양요와 신미양요를 일으켰지만 조선은 수교 요구에 저항하였다.

이후 통상 수교 거부 정책을 펼치던 흥선 대원군이 물러나자 일본은 운요호 사건을 일으켜 조선에 개항을 강요하였다. 결국 조선은 영사 재판권과 해안 측량권 등이 포함된 불평등 조약인 강화도 조약을 체결하게 되었다(1876). 이후 조선은 미국을 비롯한 서양 열강과도 잇달아 조약을 체결하였다.

◉ 동아시아 각국은 외국과 어떤 조약을 맺었나요?
What Treaties Did East Asian Countries Make with Foreign Countries?

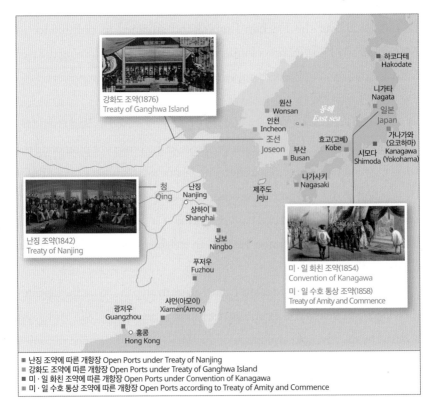

강화도 조약(1876)
Treaty of Ganghwa Island

난징 조약(1842)
Treaty of Nanjing

미·일 화친 조약(1854)
Convention of Kanagawa
미·일 수호 통상 조약(1858)
Treaty of Amity and Commence

하코다테 Hakodate
니가타 Nagata
일본 Japan
가나가와 (요코하마) Kanagawa (Yokohama)
시모다 Shimoda
원산 Wonsan
인천 Incheon
조선 Joseon
부산 Busan
효고(고베) Kobe
동해 East sea
나가사키 Nagasaki
청 Qing
난징 Nanjing
상하이 Shanghai
제주도 Jeju
닝보 Ningbo
푸저우 Fuzhou
샤먼(아모이) Xiamen(Amoy)
광저우 Guangzhou
홍콩 Hong Kong

■ 난징 조약에 따른 개항장 Open Ports under Treaty of Nanjing
■ 강화도 조약에 따른 개항장 Open Ports under Treaty of Ganghwa Island
■ 미·일 화친 조약에 따른 개항장 Open Ports under Convention of Kanagawa
■ 미·일 수호 통상 조약에 따른 개항장 Open Ports according to Treaty of Amity and Commence

03 Establishment of Nation-state in Korea

Korea-Japan Treaty Is Signed in Ganghwado Island

In the 19th century, the Western powers demanded that Joseon open trade ports as well, but Joseon refused. In particular, Joseon went to war with France and the United States, who demanded opening of its ports.

When Heungseon Daewongun, who had refused diplomatic relations, withdrew, Japan instigated a confrontation involving a ship called the Unyo and used it as an excuse to demand that Joseon open its ports. Eventually, Joseon was forced to sign an unequal Korea−Japan Treaty in 1876 commonly known as the Treaty of Ganghwa Island. It included the right of extraterritoriality and coastal surveying rights. After that, Joseon had to sign one treaty after another with Western powers, including the United States.

난징 조약 NanjingTreaty (1842)	제3조: 중국은 홍콩섬을 대영국 군주와 앞으로 그 군주 지위를 세습할 사람에게 넘겨주고 그들의 방식대로 법을 제정하여 다스릴 수 있도록 허용한다. Article 3: China hands over Hong Kong Island to the British monarchy and those who will inherit its status in the future, allowing them to make laws and rule their way.
미 · 일 화친 조약 Convention of Kanagawa (1854)	제2조: 시모다, 하코다테 두 항구에 대해 일본 정부는 미국선이 장작, 물, 식량, 석탄 등의 부족한 품물을 일본에서 조달할 경우 그 목적에 한정하여 입항을 허가한다. Article 2: For the two ports of Shimoda and Hakodate, the Japanese government authorizes American ships to enter the port only for the purpose of procuring goods such as firewood, water, food, and coal from Japan.
강화도 조약 Treaty of Ganghwa Island (1876)	제5관: 부산 외 경기, 충청, 전라, 경상, 함경 등 5도 중에서 통상하기 편리한 연해의 항구 두 곳을 골라 개항한다. Article 5: In addition to the open port of Busan, Joseon opens two more ports suitable for Japan from among the five provinces: Gyeonggi, Chungcheong, Jeolla, Gyeongsang, and Hamgyong provinces.

동아시아 각국의 조약과 개항 Treaties and Opening of Ports in East Asian Countries

국민 국가 건설을 위해 노력하다

조선에서는 외세로부터 국권을 지키려는 운동이 일어났다. 급진 개화파는 **갑신정변**을 일으켜 근대적 정치 체제를 수립하고자 하였으나 청의 개입으로 실패하였다(1884). 이후 반봉건 · 반외세를 내세운 **동학 농민 운동**이 일어났다. 조선 정부의 요청으로 동학 농민 운동을 진압하기 위해 청이 군대를 파견하자 일본도 조선에 군대를 파견하였다. 조선이 양국 군대의 철수를 요구하였으나 일본은 경복궁을 점령한 뒤 청 · 일 전쟁을 일으켰다.

청 · 일 전쟁에서 승리한 일본이 조선에 대한 간섭을 강화하자 조선은 러시아 세력을 끌어들이고 개혁을 추진하고자 하였다. 이에 일본이 조선의 왕비를 시해하였고, 고종은 러시아 공사관으로 피신하였다. 이 틈을 타 서양 열강의 이권 침탈이 본격화되자 **독립 협회**는 민중의 힘으로 자주독립을 이루고자 근대적 대중 집회를 열었다. 이후 고종은 1년 만에 경운궁으로 돌아와 **대한 제국**을 수립하고 **광무개혁**을 추진하였다.

한편 조선에 대한 러시아의 영향력이 커지는 것을 우려하던 일본은 러 · 일 전쟁을 일으켰다. 일본은 영국과 미국의 군사 지원에 힘입어 전쟁에서 승리하였고, 개혁을 통해 자강을 꾀하던 대한 제국은 결국 일본에 의해 강제 병합되었다(1910).

💿 **동학 농민 운동을 진압할 때 왜 청군과 일본군이 함께 들어왔나요?**

Why Did Qing and Japanese Troops Come Together to Suppress the Donghak Peasant Revolution?

> 갑신정변 이후 청과 일본이 체결한 톈진 조약에 '향후 조선 파병 시 사전에 서로 통고한다.' 라는 내용이 담겨 있었기 때문이에요.
> After the 'Gapsin Rebellion', Qing and Japan signed the Convention of Tientsin, which stated that they would notify each other in advance when sending troops to Joseon in the future.

청 · 일 전쟁 당시 일본군이 승리한 평양 전투
Battle of Pyongyang where Japanese
Troops Won During the Sino-Japanese War

Efforts to Build a Nation-state

As Joseon signed a series of treaties with Western powers, a movement to protect national interests from invading foreign forces took shape. Radical reformers raised a coup called the 'Gapsin Rebellion' to establish a modernized political structure and stop Qing from interfering with politics in the Korean peninsula, but it was foiled due to the intervention of Qing(1884). Later, Joseon saw the rise of the 'Donghak Peasant Revolution' which was instigated by peasants in protest of feudalism and foreign forces. The Joseon government turned to Qing and requested they send Chinese troops to quell the revolt. When Qing deployed their troops to Joseon, Japan also sent their troops to Joseon. Later on, Joseon asked both countries to withdraw their troops, but Japan seized Gyeogbokgung Palace instead, and went on to wage war with Qing.

After winning the Sino-Japanese War, Japan increased its interference in Joseon, to which the Joseon government responded by bringing in Russia and trying to push forward with reforms. In retaliation, Japan committed the atrocity of assassinating the queen of the Joseon Dynasty. Later, King Gojong took refuge in the Russian legation. Taking advantage of this gap, the invasion of Western powers began in earnest. The Independent Society held a modern mass rally to achieve independence through the power of the people. King Gojong returned to the Gyeongungung palace a year later before establishing the Daehan Empire and starting the Gwangmu Reform.

In protest of the growing influence of Russia over the Korean peninsula, Japan went on to start the Russo-Japanese War. Japan won the war with the support of the British and American military forces, and the Daehan Empire was forcefully annexed despite its efforts to build a strong empire through a series of reforms(1910).

04 동남아시아의 국민 국가 건설 운동

열강이 동남아시아를 침략하다

동남아시아는 인도와 태평양을 연결하는 해상 교통의 요지이고 향신료의 주산지여서 서양 열강의 표적이 되었다. 포르투갈은 신항로 개척 이후 동남아시아로 진출하여 향신료 무역에 참여하였으며, 에스파냐는 필리핀을 점령하였다.

네덜란드는 포르투갈의 뒤를 이어 향신료 무역을 독점하였다. 또한 동인도 회사를 앞세워 인도네시아에 진출하고 네덜란드령 동인도를 건설하였다. 프랑스는 프랑스령 인도차이나 연방을 수립하였으며, 영국은 미얀마를 식민지화하고 싱가포르와 말레이반도, 보르네오섬 북부 일부를 합쳐 말레이 연방을 구성하였다. 미국은 에스파냐와의 전쟁에서 승리하여 필리핀을 차지하였고, 프랑스는 베트남을 식민지로 만들었다. 열강은 현지인에게 고무, 커피, 사탕수수 등 특정 상품을 대량 생산하는 플랜테이션 농업을 강요하였다.

동남아시아는 시암(타이)을 제외하고 대부분 열강의 식민지로 전락하였다. 시암은 근대적 개혁에 성공하고, 영국과 프랑스 사이에서 균형 외교를 펼쳐 독립을 유지하였다.

동남아시아의 국민 국가 건설 운동 Southeast Asia's Nation-state Construction Movement

---

🏅 시암은 어떻게 동남아시아에서 유일한 독립국이 되었나요?

> 서양 열강이 동남아시아에 진출하기 시작하자 근대화 개혁을 시행하였어요. '왕과 나'라는 영화에서 율 브린너가 라마 4세 역할을 하였지요. 라마 4세의 뒤를 이어 즉위한 라마 5세 역시 서양 열강의 압박 속에서도 근대화를 이루어냈어요. 이로써 시암은 동남아시아에서 유일한 독립국으로 존속하였고, 1939년에는 국명을 타이로 바꾸었지요. '타이'는 태국어로 '자유'를 뜻해요.

라마 4세 King Rama IV

04 Movements to Build a Nation-state in Southeast Asia

Western Powers Invade Southeast Asia

Southeast Asia became the main target of the Western powers because it was the hub of maritime transportation that connected India and the Pacific Ocean, and also because it was the main source of spices. After discovering new sea routes, Portugal made inroads into Southeast Asia and participated in the spice trade, while Spain went on to occupy the Philippines.

Following Portugal, the Netherlands monopolized the spice trade. In addition, the Netherlands established the East India Company, made forays into Indonesia and established the Dutch East Indies. France established French Indochina, which is also known as the Indochinese Union, and Britain colonized Myanmar and established British Malaya by including Singapore, the Malay Peninsula, and the northern part of the island of Borneo. The US took over the Philippines after winning the Spanish–American War, and France made Vietnam its colony. The Western powers forced the locals to do plantation farming(agricultural mass production of certain crops such as rubber, coffee, sugar cane, etc.).

Almost all of Southeast Asia became colonized by the Western powers except Siam(Thailand). Siam succeeded in modern reforms and maintained its independence through balanced diplomacy between Britain and France.

....

🔹 How Did Siam Become the Only Independent Country in Southeast Asia?

When the Western powers began to enter Southeast Asia, Rama IV implemented modernization reform. In the movie '*The King and I*', Yul Brynner played the role of King Rama IV. King Rama V, who succeeded Rama IV to the throne, also achieved modernization under the pressure of the Western powers. Siam remained the only independent country in Southeast Asia, changing its name to Thailand in 1939. 'Thai' means 'freedom' in Thai.

동남아시아에서 근대 국가 수립 운동이 일어나다

베트남에서는 프랑스에 맞서 근왕 운동 1885년 베트남 황제가 프랑스의 침략에 맞서 황실을 수호하라는 명령을 내리자 전국 각지에서 유학자와 지주가 농민을 이끌고 봉기하여 전개된 운동이 일어났으나 실패하였다. 이후 **판보이쩌우**는 베트남 유신회를 조직하여 민족 운동을 전개하였다. 판쩌우찐은 '통킹 의숙' 설립에 참여하는 등 사립 학교 설립 운동을 전개하였다.

필리핀에서는 **호세 리살**이 필리핀 연맹을 조직하여 에스파냐에 저항하였으며 필리핀인이 에스파냐인과 동등한 대우를 받을 것을 요구하였다. **아기날도**는 미국·에스파냐 전쟁 중 미국을 지원하며 독립을 선언하고 필리핀 공화국을 선포하였으나 전쟁에서 승리한 미국이 필리핀을 식민지화하였다.

인도네시아에서는 **카르티니**가 여성들을 위한 교육 운동에 헌신하였고, 인도네시아 지식인들은 자바섬을 중심으로 '부티 우토모'를 결성하여 교육을 통해 민중을 계몽하여 민족의식을 높이고자 하였다. 또한 **이슬람 동맹**은 크리스트교 반대 운동을 벌여 인도네시아의 전통과 이슬람교를 지키려고 노력하였다.

🌐 동남아시아의 독립운동가는 누가 있나요?

판보이쩌우 프랑스의 침략과 베트남 멸망 과정이 자세하게 서술되어 있는 『월남 망국사』를 펴냈어요. 프랑스의 혹독한 식민 정책으로 곤경에 처한 베트남의 상황을 세계에 알리기 위한 것이었지요.
Phan Boi Chau I published "*History of the Loss of Vietnam*", which details the process of the French invasion and the destruction of Vietnam. Its goal was to inform the world about the situation in Vietnam, which was in trouble due to France's harsh colonial policy.

호세 리살 마드리드 유학 시절 출간한 소설 『놀리메 탕게레(Noli Me Tangere)』로 유명해졌어요. 이 소설에서 에스파냐의 식민지 차별 정책과 식민지 지배의 모순을 비판하였어요.
Jose Rizal I became famous for the novel "*Noli Me Tangere*" while studying in Madrid. In this novel, I sharply criticized the contradictions between Spain's policy of colonial discrimination and colonial rule.

Movements to Establish a Modernized State in Southeast Asia

The Vietnamese fought against French colonial rule in what came to be known as 'the Can Vuong Movement', but failed. Later, a Vietnamese named Phan Boi Chau organized the Vietnam Public Offering Society and launched a nationalist movement. Another Vietnamese nationalist, Phan Chau Trinh, participated in the movement to establish private schools such as Tonkin Free School.

In the Philippines, Jose Rizal resisted Spain by putting together a special organization, the La Liga Filipina, and demanded that Filipinos be treated the same as the Spanish. During the Spanish–American War, the Philippines supported the US and Filipino rebels led by Emilio Aguinaldo, proclaimed the independence of the Philippines, and declared the establishment of a republic. But after winning the war, the US colonized the Philippines.

In Indonesia, Kartini pioneered education for women. Indonesian intellectuals organized a political society, Budi Utomo(lit. Prime Philosophy) on Java island and tried to heighten nationalist consciousness by enlightening the people. The Sarekat Islam(Union of Islam) fought to protest Christianity and attempted to protect Indonesian customs and Islamic religion.

....

🕙 Who Are the Independence Activists in Southeast Asia?

카르티니 친구들과 주고받았던 편지를 모아 출간한 책 『어둠에서 빛으로』 에서 학업에 대한 열망과 학교를 세우겠다는 포부를 표현하였어요. 이후 내 이름을 딴 학교들이 생겨났지요.

Kartini I expressed my aspirations for the studies and the establishment of schools in "Out of Darkness to Light", which was published by collecting letters that I had exchanged with my friends. Since then, schools named after me have been opened.

V

세계 대전과 사회 변동

1. 세계 대전과 국제 질서의 변화
2. 민주주의의 확산
3. 인권 회복을 위한 노력

…… 누구의 죽음이라도 나를 감소시킨다.

나는 인류에 포함되어 있기 때문이다.

누구를 위해 저 종이 울리는지 알고자 사람을 보내지 말라.

종은 그대를 위해 울린다.

– 존 던(1572~1631)

V

World War and Social Changes

······ Any man's death diminishes me,

because I am involved in mankind.

And therefore never send to know for whom the bell tolls.

It tolls for thee.

–John Donne(1572~1631)

안네 프랑크의 집(네덜란드 암스테르담)
Anne Frank House(Amsterdam, Netherlands)

세계 대전과 국제 질서의 변화

01 제1차 세계 대전의 발발과 전개

제국주의 국가 간의 대립과 경쟁이 제1차 세계 대전을 부르다

19세기 후반부터 제국주의 국가 간 대립과 경쟁이 치열해지고 식민지 쟁탈전이 격화되면서 유럽 열강들은 민족과 국가의 이해관계에 따라 서로 동맹과 협상을 맺었다. 유럽에서 뒤늦게 통일을 이룬 독일은 프랑스를 고립시키기 위해 오스트리아·헝가리 제국과 이탈리아를 끌어들여 **3국 동맹**을 맺었다. 이에 맞서 프랑스도 영국과 손을 잡은 데 이어 러시아를 끌어들여 **3국 협상**을 맺었다.

발칸반도는 여러 민족과 종교가 엉켜 있어 '유럽의 화약고'로 불리는 지역이었다. 이곳에서 러시아는 오스만 제국에서 독립한 세르비아 등 슬라브 국가들을 끌어들여 **범슬라브주의**를 내세웠다. 이에 독일과 오스트리아·헝가리 제국은 **범게르만주의**로 맞서 유럽에 팽팽한 긴장감이 감돌았다.

1914년 6월 보스니아의 수도 사라예보를 방문 중이었던 오스트리아·헝가리 제국의 황태자 부처가 세르비아계 청년에게 암살 당하였다(**사라예보 사건**).

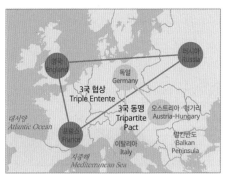

3국 동맹과 3국 협상
Tripartite Pact and Triple Entente

오스트리아·헝가리 제국은 슬라브인들이 많이 살고 있던 보스니아 헤르체고비나를 합병하였어요. 세르비아 애국 청년들이 이에 반발하여 '검은 손'이라는 비밀 단체를 결성하였지요. 한 단원이 황태자 부처가 탄 차에 폭탄을 투척하였지만 실패하였어요. 이후 길을 잘못 든 황태자의 차가 라틴 다리 옆의 카페에서 길을 돌렸어요. 검은 손 단원 프린치프가 카페에서 나오다 이를 발견하고 두 발의 총알을 발사하여 암살에 성공하였지요. 차 한 잔의 시간이 세계사를 요동치게 하였지요.
The Austro-Hungarian Empire annexed Bosnia and Herzegovina, which was heavily populated with Slavs. Young patriotic Serbians protested against this and formed a secret group called the 'Black Hand'. One member of the group threw a bomb at the car that was carrying the Crown Prince and his wife, but it failed. Later, the car took a wrong turn into a cafe near the Latin Bridge, and a member of the Black Hand, Princip, saw them as he was walking out of the cafe. He fired two shots at them and successfully assassinated them. That's how a time spent in a cafe ended up rocking the history of the world.

World Wars and Changed International Order

01 Outbreak and Progress of the First World War

Competition Among Imperialist Countries Results in the First World War

Conflicts and competition among the imperialist nations grew fiercer beginning in the late 19th century, and so did their race for colonization. European powers made alliances or negotiated with each other depending on their national interests on their quest to colonize other countries. After having united relatively late in Europe, Germany signed the Tripartite Pact with Italy and the Austro-Hungarian Empire and isolated France. In response to this, France signed the Triple Entente with Britain and Russia.

The Balkan Peninsula was called 'the powder keg of Europe' because the region was characterized by a mix of numerous ethnic groups and religions. Tension started increasing in this region when Russia joined with the Slav nations that became independent from the Ottoman Empire, including Serbia, and started a movement called Pan-Slavism. Germany and the Austro-Hungarian Empire attempted to counter this with their own Pan-Germanicism.

In June 1914, the Crown Prince of the Austro-Hungarian Empire was visiting the Bosnian capital Sarajevo with his wife when they were assassinated by a young Serbian idealist(Assassination of Sarajevo).

사라예보의 라틴 다리
Latin Bridge in Sarajevo ©Peretz Partensky

제1차 세계 대전이 총력전으로 전개되다

사라예보 사건을 계기로 오스트리아 · 헝가리 제국은 세르비아에 선전 포고를 하였고, 러시아는 세르비아를 지원하였다. 이어 독일, 프랑스, 영국 등 유럽의 여러 나라가 각국의 이해관계에 따라 연달아 선전 포고를 하면서 전쟁이 시작되었다.

동맹국 제1차 세계 대전에서 연합국의 반대 진영에 섰던 국가에는 불가리아와 오스만 제국이 가담하였고, **연합국** 3국 협상을 맺은 러시아·영국·프랑스 중심의 국가 연합에는 3국 동맹을 탈퇴한 이탈리아를 비롯하여 일본과 중국까지 가담하면서 세계 대전으로 확대되었다.

독일은 러시아가 전쟁에 본격적으로 참가하기 전에 서부 전선을 장악하여 전쟁을 빨리 끝내겠다는 계획을 세웠다. 벨기에를 차지한 후 프랑스 파리 부근까지 진격하였으나 영국, 프랑스, 러시아 등의 반격으로 계획이 뜻대로 이루어지지 않았다. 이후 전쟁은 참호를 파서 대치하는 참호전으로 전개되면서 장기전이 되었다.

언론의 통제 속에 전쟁의 참상이 잘 알려지지 않으면서 후방에서는 계속 신병을 소집하여 전쟁에 투입하였고, 부상자 치료와 군수품 생산에는 여성들을 동원하였다. 이로써 국가 전체의 힘을 총동원하는 총력전이 전개되었다.

．．．

⚙ 참호전이 무엇인가요? What Is a Trench Warfare?

제1차 세계 대전을 '삽으로 하는 전쟁'이라고 해요. 참호를 파고 그 속에 숨어 전쟁을 하였기 때문이에요. 병사들은 비가 내리면 참호 속에 물이 차올라 진흙탕 속에서 고통스러운 경험을 하였고, 쥐와 각종 벌레에 시달렸어요. 독일군이 독가스를 개발한 후에는 컴컴한 참호 속에서 숨쉬기도 힘겨운 방독면을 쓰고 지내야 하였지요. The First World War is called a 'War with a Shovel'. This was because the soldiers dug trenches and hid in them to wage war. When it rained, water filled the trenches, and the soldiers had painful experiences in the mud and were plagued by mice and various insects. After the Germans developed poison gas, they had to wear gas masks which made it difficult for the soldiers to breathe in dark trenches.

러시아군의 참호
Russian Trench

The First World War Unfolds as a Total War

In retaliation for Assassination of Sarajevo, the Austro-Hungarian Empire declared war on Serbia, and Russia promised its support to Serbia. Several European countries that had a stake in this conflict, such as Germany, France, and Britain also declared war as well, and so began a war between these nations.

Bulgaria and the Ottoman Empire sided with the Central Powers while Japan and China sided with the Allied Powers along with Italy, who broke away from the Triple Alliance and joined the Triple Entente instead. This war escalated into the First World War.

Determined to finish the war as soon as possible by seizing the Western Front before Russia became involved, Germany invaded and occupied Belgium. Germany was able to advance to Paris, but the German attempt was foiled when it faced a counterattack by Britain, France, and Russia. Then both sides of the war started building trenches to protect occupied fighting lines and soldiers, transforming the conflict into a long and drawn out bout of trench warfare.

With the horrors of the war left largely unknown to the public due to the controlled media coverage, it gradually blew up into a total war with a continuous supply of soldiers who were recruited in the rear and women who were mobilized either to produce military supplies or sent to treat the injured soldiers.

참호 건너기에 실패한 탱크 A Tank that Failed to Cross a Trench

oo 제1차 세계 대전은 과연 누구를 위한 전쟁이었을까요?

「서부 전선 이상 없다」는 독일 작가 에리히 마리아 레마르크의 소설을 원작으로 제작된 반전 영화이다. 제1차 세계 대전 중 독일군으로 자원입대한 학도병들이 겪었던 참혹한 서부 전선의 상황을 보여 준다.

열 여덟 살이 된 파울은 급우들과 함께 군에 입대하였다. 그들은 서부 전선에 배치되었다. 전투가 치열하게 전개되면서 참호 속의 급우들은 차례차례 쓰러져 갔다. 파울은 교회 근처에서 벌어진 전투에서 프랑스 병사를 죽였다. 서로 아무런 원한도 없이 전쟁의 광란 속에서 공포에 사로잡혀 무의식적으로 상대를 죽인 것이다. 파울은 죽은 병사의 주머니 속에서 나온 가족사진을 보고 망연자실하였다. 과연 누구를 위한 전쟁인가?

오랜만에 전투가 소강상태로 접어들었다. 어디선가 하모니카 소리가 들려왔다. 병사들은 모두 귀를 기울였다. 그때 어디선가 나비 한 마리가 나타나 파울의 눈앞으로 지나갔다. 파울의 눈은 나비를 따라갔다. 나비를 따라 참호에서 몸을 일으켜 나비에게 손을 내미는 순간, 온몸에 전율을 느꼈다. 파울은 나비가 내려앉듯 그렇게 내려앉았다. 그날 전선은 종일 조용했다. 전선의 지휘부는 그날도 본국에 전문을 보냈다.

"서부 전선 이상 없다."

「서부 전선 이상 없다」 영화 포스터(1930)
Poster for the Movie 'All Quiet On the Western Front'

프랑스군은 파리에서 30km 정도 떨어진 마른강 지역에서 독일군과 대치하였어요. 제1차 마른 전투에서 프랑스군이 독일군의 진격을 막음으로써 이후 전투는 참호전으로 전개되었지요.

👓 Who Was World War I for?

'*All Quiet On The Western Front*' is an antiwar film based on the novel by German writer Erich Maria Remarque. The film shows the harrowing situation on the western front of the German army during World War I.

At the age of 18, Paul joined the army with his classmates. They were deployed on the western front. As the battle fiercely unfolded, his classmates in the trenches fell one after another. Paul killed a French soldier in a battle near a church. In the frenzy of war, without any grudge against each other, they were caught up the terror and unconsciously killed their opponents. Paul was devastated when he saw a family picture taken from the pocket of a dead soldier. Who is this war for?

After a long time, the battle entered a lull. Somewhere he heard the sound of a harmonica. All of the soldiers listened. Then a butterfly appeared from somewhere and passed before Paul's eyes. His eyes followed the butterfly. As soon as Paul lifted himself up from the trench following the butterfly, and put his hand out to the butterfly, he felt a thrill all over his body. He sat down like a butterfly. The front line was quiet all day. The command of the front also sent a message to the home country that day.

"There is no problem with the western front."

> The French army confronted the Germans in the area of the Marne River, about 30 km from Paris. In the first Battle of Marne, the French army prevented the advance of the Germans, and the battles later developed into trench warfare.

마른강 지역에서 벌어진 프랑스군과 독일군의 참호전
French and German Trench Warfare near the Marne

연합국의 승리로 전쟁이 끝나다

독일은 영국 해군의 해상 봉쇄로 어려움을 겪게 되자 이를 타개하기 위해 **무제한 잠수함 작전**에 돌입하였다. 그러나 작전 수행 과정에서 많은 미국 시민들이 타고 있던 배가 침몰하였고, 이로 인해 **미국**이 연합국 측에 가담하게 되었다. 동부 전선에서 독일과 힘겨운 싸움을 벌이던 **러시아**는 11월 혁명 이후에 독일과 단독으로 강화 조약을 체결하고 전쟁에서 물러났다.

이후 독일은 서부 전선에 집중하였으나 날이 갈수록 전세는 불리해졌다. 불가리아와 오스만 제국에 이어 오스트리아 · 헝가리 제국이 연합국에 항복하면서 전쟁은 끝을 향해 가기 시작하였다.

결국 독일에서 혁명이 일어나고 새롭게 세워진 임시 정부가 연합국과 휴전 조약을 체결함으로써 세계를 전쟁의 소용돌이에 몰아넣었던 제1차 세계 대전이 막을 내렸다.

제1차 세계 대전의 전개
Unfolding of the World War I

🌀 **제1차 세계 대전 후 여성의 지위에 어떤 변화가 있었나요?**

> 제1차 세계 대전이 총력전으로 전개되면서 여성들이 후방의 공장이나 병원 등에서 일하였어요. 여성들이 전쟁 수행에 큰 역할을 하여 전쟁이 끝난 후 여성의 사회적 지위가 향상되었지요.
> As World War I developed into a total war, women worked in factories and hospitals in the rear. Women's social status improved after the war, as women played a major role in it.

The War Ends with the Victory of the Allied Powers

When stymied by the British Navy blocking the ocean, Germany launched an Unrestricted Submarine Warfare campaign to overcome the crisis. But when a British ship that was carrying a number of American passengers was attacked and sunk by a German submarine, the US joined the Allied forces to fight in the war. Russia had been engaged in a difficult battle with Germany on the Eastern Front, but it withdrew from the war when it signed its own armistice with Germany after the November Revolution.

Later, Germany fought with a focus on the Western Front, but as the days went on, the tide of the war turned away from Germany. The war started coming closer to its end when Bulgaria and the Ottoman Empire surrendered to the Allied forces, followed by the surrender of the Austro-Hungarian Empire.

Eventually, the war that had swept through the entire world came to an end when the German government underwent a revolution and the newly established government signed an armistice with the Allied forces.

How Did the Status of Women Change after World War I?

포탄 공장에서 일하는 여성 노동자
Female Worker Working in a Shell Factory

방위산업체에 종사하는 여성을 상징하는 리벳공 로지
Rosie the Riveter Symbolizes Women Working in Defense Contractors

02 러시아 혁명과 사회주의 국가의 성립

러시아에서 사회주의 혁명이 일어나다

러시아에서는 산업 혁명 이후 노동자 계급이 성장하면서 사회주의 이념을 지닌 지식인들이 활발한 활동을 전개하였다. 이들은 탄압을 받으면서도 노동자와 농민의 의식을 일깨우며 기반을 확대해 나갔다. 차르는 1905년 발생한 **피의 일요일 사건**을 무력으로 진압한 이후 시위가 격화되자 의회의 설립과 언론 및 집회의 자유를 약속하였다. 하지만 차르는 약속을 지키지 않았고 러시아의 어려운 경제 사정을 외면한 채 제1차 세계 대전에 참여하였다.

전쟁으로 러시아의 경제 상황은 더욱 악화되었고, 국민의 삶은 하루하루가 힘들어졌다. 이에 불만이 폭발하여 각지에서 노동자와 병사가 중심이 되어 **소비에트** '평의회', '대표자 회의'를 뜻하는 러시아어를 세우고 혁명을 추진하였다. 그 결과 로마노프 왕조가 무너지고 임시 정부가 세워졌다(**3월 혁명**, 러시아력 2월). 그러나 **멘셰비키** 1898년 러시아 사회 민주 노동당에 성립된 세력을 일컫는 말, '소수파'를 뜻함가 지원한 임시 정부는 개혁에 실패하였고, 국민의 뜻과는 달리 전쟁을 계속하였다. 이에 레닌을 중심으로 한 **볼셰비키** '다수파'를 뜻함가 일어나 임시 정부를 무너뜨렸다(**11월 혁명**, 러시아력 10월). 이로써 러시아에서는 세계 최초로 사회주의 혁명에 의한 소비에트 정권이 수립되었다.

⚉ **러시아 사람들은 왜 피의 일요일 사건을 일으켰나요?**
Why Did the Bloody Sunday Incident Occur?

> 저희는 가난하고, 핍박받고, 과도한 노동에 시달리고 있습니다. …… 모든 사람이 평등하게 선거권을 가지며 자유롭게 선거할 수 있도록 하여 주십시오.
> - 상트페테르부르크 노동자와 주민의 청원서(1905)

피의 일요일 사건을 그린 그림 Painting of the Bloody Sunday Incident

02 Russian Revolution and the Establishment of a Socialist State

Outbreak of a Socialist Revolution in Russia

In the wake of the industrial revolution, Russia saw the growing influence of the working class and dynamic social movements led by intellectuals with socialist ideology. These socialist intellectuals kept expanding their ground in Russia while awakening the consciousness of workers and peasants despite the oppression of the government. When the protest grew more serious after the violent suppression of Bloody Sunday in 1905, the Tsar promised the establishment of a parliament and freedom of press and assembly. But the Tsar did not keep these promises, and Russia joined WWI, ignoring its difficult economic situation.

The economic crisis went from bad to worse in Russia due to the war, and it took a toll on people's livelihoods. The growing resentment among workers and soldiers blew up into protests throughout the country until the first Soviet Union was established and introduced sweeping reform policies. Eventually, the Romanov Dynasty collapsed and a provisional government was established(March Revolution, Russian calendar February). Supported by the Mensheviks, the provisional government carried out many reform policies, but they were not successful, and the war kept on despite the people's objections. Soon the Bolsheviks launched a revolution under the leadership of Lenin and brought down the provisional government(November Revolution, Russian calendar October). With this event, a socialist revolution gave birth to the Soviet regime in Russia for the first time.

> We are poor, persecuted, and suffering from excessive labor ······ Make sure everyone has equal voting rights and can vote freely.
> - Petition from workers and residents of St. Petersburg(1905)

사회주의 국가, 소비에트 사회주의 공화국 연방이 탄생하다

11월 혁명에 성공한 레닌은 러시아 공산당을 수립하고 수도를 모스크바로 옮겼다. 그 후 독일과 휴전 조약을 맺고 개혁에 박차를 가하였다. 토지와 산업이 국유화되고, 농민에게 무상으로 토지가 분배되었으며, 노동자의 권익이 보장되었다.

레닌은 전 세계에 사회주의 이념과 혁명을 확산시키기 위해 **코민테른**을 조직하여 세계 약소민족의 독립 운동과 혁명을 지원하였다. 그러나 내란을 잠재우고 개혁을 추진하는 과정에서 경제가 악화되었다. 이를 극복하기 위해 레닌은 시장 경제 요소를 일부 도입한 **신경제 정책**(NEP)을 실시하였다. 또한 러시아를 중심으로 여러 소비에트 정부를 흡수하여 **소비에트 사회주의 공화국 연방**(소련)을 수립하였다(1922).

레닌의 뒤를 이은 **스탈린**은 중공업과 군수 산업을 집중 육성하는 경제 개발 5개년 계획을 추진하였다. 소련 곳곳에 집단 농장이 세워졌고, 국가 통제에 의한 중공업 중심의 경제 정책이 실시되었다. 소련 경제는 성장 곡선을 그려 나갔으나 스탈린이 권력을 독점하기 위해 무리하게 반대파를 제거하고 1인 독재 체제를 강화하는 과정에서 자유와 인권을 탄압하였다. 러시아 혁명의 영향으로 프랑스, 독일 등 유럽 각국에서는 사회주의 계열의 정당이 대두하였고, 소련의 지원으로 아시아 · 아프리카의 여러 나라에서 공산당이 성립하여 사회주의 운동이 활기를 띠었다.

⚙ **러시아 혁명이 세계사에 어떤 영향을 주었나요?**

How Did the Russian Revolution Influence World History?

영국 England
총파업(1926)
General Strike

중국 China
5·4 운동(1919), 중국 공산당 성립(1921)
5·4 Movement,
Established the Communist Party
of China

러시아 혁명(1917)
RussianRevolution

몽골 Mongolia
인민 공화국 성립(1924)
Establishment of the
People's Republic

베트남 Vietnam
호찌민의 베트남 공산당 결성(1930)
Ho Chi Minh Formed the
Communist Party of Vietnam

인도네시아 Indonesia
공산당 결성
Formation of the Communist
Party of Indonesia

한국 Korea
박헌영, 김단야, 조봉암 등이 조선 공산당 성립(1925)
Joseon Communist Party Was Established by
Park Hun Yeong, Kim Danya, and Cho Bong-am

The Birth of the Union of Soviet Socialist Republics

Following the successful November Revolution, Lenin formed the Communist Party of the Soviet Union and moved the capital to Moscow. Soon after, he signed an armistice with Germany, and introduced reforms. Land and industries were nationalized, and this nationalized land was distributed to peasants for free. The workers also had their rights and interest guaranteed by the regime.

Lenin went on to organize Communist International to spread socialist ideology and revolution throughout the world, and proactively supported independence movements and revolutions that took place in other smaller and weaker countries around the world. But the fast-paced radical reforms and the civil war dealt a critical blow to the national economy. To overcome the economic crisis, Lenin proposed the New Economic Policy(NEP), which partially adopted capitalist economic policy. In addition, Moscow absorbed Soviet governments and proclaimed the creation of the Union of Soviet Socialist Republics(USSR) under the leadership of Russia(1922).

Lenin's successor Stalin launched five-year plans for the national economy of the Soviet Union that were designed to proactively promote the heavy and military supply industries. Collective farms popped up everywhere around the Soviet Union, and the Soviet economy started to develop and grow in parallel with the heavy industry centered economic plans. But during this process, Stalin oppressed freedom and violated human rights while aggressively persecuting his opponents and strengthening his absolute dictatorship. The Russian revolution influenced European countries such as France and Germany where socialism-oriented political parties gained power, and the socialist movement became more dynamic as communist parties were established in many countries in Asia and Africa with the support of the Soviet Union.

03 전후 세계의 새로운 질서, 베르사유 체제

전후 문제 처리를 위해 파리 강화 회의가 열리다

제1차 세계 대전이 끝나자 전승국을 중심으로 전쟁 후의 뒷수습을 위한 국제회의가 파리에서 열렸다(1919). **파리 강화 회의**에 참석한 전승국들은 미국 대통령 윌슨이 제창한 **14개조 평화 원칙**을 바탕으로 전쟁 이후 유럽의 영토 문제, 패전국에 대한 군비 축소, 패전국의 식민지 문제 등에 대해 협의하였다.

전승국들은 패전국 중에서도 특히 독일에 전쟁의 책임을 강하게 물었다. 독일이 다시는 전쟁을 일으키지 않도록 영토를 축소하고 군비를 감축하였다. 또한 감당하기 힘들 정도로 막대한 배상금을 지불하도록 하였다. 파리 강화 회의에 따라 연합국과 독일이 맺은 조약을 **베르사유 조약**이라고 한다.

이어서 전승국들은 오스트리아 · 헝가리 제국을 해체하였다. 오스만 제국, 불가리아 등 패전국들과 개별적인 조약을 맺어 군비를 축소하게 하고 배상금을 물렸으며, 식민지를 재편하였다. 이렇게 파리 강화 회의에서 결정된 내용을 바탕으로 성립한 전후의 새로운 국제 질서를 '베르사유 체제'라고 한다.

....

◉ 파리 강화 회의의 한계는 무엇이었나요?

What Were the Limitations of the Paris Peace Conference?

일제 강점기 대한민국 임시 정부는 김규식을 파리 강화 회의에 보냈어요. 김규식은 우리나라의 독립을 탄원하였으나 받아들여지지 않았지요. 베트남의 호찌민도 『베트남 인민의 요구서』를 제출하려 하였으나 회담장 복도에서 쫓겨났어요. 이러한 사례에서 알 수 있듯 파리 강화 회의는 철저히 승전국만을 위해 개최된 회담이었습니다.

During the Japanese colonial rule, the Provisional Government of the Republic of Korea sent Kim Kyu-sik to the Paris Peace Conference. He appealed for the independence of Korea, but was not accepted. Vietnam's Ho Chi Minh also tried to submit the *"Vietnamese People's Request"* but was kicked out of the hallway of the conference hall. As we can see from these examples, the Paris Peace Conference was held strictly for the victorious states.

김규식
Kim Kyu-sik

파리 강화 회의에 파견된 대한민국 임시 정부의 대표단
The Delegation of the Provisional Government of
the Republic of Korea to the Paris Peace Conference

03 Versailles System, a New Post-War World Order

Paris Peace Conference for Solutions to Post-War Problems

After the end of WWI, an international conference was held among the victorious Allied Powers in Paris to set the peace terms for the post-war world(1919). The victorious countries that participated in the Paris Peace Conference discussed issues regarding colonies and the reduction of armaments, which the defeated states were faced with, in addition to the territorial boundary issues in Europe, all based up on the basis of the 14 Points proposed by the US President Woodrow Wilson.

In this conference, the victorious Allied Powers signed the Treaty of Versailles, which explicitly demanded that Germany take responsibility for the war. The main points of the treaty included the reduction of Germany's armed forces and territories to prevent Germany from starting another war. The treaty also established Germany's heavy liability for reparations. The treaty between the Allies and Germany following the Paris Peace Conference is called the Treaty of Versailles.

The victorious Allied Powers declared that the Austro-Hungarian Empire was to be dissolved, and they also signed treaties with defeated states individually, including the Ottoman Empire, to demand that they reduce their armed forces, reorganize their colonies, and take responsibility for the losses of and damages to the Allies. The new post-war order of the international community, established based on the agreements made during the Peace Conference in Paris, is called the Versailles System.

베르사유 체제가 새로운 국제 질서를 만들다

총력전을 전개하였던 영국과 프랑스 등의 유럽 열강은 제1차 세계 대전 이후 세력이 약화되었다. 반면 전쟁 후반에 참전하여 전쟁을 승리로 이끌었던 미국의 국제적 위상이 높아졌고, 일본도 연합국의 일원으로 승전국 대열에 올랐다.

미국 대통령 윌슨이 제시한 14개조 평화 원칙에는 식민지 지역의 여러 약소민족들에게 힘을 실어 주는 조항이 포함되어 있었다. 그것이 **민족 자결주의 원칙**이다. 또한 윌슨이 전쟁의 재발 방지를 위해 국제적 평화 기구 창설을 제안함에 따라 파리에서 **국제 연맹**이 창설되었다(1920).

그러나 국제 연맹에는 여러 한계가 있었다. 국제 연맹 창설을 제안하였던 미국이 의회의 반대로 국제 연맹에 참여하지 못하였고 소련과 독일 또한 제외되었다. 국제 연맹은 전쟁을 억제하여 세계 평화를 유지할 수 있는 군사 기구도 갖추지 못하였다. 이와 같이 **베르사유 체제**는 전후에 새로운 국제 질서로 등장하였으나 여러 가지 갈등의 씨앗을 안고 있었다.

◎ **윌슨의 민족 자결주의 원칙이 왜 한국에는 적용되지 않았나요?**

민족 자결주의 원칙은 패전국의 식민지에만 적용되었고 승전국의 식민지에는 해당되지 않았다. 오히려 승전국들은 독일과 오스만 제국의 지배를 받던 지역을 자신들의 식민지나 이권 지역으로 재분할하였다. 따라서 승전국인 일본의 식민지였던 한국도 민족 자결주의의 적용을 받을 수 없었다.

미국 제28대 대통령 윌슨
각 민족은 다른 민족이나 국가의 간섭을 받지 않고 자신의 정치적 운명을 스스로 결정해야 합니다.
28th President of the United States, Thomas Woodrow Wilson
Each people must decide for themselves their own political destiny without interference from other peoples or nations.

Versailles System Creates a New World Order

The European powers that had engaged in the total war, such as Britain and France, grew weaker after WWI. While the US, which participated in the war during the later stages and contributed to the victory, emerged as an international power player. Japan also joined the list of victorious states as a result of the victory of the Allied Powers.

The 14 Points proposed by US President Woodrow Wilson included an article that empowered many smaller and weaker states, which came to be known as the Principle of National Self-determination. President Wilson also proposed the establishment of an international peacekeeping organization to prevent the recurrence of war, which materialized in the creation of the League of Nations(1920).

However, the League of Nations had several limitations. The US could not join the League of Nations because of the objection of its Congress even though it had proposed its creation, and Germany and the Soviet Union were also excluded. The League of Nations did not have a military organization that could maintain peace by helping prevent wars throughout the world. Therefore, even though the Versailles System emerged as a new international order in the post-war world, it was holding within it the seeds of various conflicts.

⊕ Why Didn't Wilson's Principle of National Self-determination Apply to Korea?

The Principle of National Self-determination applied only to the colonies of defeated countries, and not to the colonies of victorious ones. Rather, the victorious states subdivided the regions that had been dominated by the German and Ottoman Empires into their own colonies and areas of interest. Therefore, Korea, which was a colony of the victorious state of Japan, could not be subject to the Principle of National Self-determination.

04 제2차 세계 대전의 발발과 전개

대공황이 일어나다

미국은 제1차 세계 대전 이후 세계 제일의 공업 생산력과 자본력을 바탕으로 눈부신 성장을 거듭하였다. 그러던 미국에 **대공황** 자본주의 체제에서 과잉 생산으로 시장의 수요 공급이 급격하게 붕괴되어 나타나는 경기 침체 현상이 일어났다. 1929년 10월 뉴욕 증시의 주가가 갑자기 큰 폭으로 떨어졌다. 은행은 문을 닫고, 공장과 기업이 도산하였으며, 농산물 가격이 대폭락하면서 실업자가 급증하였다.

미국의 루스벨트 대통령은 대공황에서 벗어나기 위해 정부가 나서서 경제 활동에 개입하는 **뉴딜 정책**을 추진하였다. **테네시강** 댐 개발 공사와 같은 대규모 공공사업을 벌여 실업자를 구제하고 정부가 나서서 농산물을 사들였다. 또한 노동자의 권익을 보호하고 실업 수당을 지급하는 등 사회보장 제도를 실시하여 경기를 회복해 나갔다.

한편 유럽에도 대공황의 충격이 몰려와 각국이 큰 경제적 어려움에 빠졌다. 이에 영국과 프랑스는 외국 상품에 높은 관세를 붙이는 보호 무역, 본국과 식민지를 경제 블록으로 묶는 **블록 경제**를 통해 대공황의 위기를 극복해 나갔다.

■ 파운드 블록 Pound Block
■ 달러 블록(미국) Dollar Block(US)
■ 프랑 블록 Franc Block
■ 엔 블록(일본) Yen Block(Japan)

블록 경제 Bloc Economy

💡 '뉴딜 정책'의 '뉴딜'은 무엇을 의미하나요?

루스벨트 대통령 '뉴딜(New Deal)'은 트럼프를 칠 때 새로운 카드를 내놓는 것을 의미해요. 영국 경제학자 케인스가 주장하는 '국가에 의한 유효 수요의 창출', '완전 고용', '국가에 의한 관리 통화 제도' 등을 받아들여 새로운 변화를 꾀하였지요.

04 Breakout and Unfolding of the Second World War

The Financial Crisis of the Great Depression

After WWI was over, the US was on a streak of remarkable economic growth with the support of its world's best industrial productivity and capital power. Then it was hit by the Great Depression. It all started in October 1929 when share prices on the New York Stock Exchange collapsed. It was soon followed by a skyrocketing unemployment rate because banks closed their doors, factories and companies went bankrupt, and the prices of agricultural products plunged.

Aiming to overcome the Great Depression, US President Franklin Roosevelt launched the New Deal, which had the government taking the lead in controlling economic activities. The government responded to the needs of unemployed workers for relief with large-scale public projects such as the construction of a dam on the Tennessee River and the buying out of agricultural products. The government initiated social welfare programs such as unemployment compensation and the protection of workers' rights, and the US government economy started recovering as a result.

In the meantime, Europe was not spared from the impact of the Great Depression and faced serious economic crisis itself. In response, Britain and France tried to overcome the crisis of the Great Depression by turning to protective trade and imposing high tariffs, and also by binding their mainland and colonies into a single economic bloc, thereby creating what is referred to as a Bloc economy.

🌐 What Does 'New Deal' in 'New Deal Policy' Mean?

President Roosevelt 'New Deal' means to play a new hands of cards when playing cards. I made new changes by adopting the 'creation of effective demand by the state', 'full employment', and 'currency system managed by the state', which British economist Keynes argued against.

전체주의와 군국주의가 국민을 전쟁으로 내몰다

대공황 이후 식민지가 적고 경제 사정이 취약한 국가들에서는 경제 혼란과 사회 불안을 이용하여 전체주의와 군국주의를 앞세운 세력이 권력을 장악하였다. 이탈리아에서는 대공황이 일어나기 전 이미 파시즘을 주장하는 무솔리니가 정권을 잡았다. 대공황이 일어나자 독일에서는 히틀러가 나치당을 이끌고 나치즘을 앞세워 정권을 잡았다.

일본에서는 군부 세력이 군국주의를 강화하는 한편 만주 사변을 일으켰다 (1931). 에스파냐에서는 프랑코를 중심으로 하는 군부 파시스트 세력이 독일과 이탈리아의 지원을 받아 자유주의자들과 사회주의자들이 연대한 인민 전선을 누르고 권력을 잡았다.

무솔리니는 국가 지상주의를 내세워 국가와 개인을 하나로 만들고, 국민의 열렬한 지지를 받으며 침략적인 대외 팽창을 전개하였다. 히틀러는 무솔리니와 손을 잡고 일본을 끌어들여 추축국 로마, 베를린, 도쿄를 추축으로 방공 협정을 맺은 이탈리아, 독일, 일본 3국을 형성하였다. 이탈리아는 에티오피아를 침공하였고, 일본은 중·일 전쟁을 일으켰다 (1937). 독일도 재무장을 선언하고 오스트리아를 합병한 데 이어 체코슬로바키아를 점령하였다. 이러한 상황에서 국제적 비난이 빗발치자 독일은 국제 연맹을 탈퇴하였다.

◈ 무솔리니와 히틀러는 어떻게 국민의 인기를 얻었나요?

무솔리니와 히틀러는 대공황 속에서 국민의 절망적인 상황을 자극하고 국가주의를 내세우는 대중 연설을 하여 인기를 얻었다.

국가를 떠나서는 인간과 영혼의 가치도 존재하지 않는다. …… 국가가 국민을 창조한다.
Apart from the state, neither human nor soul values exist. …… The state creates the people.

무솔리니와 히틀러
Mussolini and Hitler

우리 민족은 희망도 질서도 없는 국제주의로부터 해방되어야 하며, 민족주의에 의해 단호하고도 열정적으로 재조직되어야 한다.
Our nation must be freed from internationalism, which has neither hope nor order, and must be reorganized firmly and passionately by nationalism.

Totalism and Militarism Push People to Wars

After the Great Depression, totalitarian or militaristic regimes took advantage of social unrest and economic destabilization to seize power in countries with few or no colonies and a weak economy. In Italy, Benito Mussolini, who had been advocating Fascism even before the Great Depression, seized power. In the wake of the Great Depression, the leader of the Nazi Party, Hitler, advocated Nazism and seized power in Germany.

In Japan, the military forces took the lead in strengthening Militarism and instigated the Mukden Incident(1931). In Spain, the militaristic fascist groups under the leadership of Franco drove out the Popular Front, which was a coalition between liberalism and socialism, and seized power with the support of Germany and Italy.

A believer of statism, Mussolini brought nation and individuals together into a singular entity and launched campaigns to invade and expand its territory with the passionate support of the people. Hitler also created the Axis Powers by joining forces with Mussolini and bringing in Japan, which planted a seed of war. Italy invaded and battled with Ethiopia, and Japan fought with China in the Sino-Japanese War(1937). Germany declared re-militarization, merged Austria, and occupied Czechoslovakia. When severely criticized by the international community, Germany left the League of Nations.

. . . .

ⓐ How Did Mussolini and Hitler Gain Popularity among the People?

Mussolini and Hitler gained popularity during the Great Depression by making public speeches stimulating the desperate situation of the people and promoting nationalism.

제2차 세계 대전이 전개되다

독일은 소련과 **상호 불가침 조약**을 맺고 폴란드를 침공하였다(1939). 이에 영국과 프랑스가 독일에 선전 포고를 하면서 제2차 세계 대전이 발발하였다. 독일이 폴란드 서부를 차지하자 소련은 폴란드 동부와 **발트 3국**을 점령하였다. 이후 독일은 서부 전선으로 진격하여 프랑스 파리를 함락하였다. 프랑스인들은 이에 굴복하지 않고 레지스탕스^{저항을 뜻하는 프랑스어로, 파시즘에 대한 저항 운동을 말함}를 조직하여 곳곳에서 독일의 지배에 항거하였다.

일본은 전쟁 물자 확보를 위해 동남아시아 지역을 차지하려 하였으나 미국에 의해 경제 제재 조치를 받았다. 이에 **진주만**을 공격하여 **태평양 전쟁**을 일으켰다(1941). 전쟁이 전 세계로 확대된 가운데 미국이 태평양 전선의 **미드웨이 해전**에서 승리한 이후, 점차 전세가 연합국에 유리하게 전개되었다.

🏅 일본이 진주만을 공격한 이유는 무엇인가요?

일본군이 프랑스령 인도차이나반도에 진군하자 미국은 1940년 9월 중요한 군수 물자인 폐철의 대일 수출을 전면 금지하였고, 석유 수출 금지 조치까지 내리려 하였다. 당시 일본은 석유의 80%를 미국에서 수입하고 있었다. 이에 일본은 1941년 12월 7일 미국의 해군 기지인 진주만을 선제공격하였다. 미국 태평양 함대가 무너지면 일본은 석유를 얻을 수 있는 동남아시아를 점령할 수 있다고 보았다.

태평양 전쟁이 한창이던 1942년, 미국은 일본의 암호를 해독하여 일본이 미드웨이섬과 알류샨열도의 기지를 점령하려 한다는 계획을 알아냈다. 이후 미국의 폭격기들이 일제히 날아올라 일본의 항공 모함을 대거 침몰시키며 일본의 점령 계획을 무력화하였다.

일본의 진주만 기습(1941)
Japan Attacked on Pearl Harbor

미드웨이 해전(1942)
Battle of Midway

World War II Unfolds

German forces invaded Poland after signing the Treaty of Non-aggression with the USSR(1939). Accordingly, Britain and France declared war on Germany and World War II(WWII) began. Germany occupied western Poland, shortly before the Soviet Union invaded and occupied eastern Poland and three Baltic states. Later, German forces marched onward to the Western Front and captured Paris. The French launched a resistance movement and strongly fought back against the Germans' hostilities throughout the country.

Japan tried to occupy Southeast Asia to secure war supplies, but when its hostility sparked economic sanctions by the United States, Japan launched a surprise attack on a base at Pearl Harbor and started the Pacific War(1941). As the war spread throughout the world, the United States won the Battle of Midway on the Pacific Front, and the tide of the war turned in favor of the United States and its allies.

Why Did Japan Attack Pearl Harbor?

When Japanese troops marched on the French Indochina Peninsula in September 1940, the United States completely banned the export of scrap iron, an important military material to Japan, and attempted to ban oil exports. At the time, Japan was importing 80% of its oil from the United States. On December 7, 1941, Japan preemptively attacked Pearl Harbor, the US naval base. If the US Pacific fleet collapses, Japan believes that they can occupy Southeast Asia where oil can be obtained.

In 1942, in the midst of the Pacific War, the U.S. cracked the Japanese code and discovered a plan for Japan to capture bases on Midway Island and the Aleutian Islands. Afterwards, United States' bombers flew in unison, sinking a large number of Japanese aircraft carriers and neutralizing the Japanese occupation plan.

이탈리아, 독일, 일본이 항복하다

전쟁의 장기화로 전쟁 물자가 부족해지자 독일은 **독·소 불가침 조약**을 깨고 소련을 침공하였다. 그러나 소련의 매서운 추위와 유격대의 완강한 저항에 부딪혀 큰 피해를 입었다(**스탈린그라드 전투**, 1942).

연합국은 먼저 이탈리아에 상륙하여 파시스트 정권을 무너뜨렸다. 이후 **노르망디 상륙 작전**을 펼쳐 파리를 해방하고 독일 본토로 진격하였다. 소련군도 서쪽으로 계속 진격하며 독일을 압박하였다. 동서 양쪽에서 압박을 받게 된 독일은 연합국에 항복하였다.

미국이 일본의 **히로시마**와 **나가사키**에 원자 폭탄을 투하하고 소련군이 극동 전선에 참전하자 일본군의 전세는 극도로 불리해졌다. 이에 8월 15일 일본이 무조건 항복을 선언하여 제2차 세계 대전은 막을 내렸다(1945).

제2차 세계 대전 유럽 전선 World War II European Front

⚡ 스탈린그라드 전투, 노르망디 상륙 작전은 어떻게 전개되었나요?

↑↓ 스탈린그라드 전투(1942~1943)
Battle of Stalingrad

독일은 소련의 석유 공급 요충지인 스탈린그라드(지금의 볼고그라드)를 차지하기 위해 1942년 여름부터 1943년 2월까지 소련과 치열하게 싸웠지만 추위로 인해 물러섰어요. Germany fought fiercely with the Soviet Union from the summer of 1942 to February 1943 to occupy the Soviet oil supply center, Stalingrad(current Volgograd), but withdrew due to the cold.

Italy, Germany, and Japan Surrender

When the prolonged war created a shortage of supplies, Germany broke the Non-aggression treaty it had signed with Russia and invaded the Soviet Union, but German forces sustained significant losses due to the harsh winter and strong resistance of the Soviet forces(Battle of Stalingrad, 1942).

The allied forces landed in Italy, brought down the fascist regime, and went on to liberate Paris in the Normandy Landings operation. Then they advanced to mainland Germany. Soviet forces also continued to advance westward and pressed to Germany. Under pressure from both east and west, Germany surrendered to the Allies.

Japan also took a blow when the US dropped nuclear bombs on Hiroshima and Nagasaki, and the tide of the war grew extremely unfavorable to the Japanese troops after the Soviet forces' engagement on the Far East Front. On August 5, Japan declared an unconditional surrender, thereby ending the Second World War(1945).

....

🏵 How Did the Battle of Stalingrad and the Normandy Landings Operation Unfold?

노르망디 상륙 작전(1944)
Normandy Landings Operation

연합국은 1,200여 척의 함선과 800여 척의 상륙정, 1만여 대의 항공기를 동원하여 노르망디 상륙 작전을 전개하였고, 결국 독일군을 물리치고 파리를 해방하였어요.
The Allied Powers mobilized 1,200 ships, 800 landing ships, and 10,000 aircraft to launch the Normandy landings, eventually defeating the Germans and liberating Paris.

05 평화 확산을 위한 노력

대서양 헌장을 바탕으로 국제 연합이 성립하다

제2차 세계 대전이 한창이던 1941년 연합국을 대표하는 미국 루스벨트 대통령과 영국의 처칠 수상이 만나 전후의 평화 원칙이 담긴 **대서양 헌장**을 발표하였다. 이 원칙은 전후에 창설된 국제 연합의 이념적 바탕이 되었다.

대서양 헌장 발표 이후 국제 사회는 **카이로 회담, 얄타 회담, 포츠담 회담** 등 여러 차례 회담을 열어 전후 처리 문제를 논의하면서 전쟁을 빨리 끝내기 위해 노력하였다. 또한 전쟁이 끝난 뒤에는 독일의 뉘른베르크와 일본의 도쿄에서 군사 재판을 열어 전쟁을 일으킨 전범을 심판하였다.

국제 연합(UN)은 이러한 국제 사회의 협의와 노력을 바탕으로 51개국이 샌프란시스코에 모여 창설한 항구적인 국제기구이다(1945). 국제 연합은 침략 행위가 일어나면 군사력을 동원하여 이를 무력으로 제재할 수 있기 때문에 국제 연맹보다 훨씬 강력한 국제 평화 기구이다.

··

⚉ 전후 처리 문제를 위해 열린 국제회의에서 무엇이 결정되었나요?

What Was Decided at the International Conference on Post-War Issues?

대서양 헌장(1941. 8.) Atlantic Charter
국제 연합의 원칙 마련 Establishing Principles of the United Nations

▼

카이로 회담(1943. 11.) Cairo Conference
한국 독립을 최초로 약속 The First Promise of Korean Independence

▼

얄타 회담(1945. 2.) Yalta Conference
소련의 대일전 참전을 결정 The Soviet Union decided to participate in the war against Japan.

▼

포츠담 회담(1945. 7.) Potsdam Conference
한국의 독립을 재확인, 일본의 무조건 항복이 결정됨. Korea's independence was reaffirmed, and Japan's unconditional surrender was decided.

05 Efforts for the Spread of Peace

The United Nations Is Created Based on the Atlantic Charter

In 1941, when the Second World War was raging throughout the world, US President Roosevelt represented the allied forces at a meeting with UK Prime Minister Winston Churchill and announced the Atlantic Charter, which included the principles of post-war peace. These principles became the ideological basis of the United Nations created after the war.

The announcement of the Atlantic Charter was followed by several meetings in the international community, such as the Cairo Conference, the Yalta Conference, and the Potsdam Conference, all of which were to discuss the post-war order of the world and an early conclusion to the world war. Following the end of WWII, the victorious allied governments prosecuted war criminals who were responsible for war crimes and wartime atrocities through the Nuremberg Trials and the Tokyo War Crimes Trials.

The United Nations (UN) is a permanent international organization founded by 51 countries in San Francisco, supported by the efforts and discussions of the international community(1945). The League of Nations was the forerunner of the United Nations, but the United Nations was an international peace organization with much greater power because the UN could use military force against acts of invasion should they ever occur.

1914년 이후 일본이 점령한 모든 영토를 반환하도록 하고 적당한 시기에 한국을 자주 독립시킬 것을 결의한다.
Resolve to return all territories occupied by Japan after 1914 and to give Korea independent in due course.

카이로 회담(왼쪽부터 장제스, 루스벨트, 처칠)
Cairo Conference(From Left to Right: Chiang Kai-shek, Roosevelt, Winston Churchill)

민주주의의 확산

01 민주주의의 발전

민주주의 원칙에 입각한 신생 공화국이 탄생하다

제1차 세계 대전은 시민들이 참가한 총력전으로 전개된 전쟁이었다. 전쟁이 끝나자 전쟁 과정에서 큰 역할을 한 시민의 지위가 높아졌고, 시민들은 민주주의 원칙에 입각한 공화국 수립을 위해 노력하였다.

제1차 세계 대전 막바지에 독일에서 혁명이 일어나 빌헬름 2세가 폐위되고 민주주의 원칙에 입각한 **바이마르 공화국**이 성립되었다. 바이마르 공화국은 국민 주권주의에 의한 민주적인 헌법을 제정하였다. 이후 **바이마르 헌법**은 현대 헌법의 모범이 되었다.

오스트리아가 상실한 지역 Regions Austria Lost
러시아가 상실한 지역 Regions Russia Lost

독일에 이어 오스트리아와 오스만 제국에서도 제정이 무너지고 공화정이 탄생하였다. 베르사유 체제하에 민족 자결주의의 영향으로 러시아와 패전국의 지배를 받던 동유럽에서는 새로운 신생 독립국들이 탄생하였다.

제1차 세계 대전 이후의 독립국
Sovereign States after the World War I

◈ 바이마르 헌법이 현대 헌법의 효시로 평가받는 이유는 무엇인가요?

1919년 20세 이상 바이마르 공화국 국민들의 보통 선거로 의회가 출범하였다. 독일 의회는 사회 민주당 당수인 에베르트를 대통령으로 선출하였다. 바이마르 헌법에는 국민 주권주의에 입각한 기본권 보장, 노동자의 권리 보호, 취업·교육의 권리, 언론의 자유, 여성의 보통 선거권 등이 잘 규정되어 있어 현대 헌법에 많은 영향을 주었다.

바이마르 헌법 Weimar Constitution

Spread of Democracy

01 Development of Democracy

Birth of New Republics Built on the Principle of Democracy

The First World War was a total war fought by and prosecuted against entire populations of the involved states. Having played a significant role during the war, citizens found themselves having elevated their social status and no longer wanted a monarchy where a king or a queen was the head of the state.

At the end of World War I, a revolution broke out in Germany, which led to the abdication of Wilhelm II allowing the Weimar Republic to be founded upon the principle of democracy. A new constitution was signed into law during the Weimar Republic that officially created a parliament democracy. Commonly called the Weimar Constitution, it became the model modern constitution.

Germany was followed by Austria and the Ottoman Empire in dissolving their monarchy government systems and establishing republics. Influenced by the principle of national self-determination from the Versailles System, East Europe also saw the emergence of states that became independent from the rule of Russia and other defeated states.

🔎 Why Is the Weimar Constitution Regarded as the Beginning of the Modern Constitution?

In 1919, the people of the Weimar Republic over 20 years of age held general elections to launch parliament. The German parliament elected Ebert, leader of the Social Democratic Party, as president. The Weimar Constitution greatly influenced the modern constitution as it clearly defines basic rights based on national sovereignty, protection of workers' rights, the right to employment and education, freedom of speech, and women's general election rights.

전체주의 세력과의 대결을 통해 민주주의가 발전하다

제1차 세계 대전 후 에스파냐에서는 왕정이 무너지고 **제2 공화정**이 수립되었다(1931). 제2 공화정은 평화주의 원칙에 따라 여성에게도 참정권을 인정하는 발전된 민주주의의 모습을 보였다. 1936년 에스파냐 총선에서는 **인민 전선**이 승리하여 정권을 수립하고 교회, 지주, 부유층 등의 특권을 없애는 토지 개혁을 추진하였다.

당시 유럽은 1929년 발생한 **대공황**으로 경제가 매우 어려웠다. 그 틈을 타 **전체주의**가 유행처럼 번져 나갔다. 전체주의 세력은 국가의 발전과 팽창을 위해서라면 국민은 무조건 따라야 할 것을 요구하며 개인의 자유를 억압하였다.

에스파냐에서도 **프랑코**가 이끄는 전체주의 세력이 개혁에 불만을 품은 세력의 지지를 받아 군사 정변을 일으켰다. 에스파냐는 내전에 휩싸여 인민 전선과 전체주의로 정권을 탈취하려는 군부 세력이 치열한 접전을 벌였다. 전체주의 국가인 이탈리아와 독일은 무기를 보내는 등 적극적으로 프랑코 세력을 지원하였다.

군부 세력에 밀리게 되자 인민 전선은 국제 사회에 호소하여 **국제 여단**을 조직하였다. 전 세계 50여 개국에서 전체주의에 맞서려는 사람들이 국제 여단에 모여들었다. 의용군 숫자는 4만여 명에 이르렀고 후방에서 의료와 자원봉사를 담당한 사람들도 2만여 명에 달하였다. 그러나 1939년까지 계속된 내전은 인민 전선의 패배로 끝났다.

에스파냐 내전 중에 반군의 장갑차에 올라 환호하고 있는 국제 여단의 의용군
Members of the International Brigades Cheering on Rebels' Armored Vehicle During the Spanish Civil War ⓒAlamy Stock Photo

파시스트를 몰아내자!
Let's drive out the fascists!

Democracy Grows Through Conflict with Totalitarianism

After WWI, Spain saw the abolition of the monarchy and the proclamation of the Second Spanish Republic(1931). The republic government advanced democracy under the principle of pacifism, such as demonstrated by its policy to give women the right to vote. The Spanish Popular Front won the 1936 general election, formed a new government, and introduced land reform that stripped the church, the landowners, and the rich of their privileges.

At the time, economic conditions were extremely bad in Europe due to the Great Depression that occurred in 1929. During this time of economic crisis, Totalitarianism spread like wildfire. Totalitarianism demanded unconditional obedience to the government and oppressed people's freedoms for the sake of the development and expansion of the nation.

In Spain, totalitarian forces led by Franco triggered a military coup with the support of those dissatisfied with the reform. In this Spanish Civil War, the military forces fought fiercely to overthrow the Popular Front government that tried to protect democracy and establish a new totalitarian government. Other totalitarian regimes such as Italy and Germany supplied weapons and gave their full support to Franco's forces.

When the military forces started to prevail in the war, the Popular Front appealed to the international community and set up the 'International Brigades'. The brigades were joined by people from over 50 countries around the world who wanted to fight against totalitarianism. It is estimated that close to 40,000 members served in the International Brigades, and an additional 20,000 plus served in the rear as volunteers and medical staff. However, the civil war ended with the defeat of the Popular Front in 1939.

👓 작가들이 에스파냐 내전에 참전한 이유는 무엇인가요?

전체주의에 대항하는 많은 작가들이 민주주의를 지키고자 에스파냐 내전에 참전하였다. 대표적으로 어니스트 헤밍웨이, 앙드레 말로, 조지 오웰 등이 있다.

어니스트 헤밍웨이의 소설 『누구를 위하여 종은 울리나』의 주인공 로버트 조던은 대학교수였지만 에스파냐 내전에 참가하여 동굴에서 생활하였다. 적군의 교량을 폭파하는 임무를 맡아 수행하던 도중 조던은 마리아라는 여인을 만나 사랑에 빠지게 되었다.

조던은 적군의 교량을 폭파하던 중 적탄에 맞아 큰 부상을 입게 되었고, 마리아에게 떠나라고 설득하였다. 조던의 동료는 마리아를 억지로 말에 태웠고, 홀로 남은 조던은 적진을 향해 사격을 가하며 동료와 마리아의 탈출을 도왔다.

어니스트 헤밍웨이는 종군 기자로서 에스파냐 내전에 참여한 경험을 바탕으로 『누구를 위하여 종은 울리나』를 썼다. 그는 이 작품에서 개인과 인류의 관계, 연대 책임에 대한 문제를 다루었다. 앙드레 말로와 조지 오웰도 국제 여단의 일원으로 에스파냐 내전에 참여한 경험을 바탕으로 각각 소설 『희망』과 『카탈루냐 찬가』를 썼다.

어니스트 헤밍웨이
『누구를 위하여 종은 울리나』는 영국 시인 존 던의 시 제목이에요.
"⋯⋯ 누구의 죽음이라도 나를 감소시킨다
나는 인류에 포함되어 있기 때문이다
누구를 위해 저 종이 울리는지 알고자 사람을 보내지 말라
종은 그대를 위해 울린다"
Ernest Miller Hemingway
The title of a poem by British poet John Dunn, "*For Whom the Bell Tolls*".
"⋯⋯Any man's death diminishes me, because I am involved in mankind. And therefore never send to know for whom the bell tolls. It tolls for thee."

앙드레 말로
『희망』은 국제 여단에서 활동한 경험을 르포 형식으로 구성한 소설이에요.
Andre Malraux
"*Hope*" is a novel that utilized a reportage format to convey my experience in an International Brigade.

🔭 Why Did the Writers Participate in the Spanish Civil War?

Many writers who opposed totalitarianism participated in the Spanish Civil War to protect democracy. Typical examples include Ernest Hemingway, Andre Malraux, and George Orwell.

Robert Jordan, the protagonist of Ernest Hemingway's novel "*For Whom the Bell Tolls*", was a university professor, but participated in the Spanish Civil War and lived in a cave. While on a mission to blow up an bridge, Jordan met a woman named Maria and fell in love.

Jordan was seriously injured by an enemy's bullet in the process of detonating an enemy bridge and persuaded Maria to leave. Jordan's colleague forced Mary to ride, and Jordan, who was left alone, fired at the enemy, helping his colleague and Maria escape.

Ernest Hemingway wrote the novel "*For Whom the Bell Tolls*" based on his experience of participating in the Spanish Civil War as a military reporter. In this work, he dealt with the issues of the relationship between individuals and humanity, and the responsibility for solidarity. Andre Mallo and George Orwell also wrote novels, "*I Hope*" and "*Homage to Catalonia*" respectively, based on their experiences in the Spanish Civil War as members of the International Brigade.

조지 오웰
소설 『카탈루냐 찬가』에 의용군 체험담과 더불어 에스파냐 공산당에 대한 고발을 담았어요.
George Orwell
In the novel "Homage to Catalonia", I wrote a story about my own experiences with the International Brigade and accusations against the Spanish Communist Party.

인권 회복을 위한 노력

01 세계 대전 중에 저지른 인권 침해

홀로코스트의 대량 학살이 일어나다

제2차 세계 대전은 인류 역사상 가장 잔인한 전쟁 범죄를 낳았다. 그 대표적인 것이 **홀로코스트**(1933~1945)로 불리는 대량 학살이다. **히틀러**는 게르만족이 세계에서 가장 인종적으로 우월하다고 믿는 인종주의자였다. 그는 게르만족에게 가장 해악을 끼치는 인종으로 **유대인**을 지목하였다. 그 외에도 집시와 슬라브인 등을 열등한 민족으로 간주하여 대대적인 탄압과 학살을 자행하였다.

1935년 **뉘른베르크 법**으로 독일은 유대인의 시민권을 박탈하였다. 독일인과 유대인의 결혼이 금지되었고, 유대인의 모든 재산이 몰수되었다. 제2차 세계 대전이 시작되자 유대인들을 **게토** 중세 시대 유럽에서 유대인을 강제 격리하기 위해 설정한 유대인 거주 지역 안에서만 살도록 철저히 격리하였다.

◉ 히틀러는 유대인을 어떻게 탄압하였나요?

제2차 세계 대전 중에는 유럽 내 수백만 명의 유대인들이 아우슈비츠 등의 강제 수용소에서 굶주림에 시달리며 강제로 중노동을 하였다. 어른, 어린아이 구별 없이 하루에도 수천 명이 죽임을 당하였으며, 유대인들은 화학 무기 개발을 위한 생체 실험에 희생당하기도 하였다.

아우슈비츠에 끌려간 유대인들은 몸만 겨우 누일 수 있는 곳에 수용되었어요.
The Jews who were taken to Auschwitz were confined to a place where they could barely lie down.

아우슈비츠 수용소(폴란드) Auschwitz Concentration Camp(Poland)

Efforts for the Recovery of Human Rights

01 Human Rights Violations Committed During World War II
The Genocide of the Holocaust

One of the cruelest war crimes that happened during WWII was a genocide called the Holocaust(1933–1945). Hitler was a racist who believed the German 'Aryan' race was superior to all other races of the world. Believing that Jews were a threat to the German race and that Gypsies and the Slavs were inferior races, he decided to persecute them when he came into power.

In 1935, the Nazis signed the Nuremberg Laws and officially excluded Jews from German citizenship. Marriage between Germans and Jews was prohibited, and properties owned by Jews were confiscated. During World War II, the Nazis isolated Jews by forcefully deporting and confining them to live only in ghettos.

◉ How Did Hitler Oppress the Jews?

During World War II, millions of Jews in Europe were killed after being forced into labor and starvation in concentration camps such as Auschwitz in Poland. Thousands of adults, and even children, were killed every day, and many others lost their lives as the victims of brutal medical experiments done for the development of chemical weapons.

유대인들은 샤워하는 줄 알고 들어간 가스실에서 최후를 맞았어요.
The Jews died in gas chambers where they thought they were taking a shower.

아우슈비츠 수용소 가스실
Gas Chamber in Auschwitz

난징 대학살이 일어나다

독일이 유럽 내 유대인을 탄압하고 있을 때 아시아에서도 반인륜적인 학살이 자행되고 있었다. 일본은 루거우차오 사건을 구실로 중·일 전쟁(1937)을 일으킨 후 중국의 수도인 난징을 점령하고 민간인을 학살하였다.

중국은 2015년 난징 대학살 기념관에 보관 중인 난징 대학살 관련 기록을 유네스코 세계 기록 유산으로 등재하여 난징 대학살이 인류가 결코 잊지 말아야 할 전쟁 범죄임을 세계에 알렸다.

⚜ **난징 대학살은 왜 일어났나요?**

루거우차오는 베이징 남쪽 교외에 있는 다리로 전략적 요충지였다. 1937년 7월 다리 서쪽을 지키던 일본군 병사가 야밤에 총소리와 함께 실종되었다. 그는 20여 분 뒤 부대로 복귀하였으나 일본군은 중국군의 공격으로 사건이 일어났다고 우기며 중·일 전쟁을 일으켰다. 일본군은 12월 10일 중국군에게 항복을 요구하였고 중국군은 이에 응하지 않았다. 그러자 일본군은 12월 13일 당시 중국의 수도였던 난징에 난입하였다.

중국군 사령관은 난징을 버리고 도망갔지만 난징에는 50~60만 명의 시민과 군인이 남아 있었다. 일본군은 난징에서 6주간 대학살극을 벌였다. 장교들이 100명의 목을 베는 시합을 벌이기도 하고, 마구잡이로 성폭력을 자행하기도 하였다. 이러한 난징 대학살은 일본 군부의 조직적인 지시에 의해 이루어졌다.

제2차 세계 대전이 끝난 후 난징 전범 재판이 열렸고, 학살을 주도한 일본군들은 사형을 선고받았다.

난징을 점령한 일본군은 투항한 중국군 포로뿐만 아니라 수많은 민간인들을 대상으로 잔인한 학살을 저질렀어요.
After occupying Nanjing, the Japanese military brutally massacred many civilians as well as Chinese prisoners of war who surrendered.

난징에 입성하는 일본군 Japanese Troops Rides into Nanjing

A Massacre in Nanjing

While the Jews were being persecuted by Germany in the West, a similar atrocity against humanity was being committed in Asia by Japan. Japan used an incident that happened on the Lugou Bridge to go to war with China(1937). During this Sino-Japanese War, Japan occupied the Chinese capital city of Nanjing and slaughtered numerous innocent civilians.

China let the entire world know that the Nanjing massacre was a war crime that humanity should never forget when the Chinese government submitted the Nanjing Massacre documents that were kept at the History Institute of Nanjing University to UNESCO and had them added to the UNESCO Memory of the World Register in 2015.

◉ Why Did the Nanjing Massacre Happen?

Lugou Bridge is a bridge in the southern suburbs of Beijing and a strategic point. In July 1937, a Japanese soldier guarding the west side of the bridge disappeared at night and a gunshot was heard. He returned to the troops after about 20 minutes, but the Japanese troops started a war between China and Japan, arguing that the incident occurred due to an attack by the Chinese army. The Japanese military demanded surrender from the Chinese on December 10, but the Chinese did not respond. Then, on December 13, the Japanese troops invaded Nanjing, the capital of China.

The Chinese commander abandoned Nanjing and ran away, but 500,000 to 600,000 citizens and soldiers remained in Nanjing. The Japanese military staged a massacre in Nanjing for six weeks. Japanese military officers competed to behead 100 people and sexually assaulted women indiscriminately. The Nanjing massacre was carried out under systematic instructions from the Japanese military.

After World War II, the Nanjing war crimes trial was held, and the Japanese soldiers who led the massacre were sentenced to death.

일본군 '위안부', 인권 유린을 강요당하다

1930년대 초부터 일본은 대륙 침략을 위한 전쟁을 일으키면서 여성의 인권을 짓밟는 전쟁 범죄를 저질렀다. 일본군은 침략한 지역의 여성들을 육체적 · 정신적으로 유린하였다. 일본군 '위안부'에는 한국을 비롯하여 중국, 타이완, 필리핀, 인도네시아 등 20만여 명으로 추산되는 여러 나라의 여성들이 포함되어 있었다.

전쟁 기간에 이 여성들은 인간 이하의 생활 속에서 고통스러운 삶을 살았다. 일본군은 '위안부' 운영 사실을 숨기기 위해 패전 이후 퇴각하기 전에 이들을 학살하거나 집단 자살을 강요하였다.

💧 일본은 일본군 '위안부' 문제에 대해 사죄하였나요?

2008년 유엔 인권 위원회는 일본 정부에 일본군 '위안부' 문제에 대한 책임을 인정하라고 권고하였지만 일본 정부는 아직도 일본군 '위안부' 강제 연행과 인권 침해에 대해 공식적으로 인정하지 않고 있다.

2015년 한·일 양국 정부는 '한·일 합의'를 통해 화해 치유 재단을 설립하고 '위안부' 문제를 최종적으로 해결한다고 발표하였다. 하지만 피해자와의 논의나 동의 과정 없이 합의가 진행되었고, 일본 정부는 지불하는 돈의 성격을 피해에 대한 배상금이 아닌 인도적 지원금이라고 하였다. 이에 일본군 '위안부' 피해 여성들은 유엔 인권 원칙에 부합하는 정의로운 문제 해결을 요구하는 시위를 계속하고 있다.

일본군 '위안부'의 모습을 형상화한 평화의 소녀상(서울 종로)
Statue of Peace in the Form of a 'Comfort Women' for the Japanese Military(Jongno, Seoul)

'Comfort Women' Are Forced into Sex Slavery for Japanese Soldiers

Since the early 1930s, Japan has committed war crimes against women and violated their human rights during the war that they initiated to invade continental China. The Japanese army physically and mentally abused women in the invading area. The 'Comfort Women' for the Japanese Army included over 200,000 women from not only Korea, but also from China, Taiwan, the Philippines, and Indonesia.

During the war, these women suffered pain while living in sub-human conditions and being forced to sexually serve the Japanese soldiers. In order to hide the operation of the 'Comfort Women', the Japanese military slaughtered them or forced them to commit mass suicide before retreating after defeat.

⊚ Did Japan Apologize for the Japanese Military 'Comfort Women' Issue?

In 2008, the United Nations Commission on Human Rights recommended that the Japanese government admit responsibility for the issue of 'Comfort Women(Sex slavery)' regarding the Japanese Army, but the Japanese government still has not officially acknowledged the forced arrest of 'Comfort Women' and the human rights violations of the Japanese Army.

In 2015, the governments of both Korea and Japan announced that they would establish a Reconciliation Healing Foundation through the 'Japan-South Korea Comfort Women Agreement' and finally solved the 'Comfort Women' issue. However, the agreement was reached without discussion with or consent from the victims. The Japanese government claimed that the money they paid was humanitarian aid, not compensation for damages. Accordingly, the 'Comfort Women' for the Japanese soldiers continue to demand a just solution to the problem in line with UN human rights principles.

VI

현대 세계의 전개와 과제

우리가 중대한 일에 침묵하는 순간 우리의 삶은 종말을 고하기 시작합니다.

– 마틴 루서 킹(1929 ~ 1968)

VI

Progress and Tasks of the Modern World

1. Cold War System and the Formation of the Third World
2. Globalization and Economic Integration
3. Anti-Authoritarian Movement and Mass Movement
4. Modern World's Efforts to Solve Problems

As soon as we are silent on something important,

our lives begin to come to an end.

–Martin Luther King(1929–1968)

브란덴부르크 문(독일 베를린)
Brandenburg Gate(Berlin, Germany)

냉전 체제와 제3 세계의 형성

01 냉전 체제의 형성

미국과 소련을 중심으로 냉전 체제가 이루어지다

제2차 세계 대전이 끝난 후 동유럽의 폴란드, 체코슬로바키아, 루마니아, 유고슬라비아 등에 소련의 지원을 받은 공산 정권이 들어섰다. 이에 위기를 느낀 미국은 트루먼 독트린에 이어 **마셜 플랜**(유럽 부흥 계획)을 발표하였다.

소련도 대응에 나서 동유럽의 공산주의 국가들과 **경제 상호 원조 회의**(COMECON)를 조직하였다. 그러자 미국을 비롯한 자본주의 진영은 **북대서양 조약 기구**(NATO)를 만들어 서유럽 국가 간에 상호 군사 원조와 집단 방위 체제를 갖추었다. 소련도 동유럽 공산 국가들을 결집하여 군사 동맹인 **바르샤바 조약 기구**(WTO)를 만들었다.

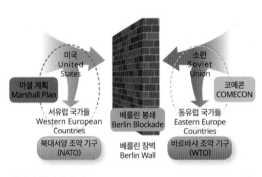

그 결과 세계는 미국 중심의 자본주의 진영과 소련 중심의 사회주의 진영이 총성 없는 전쟁을 하면서 긴장과 대립이 계속되는 상황을 이루게 되었다. 이것을 **냉전** 체제라고 한다.

냉전의 형성과 대립 The Formation and Confrontation of the Cold War

⏱ 트루먼 독트린과 마셜 플랜은 무엇인가요?

1947년 미국의 트루먼 대통령은 자유 국가들에 군사적, 재정적 지원을 하겠다는 내용의 트루먼 독트린을 발표하였어요. 마셜 플랜은 1947년 미 국무 장관 마셜이 서유럽 경제를 부흥하기 위해 제안한 원조 계획이었지요.

트루먼 독트린 발표
Truman Doctrine Announced

마셜 플랜 원조 물자에 사용된 식별 표지
Identification Mark Used on Marshall Plan Aid Supplies

Cold War System and the Formation of the Third World

01 Formation of the Cold War System

A Cold War System Is Formed Centering Around the United States and the Soviet Union

After the end of WWII, East Europe saw the emergence of communist regimes in Poland, Czechoslovakia, Romania, Yugoslavia, and others with the support of the Soviet Union. Feeling a sense of crisis in the situation, the United States declared the Truman Doctrine and launched the Marshall Plan(officially the European Recovery Program).

The Soviet Union countered the US initiatives by organizing Council for Mutual Economic Assistance(COMECON) with communist countries. Then the capitalist camps, including the United States, created the North Atlantic Treaty Organization(NATO) and established a system of collective defense and military aid between countries in Western Europe. The Soviet Union joined forces with Eastern European communist countries and created the Warsaw Treaty Organization(WTO), which was their own military alliance.

As a result, the world formed a Cold War system in which tensions and confrontations continued as the US-centered capitalist camp and the Soviet-centered socialist camp waged a 'war minus the shooting'.

◉ What Are the Truman Doctrine and Marshall Plan?

In 1947, President Truman of the US announced the Truman Doctrine to provide military and financial support to the free countries. The Marshall Plan was an aid program proposed by U.S. Secretary of State Marshall in 1947 to revitalize the Western European economy.

냉전 체제 속에 열전이 일어나다

미국과 소련을 중심으로 하는 냉전 체제는 세계 곳곳에서 긴장과 갈등을 낳아 결국에는 두 세계를 대리하는 열전 _{무력을 사용하는 전쟁}이 벌어졌다.

한반도에서는 미국과 소련이 일본군의 무장 해제를 위해 38도선이라는 군사 분계선을 그었고, 남과 북에 서로 다른 체제의 정권이 들어서면서 38도선이 분단선으로 고착화되었다.

독일은 제2차 세계 대전이 끝난 후 미국 · 영국 · 프랑스 · 소련 4개국에 의해 분할 점령되었다. 이후 냉전이 격화되면서 소련에 의해 베를린 봉쇄가 일어났고, 결국 사회주의 체제의 동독과 자본주의 체제의 서독으로 나뉘었다(1949). 1960년대에 세워진 베를린 장벽은 냉전 체제를 보여 주는 이념 대립의 대표적인 상징물이 되었다.

◉ 냉전 체제하에서 어떤 일이 일어났나요?

❶ 중국에서 항일 전쟁이 끝난 후 국민당과 공산당 사이에 내전이 벌어졌어요. 공산당은 국민당 정부를 타이완으로 몰아내고 중화 인민 공화국을 수립하였지요.
After the anti-Japanese war in China, a civil war broke out between the Kuomintang Party and the Communist Party. The Communist Party finally ousted the Kuomintang Party government to Taiwan and established the People's Republic of China.

❷ 소련의 지원을 받은 북한이 남한에 침입하며 전쟁이 일어났고, 결국 한반도는 남북으로 분단되었어요.
North Korea, supported by the Soviet Union, invaded South Korea and a war broke out, eventually dividing the Korean Peninsula into North and South Korea.

Hot Wars under the Cold War System

The Cold War system centered on the US and the Soviet Union created tension and conflicts around the world until it led to hot wars with other countries as proxies of the United States and the Soviet Union.

In the Korean Peninsula, the 38th parallel drawn as a military demarcation line by the United States and the Soviet Union for the disarmament of the Japanese army became cemented as a partition line that divided the country into two different governments in the South and the North.

In the case of Germany, it was divided and occupied by four countries, including the US, Great Britain, France, and the Soviet Union, after the end of WWII. Later, the Cold War intensified until the Soviet Union attempted the 'Berlin Blockade'. Eventually, Germany was divided into socialist East Germany and capitalist West Germany(1949). The Berlin Wall that was built in the 1960s became a symbol of ideological confrontation that represented the Cold War system.

🌐 What Happened under the Cold War?

❸ 소련이 미국에서 가까운 쿠바에 미사일 기지를 설치하려 하자 미국은 쿠바 해상을 봉쇄하였어요.
When the Soviet Union tried to set up a missile base in Cuba near the US, the US decided to place a naval blockade around Cuba.

❹ 베트남에서는 남쪽의 친미 정권을 지지하는 미국이 공산권의 확대를 막겠다는 명분으로 전쟁에 개입하였어요. 10여 년 동안 계속된 베트남 전쟁은 북베트남의 승리로 끝났어요.
In Vietnam, the United States, who supported pro-American South Vietnam, got involved to stop the spread of communism. The Vietnam War, which lasted for over 10 years, ended with the victory of North Vietnam.

6·25 전쟁 이후 중국, 한국, 일본이 변화하다

6·25 전쟁이 끝나고 대한민국과 미국은 대한민국의 군사적 안전을 보장하는 한미상호방위조약을 체결하였다(1953. 10.). 이에 따라 미군이 한국에 계속 주둔하게 되었고, 동북아시아에서 미국의 영향력이 강화되었다. 한편 중국은 북한을 포함한 아시아 공산 정권에 대한 정치적 영향력을 강화하였다.

일본은 제2차 세계 대전 후에 패전국으로서 경제난에 시달렸으나 미국이 필요한 전쟁 물자를 일본에서 수입하면서 전쟁 특수를 누리게 되어 경제 부흥의 발판을 마련하였다. 일본은 미국의 요구에 따라 정치·경제의 민주화를 수용하였다. 이에 힘입어 일본은 샌프란시스코 강화 회의를 자국에 유리하게 맺었고 제2차 세계 대전 배상 책임 문제에서도 사실상 벗어나게 되었다.

또한 신헌법이 제정되어 일본은 전쟁을 일으키거나 무력을 사용하여 국제 분쟁에 참여할 수 없게 되었다. 그러나 중국대륙을 공산당이 차지하자 미국은 일본을 반공 기지로 만들고자 하였다.

◉ 주한 미군은 어떤 역할을 하나요?

주한 미군은 대한민국에 주둔하는 미국의 군대이다. 한미상호방위조약과 주한미군 지위협정에 의해 대한민국 내에서 합법적 지위를 확보하고 있다. 2017년 미국 제8군 사령부가 미군의 세계 최대 해외기지인 평택의 캠프 험프리스로 이전하였다.

전쟁 발발시 한국에 주둔 중인 주한미군은 한국군과 함께 전선을 방어하여 오키나와, 괌, 하와이, 미국 본토의 증원군이 도착할 때까지 버티는 역할을 한다. 미국 내에서는 젊은이들을 해외에 파견하는 것을 반대하는 여론이 있다. 하지만 동북아시아의 안정이 곧 세계의 안정이라는 인식을 양국이 대체로 공유하고 있다.

미국 제8군(서울 용산구) The Eighth United States Army(EUSA, Seoul, 2021)

Changes in China, Korea, and Japan after the Korean War

After the Korean War, the Republic of Korea and the United States signed the Korea‐U.S. Mutual Defense Treaty to ensure the military safety of the Republic of Korea (October 1953). As a result, the U.S. military continued to be stationed in Korea, and the U.S. influence in Northeast Asia was strengthened. Meanwhile, China has strengthened its political influence on the Asian communist regime, including North Korea.

After World War II, Japan suffered from economic difficulties as a defeated country, but the United States imported necessary war supplies from Japan, and Japan laid the foundation for economic revival. Japan accepted the democratization of politics and economy at the request of the United States. Thanks to this, Japan signed Treaty of San Francisco in its favor and virtually escaped from the issue of World War II liability.

In addition, a new constitution was enacted to prevent Japan from starting war or participating in international disputes using force. However, when the Communist Party occupied the continent of China, the United States tried to turn Japan into an anti‐communist base.

◉ What role does the USFK play?

The United States Forces Korea(USFK) is an American army stationed in the Republic of Korea. In 2017, the U.S. 8th Army Command moved to Camp Humphreys in Pyeongtaek, the world's largest overseas base for the U.S. military.

In the event of a war, USFK stationed in South Korea, along with South Korean troops, defend the front and hold out until reinforcements from Okinawa, Guam, Hawaii, and the U.S. mainland arrive. In the United States, there is public opinion against dispatching young people abroad. However, the two countries generally share the perception that stability in Northeast Asia is stability in the world.

02 제3 세계의 형성과 냉전의 완화
제3 세계가 형성되다

냉전이 격화되면서 미국을 중심으로 하는 자본주의 국가들로 구성된 제1 세계나 소련을 중심으로 하는 사회주의 국가들로 구성된 제2 세계에는 속하지 않겠다고 하는 제3 세계 국가들이 힘을 하나로 모으기 시작하였다. 이들 국가의 대부분은 경제적으로 빈곤한 아시아·아프리카의 개발 도상국들이었다.

제3 세계가 본격적으로 등장한 것은 1955년이었다. 이해에 인도네시아 **반둥**에서 세계 인구의 과반수를 대표하지만 가난한 약소민족으로 제국주의 국가의 지배를 받았던 29개국 대표들이 모여 **아시아·아프리카 회의**(반둥 회의)를 열었다. 이회의에서는 평화 10원칙을 채택하였다.

1961년에는 유고슬라비아의 베오그라드에서 비동맹 중립 노선을 표방한 25개국이 모여 제1회 비동맹국 회의를 열었다. 제1회 비동맹국 회의는 평화 공존과 핵전쟁 확산을 막기 위해 어느 세력에도 가담하지 않을 것을 결의한 **베오그라드 선언**을 채택하였다. 이후 비동맹국 회의가 계속 열리면서 2017년에는 회원국이 120여 개국으로 늘어났다. 이들 국가는 국제 연합 회원국의 3분의 2를 차지하고, 국제 연합 총회에서 한목소리를 내는 등 영향력을 행사하고 있다.

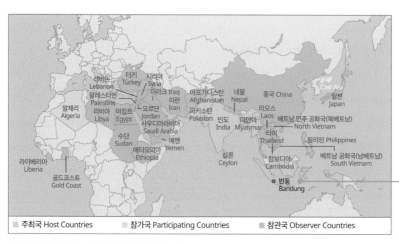

1955년 아시아·아프리카 회의에 참석한 국가
Countries Who Attended Asian-African Conference in 1955

02 Formation of the Third World and the Breakdown of Cold War

Formation of the Third World

As the Cold War intensified, third world countries began to unite among themselves because they did not want to belong to the first world, which consisted of capitalist nations including the United States, or the second world, which consisted of socialist nations including the Soviet Union. A majority of these third world countries were developing countries in Asia and Africa with poor economies.

It was in 1955 that the third world emerged in the international spotlight for the first time. In that year, delegates of 29 smaller weaker countries, which represented nearly half of the world's population but had been under imperialist rule, had a conference in Bandung, Indonesia. In this Bandung Conference, they adopted the 10-point 'declaration of the promotion of world peace and cooperation'.

In 1961, 25 countries that followed the nonaligned neutral line came together for the first Non-Aligned Movement(NAM) Summit held in Belgrade, Yugoslavia. In the first Non-Aligned Movement Summit, the participating countries adopted the Belgrade Declaration in which they promised not to join any forces in order to ensure peaceful coexistence and to stop the spread of nuclear wars. The NAM continued to hold summits until the number of member countries increased to 120 as of 2017. These countries account for two thirds of UN members and are exercising their influence as one voice in the UN general assembly.

> 아시아·아프리카 회의는 1955년 반둥에서 열려 반둥 회의라고도 불러요. 이때 채택된 10가지 평화 원칙에는 반식민주의, 민족주의, 평화 공존 등이 담겨 있어요.
>
> The Asia-Africa Conference was held in Bandung in 1955 and is also known as the Bandung Conference. The 10 principles of peace adopted at this time included anti-colonialism, nationalism, and peaceful coexistence.

냉전 체제가 완화되다

긴장과 대립의 연속이던 냉전 체제는 1960년대 들어 국제 사회가 다원화되면서 완화되기 시작하였다. 자본주의 진영에서는 **유럽 공동체**가 창설되고 서독과 일본이 경제 대국으로 성장하였으며, 프랑스가 북대서양 조약 기구를 탈퇴하고 독자 노선을 걷게 되자 미국의 영향력도 약화되었다. 사회주의 진영에서도 폴란드, 헝가리, 체코슬로바키아를 비롯한 동유럽 국가에서 소련의 간섭에서 벗어나기 위한 **자유화 운동**이 일어났고, 중국과 소련 사이에는 이념 논쟁과 국경 분쟁이 발생하였다. 이와 함께 아시아 · 아프리카의 신생 독립국을 중심으로 **제3 세계**가 형성되고 이 국가들이 비동맹 중립 노선을 선택하면서 냉전 체제가 서서히 무너지기 시작하였다.

이러한 국제 질서의 변화를 반영하여 미국 대통령 닉슨은 핵 위협이 아니라면 베트남전과 같은 아시아에서 전개되는 내란이나 침략에 대한 직접적인 개입을 자제하겠다고 선언하였다(닉슨 독트린, 1969). 1970년대로 접어들자 세계에는 **데탕트** '긴장 완화'를 의미하는 프랑스어라고 부르는 화해 분위기가 조성되었다.

◉ 닉슨 독트린은 냉전 완화에 어떤 역할을 하였나요?

1969년 1월에 취임한 닉슨 대통령은 베트남 전쟁을 수행하는 과정에서 실추된 대외 정책에 대한 국내적 합의 기반을 다시 형성하려고 하였다. 닉슨은 미국 영토인 괌을 순방하는 동안 냉전 완화를 의미하는 독트린을 공식적으로 발표했다.

제37대 미국 대통령 리처드 닉슨이 닉슨 독트린을 발표하는 모습 Richard Nixon, the 37th President of the United States, Announces the Nixon Doctrine

길지 않은 기간 동안 미국은 세 번이나 태평양을 건너 아시아에서 싸워야 했다. 일본과의 태평양 전쟁, 한국 전쟁, 그리고 아직도 끝이 나지 않은 베트남 전쟁이 그것이다. 2차 대전 이후 아시아처럼 미국의 국가적 자원을 소모하게 한 지역은 일찍이 없었다. 아시아에서 미국의 직접적인 출혈은 더는 계속되어서는 안 된다. 미국은 아시아에서의 모든 조약을 지킬 것이다. 하지만 국제 안보 문제에 관해서는 아시아 국가들에 의해 점점 더 많이 다뤄질 것이다.

The Breakdown of the Cold War

The Cold War system, marked by a series of tensions and confrontations, began to thaw in the 1960s as the international community became increasingly diversified. In the capitalist camp, the European Community (EC) was established, Germany and Japan grew into economic superpowers, and the influence of the United States grew weaker after France withdrew its troops from NATO and pursued an independent line. In the socialist camp, Eastern European countries such as Poland, Hungary, and Czechoslovakia saw the rise of impassioned liberation movements to break away from Soviet intervention, while China and the Soviet Union were locking horns with each other over ideological and territorial disputes. In Asia and Africa, newly-independent nations were forming a third world and chose to take nonaligned neutral political lines, thereby contributing to the gradual breakdown of the Cold War system.

It was under these circumstances that US President Nixon proclaimed the Nixon Doctrine that reflected the changing world order and declared that, regarding military defense, except for the threat of a major power involving nuclear weapons, the United States would expect its Asian allies to tend to their own military defense(1969). In the 1970s, the world was entering a period of eased tensions called 'Détente'.

◉ What role did the Nixon Doctrine play in alleviating the Cold War?

President Nixon tried to rebuild the basis of a domestic agreement on the Vietnam War. In 1969, Nixon officially announced the Doctrine, which means easing the Cold War, during his tour of Guam, the U.S. territory.

> During the short period, the United States had to cross the Pacific Ocean three times and fight in Asia. These are the Pacific War with Japan, the Korean War, and the Vietnam War, which has yet to end. Since World War II, there have been no regions like Asia that have consumed U.S. national resources. Direct bleeding in the United States in Asia should no longer continue. The United States will abide by all treaties in Asia. However, international security issues will be dealt with more and more by Asian countries.

03 아시아의 새로운 국가 건설
동아시아에 큰 정치적 변혁이 생기다

중국에서는 장제스가 이끄는 **국민당**과 마오쩌둥이 이끄는 **공산당** 사이에서 내전이 일어나 공산당이 승리를 거두고 **중화 인민 공화국**을 수립하였다(1949).

중화 인민 공화국은 토지 개혁과 산업의 국유화를 실시하였다. 또한 농장의 집단화를 바탕으로 공업 생산을 비약적으로 늘리려는 **대약진 운동**을 전개하였다. 그러나 대약진 운동은 실패하였고, 이로 인해 정치적 위기에 빠진 마오쩌둥은 **문화 대혁명**을 일으켰다(1966). 문화 대혁명은 자본주의를 타파하고 사회주의를 실천하자는 계급 투쟁 운동인데, 1976년까지 10년 동안 지속되었다. 문화 대혁명에 앞장선 **홍위병** 마오쩌둥의 이념을 지키는 병사. 문화 대혁명 당시 중학생부터 대학생까지 다양하게 구성된 급진적인 집단들은 중국의 전통문화를 파괴하였고, 실용적인 개혁을 추진하던 인물들을 몰아냈다.

국민당 정부는 미국의 막대한 군사적 지원을 받으면서도 부정부패로 민심을 잃어 타이완으로 밀려났다. 이후 국민당 정부는 경제 발전에 힘을 기울여 경제 성장을 이루어냈다.

한편 일본은 연합군 최고 사령부의 군정 통치하에서 **평화 헌법**을 제정하고 샌프란시스코 강화 조약을 통해 주권을 되찾았다(1951). 이후 6·25 전쟁과 베트남 전쟁으로 특수를 누린 일본은 경제 대국으로 성장하였다.

⚙ **정치 위기 타개를 위한 문화 대혁명의 대상은 누구였나요?**
Who Was the Target of Cultural Revolution for Overcoming the Political Crisis?

❶ 집회에 소환된 지식인들의 머리카락을 강제로 깎는 홍위병
❷ 문화 대혁명 당시 모자를 뒤집어 쓴 채 끌려다니는 지식인들
❸ 공자 사당의 장식을 부수고 있는 홍위병

03 the Emergence of New Nations in Asia

Major Political Changes in East Asia

In China, a civil war broke out between the Kuomintang Party led by Chiang Kai-shek and the Community Party led by Mao Zedong. The war ended with the victory of the Communitst Party, and the Chinese Communist leader Mao Zedong declared the creation of the People's Republic of China(PRC, 1949).

The People's Republic of China launched a campaign called 'The Great Leap Forward' to swiftly transform the country through rapid industrialization, collectivization of farms, nationalization of industry, and land reform. But the campaign ultimately ended in failure. Mao Zedong, who fell into a political crisis, started the Cultural Revolution(1966). The Cultural Revolution was a class struggle movement to break capitalism and practice socialism, which lasted for 10 years until 1976. Taking the lead in the Cultural Revolution, the Chinese Red Guards destroyed traditional Chinese culture and drove out those who were pursuing practical reforms.

The Kuomintang Party lost the support of the people due to corruption and graft and ended up being pushed away to Taiwan despite significant military aid from the United States. But the Party achieved economic growth through a campaign.

Japan, on the other hand, enacted the Peace Constitution under US-led military rule and regained Japan's sovereignty through the San Francisco Peace Treaty(1951). Later on, the Korean War and the Vietnam War became the springboard for Japan to achieve drastic economic growth and grow into an economic power.

❶ The Chinese Red Guards Forcibly Shaving the Hair of Intellectuals Summoned to the Rally
❷ Intellectuals Were Dragged with Their Hats Upside Down During the Cultural Revolution
❸ The Chinese Red Guards Destroying the Decorations of the Confucius Shrine

∞ 중국 국민당과 공산당은 왜 합작에서 내전으로 돌아섰나요?

중화민국의 국부인 쑨원은 군벌을 무찌르기 위해 공산당과 손을 잡았다(제1차 국·공 합작). 레닌이 주도한 코민테른은 '민족과 식민지 문제에 관한 결의'(1920)에 따라 소수 집단에 불과한 중국 공산당에게 중국 국민당에 들어가 조직 기반을 형성하도록 지시하였다. 쑨원이 숨을 거둔 후 장제스가 그 뒤를 이었다. 장제스는 북벌을 단행하여 군벌을 소탕하고, 공산당을 내몰기 위한 대추격전을 시작하였다.

마오쩌둥이 이끄는 중국 공산당 홍군 8만 5,000여 명은 국민당의 포위를 뚫고 1934년 장정을 시작하였다. 약 9,600km의 장정이 끝났을 때 홍군의 생존자는 8,000여 명에 지나지 않았다. 이러한 가운데 1936년 동북 지역의 젊은 군벌 장쉐량이 시안 사건을 일으켰다. 장쉐량은 장제스를 감금한 후 항일전을 위한 제2차 국·공 합작을 강요하였고, 장제스는 이를 수락하였다.

1945년 8월 일본이 무조건 항복을 하자, 국민당과 공산당은 다시 등을 돌리고 치열한 내전을 벌였다. 1946년에 일어난 국·공 내전은 1949년까지 이어졌다. 미국은 국민당을 지원하였고, 소련은 공산당을 지원하여 전쟁은 대리전 양상을 띠었다. 내전은 공산당의 승리로 끝났고, 국민당은 중국 본토에서 밀려나 타이완으로 물러났다.

마오쩌둥은 1949년 10월 1일 중화 인민 공화국 수립을 선포하였다. 그로부터 3개월 후인 12월 장제스는 중국 본토에서 약 150km 떨어진 타이완에서 중화민국의 총통 자리에 올랐다.

> 전 중국의 인민들은 새로운 정부의 탄생을 갈망한다. 이에 중화 인민 공화국의 수립을 선포한다.
> All Chinese people long for the birth of a new government. Accordingly, I declare the establishment of the People's Republic of China.

중화 인민 공화국 수립을 선포하는 마오쩌둥(1949)
Mao Zedong Declares the Establishment of the People's Republic of China

👓 Why Did the Kuomintang Party and the Community Party Turn from United Front Cooperation to The Chinese Civil War?

Sun Yat-sen, the national father of the Republic of China, joined hands with the Community Party to defeat the warlords(First United Front). The Comintern(Communist International), led by Lenin, instructed the Chinese Community Party, a minority group, to join the Kuomintang Party and form an organizational basis in accordance with the 'Resolution on National and Colonial Issues'(1920). After Sun Yat-sen's death, Chiang Kai-shek succeeded. He carried out the Northern Expedition to wipe out the warlords and began a pursuit battle to drive out the Community Party.

About 85,000 Red Army members of the Community Party of China, led by Mao Zedong, broke through the siege of the Kuomintang Party and began their campaign in 1934. At the end of the 9,600 km long run, there were only 8,000 survivors of the Red Army. In the midst of this, in 1936, a young warlord in the northeastern region, Chang Hsueh-liang, initiated the Xian incident. After Chang Hsueh-liang imprisoned Chiang Kai-shek, he forced Chiang Kai-shek to join forces with the Second United Front for the anti-Japanese war, which Chiang Kai-shek accepted.

When Japan unconditionally surrendered in August 1945, the Kuomintang Party and the Community Party turned their backs again and engaged in a fierce civil war. The civil war that took place in 1946 continued until 1949. The United States supported the Kuomintang Party, and the Soviet Union supported the Community Party, so the war became a proxy war. The civil war ended with the victory of the Community Party, and the Kuomintang Party was pushed out of mainland China and withdrew to Taiwan.

Mao Zedong declared the establishment of the People's Republic of China on October 1, 1949. Three months later, in December, Chiang Kai-shek became president of the Republic of China in Taiwan, about 150 kilometers from mainland China.

인도와 동남아시아에 여러 독립 국가가 세워지다

인도는 1947년 영국으로부터 독립하였으나 종교와 민족의 대립으로 힌두교도가 다수인 **인도**와 이슬람교도가 다수인 **파키스탄**으로 분리되었다. 파키스탄은 다시 분열되어 동파키스탄이 방글라데시로 독립하였다. 실론섬에서는 스리랑카가 불교 국가로 독립하였다.

프랑스는 제2차 세계 대전 이후에도 베트남을 계속 지배하려 하였으나 베트남은 **호찌민**을 중심으로 치열하게 독립 전쟁을 전개하여 프랑스를 물리쳤다. 그러나 강대국들의 냉전 논리에 따라 북위 17도선을 기준으로 북쪽에는 호찌민이 중심이 된 북베트남이, 남쪽에는 반공주의자가 이끄는 남베트남이 수립되었다.

영국의 지배를 받고 있던 미얀마, 말레이시아와 프랑스의 지배를 받고 있던 라오스, 캄보디아도 독립을 쟁취하였다. 인도네시아는 네덜란드로부터, 필리핀은 미국으로부터 각각 독립하였다.

하노이 Hanoi

북베트남(베트남 민주 공화국)은 소련·중국이, 남베트남(베트남 공화국)은 미국이 지원하였어요.
North Vietnam(Democratic Republic of Vietnam) was supported by the Soviet Union and China, and South Vietnam(Republic of Vietnam) was supported by the United States.

북위 17도선
17th Parallel
North Latitude

사이공
Saigon

베트남 전쟁 Vietnam War

동남아시아의 유일한 독립국이었던 **타이**는 입헌 혁명을 통해 입헌 군주국이 되었다. **싱가포르**는 말레이시아로부터 독립하고 경제적으로 비약적인 발전을 이루어 선진국 대열에 들어서게 되었다.

독립 영웅 네루와 호찌민은 누구인가요?

네루 1947년부터 1964년까지 인도의 총리를 지냈어요. 간디와 달리 무력 투쟁으로 영국에 맞서 싸웠지요.
Nehru I served as Prime Minister of India from 1947 to 1964. Unlike Gandhi, I struggled against England by force of arms.

India and Southeast Asian Countries Establish Independent States

India became independent from British rule in 1947, but religious and ethnic conflicts divided the country into Hindu India and Islamic Pakistan. Pakistan split again, and East Pakistan became the independent Bangladesh. Sri Lanka became an independent Buddhist country in the island of Ceylon.

In Vietnam, France tried to continue its colonial rule over the country after the end of WWII, but the Vietnamese fought and defeated France under the leadership of Ho Chi Minh in the First Indochina War. However, following the logic of the Cold War, the country was divided by super powers at the 17th parallel into North Vietnam, which was under the leadership of Ho Chi Minh, and South Vietnam, which was under the leadership of anticommunists.

Myanmar became independent from Britain, and Laos and Cambodia achieved independence from France. Indonesia gained independence from the Netherlands and the Philippines became independent from the United States.

Thailand had been the only independent country in Southeast Asia, but it became a constitutional monarchy after a revolution. Singapore achieved its independence from Malaysia and recorded rapid economic growth until it became an advanced country.

🔎 **Who Are the Heroes of Independence, Nehru and Ho Chi Minh?**

호찌민 인도차이나 공산당을 창설하여 베트남의 독립 운동을 이끌었어요. 1975년 북베트남이 베트남 전쟁에서 승리하여 베트남 사회주의 공화국으로 거듭났지요.

Ho Chi Minh I founded the Indochina Communist Party to lead the independence movement in Vietnam. In 1975, North Vietnam won the Vietnam War and became the Socialist Republic of Vietnam.

서아시아에서 이스라엘과 아랍이 대립하다

제2차 세계 대전이 끝난 후 서아시아에는 홀로코스트로 큰 피해를 입었던 유대인들이 **시오니즘** 팔레스타인에 민족 국가를 세울 것을 제창한 사상 으로 뭉치면서 **이스라엘**을 건국하였다(1948). 시리아, 요르단 등 여러 국가도 식민 지배에서 벗어나 독립국이 되었다.

이스라엘이 건국되기 이전부터 수천 년 동안 팔레스타인에 살고 있던 아랍인들은 **팔레스타인 해방 기구**를 중심으로 이스라엘에 대항하였다. 아랍 국가들도 가세하여 네 차례에 걸친 **아랍·이스라엘 전쟁**이 벌어졌으나 모두 이스라엘에 패배하였다. 특히 제3차 아랍·이스라엘 전쟁에서 이스라엘은 영토를 4배 이상 확장하여 **시나이반도**와 가자 지구 등을 차지하였다. 한편 제4차 아랍·이스라엘 전쟁에서 패배한 아랍 국가들은 석유 수출국 기구(OPEC)의 석유 동결 조치를 단행하였다. 이로 인해 석유 가격이 치솟아 세계가 심각한 석유 파동을 겪었다.

아랍·이스라엘 전쟁에 따른 영토 변화
Territorial Changes Following the Arab-Israeli War

💧 아랍·이스라엘 전쟁의 발단은 무엇이었나요?

아랍인과 유대인에 대한 엇갈린 영국의 외교는 현재의 이스라엘-팔레스타인 분쟁의 계기가 되었고, 급기야는 아랍·이스라엘 전쟁으로 이어졌다.

영국은 메카의 통치자인 후세인이 요구한 모든 지역에서 아랍 국가들의 독립을 인정하고 지지할 각오가 되어 있습니다. - 맥마흔의 서한, 1915

이집트 주재 영국 고등 판무관, 헨리 맥마흔

영국 정부는 유대 민족을 위한 국가가 팔레스타인에 수립되는 것을 적극적으로 찬성하고, 이러한 목적을 실현하기 위해 최선의 노력을 기울이겠습니다. - 밸푸어 선언, 1917

영국의 외무 장관, 아서 밸푸어

Israel and Independent Arab States Coexist in West Asia

After the end of World War II, the Jews, who suffered severe persecution under the Nazis, united under Zionism and established Israel(1948). Many other countries, including Lebanon, Syria, and Jordan, ended their colonial rule and became independent states.

The Arabs who had lived in Palestine for thousands of years before the establishment of Israel resisted under the leadership of the Palestine Liberation Organization. Other Arab states joined the struggle against Israel, but they were all defeated in the four Arab-Israeli wars. In particular, after winning the third Arab-Israeli War, Israel seized the Sinai Peninsula and the Gaza Strip, thereby expanding its territory fourfold. After having been defeated in the fourth Arab-Israeli War, the Arab oil producers of OPEC(Organization of the Petroleum Exporting Countries) decided to cut down oil production and imposed an embargo against nations that supported Israel in the fourth Arab-Israeli War. This action caused a serious oil shortage crisis throughout the world due to skyrocketing oil prices and negative economic growth rates.

❷ What Was the Beginning of the Arab-Israeli War?

Britain's confusing diplomacy between Arabs and Jews was the trigger for the current Israeli-Palestinian conflict, which eventually led to the Arab-Israeli War.

> Britain is determined to recognize and support the independence of Arab states in every region demanded by Hussein, the ruler of Mecca.
> - McMahon's letter, 1915

Henry McMahon, British High Commissioner in Egypt

> The British government actively supports the establishment of a nation for the Jewish people in Palestine and will make every effort to realize this purpose.
> - Balfour Declaration, 1917

Arthur Balfour, British Foreign Minister

04 아프리카의 저항 운동과 독립 국가의 탄생

아프리카에서 서양 문물을 수용하며 저항 운동을 전개하다

제국주의 열강의 침략이 확대되자 아프리카 곳곳에서 저항이 일어났다. 나미비아에서는 헤레로족이 독일에 맞서 무장봉기하였으나 독일군에게 진압되었다. 탄자니아도 독일의 식민 지배와 수탈에 맞서 **마지마지 운동**을 벌이는 등 저항하였으나 실패로 끝났다.

에티오피아에서는 **메넬리크 2세**가 철도와 학교를 설립하고 신식 군대를 창설하는 등 근대화 개혁을 실시하였으며, 이탈리아를 아도와 전투에서 격퇴한 후 독립을 인정받았다. 수단에서는 **무함마드 아흐마드**가 토지 개혁을 주장하며, 군대를 모아 영국의 침략에 저항하는 전쟁을 벌였으나 결국 실패하였다.

아프리카 각지의 국민 국가 건설 운동 Nation-state Building Movements in Africa

💧 **탄자니아의 마지마지 운동이 무엇인가요?**

독일은 식민 지배를 위해 동아프리카의 부룬디, 르완다 및 탄자니아에서 가혹한 탄압 정책을 시행하였다. 이에 탄자니아의 주술사 킨지키틸레는 기장과 옥수수를 혼합하여 물을 만들고, 자신이 만든 요술 약을 마시면 총에 맞아도 부상을 당하지 않는다며 반란을 부추겼다. 탄자니아 병사들은 이 '마지(Maji)'라는 요술 약을 마시거나 뿌린 후 독일에 맞서 싸웠다. '마지(Maji)'는 스와힐리어로 '물'이라는 뜻이다. 이 요술 약은 단순한 물에 불과했기에 병사들은 독일군의 총탄에 죽어갔다. 비록 마지마지 운동은 실패하였지만 탄자니아라는 국가의 정체성을 확립하고 반식민지 의식이 확산하는 데 영향을 주었다.

탄자니아 마헨지에서의 전투
Battle at Mahenge, Tanzania

04 Resistance Movement and Independence in Africa

Acceptance of Western Civilization and the Development of a Resistance Movement in Africa

Increasing invasions by imperialist powers were met by resistance everywhere throughout Africa. In Namibia, the Herero raised an armed revolt against Germany but was suppressed by the German army. Tanzania also resisted Germans' colonial rule and exploitation by leading the Maji Maji Rebellion, but it ended in failure as well.

In Ethiopia, Emperor Menelik II carried out modernization reforms by building railroads, schools, and modernizing the military, and achieved independence after defeating Italy in the Battle of Adowa. In Sudan, Muhammad Ahmad demanded land reform and raised an army to fight against the invading British army, but ended in failure.

◈ What Is Maji Maji Rebellion in Tanzania?

Germany implemented harsh repression policies for colonial rule in Burundi, Rwanda, and Tanzania. Tanzanian shaman Kinjikitile made water from a mixture of millet and corn, and encouraged a revolt by saying that drinking this magic potion he had made would turn enemy bullets into water. Tanzanian soldiers fought against Germany after drinking or spraying a magic potion called 'Maji' upon themselves. 'Maji' means 'Water' in Swahili. This magic medicine was just water, thereby the soldiers were killed by the Germans. Although the Maji Maji - Rebelion failed, it has influenced the spread of anticolonial consciousness and helped in establishing the national identity of Tanzania.

제국주의 세력에 저항하며 민족의식을 키우다

19세기 남아프리카 지역에서는 샤카 줄루가 주변 부족을 통합해 **줄루 왕국**을 건설하였다. 줄루 왕국은 침략해 온 영국군을 **이산들와나 전투**에서 격퇴하였으나, 이후 기관총으로 중무장하고 다시 쳐들어온 영국군에 패하여 식민지로 전락하였다.

아프리카의 저항 운동은 주로 부족 단위로 이루어져 제국주의 세력을 이길 만한 힘을 갖추지 못했기 때문에 대부분 가혹하게 진압되는 등 실패로 끝났다. 그러나 이러한 열세에도 불구하고 아프리카인들의 저항은 계속되었고 제국주의에 맞서 싸우며 점차 민족의식도 커져 갔다.

줄루족은 어떻게 영국군을 격파할 수 있었나요?

줄루 왕국의 왕 샤카는 이클와라는 단창을 만들어 병사들의 무기로 삼았고, 병사들이 더 신속하게 움직일 수 있도록 맨발로 다닐 것을 명령하였다. 화약 무기가 없었던 줄루족은 지형을 이용하였다. 주변의 계곡을 따라 이동하면서 적이 포위되었다고 생각하면 일제히 사방에서 공격하는 전술을 사용한 것이다. 이러한 전술로 1838년에는 현재의 남아프리카 공화국 북부의 움폴로 지방에서 보어인을, 1879년에는 동북부의 이산들와나에서 영국 정규군을 격파하였다.

그러나 줄루족은 로크스 드리프트에서 영국군에 대패하였고, 울룬디 전투에서는 거의 전멸하다시피 하였다. 창을 든 군대가 총과 대포를 쏘는 군대를 이길 수는 없었던 것이다. 1883년에는 줄루 왕국의 수도가 불타고, 줄루 왕국도 사라졌다.

줄루족의 전술 Zulu's Tactics

African Raises National Consciousness by Resisting Imperialist Powers

In 19th century South African regions, Shaka Zulu founded the Zulu Kingdom by unifying neighboring tribes. When Britain invaded, the Zulu Kingdom fought and defeated the British in the Battle of Isandlwana, which eventually became a British colony after they were defeated when British forces invaded again, this time with machine guns and cannons.

Most nationalist movements in Africa were brutally suppressed and ended in failure because, Africans being mostly tribal soldiers, lacked the military technology to fight against imperialist powers. Despite this weakness, African resistance continued, and during the process their national consciousness grew stronger.

How Did the Zulus Defeat the British Army?

Shaka, King of the Zulu Kingdom, made a javelin called the Iklwa and used it as a weapon for the soldiers. He ordered them to walk barefoot so that the they could move more quickly. The Zulus, who had no gunpowder weapons, moved along the surrounding valley and used the tactic of attacking from all directions at once when the enemy was surrounded. This tactic defeated the Boer in 1838 in the northern Umfolozi region of South Africa and the British regular army in Isandelwana in the northeast in 1879.

However, the Zulus were defeated by the British at nearby Rorke's Drift, and almost wiped out at the Battle of Ulundi. This is because their army with spears couldn't beat the opposing army using guns and cannons. Eventually, in 1883, the capital of the Zulu kingdom was burned, and the Zulu kingdom disappeared.

아프리카 독립 국가의 탄생으로 아프리카의 해가 생겨나다

식민 착취의 대표적 지역인 황금 해안에 위치한 가나가 독립하면서 아프리카 독립에 불이 붙기 시작하였다. 1950년대 들어 북부 아프리카의 여러 나라가 민족주의 운동을 일으켜 독립을 쟁취하였다. 1960년에는 17개국이 독립하여 이 해를 아프리카의 해라고 부르게 되었다. 1963년까지 알제리를 비롯하여 아프리카 대부분 지역이 독립했다.

아프리카 독립국들은 1963년 아프리카 통일 기구를 설립하여 아프리카 해방 운동을 지지하는 등 정치·경제적 통합을 다졌다. 그러나 아프리카의 국경선이 서양 열강이 설정한 식민지 영토 선을 토대로 정해진 것이어서 독립 후에도 부족 사이에 분쟁과 내란이 계속되었다. 또한 식민 지배의 후유증 속에 빈곤과 기아, 전염병의 악순환으로 어려움을 겪었다. 특히 남아프리카 공화국에서는 백인의 흑인에 대한 심각한 인종 차별인 아파르트헤이트가 자행되었다.

⊛ 알제리는 프랑스로부터 어떻게 독립하였나요?

알제리인들은 프랑스의 식민 지배에서 벗어나기 위해 민족 해방 전선을 출범하였다. 그리고 1954년부터 8년에 걸쳐 독립 전쟁을 전개하였다. 프랑스는 알제리의 독립을 막기 위해 50만여 명의 군대를 파견하여 알제리 민족 해방 전선을 탄압하였다. 프랑스의 강경 진압에 대한 세계 여론이 악화되자 새로 당선된 샤를 드골 프랑스 대통령은 알제리 민족 해방 전선에 정전 평화 협상을 제의하였다(에비앙 협정). 결국 1962년 독립의 찬반을 묻는 국민 투표를 통해 알제리가 독립하였다.

프랑스와의 전쟁에서 승리하여 기뻐하는 알제리 시민들
Algerian Citizens Rejoicing after Winning the War with France

프랑스의 식민 지배가 유지되기를 바란 알제리 거주 프랑스 이민자들이 100만여 명에 달하였기 때문에 알제리의 투쟁 과정은 더 어려웠어요.
Algeria's struggle was even more difficult, as there were more than 1 million French immigrants living in Algeria who wanted to maintain French colonial rule.

Birth of Independent African States in the Year of Africa

As Ghana, located on the Golden Coast, a representative region of colonial exploitation, became independent, it triggered an independence movement throughout Africa. In the 1950s, numerous countries in the northern part of Africa saw the rise of nationalist movements and eventually achieved independence. The year of 1960 came to be known as 'the Year of Africa' because in this particular year alone, as many as seventeen African nations became independent. By 1963, Algeria and most of Africa were independent.

After gaining independence, African nations came together and formed the Organization of African Unity in 1963 and sought political and economic solidarity while supporting other independence movements that took place in Africa. However, skirmishes and civil wars continued among African tribes even after they became independent, largely because their national borders were decided based on the colonial boundaries set by the Western powers in the past. They also suffered from a vicious cycle of poverty, famine, and contagious diseases. The Republic of South Africa had it particularly hard due to Apartheid policies that caused serious racial discrimination against the blacks by the whites.

How Did Algeria Become Independent from France?

The Algerians launched the National Liberation Front to escape from French colonial rule. And they waged a war of independence for eight years beginning in 1954. To prevent the independence of Algeria, France dispatched more than 500,000 troops, suppressing the National Liberation Front. As world public opinion about the French repression worsened, the newly elected French President Charles de Gaulle proposed an armistice peace negotiation with the National Liberation Front(Evian Agreement). Eventually, in 1962, Algeria became independent through a referendum regarding independence.

세계화와 경제 통합

01 유럽 연합의 출범

유럽 통합 운동이 전개되다

유럽은 두 차례 세계 대전을 겪은 후 경제적으로 큰 타격을 입었다. 미국의 마셜 플랜으로 경제 부흥을 이루었지만 세계가 미국과 소련에 의해 냉전 구도를 형성하면서 유럽의 국제적 영향력은 크게 감소하였다.

유럽 국가들이 개별적으로 미국과 소련의 풍부한 자원과 경제력에 맞서 경쟁하기에는 역부족이었다. 또한 제국주의 시대에 유럽 각국이 지배하였던 식민지들이 독립하여 제3 세계를 이루고 비동맹 중립 노선을 택하며 한목소리를 내는 것도 유럽을 자극하였다. 이에 유럽의 발전과 미래를 위해 유럽을 하나로 통합하려는 운동이 일어났다.

유럽 통합 운동은 1952년부터 시작되었다. 프랑스, 서독, 이탈리아, **베네룩스 3 국** ^{1944년 관세 동맹을 체결한 벨기에, 네덜란드, 룩셈부르크}이 **유럽 석탄 · 철강 공동체**(ECSC)를 만들었다. 1957년에는 유럽 원자력 공동체(Euratom)와 **유럽 경제 공동체**(EEC)를 설립하여 회원국들 사이의 무역 장벽을 제거하였고, 노동력, 자본, 기업의 자유로운 이동을 보장하였다.

유럽 공동체(EC)는 유럽 석탄 · 철강 공동체, 유럽 원자력 공동체, 유럽 경제 공동체가 통합된 기구예요. 1967년 유럽 경제 공동체 가입국 6개국에 의하여 설립되었고, 1973년에 영국 · 덴마크 · 아일랜드가 가입하면서 확대되었어요.
The European Community(EC) is an integrated organization of the ECSC, the Euratom, and the EEC. The EC was founded in 1967 by members of the EEC, and expanded in 1973 with the membership of the United Kingdom, Denmark, and Ireland.

유럽 경제 공동체를 조직한 회원국 Members of the European Economic Community

2

Globalization and Economic Integration

01 Creation of the European Union

Movement to Integrate Europe

Two world wars dealt a devastating economic blow to countries in Europe. Europe was able to revive its economy thanks to the Marshall Plan, but Europe experienced rapidly weakening international influence as the world was brought into the Cold War system by the United States and the Soviet Union.

Individual European countries found themselves with economies that were too weak to compete with the rich resources and economic powers of the US and the Soviet Union. On top of that, the countries that used to be under European rule during the imperialism period were uniting as a third world that followed their own independent political line with each other. All of these factions were calling for European countries to unite as well. Eventually, Europe saw the rise of a movement to unite Europe into a single bloc for its growth and future.

The movement to unite Europe kicked off in 1952 when France, Germany, Italy, and three Benelux states organized the European Coal and Steel Community(ECSC). A few years later, in 1957, came the birth of the European Atomic Energy Community(Euratom) and the European Economic Community(EEC). Member countries brought down trade barriers and guaranteed free movement of labor forces, capital, and companies.

유럽기 The Flag of Europe

유럽기는 1986년에 유럽 연합을 상징하는 깃발로 채택되었어요. 하나의 원을 이루고 있는 별들은 유럽 시민의 단결과 연대를 상징해요.
The European flag was adopted as a symbol of the European Union in 1986. The stars in a circle symbolize the unity and solidarity of European citizens.

유럽 연합의 시대가 열리다

1992년 2월, 유럽 공동체(EC) 12개 회원국이 네덜란드 마스트리흐트에서 유럽 연합에 관한 조약을 정식 조인하였다(마스트리흐트 조약). 유럽 공동체 회원국들은 마스트리흐트 조약을 통해 유럽 중앙은행을 설립하고 유럽 내에 단일 통화를 도입하기로 약속하였다. 이 조약에는 유럽 의회의 권한을 확대하며, 외교·안보 분야에서 회원국 간 결속을 강화한다는 내용도 담겨 있었다.

마스트리흐트 조약에는 정치적인 권한의 상당 부분을 통합 기구에 위임한다는 계획이 담겨 있어 각국의 반대가 심하였다. 그러나 독일을 끝으로 비준에 성공하면서 유럽 공동체의 명칭은 유럽 연합(EU)이 되었다. 이로써 하나가 된 유럽이 본격적으로 출범하게 되었다.

유럽은 2002년부터 유로(EURO)라는 단일 화폐를 사용하고 있다. 유로화는 현재 달러(USD)와 함께 세계에서 가장 영향력 있는 화폐이다. 유럽 연합이 출범하여 단일 통화를 사용하는 하나의 유럽이 세계를 움직이는 새로운 축으로 등장하였다.

⊙ 유로(EURO) 속에 숨어 있는 여인은 누구일까요?

'유럽'이라는 이름은 그리스 신화에서 비롯되었어요. 어느 날 제우스는 페니키아의 공주 에우로페를 보고 한눈에 반하였지요. 제우스는 황소로 변신하여 에우로페를 납치해 태우고 다녔어요. 그때 돌아다닌 지역을 에우로페의 이름을 따 유럽이라고 부르고, 유럽의 단일 화폐는 유로라고 해요. 20유로 화폐의 '초상화 창'에 빛을 비추면 에우로페가 나타난답니다. 위조 지폐 방지를 위해 그렇게 만들었지요. 2유로 동전에서는 황소로 변한 제우스가 에우로페를 태우고 가는 모습을 볼 수 있어요.

20유로 지폐와 2유로 동전
20 Euro Bill and 2 Euro Coin

에우로페의 납치(프라도 미술관)
The Rape of Europa(Prado Museum)

The Era of the EU Opens

In February 1992, twelve member states of the European Community(EC) officially signed a treaty regarding the European Union in Maastricht, the Netherlands(Maastricht Treaty). In this Treaty, Member States promised to establish a European Central Bank and pledged to introduce a single currency within Europe. In addition to this, the participants agreed to strengthen the powers of the European Parliament and the security of the EU and its member countries.

The Maastricht Treaty was met by strong objections from various countries because the treaty proposed delegating important powers to integrated organizations. But the treaty was ratified when Germany became the last to sign it, and it effectuated the official establishment of the European Union(EU) that united Europe into a single world.

Europe has been using a single currency called the Euro since 2002. As of today, the Euro is one of the most influential currencies in the world along with the US dollar. The beginning of the EU signified the emergence of Europe under a single European currency as a new axis that moved the world and opened a new chapter in history.

Who Is the Woman Hiding in the EURO?

The name 'Europe' comes from Greek mythology. One day, Zeus saw the Phoenician princess Europa and fell in love immediately. Zeus transformed into a bull, kidnapped Europa and carried her around. At that time, the region they traveled around is called Europe after Europa, and the currency in Europe is called the Euro. If we shine a light on the portrait window of the 20 euro bill, we will see Europa. This is to prevent counterfeit bills. In the 2 euro coin, we can see Zeus, who turned into a bull, carrying Europa.

브렉시트로 유럽 연합의 갈등이 시작되다

유럽 연합의 회원국 수는 꾸준히 증가하여 28개국으로 확대되었다. 그런데 2016년 유럽 연합의 회원국이었던 영국이 국민 투표를 통해 유럽 연합 탈퇴를 결정하였다. 이것을 브렉시트라고 한다.

영국이 유럽 연합 탈퇴를 결정한 이유는 세 가지로 요약할 수 있다. 우선 유럽 연합의 재정이 악화되어 유럽 연합의 주요 국가인 영국이 유럽 연합에 내야 하는 분담금 부담이 커졌다. 두 번째로 유럽 연합의 과도한 규제가 영국 국민의 불만을 가져왔다. 마지막으로 이주민이 취업을 위해 영국으로 대거 건너오면서 이주민에 대한 복지 지출로 재정 부담이 커지고 노동 시장에서 영국 노동자와 이주민 간의 경쟁과 갈등이 심화되었다.

영국은 2018년에 브렉시트를 단행할 예정이었지만 의회의 반대로 총 세 차례 연기되었다. 이후 유럽 연합 정상 회의의 승인, 유럽 의회의 동의, 영국 내부의 법안 통과 등을 거쳐 2020년에 브렉시트가 단행되었다. 영국의 유럽 연합 탈퇴가 이뤄지면서 1993년 유럽 연합이 정식으로 출범한 이래 25년 만에 처음으로 탈퇴하는 회원국이 나오게 되었다.

영국과 유럽 연합 국가들
The UK and the European Union countries.

◉ **유럽 연합의 공식 언어는 무엇인가요?**

유럽 연합은 24개의 언어를 공식 언어로 정하고 있다. 유럽 의회는 문서와 본회의 관련 자료 등을 모든 언어로 번역한다. 이에 해당하는 언어는 그리스어, 네덜란드어, 덴마크어, 독일어, 라트비아어, 루마니아어, 리투아니아어, 몰타어, 불가리아어, 스웨덴어, 스페인어, 슬로바키아어, 슬로베니아어, 아일랜드어, 에스토니아어, 영어, 이탈리아어, 체코어, 크로아티아어, 포르투갈어, 폴란드어, 프랑스어, 핀란드어, 헝가리어 등이다.

Brexit Initiates the European Union Conflict

The number of member states of the European Union has steadily increased to 28 countries. However, in 2016, Britain, a member of the European Union, decided to withdraw from the European Union through a referendum. This is called Brexit.

There are three reasons why Britain decided to withdraw from the European Union. First of all, the European Union's finances deteriorated, increasing the burden of contributions Britain, a major European Union country, has to pay to the European Union. Second, excessive regulation by the European Union brought about dissatisfaction from the British people. Finally, as a large number of migrants for employment purposes came to the UK, the financial burden increased due to welfare expenditures for migrants, and competition and conflict between British workers and migrants intensified in the labor market.

The UK was scheduled to carry out Brexit in 2018, but it was postponed three times due to parliamentary opposition. Since then, Brexit has been implemented in 2020 after the approval of the European Union Summit, the consent of the European Parliament, and the passage of legislation inside the UK. With Britain's withdrawal from the European Union, it became the first member state to withdraw in 25 years since the European Union was officially launched in 1993.

◉ **What is the official language of the European Union?**

The European Union has designated 24 languages as its official language. The European Parliament translates documents and materials related to the plenary session into all languages. The corresponding languages are Greek, Dutch, Danish, German, Latvian, Romanian, Lithuanian, Malta, Bulgarian, Swedish, Spanish, Slovakia, Slovenian, Irish, Estonian, English, Italian, Czech, Croatia, Polish, French, Finnish, Hungarian, etc.

02 사회주의권의 붕괴와 경제 개방

고르바초프, 개혁·개방 정책을 도입하다

소련은 공산당의 일당 독재 지배 체제 아래에서 자유를 억압하는 통제된 사회를 유지하였다. 1985년 공산당의 서기장으로 선출된 고르바초프는 소련의 사회와 경제를 회복하기 위해 자본주의적 시장 경제 체제를 도입하는 개혁·개방 정책을 추진하였다. 생필품을 제외한 상품의 가격을 자유화하고, 국영 기업을 민영화하였다. 또한 민주적인 대통령제를 도입하여 소련 최초의 대통령으로 당선되었다. 고르바초프는 한창 자유화 바람이 불어오고 있는 동유럽 국가에도 더 이상 군사적으로 간섭하지 않을 것을 분명히 하였다. 1989년에는 미국과 몰타 회담을 열고 냉전 종식을 선언하였다.

시장 경제 체제를 도입하는 과정에서 경제가 어려워지자 공산당 강경 보수파가 쿠데타를 일으켰다(1990). 옐친은 쿠데타를 저지하고 러시아 연방 대통령에 취임한 후 소련의 공식적인 해체를 선언하였다(1991). 소련이 해체된 후 옛 소련에서 분리 독립한 11개 공화국이 러시아를 중심으로 독립 국가 연합(CIS)을 이루었다.

소련의 해체와 독립 국가 연합
Dissolution of the Soviet Union and the Commonwealth of Independent States

지도 설명:
- 라트비아 Latvia
- 리투아니아 Lithuania
- 에스토니아 Estonia
- 벨라루스 Belarus
- 몰도바 Moldova
- 우크라이나 Ukraine
- 흑해 Black Sea
- 러시아 Russia
- 조지아 Georgia
- 아르메니아 Armenia
- 카자흐스탄 Kazakhstan
- 우즈베키스탄 Uzbekistan
- 아제르바이잔 Azerbaijan
- 투르크메니스탄 Turkmenistan
- 카스피해 Caspian Sea
- 타지키스탄 Tajikistan
- 키르기스스탄 Kyrgyzstan
- 0 500km
- ── 독립 국가 연합(CIS) Commonwealth of Independent States

🌀 옐친은 어떻게 쿠데타를 저지하였나요?

소련 동포들은 부끄러움과 양심을 상실한 채 극우적인 옛 것만을 고집하는 쿠데타 주동자들의 횡포를 결코 허용하지 않을 것입니다. 우리는 군인들이 시민들을 위해 싸우고 쿠데타 세력에 이용되지 말 것을 간곡히 당부합니다.

탱크 위에서 연설하는 옐친(왼쪽)
Yeltsin Speaks on a Tank(Left)

02 Fall of the Socialist Camp and the Opening of the Economy

Gorvachev Introduces Glasnost and Perestroika Policies

Russians lived in a controlled society where freedom was suppressed under the dictatorial rule of the Soviet Union's Communist Party. When Gorbachev was elected as the Secretary of the Communist Party in 1985, he carried out glasnost and perestroika policies to introduce a capitalist market economy system for the sake of recovering the economy and rebuilding Soviet society. As a part of this effort, he deregulated commodities prices and privatized Soviet state-owned companies. He also adopted a democratic presidential system and became the first elected President of the Soviet Union. Gorbachev made it clear that he would not interfere any more in the Eastern European countries that were experiencing a wave of liberalization movements. Then in 1989, he had a summit with the US president in Malta where he declared the end of the Cold War.

The economy declining during the process of introducing a market economy system blew up into a coup instigated by a hard-liner communist conservative camp(1990). After swearing into office, Yeltsin declared that the Soviet Union was dissolved in order to overcome the crisis (1991). The dissolution of the Soviet Union was followed by the formation of the Commonwealth of Independent States(CIS), which consisted of eleven republics that became independent from the former Soviet Union under the leadership of Russia.

⊘ How Did Yeltsin Stop the Coup?

> Soviet Union compatriots will never allow the tyranny of coup leaders who have lost their shame and conscience and insist on the far-right old things. We earnestly urge soldiers to fight for citizens and not be used by coup forces.

사회주의권이 붕괴하고 경제 개방이 이루어지다

1950년대 후반부터 동유럽 공산권 국가에서 자유화 운동이 일어났다. 그러나 소련은 무력을 동원하여 이를 강제로 진압하였다.

1980년대 들어 폴란드의 **바웬사**는 자유 노조 운동을 일으켜 동유럽 자유화 운동에 선구적인 역할을 하였다. 고르바초프가 동유럽 내정에 간섭하지 않겠다고 선언한 이후 동유럽의 자유화 운동은 더욱 활발하게 일어났다. 그 결과 동유럽 대부분의 나라에서 공산당 일당 독재가 폐지되고 자유 선거가 시행되었으며, 사회주의권은 붕괴되었다. 동유럽 국가들은 자본주의 시장 경제를 수용하여 경제 개방에 나섰다.

1989년에는 독일에서 **베를린 장벽**이 무너졌고, 다음 해에는 동독이 독일 연방에 가입하는 형태로 독일이 통일되었다(1990).

....

독일의 통일은 어떻게 시작되었나요?

제2차 세계 대전에서 패전국이 된 독일은 소련군이 진주한 동독과 연합군이 진주한 서독으로 나뉘어 분할 통치되었다. 1980년대 동유럽에 개혁과 자유화 바람이 불면서 동독 전역에서는 반정부 시위가 이어졌고, 서독으로 탈출하는 동독 주민들이 늘어났다.

1989년 11월 9일 동독 정부는 동독 주민들을 달래기 위해 외국 여행의 규제를 완화한다는 내용의 법령을 발표하였다. 그러나 이 법령은 동독 정치국원의 실수로 "지금부터 서독을 포함한 외국 여행을 자유화한다."라는 내용으로 잘못 전해졌다. 이 소식을 들은 수천 명의 사람들이 베를린 장벽 앞으로 몰려들었고, 국경 수비대는 머뭇거리다 국경을 개방하였다.

> 베를린 장벽이 무너지면서 독일의 통일이 시작되었어요.
> The fall of the Berlin Wall marked the beginning of German unification.

베를린 장벽에 모여든 사람들
People Gathered at the Berlin Wall

The Collapse of the Socialist Camp and the Opening of the Economy

From the late 1950s, Eastern European communist countries fought hard through active democratization struggles. However, the Soviet Union used force to forcibly suppress them.

In 1980, the Polish politician Lech Walesa spearheaded the movement to liberalize Eastern Europe, taking the lead in a union strike. After Gorbachev declared non-intervention in Eastern European politics, the liberalization movement in Eastern Europe became more active. As a result, communist dictatorships were abolished in most Eastern European countries, free elections were held, and the socialist camps collapsed. Eastern European countries moved forward to an open economy by embracing capitalist market economy.

In 1989, the Berlin Wall was brought down in Germany, and in the following year, East Germany and West Germany became united when East and West Germany joined the Federal Republic(1990).

◉ How Did German Unification Begin?

Germany, which was defeated in World War II, was divided into East Germany where Soviet troops were stationed and West Germany where Allied forces were stationed. In the 1980s, as movement of reform and liberalization became active in Eastern Europe, anti-government protests continued throughout East Germany, and more East Germans fled to West Germany.

On November 9, 1989, the East German government issued a decree stating that it would ease restrictions on foreign travel to appease the residents of East Germany. However, this decree was misrepresented by the mistake of a political officer in East Germany, saying, "From now on, foreign travel, including West Germany, is liberalized." Thousands of people who heard this flocked to the Berlin Wall and the border guards hesitated to open the border.

👓 동유럽의 자유화는 어떻게 진행되었나요?

©Libor Hajsky

❶ 체코슬로바키아의 민주화 시위
'프라하의 봄'이라 불리는 민주화 투쟁이 소련에 의해 진압되었지만 1980년대 후반 체코슬로바키아 사회주의 공화국은 민주화 세력에 의해 무너졌어요. 이후 체코슬로바키아는 체코와 슬로바키아로 분리 독립되었지요.

©AFP

❷ 루마니아 혁명
1980년대에 루마니아는 차우셰스쿠 공산당 정권의 경제 실패와 일당 독재에 시달리고 있었어요. 군부 세력이 시민 편에 합세하여 차우셰스쿠의 친위대를 타도하자 그는 북한으로 탈출하려 했지만 150여 발의 총탄을 맞고 사형당하였어요.

©Lehtikuva, Jorma Pussa

❸ 연설하는 바웬사
폴란드에서는 역사상 최초의 자유 선거를 통해 노조 지도자이자 정치가인 바웬사가 대통령에 당선되었어요. 폴란드 제3 공화국은 1990년에 폴란드 망명 정부의 국새와 대통령기를 바웬사에게 넘겨 주고 해체되었지요.

©Bojár Sándor

❹ 부다페스트 학생 시위
민주 포럼을 중심으로 개혁 운동을 전개하여 헝가리 공화국을 수립하였어요.
시인 김춘수는 「부다페스트에서의 소녀의 죽음」에서 "수 발의 소련제 탄환은 땅바닥에 쥐새끼보다도 초라한 모양으로 너를 쓰러뜨렸다."라고 학생 시위를 묘사하였어요.

🔭 How Did Liberalization in Eastern Europe Proceed?

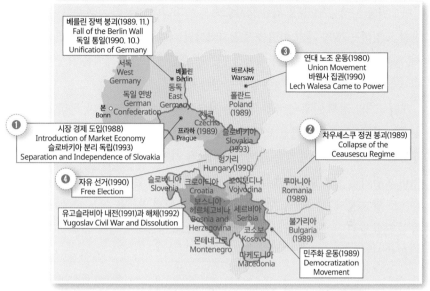

베를린 장벽 붕괴(1989. 11.)
Fall of the Berlin Wall
독일 통일(1990. 10.)
Unification of Germany

서독
West
Germany

베를린
Berlin

바르샤바
Warsaw

❸ 연대 노조 운동(1980)
Union Movement
바웬사 집권(1990)
Lech Walesa Came to Power

독일 연방
German
Confederation

본
Bonn

동독
East
Germany

폴란드
Poland
(1989)

체코
Czecha

❶ 시장 경제 도입(1988)
Introduction of Market Economy
슬로바키아 분리 독립(1993)
Separation and Independence of Slovakia

프라하 (1989)
Prague

슬로바키아
Slovakia
(1993)

❷ 차우셰스쿠 정권 붕괴(1989)
Collapse of the
Ceausescu Regime

헝가리
Hungary(1990)

❹ 자유 선거(1990)
Free Election

슬로베니아
Slovenia

크로아티아
Croatia

보이보디나
Vojvodina

루마니아
Romania
(1989)

유고슬라비아 내전(1991)과 해체(1992)
Yugoslav Civil War and Dissolution

보스니아
헤르체고비나
Bosnia and
Herzegovina

세르비아
Serbia

불가리아
Bulgaria
(1989)

몬테네그로
Montenegro

코소보
Kosovo

마케도니아
Macedonia

민주화 운동(1989)
Democratization
Movement

동유럽의 민주화 Democratization in Eastern Europe

❶ Democratization Protests in Czechoslovakia

The struggle for democratization, called the 'Spring of Prague', was suppressed by the Soviet Union, but in the late 1980s the Czechoslovak Socialist Republic was overthrown by democratic forces. After that, Czechoslovakia was divided into Czech Republic and Slovakia.

❷ Romanian Revolution

In the 1980s, Romania was suffering from economic failure and the one-party dictatorship of the Ceausescu Communist Party regime. When military forces joined with the citizens and defeated Cauchescu's bodyguards, he tried to escape to North Korea, but he was shot over 150 times and executed.

❸ A Speech by Lech Walesa

In Poland, union leader and politician Lech Walesa was elected president through the first free elections in history. The Third Republic of Poland handed over the seal of state and presidential flag of the Polish government-in-exile to Walesa in 1990 and was dissolved.

❹ Budapest Student Protest

The Hungarian Republic was established by carrying out a reform movement around the Democratic Forum.
Poet Kim Chun-soo described the student demonstration in 'The Girl's Death in Budapest', saying, "Several Soviet bullets knocked you down in a shabbier shape than a rat on the ground".

중국이 경제 대국으로 성장하다

마오쩌둥 사망 후 정권을 잡은 **덩샤오핑**은 1970년대 말부터 자본주의 시장 경제를 도입하는 **개혁·개방 정책**을 추진하였지만 정치적인 자유는 허용하지 않았다. 1989년 대규모의 시위대가 베이징 톈안먼 광장에서 민주 개혁을 요구하였지만 공산당 지도부는 이를 탄압하였다(**톈안먼 사건**).

개혁·개방 정책 이후 중국의 경제는 지속적으로 성장하고 있다. 중국은 1997년에는 영국으로부터 **홍콩**을, 1999년에는 포르투갈로부터 **마카오**를 반환받았다. 홍콩과 마카오는 중국에 많은 경제적인 이득을 가져다주고 있다. 2008년에는 베이징 올림픽을 성공적으로 개최하였다. 우주 개발에도 힘을 기울여 2019년 세계 최초로 달 뒷면에 탐사선을 착륙시켰다. 눈부신 경제 발전을 이룬 중국은 미국, 유럽 연합 등과 어깨를 나란히 하는 경제 대국으로 성장하여 세계 경제에 큰 영향력을 미치고 있다.

개혁주의자 후야오방의 명예를 회복하라! 부정부패를 척결하라! 보통 선거를 시행하라! 다당제를 도입하라!
Restore the honor of the reformist Hu Yaobang! Fight for corruption! Conduct general suffrage! Introduce a multiparty system!

톈안먼 사건(1989) Tiananmen Square Protest ©AFP

◉ **덩샤오핑은 왜 개혁·개방 정책을 추진하였나요?**

마오쩌둥 시대의 대약진 운동, 문화 대혁명으로 경제 위기가 닥치자, 덩샤오핑은 경제 위기를 극복하기 위해 개혁·개방 정책을 추진하였다. 개혁 정책으로는 인민공사 폐지, 기업의 이윤 추구 인정 등을 추진하였고, 개방 정책으로는 외국 자본 도입, 경제특구 설치 등을 실시하였다.

덩샤오핑 개혁·개방을 추진하는 근거로 실용주의 노선을 택하였어요. 검은 고양이든 흰 고양이든 쥐만 잘 잡으면 되는 것처럼 자본주의든 공산주의든 중국 인민을 잘 살게 하는 것이 제일 좋은 것입니다.

China Grows into an Economic Super Power

Deng Xiaoping, who took power after the death of Mao Zedong, pushed forward with open door and reform policies that embraced a capitalist market economy beginning from the late 1970s after the failed Cultural Revolution. In 1989, a large number of protesters rallied in Tiananmen Square in Beijing and demanded democratic reform, only to be cracked down upon by the Communist Party leaders(Tiananmen Square Protest).

After the Chinese economic reform policy, the Chinese economy kept growing. Then in 1997, China had Hong Kong returned from Britain, and Macao from Portugal in 1999. Hong Kong and Macao brought many economic benefits to China. China successfully hosted the 2008 Beijing Olympic Games. In 2019, China landed a communication satellite on the dark side of the moon for the first time in the world. Having achieved remarkable economic development, China has grown to become a major economic superpower on par with the United States and the EU, and is generating a great influence on the world economy.

◉ Why Did Deng Xiaoping Promote the Open Door and Reform Policies?

When economic crisis occurred due to the Great Leap Forward Movement and the Cultural Revolution in the Mao Zedong era, Deng Xiaoping pushed for reform and opening policies to overcome it. As a reform policy, he promoted the abolition of the People's Commune and recognition of the pursuit of profits by enterprises. As an opening policy, foreign capital was introduced and special economic zones were established.

Deng Xiaoping I took the pragmatism as a basis for promoting open door and reform policies. Whether it's a black cat or a white cat, we just need to catch mice. It is best to make the Chinese people live well, whether capitalism or communism.

03 신자유주의 경제 체제의 형성

세계화 속에서 신자유주의 경제 체제가 형성되다

사회주의권이 무너지면서 시장 경제 원리를 기반으로 한 자본주의 체제가 확대되었다. 세계를 '국경 없는 시장'으로 통합하려는 세계화의 물결 속에서 거대 금융과 자본을 가진 선진 자본국들의 주도로 신자유주의 경제 체제가 형성되었다.

신자유주의 경제 체제를 앞장서서 도입한 나라는 미국과 영국이다. 두 나라는 1970년대 말부터 자국의 경제 불황을 극복하기 위해 신자유주의를 추진하였다. 신자유주의 경제 체제가 형성되면서 상품의 이동에 대한 국가 간 장벽이 낮아지고 전 지구촌이 상품 시장과 금융 시장의 대상이 되어 자본과 노동이 자유롭게 이동하였다.

1995년 출범한 세계 무역 기구(WTO)는 관세 및 무역에 관한 일반 협정(GATT)에 없는 관세 인하 요구, 지적 재산권 요구 등 세계 무역 분쟁 조정 기능을 가지고 있어 한층 강화된 신자유주의 경제 체제를 이끌어 나가게 되었다.

자유 무역이 추진되며 기업들은 가격 경쟁에서 이길 수 있는 저렴하고 품질 좋은 제품을 개발하기 위해 치열한 경쟁을 벌였다. 산업의 효율성을 향상하는 과정에서 일부 국가는 놀라운 경제 성장을 이루었다. 그러나 개발 도상국들의 경제가 선진국의 기술과 자본에 의해 크게 흔들리고 종속되는 문제점도 나타났다.

....

◉ 신자유주의가 무엇인가요?

What Is the Neoliberal Economic System?

대처와 레이건
Thatcher and Reagan

신자유주의 경제 이론은 무질서한 시장을 방임하지 않는다는 점에서 고전적 자유주의 이론과는 차이가 있어요. 영국의 대처 총리는 지나친 사회 복지 정책의 비효율성을 극복하기 위해 저비용·고효율 정책을 추진하였고, 미국의 레이건 대통령은 자본이 개방된 시장에서 자유롭게 이동하도록 하였어요.

Neoliberal economic theory differs from classical liberal theory in that it does not neglect disorderly markets. British Prime Minister Thatcher pushed for low-cost, high-efficiency policies to overcome the inefficiencies of excessive social welfare policies, while U.S. President Reagan allowed capital to move freely in open markets.

03 Formation of the Neoliberal Economic System

Neoliberal Economic System Is Formed Amidst the Globalization Trend

As the socialist camp spiraled down the drain, the capitalist system built on the market economy began to spread wide. Advanced countries with large financial and capital powers took the lead in the formation of the neoliberal economic system while the trend of globalization tried to integrate the world into a single borderless market.

The United States and Britain are the two countries that spearheaded the introduction of a neoliberal economic system. These two countries turned to neoliberalism as a solution to overcome their economic recession beginning in the late 1970s. When a neoliberal economic system is established, it can lower the national barriers for the movement of goods, and capital and labor can move freely since the entire global village becomes the target of the commodity and financial markets.

The World Trade Organization(WTO) that was created in 1995 was able to guide the strengthened neoliberal economic system because it has an active international dispute settlement mechanism that General Agreement on Tariffs and Trade(GATT) doesn't.

Free trade was introduced and motivated companies to compete fiercely with each other to develop affordable, high quality products that could help them win the price war. Some countries recorded remarkable economic growth while trying to improve the efficiency of their industries. However, it entailed problems such as the economies of developing countries that became rattled by and dependent upon the technology and capital of advanced countries.

신자유주의 체제에도 그늘은 있다

세계화는 국가 간 시장을 하나로 통합하여 상품, 자본, 기술, 서비스 등의 자유로운 흐름을 방해하는 장벽을 제거하였다. 이로 인해 전 세계의 소비자들은 품질 좋은 상품을 만족스러운 가격에 구입할 수 있는 기회를 더 많이 가지게 되었다. 선진국은 국경을 뛰어넘어 더 수익성 높은 곳에 투자할 기회를 얻게 되었다.

풍부한 자원과 노동력을 갖추고도 기술과 자본의 부족으로 빈곤에 허덕이던 개발 도상국들은 선진국의 자본 투자와 기술 제공에 힘입어 새로운 발전의 기회를 맞게 되었다. 대표적으로 중국이나 인도는 세계화 물결에 합류하여 꾸준한 경제 성장을 이루었고, 빈곤 인구도 지속적으로 감소하였다.

세계화는 자본력, 정치력, 외교력, 기술력, 정보력 등을 고루 갖춘 선진국에는 유리하지만, 선진국과 공정한 경쟁이 불가능한 개발 도상국에는 불리하다는 부작용도 있다. 세계화로 개별 국가의 정부 역할이 축소됨으로써 개발 도상국들은 취약한 자국의 산업과 자산을 보호하기 어렵고 막강한 힘을 갖춘 다국적 기업의 침투를 제지할 수도 없게 되었다. 신자유주의 경제 원리가 적용되면서 기업과 개인의 능력을 최대한 발휘할 수 있는 풍토가 마련되었지만, 극소수에게 부가 집중되면서 빈부의 양극화 현상이 심화되었다.

⊙ 자본의 세계화로 인한 규제 완화의 부작용을 어떻게 극복해야 할까요?
   How should we overcome the side effects of deregulation caused by the globalization of capital?

노벨 경제학상을 수상한 로버트 쉴러 예일대학교 교수
Robert Schiller, Professor at Yale University, Nobel Memorial Prize in Economic Sciences

자본주의 경제는 규제가 없으면 제대로 작동하지 못한다. 우리에게는 착한 행동을 강요할 누군가가 필요하다. 왜냐하면 모두가 선의와 공익 정신을 지니고 있는 것도 아니고 모두가 관대한 것도 아니기 때문이다. 따라서 우리에게는 사람들이 할 수 있는 행동을 제한하는 규칙이 있어야 한다.
The capitalist economy does not work properly without regulation. We need someone to force good behavior. This is because not everyone has a spirit of good faith and public interest, and not everyone is generous. Therefore, we must have rules to limit what people can do.

There is also a Shadow in the Neoliberal Economic System

Globalization has eliminated barriers that hinder the free flow of goods, capital, technology, and services by integrating markets between countries into one. This has given consumers around the world more opportunities to purchase quality products at satisfactory prices.

Developed countries have the opportunity to cross borders and invest in more profitable places. Developing countries, which had abundant resources and labor but suffered from poverty due to lack of technology and capital, faced new opportunities for development thanks to capital investment and technology provision by developed countries. Representatively, China and India joined the wave of globalization to achieve steady economic growth, and the poor population continued to decline.

Globalization is advantageous for developed countries with capital, political power, diplomatic power, technology, and information power, but there is also a side effect that it is disadvantageous for developing countries that cannot compete fairly with developed countries. As individual countries' government roles have been reduced by globalization, developing countries have difficulty protecting their vulnerable industries and assets and cannot stop the penetration of powerful multinational corporations. With the application of neoliberal economic principles, a climate was established to maximize the capabilities of companies and individuals, but the polarization between the rich and the poor intensified as wealth was concentrated on very few.

지역 단위 경제 협력체의 교류가 활발해지다

신자유주의 경제 체제하에서 지리적으로 가깝고 경제적으로 상호 의존도가 높은 지역끼리 블록을 형성하여 지역 단위의 **경제 협력체**를 구성하는 일이 늘어나고 있다. 대표적인 경제 협력체에는 **유럽 연합(EU), 아시아·태평양 경제 협력체(APEC), 동남아시아 국가 연합(ASEAN), 브릭스(BRICS)** 등이 있다. 신흥 공업국들이 모인 브릭스는 세계에서 가장 큰 시장을 자랑한다.

선진 경제국 협의체로 처음 구성된 G8은 우리나라를 비롯한 신흥 경제 주요 국가 12개국이 추가되어 G20으로 확대되었고, 2010년에는 우리나라에서 G20 정상 회의가 개최되었다. 하지만 이러한 지역 단위 경제 협력체는 회원국들에만 혜택을 주고 비회원국들에 대해서는 차별을 하여 무역 갈등을 가져오기도 한다.

세계 무역 기구 출범 이후 국가와 국가 사이에 상호 이익 추구를 위해 **북미 자유**

무역 협정(NAFTA) 등 **자유 무역 협정(FTA)**도 이루어지고 있다. 우리나라의 경우 칠레, 싱가포르, 유럽 연합, 미국 등과 자유 무역 협정을 체결하였다.

2010년 서울 G20 정상회의에 모인 세계 각국 정상들
World Leaders at the 2010 G20 Seoul Summit ©Presidencia de la Nacion Argentina

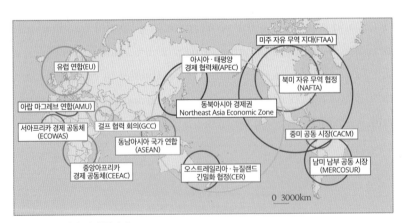

세계의 주요 지역 경제 협력체
Major Regional Economic Integration in the World

Dynamic Exchange of Regional-unit Cooperative Organizations

Under the neoliberal economic system, countries that are geographically close and economically interdependent are increasingly forming regional blocs and regional-unit economic cooperative organizations. Some of the most well-known economic cooperative organizations include the European Union, the Asia-Pacific Economic Cooperation(APEC), the Association of Southeast Asian Nations(ASEAN) and BRICS, which is an organization of newly emerging industrial countries that boast the world's largest market.

The G8 was first established as a consultative body of advanced economic powers, but was expanded to the G20 by adding 12 more countries, including Korea. In 2010, the G20 Summit was held in Korea. However, these regional economic cooperative organizations are blamed for having caused trade disputes as well, because they provided benefits only to member countries and discriminated against non-member countries.

Since the creation of the World Trade Organization, Free Trade Agreements(FTA) such as the North American Free Trade Agreement(NAFTA) have also been established to pursue mutual benefit. In the case of Korea, an FTA was signed with Chile, Singapore, the European Union, and the United States.

'브릭스(BRICS)'라는 이름은 브라질(Brazil), 러시아(Russia), 인도(India), 중국(China), 남아프리카 공화국(Republic of South Africa)에서 한 글자씩 따와 지었어요. The BRICS is named after the letters in Brazil, Russia, India, China, and the Republic of South Africa.

브릭스 BRICS ⓒAgencia Brasil

탈권위주의 운동과 대중 운동

01 탈권위주의 운동의 전개

68 운동이 일어나다

1960년대에는 청년층이 기성세대의 문화와 가치관에 저항하는 사회 분위기가 형성되었다. 이는 기존의 권위주의적 질서와 체제에 저항하는 **탈권위주의 운동**으로 이어졌다. 이러한 **탈권위주의 운동**의 대표적인 사건이 프랑스에서 일어난 **68 운동**이다. 프랑스 학생들은 1960년대에 아시아·아프리카·남아메리카에서 일어난 민족 해방 운동과 1968년 체코슬로바키아에서 일어난 **프라하의 봄**에 자극을 받았다. 68 운동은 실패하였으나 다른 지역의 탈권위주의 운동에 영향을 주었다. 또한 상업주의와 권위주의에서 비롯된 부정부패와 기존의 낡은 가치에서 벗어나야 한다는 과제를 던져 주었다.

미국의 사회학자 월러스틴은 "이제껏 세계 혁명은 둘뿐이었다. 하나는 1848년 (프랑스의 2월 혁명)에, 그리고 또 하나는 1968년에 일어났다. 둘 다 역사적인 실패로 끝났다. 둘 다 세계를 바꾸어 놓았다." 라고 말하였다. 68 운동이 세계사에서 매우 중요한 사건이었음을 밝힌 것이다. 68 운동을 시작으로 다양한 가치관이 꽃을 피우며, 진보적인 사상이 사회 곳곳에서 힘을 얻기 시작하였다.

> 금지하는 것을 금지한다!
> It is forbidden to forbid!

> 이건 우리 모두의 문제이다!
> This concerns all of us!

벽에 적힌 68 운동 구호
68 Revolts Slogan Written on the Wall ⓒEspencat

68 운동 대학생 시위
College Students Protest of 68 Revolts ⓒJean-Pierre REY

Anti-Authoritarian Movement and Mass Movement

01 Unfolding of the Anti-Authoritarian Movement

The 1968 Revolts in France

In the 1960s, there was a social atmosphere in which young people resisted the culture and values of the older generation. This led to an anti-authoritarian movement that resisted the existing authoritarian order and system. One historic anti-authoritarian movement is the series of events that happened in Paris, France, with younger generations, including students, that came to be known as the 'May 1968 events in France'. The students were inspired by the national liberation movements that happened in the 1960s in Asia, Africa, and South American countries. They were also greatly inspired by the Prague Spring in Czechoslovakia in 1968. Their revolts ended in failure, but this affected the de-authoritarian movement in other regions. The revolts were a challenge to the conservative values that tried to maintain old order, corruptions committed by authoritarianism, and commercialism.

As the American sociologist Wallerstein said, "There have been only two world revolutions so far. One occurred in 1848(the February Revolution in France), and the other in 1968. Both ended in historical failure, but both changed the world." He revealed that May 68 was a very important event in world history. Beginning from the May 68 events in France, new values began to proliferate, and progressive ideas began to gain power throughout society.

'68년 5월, 연장된 싸움의 시작'이라고 적혀 있어요.
The May 68 Poster says, 'May 68, the beginning of an extended fight.'

68 운동 포스터 May 68 Poster

민권 운동이 결실을 맺다

1960년대에는 시민의 권리를 되찾기 위한 민권 운동이 활발하게 일어났다. 가장 대표적인 사례가 미국에서 일어난 흑인 민권 운동이다. 1865년에 연방 헌법 수정 조항 제13조가 통과되면서 노예제가 폐지되었지만, 흑인들은 여전히 심각한 인종 차별에 시달리고 있었다. 법에 따라 흑인은 학교, 공공시설, 식당은 물론 버스 등의 교통수단을 이용할 때도 백인과 철저히 분리되었다. 1954년 미국 대법원은 흑인과 백인에게 각각 별개의 교육 시설을 제공하는 것은 위헌이라고 결정하였지만 인종 차별 관행은 계속되었다.

마틴 루서 킹 목사는 로자 파크스 체포 사건을 계기로 시작된 버스 승차 거부 운동을 흑인 차별에 대한 조직적인 저항 운동으로 확대하였다. 결국 버스 회사들이 여기에 굴복하여 버스 내의 흑인 전용 칸을 폐지하자, 흑인 민권 운동은 힘을 얻어 다른 지역으로 널리 전파되었다. 7만 명이 넘는 학생들이 인종 차별에 반대하는 흑인 민권 운동에 참여하였고, 20개 주의 100개가 넘는 도시에서도 민권 운동이 일어났다. 이에 힘입어 마틴 루서 킹 목사는 워싱턴에서 대규모 평화 행진을 전개하였고 1964년 의회는 **민권법** 인종, 피부색, 종교, 국적, 성별에 의한 차별을 금지하기 위한 법안을 통과시켰다.

🏀 로자 파크스는 왜 체포되었나요?

로자 파크스는 1955년 12월 1일 버스의 흑인 지정석에 앉아 있었는데 백인을 위해 자리를 양보하라는 요구를 받았다. 로자 파크스는 이를 거부하였고 법률 위반으로 체포되어 재판에 회부되었다.

로자 파크스
버스 좌석 양보를 거절했다는 이유로 저와 제 남편은 직장을 잃었어요. 이후 저는 이 사건을 알리기 위해 전국을 돌며 연설하였지요.
Rosa Parks
I and my husband lost jobs because I refused to give up a bus seat. Afterwards, I made a speech to publicize this incident around the country.

Civil Rights Movement Bears Fruit

The 1960s was a time in history marked by a proactive civil rights movement aimed to recover the rights of citizens. One of the most significant examples is the black civil rights movement that happened in the United States. Black people in America were liberated from slavery when the 13th Amendment to the Federal Constitution passed in 1865, but they still suffered serious racial discrimination. By law, blacks were completely segregated from the whites in schools, public facilities, and restaurants, and even on public transportation such as buses. The US Supreme Court ruled that providing separate educational institutions for blacks and whites was illegal and unconstitutional in 1954, but racial discrimination still remained the norm.

The Montgomery Bus Boycott was the beginning of a more organized and large-scaled resistance movement against discrimination under the leadership of Rev. Martin Luther King. Eventually, bus companies gave in and eliminated the 'colored section' and 'white-only section' in buses. Encouraged by this victory, the black civil rights movement spread to other regions like wildfire. Over 70,000 students are recorded to have participated in the black civil rights movement against discrimination, and over 100 civil rights movements were recorded to have taken place in more than 20 states. Rev. Martin Luther King organized the 'March on Washington for Jobs and Freedom' in Washington DC, and finally, the US Congress passed the Civil Rights Act in 1964.

....

◉ Why Was Rosa Parks Arrested?

On December 1, 1955, Rosa Parks got on the bus after work and sat in a seat designated for blacks, but was asked to give up the seat for a white man. she refused and was arrested for violating the law and brought to trial.

∞ 넬슨 만델라와 마틴 루서 킹은 인종 차별 철폐를 위해 무엇을 하였나요?

• 남아프리카 공화국의 인권 운동가 넬슨 만델라

1948년 남아프리카 공화국에서는 흑인을 차별하고 백인과 분리한다는 내용의 '아파르트헤이트'란 정책을 만들었다. 아파르트헤이트에 따르면 흑인과 백인 간의 결혼은 불법이었고, 흑인들은 전기도 들어오지 않는 좁은 지역에 모여 살아야 하였다.

이에 흑인 민권 운동가였던 만델라는 아프리카 국민 회의를 중심으로 인종 차별 정책에 저항하는 운동을 전개하였다. 그러다 그는 죽을 때까지 감옥에 갇히는 형벌을 선고받았고, 감옥에 갇힌 지 27년이 지난 1990년에 풀려났다. 흑인들의 민권을 위해 투쟁한 만델라는 노벨 평화상을 받았고, 1994년에 선거를 통해 남아프리카 공화국의 첫 흑인 대통령이 되었다.

> 넬슨 만델라
> 진정한 자유란 단지 사슬을 벗기는 것이 아니라 타인의 자유를 존중하고 보장하는 삶을 사는 것을 의미합니다.
> Nelson Mandela
> True freedom means not merely casting off one's chains, but living in a way that respects and enhances that freedom.

• 미국의 인권 운동가 마틴 루서 킹

미국의 인권 운동가이자 목사였던 마틴 루서 킹은 흑인 차별에 맞서 '버스 승차 거부 운동'을 이끌었다. 그는 평화적인 방법으로 흑인들의 불평등한 제도를 개선하기 위해 노력했으며, 그 공로를 인정받아 노벨 평화상을 수상하였다.

이후 마틴 루서 킹 목사는 암살을 당해 흑인 민권 운동을 계속 할 수 없었으나 그가 뿌린 씨앗은 2008년 버락 오바마가 미국 역사상 최초로 흑인 대통령이 되는 결실로 이어졌다.

> 마틴 루서 킹
> 나에게는 꿈이 있습니다. 언젠가 이 나라가 일어나 모든 인간은 평등하게 태어났다는 것을 분명한 진실로 받아들이는 날이 오리라는 꿈입니다.
> Martin Luther King
> I have a dream that one day this nation will rise up and live out the true meaning of its creed. We hold these truths to be self-evident that all men are created equal.

👓 What Did Martin Luther King and Nelson Mandela Do to Eliminate Racism?

• South African Human Rights Activist Nelson Mandela

In 1948, South Africa created a policy called apartheid that discriminated against blacks and separated them from whites. According to Apartheid, marriage between blacks and whites was illegal, and blacks had to live in small areas without electricity.

Accordingly, Mandela, a black human rights activist, launched a campaign to resist racial discrimination policies, centered on the African National Congress. He was sentenced to imprisonment until his death and was released in 1990, after 27 years of imprisonment. Mandela, who fought for the human rights of blacks, won the Nobel Peace Prize and became South Africa's first black president through an election in 1994.

• American Human Rights Activist Martin Luther King

Martin Luther King, a human rights activist and pastor in the United States, led the 'Montgomery Bus Boycott' against discrimination against blacks. He tried to improve the unequal system of black people in a peaceful way, and was awarded the Nobel Peace Prize in recognition for his contribution.

Martin Luther King was unable to continue his campaign for black human rights movement, as he was assassinated. But the seeds he sowed led to Barack Obama becoming the first black president in U.S. history in 2008.

노예 해방 선언 100주년 기념 집회에서 연설하는 마틴 루서 킹
Martin Luther King Speaking at a Rally Celebrating the
Centenary of the Declaration of Emancipation

여성 운동이 활발히 전개되다

여성의 참정권이 인정된 이후 여성들은 성 평등 운동과 여성의 권리를 주장하는 운동을 활발히 전개하였다. 그 선구적인 역할을 한 여성이 프랑스의 여권 운동가 시몬 드 보부아르이다. 보부아르는 남성이 만들어 낸 여성 이미지에 따라 여성이 남성을 위한 아내, 어머니, 성적 대상으로 살도록 사회적 역할을 부여받았다고 보았다. 그녀는 여성이 스스로 변혁의 주체가 되어야 한다고 주장하였다.

미국의 언론인인 베티 프리단도 여성 스스로 여성의 정체성에 대한 자각이 필요하다고 주장하였다. 이후 여성 운동은 사회주의, 자유주의, 급진주의 이념과 미국의 베트남 전쟁 참전을 반대하는 반전 시위의 영향을 받으며 발전하였다. 여성 운동가들은 모든 성은 평등하므로 여성 스스로 억압에서 벗어나 평등을 이루고 독립적인 자아 정체성을 형성해야 한다고 주장하였다.

....

◎ 보부아르는 왜 여성은 만들어졌다고 말했나요?

시몬 드 보부아르는 프랑스의 실존주의 작가이자 여권 운동의 선두 주자이다. 1949년 여성을 '타자', 즉 '제2의 성'으로 인식한 『제2의 성』을 출간하였다. 당시 대부분의 남성들은 이 책에 대해 혹평하였지만, 이 책은 여성들에게 그동안 사회에서 받아온 속박 속에서 벗어나 세상 밖으로 나가라는 메시지를 주었다.

보부아르의 이론에 의하면 남성은 세상의 주체이자 인식의 주체인 '제1의 성'이다. 반면 여성은 주체인 남성의 대상, 즉 타자(他者)로서 존재하는 '제2의 성'이다. 보부아르는 여성이 '타자'에서 벗어나기 위해 스스로 변혁의 주체가 되어야 한다고 역설하였다.

시몬 드 보부아르
여성은 여성으로 태어나는 것이 아니라 여성으로 만들어집니다.
Simone de Beauvoir
One is not born, a woman, but becomes one.

『제2의 성』 *"The Second Sex"*

Dynamic Unfolding of the Feminist Movement

Recognition of women's suffrage invigorated the women's movement for gender equality and women's rights. One of the pioneering feminist activists was the French feminist activist Simone de Beauvoir. She claimed that women were socially conditioned to play a role as a wife, mother, and sexual object all based on the image of women created and fashioned by men to suit their needs. She also stressed that women must be the primary agents in bringing about changes.

In America, a journalist, Betty Friedan, also argued that women must awaken their awareness of themselves as a woman. Later, the feminist movement evolved under the influence of socialism, liberalism, and radicalism as well as the anti-war protests against the US involvement in the Vietnam War. Feminist movement activists advocated gender equality, and claimed women must break themselves free from oppression, achieve gender equality, and form their own independent, self-identity.

◉ Why Did Beauvoir Say that Women Are Made?

Simon de Beauvoir is a French existentialist writer and a leader in the feminist movement. In 1949, she published "*The Second Sex*", which recognized women as 'the other', or 'second sex.' At the time, most men criticized this book, but it gave women a message to get out of the bondage they had received from society and go out into the world.

According to Beauvoir's theory, men are the subject of the world and the subject of perception, the 'first sex'. On the other hand, women are the 'second sex' that exist as the object of the man, that is, the other. She insisted that women must become the subject of transformation by themselves in order to escape from the 'other'.

현대 세계의 문제 해결을 위한 노력

01 반전 평화 운동의 전개

대량 살상 무기 개발을 반대하는 운동이 일어나다

제2차 세계 대전은 인류에게 깊은 상처를 남겼다. 만약 세계 대전이 또 일어난 다면 국가마다 개발한 대량 살상 무기로 인류가 함께 멸망할 수 있다는 위기감이 팽배해졌다. 이에 세계 평화를 위해 **국제 연합(UN)**이 창설되고 핵무기, 화학 무기 등 대량 살상 무기 개발을 반대하는 운동이 전개되었다.

그러나 냉전 구도가 굳어지면서 첨예하게 대립각을 세우게 된 미국과 소련은 여전히 대량 살상 무기 개발에 힘을 기울였다. 결국 **쿠바 미사일 위기**가 발발하고 전 세계 사람들이 핵전쟁의 공포를 겪은 후에야 비로소 **핵 확산 금지 조약(NPT)**이 체결되었다(1968). 핵 확산 금지 조약에 따르면 핵보유국은 비핵 국가에 핵무기와 관련한 어떠한 원조도 할 수 없으며, 비핵 국가는 핵무기와 관련된 어떠한 것도 스스로 제조할 수 없다는 내용이 담겨 있다.

🔍 **쿠바 미사일 위기는 왜 발생하였나요?**
Why Did the Cuban Missile Crisis Occur?

쿠바 미사일 위기 당시 소련의 서기장이었던 흐루쇼프와 미국의 대통령이었던 케네디가 힘을 겨루는 모습을 풍자한 그림이에요. 1962년 소련은 핵탄두 미사일을 쿠바에 배치하려는 시도를 하였어요. 미국 해안에서 불과 145km 떨어진 곳에서 미사일이 만들어질 수 있는 상황이었지요. 이에 미국과 소련이 대치하였고, 세계는 핵전쟁이 일어날지도 모른다는 공포에 숨을 죽여야 하였어요.

쿠바 미사일 위기 풍자화
Satirical Painting of Cuban Missile Crisis

Modern World's Efforts to Solve Problems

01 Anti-War Peace Movement

Movement against the Development of Weapons of Mass Destruction

World War II left scathing wounds on humanity. There has been a growing sense of crisis that, if another world war ever happened, the human race could be annihilated by the weapons of mass destruction developed by countries around the world. As a result, the United Nations(UN) was created to ensure peace in the world, and it has been campaigning against the development of weapons of mass destruction such as nuclear and chemical weapons.

However, the deepening Cold War system contributed to a sharper conflict between the US and the Soviet Union, thereby motivating them to race with each other in the development of weapons of mass destruction. Eventually, the situation led to the Cuban Missile Crisis, and it was only after people around the world experienced the panic of nuclear war that the Treaty on the Non-Proliferation of Nuclear Weapons(NPT) was signed(1968). Under the NPT agreements, nuclear–weapon capable states are not to aid or transfer nuclear weapons to non–nuclear weapon capable states and the non–nuclear weapon capable states are not to acquire or develop nuclear weapons.

It is a satirical picture of Khrushchev, the secretary of the Soviet Union, and Kennedy, the president of the United States, fighting for power during the Cuban Missile Crisis. In 1962, the Soviet Union attempted to deploy a nuclear-tipped missile in Cuba. Missiles could have been stationed just 145 kilometers off the coast of the United States. The US and the Soviet Union confronted each other, and the world had to hold their breath in fear that a nuclear war might occur.

베트남 전쟁으로 반전 평화 운동이 확산되다

1960년대에는 젊은 세대를 중심으로 베트남 전쟁에 참전한 미국을 비판하는 움직임이 일어났다. 미국이 밀림을 제거하기 위해 사용한 네이팜탄과 고엽제로 인한 피해가 알려지면서 반전 평화 운동은 전 세계로 확산되었다. 버클리대학교를 비롯한 100여 개 대학의 학생들이 반전 시위를 이끌었고, 비틀스, 밥 딜런 등 가수들과 이들을 추종하는 사람들이 동참하였다. 지식인, 여성, 흑인 민권 운동가 등도 미국의 비도덕성과 베트남 전쟁의 폭력성을 비판하며 전쟁을 멈출 것을 요구하였다.

1970년대에는 미국이 통킹만 사건을 조작하여 베트남 전쟁에 참전하였다는 사실이 미국 유력 언론에 의해 폭로되었다. 베트남전 당시 미국 국방 장관이었던 로버트 맥나마라는 1995년 회고록에서 이 사건이 미국의 자작극이었음을 고백하였다. 그의 고백에 반전 평화 운동의 불길이 더욱 거세졌고 반전 여론이 높아지자 미국은 베트남에서 철수하였다.

⊚ **미국이 통킹만 사건을 조작한 이유는 무엇인가요?**

통킹만 사건은 1964년 베트남 동쪽 통킹만에서 일어난 북베트남 경비정과 미군 구축함의 해상 전투 사건이다. 미국은 북베트남 어뢰정 3척이 미국 구축함을 선제공격하였다고 주장하였다. 이 사건을 빌미로 미국은 베트남 전쟁에 개입하였다.

우드스톡 페스티벌
Woodstock Festival
©James M Shelley

1969년 미국 뉴욕 북부에서 열린 우드스톡 페스티벌에 수십만 명이 모여 반전과 평화를 노래하였어요.
Hundreds of thousands of people gathered at the Woodstock Festival in northern New York in 1969 to sing anti-war and peace songs.

Vietnam War Triggers the Spread of the Anti-War Peace Movement

In the 1960s, the anti-war movement against the US, who participated in the Vietnam War was spreading throughout the world. The anti-war movement was triggered by the serious damages resulting from the defoliants and napalm that the US military had used indiscriminately to clear large stretches of dense jungle in Vietnam. Students from over 100 colleges, including UC Berkeley, took the lead in the movement, and the movement grew exponentially when singers including Bob Dylan and British pop group. The Beatles and their young fans joined the movement. Intellectuals, women, and black human rights activists also joined the movement and demanded that they stop the war while criticizing the immorality and racial discrimination that was happening in Vietnam.

In the 1970s, an influential news media outlet exposed that the US used the 'Gulf of Tonkin Incident' as an excuse for the US to engage more directly in the Vietnam War. Robert McNamara, who was the US Defense Secretary during the Vietnam War, confessed in a memoir in 1995 that the incident wasn't true. After his confession, the antiwar movement intensified until finally it resulted in the US withdrawing from Vietnam.

⦿ Why Did the US Fabricate the Gulf of Tonkin Incident?

The 'Gulf of Tonkin incident' was a maritime battle between a North Vietnamese patrol boat and US destroyer in Tongkin Bay in eastern Vietnam in 1964. The United States claimed that three North Vietnamese torpedoes attacked the U.S. destroyer first. Under the pretext of this incident, the United States intervened in the Vietnam War.

반전 평화 운동이 전 세계로 퍼져 나가다

1980년대에는 유럽을 중심으로 반핵 운동이 전개되었다. 북대서양 조약 기구 회원국들이 미국의 핵무기를 자국에 배치하려 하자, 1981년 북대서양 조약 기구 본부가 있는 브뤼셀에서 '폴란드에서부터 포르투갈까지 핵무기 없는 유럽을'이라는 슬로건을 내건 반핵 시위가 일어났다. 1982년에는 국제 연합에서 군비 축소 특별 총회가 열리자 국제 연합 본부가 있는 뉴욕에 100만여 명이 집결하여 반핵의 목소리를 더욱 크게 외쳤다. 그 결과 미·소 양국 간에 '중거리 핵전력 조약(INF Treaty)'이 체결되어 핵탄두를 장착한 중거리 지상 발사 미사일 수천 개가 철폐되었다(1987).

2000년대까지 지구촌에는 크고 작은 지역 분쟁이 발생하였다. 소련의 아프가니스탄 침공, 이란·이라크 전쟁, 코소보 전쟁, 걸프 전쟁, 이라크 전쟁 등이 발발할 때마다 반전 평화 운동은 비정부 기구를 중심으로 활발히 전개되었다. 특히 2003년에는 전 세계 600여 도시에서 2,000만 명이 거리로 쏟아져 나와 미국의 이라크 침공을 반대하는 대대적인 반전 투쟁을 전개하였다.

📍 1980년대부터 2000년대까지 어떤 전쟁이 일어났나요?
What Kind of War Took Place from the 1980s to the 2000s?

1980
이란·이라크 전쟁(1980~1988) 이라크의 이란 침공으로 시작되었어요. 화학 무기 사용 등에 의해 100만여 명의 사상자가 발생하였지요.

코소보 전쟁(1988~1999) 발칸반도에 위치한 코소보에서 세르비아군이 알바니아계 사람들을 상대로 '인종 청소'를 내세우며 저지른 전쟁이에요.

1990
걸프 전쟁(1991) 이라크의 쿠웨이트 침공을 계기로 다국적군이 참여한 국제 전쟁이에요.

2000
이라크 전쟁(2003) 미국과 영국 등 연합군이 이라크의 대량 살상 무기 제조를 이유로 이라크와 벌인 전쟁이에요. 이에 영국, 독일, 스웨덴, 러시아, 한국, 일본, 요르단, 시리아, 이집트 등 세계 곳곳에서 반전 평화 집회가 열렸지요.

Anti-Nuclear Peace Movement Spreads Throughout the World

The 1980s saw the rise of anti-nuclear movements centering in Europe. When NATO member states wanted to deploy US nuclear weapons in their own countries, it triggered anti-nuclear demonstrations in 1981 in Brussels, where the NATO headquarters was located, under the slogan 'a nuclear-free Europe from Poland to Portugal'. Then in 1982, when the UN Special Committee for the Reduction of Arms met, a million people took to street in New York where the UN headquarters was located and rallied in protest of nuclear weapons. As a result, the INF Treaty was signed between the US and the Soviet Union and thousands of medium-range ground-launched missiles with nuclear warheads were dismantled(1987).

Until the 2000s, there were various small and large skirmishes throughout the globe, such as the Soviet invasion of Afghanistan, the Iran-Iraq War, the Kosovo War, the Gulf War, and the Iraq War. Each time a war broke out, it was followed by an antiwar peace movement under the leadership of NGOs. In 2003 in particular, over 20 million people took to the streets in over 600 cities around the world as part of an anti-war movement, and demonstrated against the US invasion of Iraq.

> Iran-Iraq War(1980-1988) It started with Iraq's invasion of Iran. More than 1 million casualties were incurred due to the use of chemical weapons.

> Kosovo War(1988-1999) This was initiated by the Serbian army in Kosovo in the Balkans, claiming to 'clean up the race' against Albanians.

> Gulf War(1991) This was an international war in which multinational force participated in the wake of Iraq's invasion of Kuwait.

> Iraq War(2003) The United States, Britain and other coalition forces waged war against Iraq for making weapons of mass destruction. As a result, anti-war peace rallies were held in Britain, Germany, Sweden, Russia, Korea, Japan, Jordan, Syria, and Egypt.

02 지역 갈등 해결을 위한 노력

지역 갈등이 세계 곳곳에서 일어나다

지금도 영토, 민족, 종교, 부족, 자원 등의 문제로 세계 곳곳에서 지역 분쟁이 계속되고 있다. 아프리카에서는 1960년대 이후 많은 독립국이 세워졌지만 정권을 차지하기 위한 쿠데타와 부족 간의 다툼으로 르완다 내전이나 소말리아 내전 등이 발생하였다.

서아시아에서는 팔레스타인 지역을 차지한 이스라엘과 이를 지원하는 서방 국가들에 대한 불만이 커졌다. 이로 인해 미국에서 9·11 테러가 일어나 세계가 테러의 공포에 휩싸였다. 시리아에서는 독재 정권과 이에 맞서는 세력 사이에 내전

이 벌어졌다. 여기에 수니파 무장 단체 '이슬람 국가(IS)' 등이 개입하면서 반인륜적인 전쟁 범죄가 일어났다.

동남아시아에서는 미얀마 민주주의의 상징이었던 아웅 산 수치의 묵인 아래 소수민족 로힝야에 대한 집단 학살과 성폭력 등의 탄압이 일어나 국제 사회를 들끓게 하였다.

9·11 테러 September 11 Attacks ⓒRobert

◉ 로힝야족이 탄압을 받은 이유는 무엇인가요?

로힝야족은 주로 미얀마 서부 라카인주에 거주하는 이슬람 계열의 소수민족이에요. 불교도가 대다수인 미얀마에서 이슬람 계열의 로힝야족은 박해를 받았어요. 버마(미얀마) 정부는 로힝야족의 토지를 몰수하였고 결혼의 자유도 박탈하였지요. 로힝야족 반군이 경찰 초소를 습격하자 버마 정부는 이를 강력하게 진압하였어요. 그 과정에서 민간인에 대한 탄압이 일어났고 수만 명의 난민이 발생하였지요.

미얀마의 라카인주 Rakhine State in Myanmar

02 Efforts to Resolve Regional Conflicts

Regional Conflicts Happen Throughout the World

The world is still plagued by various regional conflicts and disputes over territories, nations, religions, ethnicity, and natural resources. In Africa, even though many African countries have gained their independence since the 1960s, they are still going through a tumultuous time due to increasing numbers of skirmishes and conflicts among African tribes and military coups instigated by groups trying to seize power, such as seen in the Rwandan Civil War and the Somali Civil War.

In West Asia, the growing hostility against Israel's attacks on the Palestinian territories and the Western nations that are supporting the attacks has been escalated into terrorist attacks such as the September 11 Attacks, which caused the entire world to tremble with fear. Then there is the Syrian Civil War between the Islamist Sunni militant group the Islamic State(IS) and the Syrian government, where war crimes against humanity are committed

In Asia, Myanmar's armed forces and police enraged the international community when they committed sexual assault and ethnic cleansing against the minority group of the Rohingya people while their symbol of democracy, Aung San SuuKyi, remained mostly silent.

....

⊛ Why Are the Rohingya People Persecuted?

The Rohingya are an Islamic minority ethnic group living primarily in the state of Rakhine in western Myanmar. In Myanmar, where the majority of Buddhists are, the Rohingya have been oppressed by the Burmese(Myanmar) government. The Burmese government also confiscated their land and deprived them of freedom of marriage. When the Rohingya rebels attacked a police post, the Burmese government strongly suppressed it. In the process, repression of civilians occurred and tens of thousands of refugees were generated.

지역 분쟁 조정을 위해 노력하다

국제 사회는 공조를 통해 테러에 공동 대처하고 있다. 국제 연합도 지역 간 분쟁을 조정하기 위해 동티모르 지역에 유엔 평화 유지군을 파견하는 등 강경 조치를 취하기도 하였지만 깊어진 상처와 갈등은 쉽게 아물지 못하고 있다.

한국은 이라크군이 쿠웨이트를 점령하였을 때 36개국 다국적군의 일원으로 참전한 이후 유엔 평화 유지군 활동에 본격적으로 참여하였다. 상록수 부대는 소말리아에서 한국군 최초로 도로 공사, 주민 지원 등 '평화 유지 활동(PKO)'을 수행하였다.

현대 세계에서는 어떤 지역 분쟁이 있었나요?

❶ 북아일랜드 분쟁
북아일랜드에서 구교도(가톨릭)는 취업과 선거권 제한 등 각종 차별을 받았어요. 이로 인해 신·구교파 간에 충돌이 발생하여 1969년부터 30년간 3,700여 명의 사망자가 나왔어요.

❷ 카슈미르 분쟁
카슈미르 영유권을 두고 인도와 파키스탄은 두 차례의 전쟁을 벌였어요. 지금은 휴전 상태이지만 분쟁은 계속되고 있지요.

❸ 보스니아 내전
보스니아-헤르체고비나의 독립 선언(1992)에 반대한 보스니아 내 세르비아인들이 인종 청소를 자행하며 보스니아 내전이 확대되었어요. 1993년 초에는 크로아티아-보스니아 내전으로 확대되었지요. 보스니아 내전으로 10만 명이 사망하였어요.

❹ 동티모르 독립 운동
동티모르 국민들이 인도네시아로부터 독립하려 하자 인도네시아군과 민병대는 동티모르 전역에서 1,500여 명을 학살하였어요. 이에 국제 연합은 동티모르 국민들을 구하기 위해 평화 유지군을 파견하였는데, 한국도 동참하였어요.

세계의 지역 갈등과 분쟁 지역
Regional Conflict and Conflict Areas in the World

Efforts to Resolve Regional Disputes

The international community is collectively responding to the terrorism problem through mutual cooperation. The UN is also trying to resolve regional disputes by taking strong actions, such as sending the UN peacekeeping troops to East Timor, but the deep wounds and conflicts remain difficult to heal.

In the case of Korea, Korean soldiers were deployed when the Iraqi military forces invaded Kuwait as a part of the coalition of forces from 36 countries and participated in the UN peacekeeping operations. The Korean Sangnoksu Unit was also deployed to Somalia for Peace keeping operations(PKO) such as the construction of roads and supporting residents for the first time in the history of the Korean military.

⊚ **What Kind of Conflicts Are Happening in the World Right Now?**

❶ The Troubles
In Northern Ireland, Catholics faced various forms of discrimination, including restrictions on employment and voting rights. This resulted in a conflict between the new and old denominations, killing 3,700 people over 30 years from 1969.

❷ Kashmir Conflict
India and Pakistan fought twice over sovereignty of Kashmir. The two countries are in a state of truce now, but the conflict continues.

❹ Timor-Leste Independence Movement
When the people of East Timor tried to become independent from Indonesia, Indonesian troops and militias slaughtered more than 1,500 people across East Timor. The United Nations sent peacekeepers to save the people of East Timor, as did South Korea.

❸ Bosnian War
The Bosnian War escalated as Bosnian Serbs, who opposed the Bosnia-Herzegovina Declaration of Independence(1992), carried out ethnic cleansing. In early 1993, the war expanded to the Croatian–Bosnia War. 100,000 people were killed in the Bosnian War.

분쟁 지역의 난민이 사회적 문제가 되다

　세계 곳곳에서 지역 분쟁이 일어날 때마다 내란과 분쟁을 피해 고국을 탈출하는 난민들이 속출하고 있다. 전 세계적으로 국제 난민은 약 2,500만 명으로 추산된다.

　2010년 아랍권을 휩쓸었던 '아랍의 봄' 민주화 혁명 이후에 난민이 폭발적으로 발생하였다. 독재 정권을 물리치자는 시민들의 외침은 튀니지를 시작으로 북아프리카의 리비아, 이집트, 서아시아의 시리아와 예멘까지 확산되었다. 독재 정권이 이를 무력으로 진압하려 하자 반정부 세력이 반발하여 내전이 발생하였다. 이로 인해 시리아, 이라크, 아프가니스탄, 소말리아, 나이지리아 등에서 난민이 발생하였고, 이들은 지중해를 건너 유럽으로 죽음의 항해를 하게 되었다.

　시리아 난민은 2018년 초까지 터키를 거쳐 그리스, 불가리아로 이동하였다. 그러나 유럽 연합과 터키가 난민 송환 협정을 맺으면서 이 경로로 이동할 수 없게 되자 난민들은 마케도니아, 세르비아 등 유럽 연합 비회원국에 들어간 후 유럽 연합 회원국인 헝가리를 거쳐 오스트리아, 독일 등으로 들어가는 길을 택하였다. 아프리카 난민들은 '**보트 난민**'이 되어 목숨을 건 유럽행을 시도하다가 배가 침몰하여 죽음을 맞이하기도 하였다.

일부 국가에서는 난민과 일자리를 나누고 난민에게 복지 비용을 지불하는 문제 등에 대한 불만이 고조되어 난민 수용 반대 시위가 열리기도 하였어요.
In some countries, protests against the acceptance of refugees were held due to mounting complaints about sharing jobs with refugees and paying welfare fees to refugees.

2015년에는 가족과 함께 소형 보트로 지중해를 건너다 보트 전복으로 목숨을 잃은 3살 시리아 난민 어린이 쿠르디의 사연이 보도되었어요.
In 2015, the story of Kurdi, a 3-year-old Syrian refugee child who died in a small boat that overturned while crossing the Mediterranean Sea with his family was reported.

Refugees from Conflict Regions Emerge as a Social Problem

Every time there is a regional dispute somewhere in the world, it creates a wave of refugees who escape from their homes to avoid civil war or conflict. It is estimated that there are about 25 million refugees around the world as of now.

It was the year 2010 when the democratization revolution called the 'Arab Spring' was sweeping throughout the Arab world and the number of refugees started to increase drastically. It started in Tunisia with citizens against the dictatorship and spread to Libya and Egypt in Africa, and West Syria and Yemen in West Asia. Before long, it escalated into civil wars between the antigovernment protesters and dictatorship regimes that tried to suppress them with military force. Consequently, citizens of Syria, Iraq, Afghanistan, Somalia, and Nigeria took off on a voyage of death to Europe by crossing the Mediterranean Sea.

The Syrian refugees escaped the civil war to Turkey before moving on to head to Greece and Bulgaria until early 2018, but this route was practically blocked when the EU signed a refugee agreement with Turkey. Then the Syrian refugees bypassed the route and entered the EU non-member countries such as Macedonia and Serbia in the western part of the Balkan Peninsula before making their way into EU member countries such as Austria and Germany via Hungary. Some African refugees risked their lives when they attempted to enter Europe as a group of 'Boat people' only to be killed when the boat capsized.

❶ 체코에서 열린 난민 수용 반대 시위 Protest against Accepting Refugees in the Czech Republic ©AFP/File Michal Cizek ❷ 쿠르디를 추모하는 벽화(독일 프랑크푸르트암마인) Mural of Alan Kurdi(Frankfurt am Main, Germany) ©Plenz

👀 '아랍의 봄' 이후 발생한 난민 사태를 어떻게 해결해야 할까요?

'아랍의 봄'은 2010년부터 2011년까지 독재 정권을 무너뜨리기 위해 일어난 서 아시아와 북아프리카의 민중 혁명을 말한다. '재스민 혁명'이라고도 부르는데, 이 는 아랍의 봄'이 2010년에 재스민이 많이 피는 튀니지에서 시작되었기 때문이다.

한 튀니지 청년이 대학 졸업 후 노점을 하고 있었는데, 경찰의 단속에 분노해 분 신자살하였다. 이 사건을 계기로 시위가 일어났고, 튀니지 대통령은 망명하였다. 튀니지 혁명의 불길은 이집트, 알제리, 예멘, 요르단, 시리아, 이라크, 쿠웨이트로 확산하였다.

리비아의 독재자 알 카다피는 시위대에 무차별로 발포하였다. 유엔군과 과도 정부군의 공격으로 카다피 정권은 무너졌지만 혼란은 이어졌다.

시리아 내전은 시아파 출신의 바샤르 알아사드 대통령이 다수의 수니파를 누 르고 정권 유지를 위해 강압적으로 통치하였다. 십여 명의 학생들이 '재스민 혁 명'의 구호를 벽에 썼다가 고문을 당하였다. 이에 반발하여 평화 시위가 일어나자 정부는 무력으로 진압하였고, 시민들은 무장 투쟁에 나섰다. 시리아 내전으로 36 만 명 이상이 사망하고 558만여 명의 난민이 발생하였다.

일부 유럽 연합 회원국에서는 '반난민, 반이슬람' 등의 구호를 내세운 우파 세력 이 정권을 잡았다. 영국에서는 난민에게 일자리를 나누는 것에 대한 불만이 고조 되었는데, 이는 영국이 유럽 연합을 탈퇴하는 원인이 되기도 하였다.

국제 사회는 난민 문제를 해결하기 위해 먼저 지역 분쟁 해결에 나서야 한다. 난 민을 위해 일자리를 창출하고 교육 정책도 마련해야 한다. 난민을 차별하지 않고 난민의 고유문화를 존중하는 데도 힘써야 한다. 난민이 가져온 새로운 전통과 문 화는 조화로운 다문화 사회 조성에 기여하기도 한다.

> 내전으로 고통받고 있지만 우리는 희 망을 노래할 거예요.
> We are suffering from civil war, but we will sing hope.

레바논에 있는 시리아 난민 어린이들
Syrian refugee children in Lebanon

◌◌ **How should we resolve the refugee crisis that occurred after the 'Arab Spring'?**

'Arab Spring' refers to the popular revolution in West Asia and North Africa that took place from 2010 to 2011 to overthrow the dictatorship. It is also called the 'Jasmine Revolution', because the 'Arab Spring' began in Tunisia, where Jasmine blooms a lot, in 2010.

A Tunisian young man was working as a street vendor after graduating from college, and he burned himself to death in anger at the police crackdown. Protests broke out in the wake of this incident, and Tunisian President fled to Saudi Arabia. The flames of the Tunisian Revolution spread to Egypt, Algeria, Yemen, Jordan, Syria, Iraq, and Kuwait.

Libya's dictator Al-Qadafi fired indiscriminately at protesters. The attack of the UN and transitional government forces collapsed the Al-Qadafi regime, but confusion continued.

In the Syrian Civil War, President Bashar Al-Asad from Shia defeated the majority of Sunnis and ruled coercively to maintain the regime. A dozen students were tortured for writing slogans for the 'Jasmine Revolution' on the wall. In opposition to this, when a peaceful protest broke out, the government suppressed it with force, and the citizens went on an armed struggle. The Syrian civil war killed more than 360,000 people and caused 5.58 million refugees.

In some European Union member countries, right-wing forces with slogans such as 'anti-refugee, anti-Islam' took power. In the UK, complaints about sharing jobs with refugees have risen, which has also contributed to Britain's withdrawal from the European Union.

The international community must first resolve regional disputes to resolve refugee problems. Jobs should be created and educational policies should be prepared for refugees. We should also strive to respect the refugee's unique culture without discriminating against refugees. The new traditions and cultures brought about by refugees also contribute to the creation of a harmonious multicultural society.